guc

NEW YORK STATE
HISTORICAL ASSOCIATION SERIES

DIXON RYAN FOX

EDITOR

———

NUMBER IV

THE COUNTRY PRINTER

BY

MILTON W. HAMILTON

JAMES D. BEMIS, 1783-1857

"The Father of the Press of Western New York"

THE
COUNTRY PRINTER

New York State, 1785-1830

BY

MILTON W. HAMILTON

NEW YORK: MORNINGSIDE HEIGHTS

COLUMBIA UNIVERSITY PRESS

1936

FOREIGN AGENTS

OXFORD UNIVERSITY PRESS
HUMPHREY MILFORD, AMEN HOUSE
LONDON, E. C. 4, ENGLAND

KWANG HSUEH PUBLISHING HOUSE
140 PEKING ROAD
SHANGHAI, CHINA

MARUZEN CO., LTD.
6 NIHONBASHI, TORI-NICHOME
TOKYO, JAPAN

OXFORD UNIVERSITY PRESS
B. I. BUILDING, NICOL ROAD
BOMBAY, INDIA

FOREWORD

SEVERAL comprehensive histories of American journalism have traced the growing power of the press as a factor in our culture and civilization, especially as an influence working toward political democracy. Its immense importance was recognized even in the colonial era, certainly in the early days of the Republic. Thomas Jefferson, perhaps with some extravagance, declared that if obliged to do without either government or newspapers he would choose to retain the latter. The press as an institution and an influence is usually identified with the great dailies published in the chief cities of a country; most of those in the American metropolis have had their individual histories—perhaps biographies were a better word—set forth at full length in competent accounts. But, as Dr. Hamilton points out, historical scholars have paid little heed to the "Gazettes," "Repositories," "Messengers," and the like, instituted and arduously carried forward in the rural counties of New York State by nearly seven hundred printers during the half-century following the Revolution. These cultural pioneers played their important rôles in every section of the state and Dr. Hamilton has made a rich contribution to our history in turning the light of his inquiry upon their personalities and careers.

The printing press is a social instrument, especially when in the regular production of a newspaper it keeps the diary of the community, maintains a forum for its discussions, and provides an exchange for its commerce. It is a public institution and yet at the same time a private undertaking. Seldom in those early days, or later, was a printer "called" to a community with general and responsible assurances of support, as a minister or a teacher is called. Each risked not only his time and effort but the capital tied up in an extensive and cumbersome equipment. No pioneers needed more courage to face disappointment than this vanguard of editor-publishers moving on their own frontier just behind that of the homemakers. Throughout the author's text may be discerned a trace of sentiment, and his readers will doubtless take no little satisfaction that the memory of these printers, brightened by his research, is also garlanded with his appreciation. There are heroes of the civil state no less than of the battlefield.

Neither the author nor anyone else would maintain that all printers were conscious of heroic quality. In aspect and manner they were usually as unheroic as possible; Thurlow Weed, who knew the early journeymen as well as any man, recalled that half of his acquaintances among them drank themselves into poverty or worse disaster; their political principles were oftentimes for sale. Nevertheless, there must have been few who did not realize that they bore a close relation to American progress and who worked now and then in the elation of public service.

Certainly no corps of public servants ever had a more faithful and understanding chronicler than these forgotten journalists now reviewed in Dr. Hamilton's book. It is a privilege for the New York State Historical Association to add this history to its Series. There is an added satisfaction that it is the patronage of a great metropolitan publisher, Mr. William T. Dewart of the New York *Sun,* which has made its publication possible.

UNION COLLEGE
June 1, 1936

DIXON RYAN FOX
President, New York State
Historical Association

PREFACE

W HILE there have been numerous histories of journalism, and excellent "biographies" of important
newspapers, little attention has been given to the
beginnings of the country press in America. In New York the
first country newspaper was issued at Poughkeepsie in 1785—
if we exclude an earlier journal at Albany and the exiles from
New York City which were printed at Poughkeepsie, Fishkill,
and Kingston during the Revolution. Within the next thirty-five
years a remarkable development took place, and newspaper
presses were established throughout the state. By 1830 this
phase of rapid growth was over, and the country newspaper in
New York had emerged from the pioneering stage. During
this period, however, the country press played a rôle in politics
and in community life which is worthy of our attention.

The agent in this journalistic development was the country
printer, the printer-editor-publisher, who was a distinctive
character in his community. As a politician, as an exemplar of
the traditions and customs of his trade, and as a pioneer in the
spread of culture he became a citizen of importance. An appreciation of his work is necessary for an understanding of rural
life in the early days of our Republic.

It is the purpose of this study to point out the singular position occupied by the country printer before 1830 in the life of
his time and to describe the technical development of journalism within his sphere. The lack of such a study has been due no
doubt to the scattered and elusive nature of the sources. Relying largely on the files of newspapers, the author has assembled
data concerning a large number (more than 650) of printers,
editors, and publishers who were active in this period. These
data, which are given separately in the Appendix, supply much
of the material for the topical discussion of the printer and the

newspaper in the text. It is expected that the latter will provide a composite portrait of the country printer, and an estimate of the influence of the country press.

The subject was first brought to my attention by Dr. Dixon Ryan Fox, then Professor of History at Columbia University, in a seminar in American social history. The research was carried on under his able direction, and its completion owes much to his inspiring counsel and encouragement. To him as a teacher and as an exemplar of scholarship I owe a debt which the present effort can but partially discharge.

I am also indebted to other workers in this field of research: to Mr. Clarence S. Brigham, Director of the American Antiquarian Society, who not only assisted me in the use of the Society's remarkable collections but made available the fruits of his own research; to Mr. Joseph Gavit, Senior Librarian of the New York State Library, who was always ready to send needed information and to verify my data; to Dr. Victor Hugo Paltsits, Chief of the American History Division of the New York Public Library; and to Mr. Henry Lewis Bullen, of the American Typefounders Library, whom I consulted on the technical side of printing, and who was kind enough to read Chapter I in manuscript. I have had the advice of Dr. Richard B. Morris in regard to the legal material in Chapter V.

The wide range of my research accounts for my indebtedness to many libraries and librarians. In these instances I can only list the institutions, trusting that the individuals involved will consider that as an acknowledgment of their co-operation.

The collections of newspapers in the following historical societies were used: American Antiquarian Society, Buffalo Historical Society, Cayuga County Historical Society, Greene County Historical Society, Jefferson County Historical Society, Long Island Historical Society, Madison County Historical Society, New Jersey Historical Society, New York Historical Society, New York State Historical Association—Headquarters House, Oneida Historical Society, Onondaga Historical Association, Ontario Historical Society, and Rochester Historical Society.

Collections in the public libraries of the following places were used: Batavia, Buffalo, Canandaigua, Cazenovia, Cooperstown, Cortland, East Hampton, Fredonia, Ithaca, Jamestown, Kingston, Newburgh, Norwich, Ogdensburg, Oswego, Oxford, New York, Poughkeepsie, Sag Harbor, Troy, Utica, Walton, and Waterloo. Other collections were found in the Cornell University Library, Harvard University Library, Hobart College Library, New York State Library, and the Congressional Library. In addition the private collections of Mr. John N. Bogert of Binghamton and Mr. William H. Hill of Fort Edward were made available for my use.

My initial researches were conducted in the Columbia University Library and the Syracuse Public Library. Valuable material was sent to me by research librarians of the Burton Collection of the Detroit Public Library, the Public Library of Cincinnati, and the Ohio State Archeological and Historical Society, of Columbus, Ohio. I received information from Mr. A. W. Anderson, of Jamestown, Mr. E. P. Alexander, of Ticonderoga, Mr. William H. Arnold, of Elmira, Mr. Archie D. Gibbs, of Norwich, Mr. Douglas C. McMurtrie, of Chicago, Dr. Lawrence C. Murphy, of the University of Illinois, Mr. Morton Pennypacker, of Kew Gardens, L. I., and Mrs. Amy VerNooy, of Poughkeepsie.

In my quest for facts about individual printers I was led to visit many newspaper offices and to interview many persons. Some descendants of the early printers were helpful, notably Mrs. Charlotte Prentiss Browning, the daughter of Col. John H. Prentiss, of Cooperstown. Mr. John N. Bogert, of Binghamton, supplied information about Col. James Bogert; Mr. Guilford Francis, of Buffalo, concerning Simeon Francis; and Mr. Henry M. Allen, of Auburn, concerning Isaac S. Allen. Others have supplied minor details about various printers, for which I am duly grateful.

My thanks are again due to Dr. Fox as editor and to the New York State Historical Association for publishing the work in their series; to the staff of the Columbia University Press for their co-operation; and to Mr. William T. Dewart for generously supplying the publication fund. Finally, I am indebted to Prof. John A. Krout of Columbia University for his careful reading and criticism of the manuscript in preparing it for publication. Throughout the work I have had the helpful services and criticism of my wife, who contributed much toward its completion.

Milton W. Hamilton

Reading, Pennsylvania
March 16, 1936

CONTENTS

lishment in neighboring towns; Migration of printers
—the pioneer; Co-operation of printers; Agreement
upon prices; A printers' convention.

THE
COUNTRY PRINTER

I

THE ART PRESERVATIVE

OUR printing-house often wanted sorts, and there was no letter-founder in America; I had seen types cast at James's in London, but without much attention to the manner; however, I now contrived a mould, made use of the letters we had as puncheons, stuck the matrices in lead, and thus supplied in a pretty tolerable way all deficiencies. I also engraved several things on occasion; I made the ink; I was ware-houseman, and everything, and, in short, quite a factotum.—FRANKLIN, Autobiography.

> Ours is the Heaven descended art,
>   To give fair knowledge birth,
> To mend the human heart,
>   And civilize the earth.

SAMUEL WOODWORTH, "The Art of Printing" *(1810)*.

> Arise, ye favor'd sons of light,
>   Professors of our Heaven-born art,
> And in the chorus all unite,
>   While joy expands each throbbing heart;
> The Art of Printing shall endure
>   And Independence be secure.

SAMUEL WOODWORTH, "Printing and Independence" *(1811)*.

THE process of making impressions from type has always been a fascinating one, as one realizes when he observes the crowds which never fail to gather where the great newspaper presses of today may be viewed through large, plate-glass windows. The sight of complicated machinery performing with almost human skill is not the only attraction, for mankind has not yet ceased to marvel at the miraculous transformation of white paper into a bearer of human thought. Probably everyone has experienced the desire to print, just as he has felt the urge to create and the instinct to acquire, but these impulses have often been sublimated to an interest in what others get, create, or perpetuate. The "art preservative of arts" remains the greatest agency of this common interest.

For fifty years after the Revolutionary War the processes of printing in the United States showed little variation from their colonial antecedents. Although the English colonists early made use of the press, the first one being set up in Cambridge in 1639, the spread of printing establishments was not rapid.[1] In 1671 Governor William Berkeley rejoiced that there were no printing presses in Virginia; and in 1665 the Duke of York's new colony had to depend upon Cambridge for its printing. William Bradford's first press in New York was not established until 1693, although in 1685 he had printed in Pennsylvania.[2] That these early presses were not idle is indicated by the one hundred and fifty-seven titles issued by the Cambridge press during the first thirty-one years of its existence and the four hundred printed by Bradford during his fifty

[1] Wroth, Lawrence C., *The Colonial Printers*, p. 16. This first press is supposed to have been carried later to Rutland, Vt., then sold and carried to Elizabethtown, N. Y., where it was said to have been used in 1826. It is now preserved in the Museum of the Vermont Historical Society, Montpelier, Vt. See *Saratoga Sentinel,* June 6, 1826.

[2] Wertenbaker, T. J., *The First Americans,* p. 239, n. 2; Thomas, Isaiah, *History of Printing in America* (1874), I, 38, 69, 290.

years in New York.[3] There were few printing offices in the province of New York during the eighteenth century; and the press set up at Albany in 1771 was the only one outside New York City before the Revolution.[4] Colonial printers usually obtained their presses from England as did Benjamin Franklin when he wished to open his office in Philadelphia. Presses made in America did not become common until the nonimportation agreements of the struggle over taxation gave an impetus to colonial manufacturing.[5]

Tradition has it that the first American-built press was that of Christopher Sower of Germantown, Pa., made in 1750. It was probably a homemade contrivance, however, and it did not represent the beginning of regular manufacture. The construction of presses in America really began in 1769, when Isaac Doolittle, a clockmaker of New Haven, built a press for William Goddard, of Philadelphia.[6] During the same year the first regular manufacture of types in America was undertaken in Connecticut, by Abel Buell, who received aid from the legislature of that colony to carry on the work.[7] Soon several foundries were established, the best known being those carried on by Benjamin Franklin and later by his grandson Benjamin Franklin Bache, by Binny and Ronaldson of Philadelphia, and by Elihu White and Company of Hartford and later of New York.[8]

The presses varied in make and minor details but were of uniform plan. They were not very different from the crude instruments of Gutenberg and Caxton. The upright frame, the central screw, the platen and bed were fundamental. In the eighteenth century they were constructed chiefly of wood, but

[3] Wertenbaker, *op. cit.*, p. 237; Wroth, *op. cit.*, p. 29; Paltsits, V. H., sketch of William Bradford in the *Dictionary of American Biography*, II, 564.

[4] Heartman, C. F., *Check List of Printers in the United States, From Stephen Daye to Close of the War of Independence* (1915).

[5] Wroth, L. C., article on North America, in Peddie, R. A., *Printing; a Short History of the Art*, p. 319 ff.; Thomas, *op. cit.*, I, 35-36, states that after 1775 good presses were made in America.

[6] Wroth, *The Colonial Printers*, pp. 66-67.

[7] *Ibid.*, pp. 80-83.

[8] Pasko, W. W., *American Dictionary of Printing*, pp. 556-557.

more metal parts appeared as the models were improved. Several of the early presses are now preserved in museums and historical societies, and the difficulties of eighteenth-century presswork are explained by their crude structure. One is the so-called Blaeu press used by Isaiah Thomas, historian of American printing, which is now on view in the building of the American Antiquarian Society, at Worcester, Mass.

The press generally used by the country printers of New York after 1800 was of American construction, built by a Scotchman, Adam Ramage, of Philadelphia, who arrived in this country in 1795. Prior to his coming there was no standard model in America; many variations of English presses were constructed to order, the ironwork being supplied by a blacksmith.[9] The Ramage press became standard during the first decades of the nineteenth century and was so well known that Van Winkle's *Printer's Guide* in 1818 declared that "any description of it [was] unnecessary." [10] Since this is the apparatus to which we shall frequently refer in subsequent paragraphs, an examination of its chief features seems necessary. Fortunately there is available a description of the Ramage press by a printer who received his training in its operation:

The press was formed by two heavy upright pieces of timber, standing about seven feet high,[11] called the "cheeks," which stood three or four feet apart, and were held together by a crosspiece at top and bottom. Running through the center of the "cheeks," was a carriage way, or "ribs," resting on another crosspiece called the "winter piece." These rib pieces, conveniently set apart one from the other, extended out each side of the press of sufficient length to accommodate the "bed" to run backward and forward when the printer was working off the "form" he was engaged in, whether of book, handbill, or newspaper. Next is the "bed" of the press, which ran out and in on the ribs, and which

---

[9] *Ibid.*, pp. 255, 285. Follett, Frederick, *The History of the Press of Western New York*, p. 47, says that until 1824 the Ramage press was the only one used in that section. This important work of Follett, so frequently quoted, has been used in the 1920 reprint, unless the date of the rare, original (1847) edition is given.

[10] Van Winkle, *Printer's Guide*, pp. 201-202.

[11] Pasko, *op. cit.*, pp. 253-254, gives the measurement of early presses as six feet one inch high, and one foot eleven inches between the cheeks. Length with frisket thrown out, about eight feet.

received the form of the type that was made up to be printed. This bed ran on straight, polished ribs of steel, the ribs being the same, and both were oiled. To the bed were attached two frames with joints—the larger one that folded down on the form, and on which the unprinted sheet was laid, was the "tympan," and the upper one, that folded down on the "tympan," and held the sheet while it was being printed was the "frisket." Now to make the impression, a large screw with a coarse t[h]read was placed in a box and that box was fastened into a crosspiece between the cheeks, called the "summer piece." The screw, which worked in the box, had a long point and worked in the center of a square follower, which was kept in its place by springs, and was called the "platen." Fixed to the screw immediately under the "winter piece" [summer piece] was a lever of iron, crooked in a half circle at the eye where it was attached to the screw, and had a long bar, the end of which was supplied with a large, round, wood handle. This bar swung transversely across the press from side to side, so as to give the power of the screw, and when the press was in repose its place was against the back cheek of the press, where it was held by a "stop." To make the "pull," i.e. the impression, the form being on and "locked up," the pressman, first flying the frisket and holding down the tympan, quick as thought runs under the carriage [sic]. This he does by seizing with his left hand a crank handle, the axle of which runs across under the bed of the press, and was geared or fastened to the bed by leather straps —now the pressman seizes the bar with his right hand, and swinging his body with his whole weight brings down the "platen," which gives the impression. The bed is now run back by a reverse motion on the crank, and the printed sheet is taken off.—I should say here that the tympan is covered with cotton cloth stretched tight, where the paper to be printed was laid on, and that back of the tympan cloth was another inside frame covered with cloth, and between the two was inserted a piece of good broadcloth, to soften the pull upon the face of the type in the form, and at the same time to give a clearer impression.[12]

Some obscurity in the foregoing quotation may justify a restatement. The operations described can be summarized as follows: the paper to be printed was laid upon the "tympan," a kind of frame hinged to the press. At the other end of the tympan another frame, the "frisket," was hinged, and this was folded down to hold the paper in place. Both of these were then folded over, using the hinge of the tympan, until the paper rested on the block of type in the "bed" of the press. Previous

---

[12] Scrantom, Edwin, in *Rochester Democrat and Chronicle,* Feb. 21, 1871.

to this operation, the type had been inked, either with the pad-like balls or with a roller. Now the type, bed, and frames holding the paper were run forward on the carriage by turning the crank at the side, until they were beneath the "platen," the block by which pressure was applied. The pressman next pulled the large lever, which, acting by means of the screw at the top of the press, lowered the platen on the tympan and made the impression. Since the platen was often but half the size of the form, the crank would be given a turn to slide the other half of the form beneath it, and a second pull would be given to complete the impression on this sheet.

Next the crank would be given a turn in the opposite direction, and the form would be run out from under the platen. The tympan and frisket would then be lifted in turn and the printed sheet removed. Then the operation would be repeated, and so on for each sheet printed. The succession of these operations, constantly repeated, with two or three persons co-operating in team fashion, soon became quite rapid.

The first Ramage presses were probably as crude as the homemade article of the carpenter, joiner, and blacksmith, but as improvements and inventions were made, they were gradually incorporated into the Ramage product. Ramage introduced iron into his presses when it became common in others, and the iron or brass platen and bed replaced the platen of wood and the bed of stone under a wooden coffin.[13] In 1807 he enlarged the diameter of the screw, thus increasing the pressure that could be brought to bear on the platen.[14] By an adaptation of the principle of the Ruthven (Edinburgh) press (noted by Van Winkle in 1818) it was possible for him to use a type form which remained stationary and a platen as large as the form, making only one pull necessary for each impression.[15]

In 1813 Clymer's Columbian Hand Press appeared, with its

[13] Pasko, *op. cit.*, p. 255; Munsell, *Typographical Miscellany*, pp. 128-129; 136; Bullen, H. L., "Evolution of the American Printing Press," *The American Printer*, July, 1926.
[14] Wroth, *op. cit.*, pp. 68-69.
[15] Van Winkle, *op. cit.*, p. 196.

abandonment of the screw in favor of the lever, surpassing in some respects the improved English press of Lord Stanhope, but few of Clymer's presses were sold in this country. In the same year John I. Wells, of Hartford, substituted a toggle joint for the screw to secure the necessary pressure. This principle was also used in the press patented by Samuel Rust and Peter Smith, of New York, in 1821.[16]

These practical improvements were of great interest to the country printer, who recognized their value in promoting better printing even though they never reached his modest office. He was eager, too, for news of foreign inventions introduced into this country. In 1811 it was reported that Francis Shields, of London, was to set up his press manufactory in New York to manufacture the Stanhope press.[17] At the time Messrs. Bruce, of New York City, owned the only Stanhope press in this country, but American printers had probably read descriptions of it in Stower's *Printer's Grammar,* published in London in 1808.[18] In 1825 it was reported that the New York *Daily Advertiser* and the *American* were to be printed on the London-made "Napier's Imperial Printing Machine," capable of two thousand sheets an hour, a speed which seemed phenomenal to the country printer.[19]

Central and western New York obtained presses from several sources; new ones could be purchased in New York City, Albany, Philadelphia, and Boston, while the supply of second-hand machines seems always to have been adequate. In 1826 the Auburn *Free Press* was worked on a new "improved" Washington Press, obtained from Rust & Turner, of New

---

[16] Bullen, *loc. cit.*

[17] Brooklyn *Long Island Star,* Oct. 23, 1811. In references and quotations from newspapers throughout this work the following practice is followed. The exact title of the paper (omitting the initial "The"; and sometimes lengthy subtitles in the text) is given in italics. The location of the newspaper is not italicized, unless it appears in the title (e.g., *Catskill Recorder*). When necessary for identification, the place name precedes the italicized title (e.g., Kingston *Plebeian*). This conforms with the practice in the Appendix.

[18] Stower, C., *Printer's Grammar,* pp. 499-507. This work was dedicated to Lord Stanhope.

[19] *Onondaga Register,* Oct. 12, 1825; *Saratoga Sentinel,* Sept. 13, 1825. This was a cylinder press.

York.[20] In 1828 the *Madison Farmer* of Hamilton was begun on a "Smith's improved patent imperial" press purchased of A. W. Kinsley & Co., of Albany.[21] A "Smith's Patent" was also used to print the *Rochester Daily Advertiser*.[22] The *Freeman's Journal* of Cooperstown at about the same time made arrangements to procure a "New England Press" from Boston, but due to the failure of the Boston firm to deliver it as promised, another press was purchased in New York.[23] Other presses in use at this time were "Well's Press," and "Dodge's Patent," the latter being used in Brooklyn.[24] By 1830 improved hand presses were generally used by country printers, even in the western counties.

The cost of these presses to the printer varied greatly. Although a secondhand press could be secured cheaply in some communities, the printer in the back country often had to pay a high price to cover transportation charges. If he established his office in a remote district the value of his equipment was correspondingly enhanced. In 1797, for example, David Frothingham of Sag Harbor, L. I., was able to mortgage his press for eleven pounds, although it was then considered "an old press."[25] During the following year a "Printing Office," composed of a comparatively new press, cases and four fonts of type was offered for sale in Poughkeepsie for $200.[26] Secondhand presses could be obtained on reasonable terms in New York City. In 1816 the proprietor of the Potsdam *Gazette* purchased in New York a press of the Ramage design for $150, but ten years later a genuine Ramage, probably secondhand, was obtained in the same place for $40.[27] An unusually high price was recorded in 1818, when an Elmira

[20] *Free Press*, May 31, 1826.
[21] *Madison Farmer*, Dec. 3, 1828.
[22] *Rochester Daily Advertiser*, Mar. 30, 1827.
[23] *Freeman's Journal*, Jan. 1, 1827.
[24] Van Winkle, *op. cit.*, pp. 201-202. These names of presses signified the manufacturers rather than entirely new models. The "Ramage," too, was not distinctive but was merely the product of the Philadelphia pressmaker.
[25] MS in Long Island Collection of Morton Pennypacker, East Hampton Library.
[26] *Poughkeepsie Journal*, Sept. 18, 1798.
[27] Munsell, *Typographical Miscellany*, pp. 13-14.

printer paid $1,700 for an old press and sufficient types to print his paper.[28] If the prospective buyer of a press expected to make a substantial investment in his equipment, he was extremely cautious in dealing with the distant manufacturer. The printer of the Cooperstown *Freeman's Journal,* for instance, in his negotiation for a press from Boston, deposited money for payment with an agent in Albany, a way station in the course of its delivery. Even then he was not satisfied with the treatment which he had received, and canceled his order.[29] Prices declined considerably after the first quarter of the nineteenth century. In 1844 the largest Ramage, which had sold originally in America for $400, was quoted at $165, while the Washington and Smith presses of similar size cost only $120.[30]

Presses capable of satisfactory work were often used with such worn or damaged type that good printing was impossible. It was not uncommon for the country printer to start with type one-third or one-fourth worn, and no improvement so elated him as that "new dress" provided by the purchase of a new font. Elias Williams started the *Genesee Intelligencer* in 1807 with a secondhand press and a box of old type in pi, which he spent the winter in sorting.[31]

The main body of the paper was printed in brevier or small pica. Great primer or double pica could be used for headings, advertising, or perhaps to occupy space whenever there was a scarcity of news.[32] Later advertisements of type for sale showed a wider variety, with minion, nonpareil, Bourgeois, canon, and English added to the usual pica and primer.[33] The chief sources for new types were J. Ronaldson's foundry, in Philadelphia, and D. and G. Bruce's foundry, in New York.

[28] Letter of Rev. James Durham in *Elmira Gazette,* July 14, 1853.

[29] *Freeman's Journal,* Jan. 1, 1827.

[30] Pasko, *op. cit.,* p. 255.

[31] Follett, *op. cit.,* p. 56.

[32] *Long Island Courier,* Apr. 22, 1801; A. Spooner's autobiographical letter in Tooker, "Early Sag Harbor Printers," *Sag Harbor Express,* Jan. 23, 1902.

[33] There were numerous advertisements of used type for sale, for example in Troy *Farmer's Oracle,* Feb. 20, 1798; Auburn *Advocate of the People,* Nov. 12, 1817; *Chautauqua Phenix,* Dec. 5, 1828, and *Cooperstown Federalist,* Aug. 10, 1811.

In 1820 James D. Bemis, of Canandaigua, was the agent for both of these foundries in western New York.[34] The Troy *Northern Budget,* however, in 1805 announced its acquisition of new type from the "celebrated foundry of Dr. Wilson of Glasgow." [35]

Display types came into use later in the period and were chiefly employed for political handbills and advertising. In addition, woodcuts for illustration and decoration were more commonly used. Occasionally the handbill found a place in the regular issue of the newspaper. In an election issue of the *Long Island Patriot* for April 25, 1821, the billboard set-up employed ¾ inch letters and woodcuts of a ship and an eagle, eight inches in height. In the earlier days, and especially in the case of the pioneer printer, the woodcut was sometimes a home-made affair. Franklin Cowdery at Moscow used his jackknife to cut the head for his paper from a hickory stick.[36] Figured heads were common and much desired, especially if they gave

[34] Canandaigua *Ontario Repository,* Aug. 29, 1820.
[35] *Northern Budget,* June 11, 1805.

THE CURRENT PHILADELPHIA PRICES OF TYPES PER POUND

Pt.	Name	*1801*	*1806*	*1811*	*1819*	*1827*	*1829*	*1831*
12	Pica	0.35	0.44	0.55	0.44	0.42	0.36	0.36
11	Small pica	.40	.48	.58	.48	.46	.38	.38
10	Long primer	.47	.56	.66	.56	.50	.40	.40
9	Bourgeois	.56	.66	.76	.66	.58	.46	.46
8	Brevier	.67	.76	.86	.76	.70	.56	.56
7	Minion	...	1.03	1.13	1.00	.88	.70	.70
6	Nonpareil	1.12	1.40	1.75	1.40	1.20	.90	.90
5½	Agate	...	...	...	...	1.44	...	1.10
5	Pearl	...	...	...	1.75	1.75	1.50	1.40

The above quotations are found (except for 1829) in Pasko, *op. cit.,* pp. 557, 552-553; and Mackellar, Thomas, *The American Printer,* pp. 23-27. For 1829 the data were found in an advertisement of Richard Ronaldson, Philadelphia, in *Onondaga Register,* Sept. 9, 1829. This advertisement also carried, in addition to the above: "Long letter plain" .30, Double Gt. Primer .32, Double English .32, Double Small Pica .34, English .34 and Leads and Quotations .30. Old type received for 9 cents per lb.

In 1819 James Ronaldson's advertisement listed, in addition to those above; English .42, Great Primer and all longer .41, scabbards and quotations .40. "Credit 60, 90, and 120 days. Old type received in exchange at $16 per 112 pounds." Munsell, *Typographical Miscellany,* p. 140.

[36] Letter of D. Munger in *Detroit Daily Advertiser,* Dec. 12, 1857. Clipping in the scrapbook of Henry O'Reilly, New York Historical Society.

point to the slogan above the date line. The following quotation from a Kingston paper well illustrates this practice:

We have this week the pleasure of introducing to the notice of our readers an emblematick representation of the celebrated *Antony Von Corlaer* seated near a tankard of racy October, enjoying his comfortable pipe over a sheet of the latest news. For this ingenious conception, we are indebted to My[n]heer Gerrit Lansing of New York, a clever little Dutchman, who in the maternal line has the honor of being descended from the ancient Esopus stock. The lines underneath, it is scarcely necessary to say, are borrowed from the title-page of *Knickerbocker's History of New York;* which for the benefit of such as do not understand the vernacular tongue may be translated,—

The truth that doth in darkness lie,
Comes forth with clearness to the eye.[37]

Other cuts and illustrations used were the head of Franklin, the postboy, the sentinel, the Hudson packet boat, and even (in the case of the Hudson *Bee*), a beehive or a single bee. Cuts for advertising, as everyone familiar with the history of the newspaper knows, had been used in Colonial days. Runaways, ships, hats, horses, and other emblems, small enough to occupy one end of a column width advertisement multiplied as rapidly as the printer's supply of type.

The political cartoon had been used in the colonial press, but it was too costly for the average country newspaper before 1830. The *Troy Budget* for November 4, 1828, however, ran a two-column cartoon predicting Jackson's victory at the polls. In the foreground was "Old Hickory" on a galloping horse, while in the distance was the Capitol from which tiny figures of Adams and his cabinet were scurrying.[38]

Type for musical scores was rare, but the country printer

---

[37] "De warheid die in duister lag—
    "Die kommt met klaarheid aam de dag."—*Ulster Sentinel,* Oct. 4, 1826.

[38] Another example of the political cartoon was found in the Hudson *Northern Whig,* Nov. 28, 1809, reprinted from the Albany *Balance.* This represented a man picking a goose, with the caption, "State Printing," and beneath the legend, "The public is a goose, and a man is a d—d fool that will not have a hand in picking her.—Sir Solomon Faucet [Southwick]." This occasioned the libel suit of *Croswell* vs. *Southwick.*

who had obtained it to set up a songbook or hymnbook occasionally introduced it into his paper. As early as 1828, the *Ithaca Journal* used this type to print the melody of "Oh! No, We Never Mention Her," by T. H. Bailey. The lines of the staff which extended across two columns of the paper were broken to permit the insertion of the notes or signs.[39] Such enterprise indicated that the country printer was gradually overcoming the limitations of his primitive, early equipment.

Most printers were skillful compositors. The composing stick, as well as the "stone" on which the "matter" was set up, was the tool with which the apprentice became familiar early in his career, and even when he reached the position of master he was reluctant to abandon typesetting. He was seldom satisfied until he had demonstrated his ability to compose articles, editorials, or advertising matter directly into type, without relying upon written copy.[40] The boy or journeyman who worked swiftly at the "case" was much in demand, and later when the labor was divided in the larger establishments, piecework rates were intended to encourage rapid composition.[41]

When the type had been set, the form was locked and placed on the movable carriage of the press. Now came the laborious task of inking, in which there was little improvement before 1829 when the roller began to be used.[42] Inking the types preparatory to each impression was done with two "balls" of leather, usually of green sheepskin but later of dressed deerskin, stuffed with wool and attached to wooden handles.[43] Ink, previously prepared on a board, was applied to the balls by rubbing and transferred to the type by a kind of tattoo beating of the balls as the form slid from beneath the platen. This beating was generally performed by a boy, while a man pulled at the press. The process resulted in a satisfactory inking job, but the composition roller was much more efficient and saved

[39] *Ithaca Journal*, Aug. 20, 1828; also Nov. 26, 1828, and Sept. 1, 1830.
[40] Weed, *Autobiography*, p. 70.
[41] Munsell, *Typographical Miscellany*, pp. 89-90.
[42] Follett, *op. cit.*, pp. 47-48.
[43] Weed, *Autobiography*, p. 22.

considerable time and labor. It was reported that the composition roller which had been invented in Lewes, Eng., was used first in this country in the office of Orsamus Turner in Lockport about 1829.[44] These rollers were made of a combination of glue and molasses. Crude though they were, they proved superior to the "skin rollers" which had been tested in New York in 1815.[45]

Primitive tools and methods were not the only handicaps under which the pioneer printer labored. Except in the larger towns or those served directly by New York and Albany, the supply of print paper was always a problem. Frequently the printer of a newspaper was compelled to issue a sheet of reduced size, with consequent reduction in the news and other matter, because he had been unable to obtain sufficient paper.[46] In its pioneering days, many a small establishment also had to endure taunts of rival editors that it was a "dingy 7 by 9 sheet," that it was printed on "blue" paper, or that it was not issued regularly. These strictures were keenly resented when the printer felt that he was being judged under adverse conditions over which he had no control, and he sometimes sought to forestall criticism by an apology. Said Elihu Phinney of Cooperstown, "the editor regrets that it is not in his power to begin the publication of the *Herald* on white paper; but unfortunately it could not be procured." [47] At Newport, Genesee County, Franklin Cowdery began one of his numerous enterprises in 1824, and a generous neighbor apologized for him: "The circumstances under which Mr. Cowdery commences his paper, and the difficulty of obtaining suitable materials at this season of the year, is a sufficient apology for the ordinary

[44] Letter of D. Munger, *loc. cit.;* Pool, Wm., *Landmarks of Niagara County,* p. 121 n.; and Follett, *op. cit.,* pp. 47-48.

[45] Munsell, *Typographical Miscellany* (annotated copy in American Antiquarian Society), opposite p. 123; D. Munger's letter, *loc. cit.* Mackellar, *The American Printer,* gives a recipe for making the composition roller.

[46] That it was not confined to one period is shown by the following cases, in which a cessation of regular issue was occasioned by paper shortage: *Poughkeepsie Journal,* Apr. 23, 1799; Geneva *Expositor,* May 27, 1807; *Auburn Gazette,* Mar. 25, 1818; *Jamestown Journal,* Feb. 7, 1827; *Chautauqua Republican,* Feb. 11, 1829.

[47] *Otsego Herald,* Apr. 3, 1795.

appearance of the *Patriot,* which he promises to improve in a few weeks." [48]

Since the printer rarely invested in a large supply of paper, he was constantly dependent upon the paper maker. Therefore, in order to understand the conditions under which he labored, it is necessary for us to mention briefly the paper-making industry. New York City was the natural source of supply for the towns of the Hudson valley, although the first paper-making establishment in the state was at Hempstead, L. I., in 1768. [49] In 1799 several issues of the *Poughkeepsie Journal* were reduced in size because the regular supply of paper from New York was delayed on board a Poughkeepsie sloop. [50] In this same year, however, there was a paper mill started in Mount Pleasant in Westchester County. [51] Mills in the towns of the Hudson valley were soon established. Hudson, Columbia County, had one in 1800, remodeled from an old grist mill and operated by George Chittenden of the firm which published the *Balance.* [52] Catskill and Newburgh boasted mills of their own in 1804, while northern New York had not long to wait. [53]

As early as 1789 the source of supply for the northern part of the state was Bennington, Vermont, where the paper maker was reputed to have relied upon the cast-off rags of the Indians to supply his mill. [54] The firm of Webster, Ensign and Seymour, of Troy, began paper making in 1793, while S. & A. Hawley were operating a mill at "Moreau, near Fort Edward" in 1808. [55] Schoharie followed in 1809, and Schenectady in 1812. [56]

---

[48] Rochester *Telegraph,* Feb. 17, 1824.

[49] Weeks, L. H., *A History of Paper Manufacturing in the United States, 1690-1916,* p. 156.

[50] *Poughkeepsie Journal,* Apr. 23, 1799.

[51] *Mount Pleasant Courier,* June 19, 1799.

[52] Munsell, *Typographical Miscellany,* p. 147.

[53] *Catskill Recorder,* 1804-1806; Newburgh *Recorder of the Times,* Aug. 29, 1804.

[54] Munsell, Joel, *Chronology of Paper and Papermaking,* p. 32.

[55] Woodworth, J., *Reminiscences of Troy,* p. 46; Hill, Wm. H., *A Brief History of the Printing Press in Washington, Saratoga and Warren Counties,* p. 94.

[56] Schenectady *Cabinet,* Dec. 23, 1812; Munsell, *Typographical Miscellany,* p. 109.

Central and western New York had some mills at a comparatively early date, which were compelled to serve a large area. Pioneering paper makers established themselves at Martinsburgh in 1809, and at Oriskany and Watertown in the following year. These mills appear to have been fairly permanent and successful.[57] The principal mill in western New York, however, was at Dansville, where Nathaniel Rochester was instrumental in setting up the "Eagle" mill in 1810.[58] Six years later Ontario County had its own mill, and one was opened at Waterloo in Seneca County in 1826.[59] The region of Niagara Falls entered the paper industry in 1823; Fredonia, Chautauqua County, had a well known establishment in 1828, and Ebenezer Mack offered his "share" of the Ithaca mills for sale in 1826.[60] The existence of other establishments is revealed by newspaper accounts of paper-mill fires such as those at Batavia in 1820, Schoharie in 1821, Mount Pleasant in 1822, and at Rochester in 1827.[61] The foregoing enumeration does not exhaust the list of mills, for Isaiah Thomas reported that there were twelve paper manufactories in the state in 1810, while Tench Coxe placed the number at twenty-eight in 1813.[62]

Some of these mills apparently did a considerable business, making paper for all purposes. That at Saugerties, the first to use a Foudrinier machine in this country, was reported in 1828 to be "probably the most extensive in the United States. When all the works are in operation, it will employ about 360 persons, and is capable of turning out 28,000 square feet of paper in an hour." [63] Isaiah Thomas noted that most of the mills in New England had two vats and thus would require about $10,000 in capital, and the labor of twelve or more men, boys,

---

[57] Weeks, *op. cit.*, pp. 152-156. Otsego County had a mill in 1806.

[58] *Ibid.*, pp. 148-149.

[59] *Ontario Repository*, Jan. 16, 1816; *Palmyra Register*, Oct. 6, 1819; Waterloo *Seneca Farmer*, Mar. 1, 1826.

[60] Weeks, *op. cit.*, pp. 154-155; *Chautauqua Republican*, Dec. 31, 1828; Auburn *Free Press*, Dec. 25, 1826.

[61] Munsell, *Chronology*, p. 48; *Niagara Patriot*, Jan. 25, 1820; *Rochester Album*, Dec. 25, 1827.

[62] Weeks, *op. cit.*, pp. 107-109; Thomas, *History of Printing*, II, 530-537.

[63] Cooperstown *Freeman's Journal*, May 26, 1828; Weeks, *op. cit.*, p. 156. It was established in 1827.

and girls. There were some mills in New York which had three vats and so were proportionately larger.[64] Thus it was not surprising that mills increased with less rapidity than printing offices.

Since the printer usually chose his location because of the population and political advantages in the area to be served, rather than because of proximity to a paper mill, he encountered numerous difficulties in procuring his supply of paper. After an exasperating experience in connection with delayed delivery from Dansville (one hundred miles distant), the printer in Jamestown had to borrow from his neighbor and competitor.[65] In 1818 the *Auburn Gazette* failed to receive its paper supply from Schenectady, since the thaw of March had made the roads impassable for the "waggoner." [66] And we are told that the pioneer printer at Martinsburg, Lewis County, was once reduced to carrying on his back a bundle of paper from Utica.[67] Transportation was not the only problem. During the winter months extremely cold weather might cause a cessation of manufacture.[68]

As neither money nor materials were abundant, the printer became a solicitor for the means of making paper. The advertisement for "rags" appeared in various forms, sometimes with a caption designed to catch the attention of housewives. The following is a quaint attempt at variety in such appeals.

Save Your Rags. / and / Since you refuse to let the printer have any money, do be so good as to assist him in stopping a *paper mill money call,* by letting him have immediately, *All* the linen and cotton *RAGS* you now have on hand. He will allow as much for them as you can get from any other person, and you can thus easily, meet a demand, to pay which without rags, he may possibly have to *send* to somebody *Greeting,* to get money!!![69]

[64] Thomas, *History of Printing,* II, 531. Estimated loss in the Rochester fire was $5,000.

[65] *Chautauqua Republican,* Feb. 11, 1829.

[66] *Auburn Gazette,* Mar. 25, 1818.

[67] Haddock, *History of Jefferson County,* p. 302.

[68] *Jamestown Journal,* Feb. 7, 1827.

[69] *Angelica Republican,* Mar. 6, 1821.

For clean cotton or linen rags the rate was generally two or three pence per pound, although there was a quotation as high as four pence in 1804.[70] Twenty years later the same materials were quoted at five dollars per hundred pounds.[71] Certain types of rags, such as cotton waste, cotton bagging, nets, and woolen rags, were not acceptable.[72] Even these lower grades had their uses, however, and the printer at Sag Harbor, L. I., mentioned old nets and sailcloth in his call for rags.[73] That the printer did not always secure rag paper of good quality is evident from the following complaint of a Poughkeepsie publisher. "We owe our readers an apology for the bad appearance of the paper of this week. The fault is not ours. The paper itself is so very thin, soft and spongy, that it does not hold a good impression."[74]

There were a few mills which experimented with paper made from straw, hay, "corn husks and flag leaves," and the interest of the country printer in such experimentation was another evidence of the scarcity of rags and the high cost of rag paper.[75] Fortunately, however, straw paper was not used for newspapers in this period.[76] The printer urged his readers to save rags as a patriotic duty and extolled paper making as a home manufacture which all should encourage.[77]

[70] *Catskill Packet,* July 1, 1793; Newburgh *Recorder of the Times,* Aug. 29, 1804.

[71] *Newburgh Gazette,* July 31, 1824.

[72] *Ibid.*

[73] *Frothingham's Long Island Herald,* June 28, 1791, *et seq.*

[74] Poughkeepsie *Dutchess Intelligencer,* Aug. 18, 1830.

[75] Jamestown *Chautauqua Republican,* Dec. 31, 1828.

[76] The excellent state of preservation of these old files, largely due to the durability of the paper, is one of the advantages of the researcher in this period. Since the Civil War the employment of cheap paper, often entirely of wood pulp, has rendered difficult the use of newspaper files and created for libraries the problem of their preservation.

[77] Woodworth, *Reminiscences of Troy,* p. 46.

II

THE ART AND MYSTERY

'TIS *twelve o'clock—and now, with loud acclaim,*
      Lo, the freed 'prentice issues from his frame,
His seven years servitude at length is o'er;
His buried wife can harass him no more.
At him as slippers fly from ev'ry hand,
He also flies—'twere dangerous to stand!
And, as he marks from whence those gifts are thrown,
He runs around or bobs behind the stone.
Nor slippers only—in the hot pursuit
One free translator delegates a boot.
T' express with force, in its peculiar way,
Congratulation on this happy day.
The youth, perplexed—hemmed in on every side—
Seeks for a shield, and snatches a broadside!
Alas! the riot robs him of his sense:
How can a sheet of paper yield defense?
Now comes the wash—the cross attacks the chase,
While mallets beat the boards in many a place,
And quoin-drawers play confusions double bass.
At length, exhausted with their strains, the band
Forego their labours, and quiescent stand,
When forth steps one, who bears above his brains
A vessel to receive their hard-earn'd gains.
The hint is ta'en—the new loos'd 'prentice stands
A crown—and drops of brandy cheer all hands.
He drinks their health—and then with air polite,
Invites them all to bon souper at night.

G. BRIMMER, "The Composing Room."

N O CRAFTSMAN has had a greater sense of his own importance than the printer. With the development of his trade and the increased use of printing he came to feel that his peculiar skill was an indispensable factor in the advancement of learning. Although he was often scorned as a mechanic and was humiliated at times by the inferiority of his tools and the grime of his calling, he was ever buoyed by the thought that his was an intellectual fraternity, long established and animated by high ideals. Printers, therefore, longer than many other craftsmen continued in modified form the practices of the medieval guilds.

Traditionally the printing office housed a "chapel." There was a restricted membership, and the rites and customs were guarded and preserved. Those privileged to enter the chapel were forced to conform to an ancient ritual and swore to perpetuate it. Originally as sacred as the bonds of a fraternity and enforced with the severity of guild regulations, which guaranteed the economic security of the group, these obligations later became mere customs, honored out of respect for the traditions of the craft.[1]

The purpose of the chapel was undoubtedly the governance of the workers of the craft who were gathered in the office; just as the guild regulations had for their object the welfare of master and trade. According to an English writer of the seventeenth century, "There have been formerly Customs and By-Laws made and intended for the well and good Government of the Chappel; and the Penalty for the breach of any of these Laws and Customs is in the Printer's Language called a Solace."[2]

Violations of the rules of good conduct in the office resulted in a trial, the decision in which was made by a plurality of the

---

[1] De Vinne, Theo. L., ed., *Moxon's Mechanick Exercises; or, the Doctrine of Handy Works Applied to the Art of Printing*, II, 356-363. This is a literal reprint of the original work by Joseph Moxon, printed in London in 1683.

[2] *Ibid.*

votes of the chapel. In the event of such violation it was reported to the "oldest Freeman," or "Father of the Chappel."
After judgment had been rendered the offender had to buy off
his solace, which might vary from twelve pence to one pence.
If the delinquent proved obstinate and would not pay his fine,
then he was forcibly "solac'd." [3]

The manner of Solacing, thus:
The Workmen take him by force, and lay him on his Belly athwart the
Correcting-Stone, and hold him there while another of the Work-men,
with a Paperboard, gave him 10 1. and a Purse, viz. Eleven blows on
his Buttocks, which he laid on according to his mercy...[4]

The offenses, for which "solaces" were imposed were at first
nine, but the number was later increased. Some penalties, such
as those for swearing, fighting, using abusive language, or being drunk in the chapel, were obviously designed to maintain
order. Others were intended to secure greater care and attention to duty. It was a punishable offense for the workman "to
leave his candle burning at night," to drop his composing stick
and allow another to pick it up, to let "three letters and a
Space to lye under the Compositor's Case," to "let fall his
Ball or Balls, and another take it up," or to "leave his Blankets
in the Tympan at Noon or Night." [5]

Other solaces were more or less formal taxes, or time-
sanctioned customs of no practical value, though amusing for
sport or sentiment. Mentioning the sharing of drinks or chapel
money before Saturday night was a solace. So, too, was sing-
ing in the chapel, or bringing a wisp of hay to a pressman.[6]
Of this sort, also, was the survival in this period of the custom
of a treat by the master and old journeymen, whenever signature "o" was put to press.[7] Other customs were for special
occasions. *Benvenue* (welcome) was paid by one who joined
the chapel. A survival of this was the requirement that a new
journeyman should pay "footing," a treat to all hands by the

[3] *Ibid.*
[4] *Ibid.*
[5] *Ibid.*
[6] *Ibid.*
[7] Weed, *Autobiography*, p. 58.

newcomer.[8] It would be a mistake to assume that all such customs were kept in their pristine form in the American country printing offices. Yet reminders of them crop out. Who cannot imagine the persistence of such a custom as this: knocking loudly with the "back corner of the Composing stick against the lower ledges of the lower case" to signify disbelief in a man's statement.[9]

Drinking and gambling were also bound up with solaces, and the money thus exchanged was often used for drinks. To gamble was a solace, but printers had their own peculiar form known as "jeffing," or playing at quadrats, and in this period it was common to "jeff" for beer, as Thurlow Weed testified.[10]

For the manner of how they play with them is thus; they take five or seven more *m* quadrats (generally of the English Body) and holding their Hand below the Surface of the Correcting Stone, shake them in their Hand, and toss them up upon the Stone, and then count how many Nicks upwards each man throws in three times, or any other number of times agreed on. And he that throws most Wins the Bett of all the rest, and stands out free, till the rest have try'd who throws fewest Nicks upwards, in so many throws; for all the rest are free and he pays the Bett.[11]

This was the printer's form of dice, or the modern "craps." Masters opposed this practice because it damaged the type faces. Occasional hazing of apprentices or new journeymen was also indulged in as an ancient rite of the chapel. In the larger offices these customs were longer observed, since they had their justification in the preservation of order.[12] Upon the journeymen and apprentices of the entire country, however, they had a persistent though declining influence.

With a few exceptions the printer learned his trade as an

---

[8] *Ibid.*

[9] Stevens, George A., *New York Typographical Union No. 6*, pp. 122-123.

[10] Weed, *Autobiography*, p. 58.

[11] Stevens, *op. cit.*, p. 122.

[12] *Ibid.*, p. 126. In England some masters preferred the chapel as a means of preserving order, while others opposed it as encouraging drinking. New York City printers in 1850 recommended the chapel as a means of governing the office through the employees themselves.—Commons, John R., ed., *Documentary History of American Industrial Society*, VII, 126-128.

apprentice, bound to a master printer. One hundred years ago parents and guardians sought for the young man in whom they were interested a good trade, in which, if he were industrious, he might win his way to an approved position in society. Driven, too, by economic necessity in an era of large families and education for the few, they counted it fortunate if a boy's training and support might be insured over a term of years. Care and judgment had to be exercised in finding a responsible master, and here the printer often fell under suspicion because of his migratory habits, but the strength of the bond was relied upon to overcome the natural difficulties of the ordained relationship. Under these circumstances the indentures were an unusually important factor in the development of the craft.

When the apprentice was bound to a master, the law required the execution of a legal document, a formal contract or covenant, in which were stated the obligations and duties of each to the other. It specified the term of the indenture, the nature of the service to be performed, and the character of the support and training to be given the boy. It was executed and signed by the boy, his parent or guardian, and the master, and was properly witnessed. In colonial times the contract was registered in a book kept for this purpose by the town authorities and thus became a public document. This public record seems to have lapsed after the Revolution, as other regulations also broke down, and there was frequently but one copy of the indenture, which might be delivered to the apprentice upon its expiration and his discharge.[13]

In the words of the indenture, throughout its term

the said Apprentice his Master faithfully shall serve, his secrets keep, his lawful commands every where readily obey: he shall do no damage to his said Master nor see it done by others, without letting or giving notice thereof to his said Master. He shall not waste his Master's goods, nor lend unlawfully to any: He shall not commit fornication, nor con-

[13] Seybolt, R. F., *Apprenticeship and Apprenticeship Education in Colonial New York and New England*, pp. 75-78; pp. 88-98. The original indenture of Henry O'Reilly is in the Rochester Historical Society; and J. N. Bogert of Binghamton has that of his uncle, John N. Bogert, to Col. James Bogert of Geneva (1819). The latter has a note as to its expiration.

tract matrimony within the said term: at Cards, Dice, or any unlawful game he shall not play, whereby his Master may have damage: With his own goods, nor the goods of others, without license from his said Master, he shall neither buy nor sell: He shall not absent himself day nor night from his said Master's service, without leave; nor haunt ale-houses, taverns, or play-houses; but in all things behave himself as a faithful Apprentice ought to do, during the said term.[14]

According to the printed form then used, the master should "use the utmost of his endeavors to teach, or cause to be taught or instructed, the said Apprentice, in the [Art] trade or mystery of a" printer. Likewise he was to "procure and provide for him sufficient meat, drink ... fit for an Apprentice." The blank in the last statement was filled in with the particular conditions upon which the parties might agree. John N. Bogert was to receive "washing, mending and apparel, as also medicine, nursing and medical aid." [15] Henry O'Reilly's mother inserted, "and clothing and to have him instructed in reading, writing and arithmetic." [16] In general, food, clothing, care, the rudiments of education, and training in his trade were promised to the apprentice.

As time went on it became customary to add some pecuniary remuneration to the obligation due the apprentice. Perhaps it was felt that the balance of the bargain was too strongly in favor of the master or that there would be greater security in the arrangement if the transition from bound boy to journeyman were more gradual. At any rate the old conditions were breaking down. About 1840 in Philadelphia twenty-five or thirty dollars yearly constituted this remuneration.[17] In Buffalo in 1812 Eber D. Howe agreed to an indenture for four years at forty, fifty, sixty, and eighty dollars per year respectively.[18] In Vermont in 1826 Horace Greeley had it

[14] The indenture of John N. Bogert.

[15] *Ibid.*

[16] The indenture of Henry O'Reilly. Since O'Reilly is referred to so frequently, it should be noted that later in life he changed the spelling of his name to "O'Rielly." In using the former spelling the author follows the practice of this period and also of the *Dictionary of American Biography.*

[17] Whitney, James S., *Apprenticeship,* pp. 10-11.

[18] Severance, F. H., "The Periodical Press," in the Buffalo Historical Society *Publications* XIX, 181, quotes the letter of Howe. Cf. McKinstry, L., "The

stipulated that he was to get forty dollars per year after his first six months, although the printer at first offered only twenty.[19] Henry O'Reilly's indenture had the additional condition that he was to receive "a reasonable compensation during the last year of his apprenticeship."[20] Occasionally the apprentice was to receive wages in lieu of his board or clothing. A further breaking down of regulations after this period was shown by a Pennsylvania law of 1865, which stated that an indenture was unnecessary if a contract could be proved.[21]

Similar variations in practice are found with reference to the length of the term of service. It is difficult to get definite information on this, for there are not available enough printers' indentures from which to generalize. Some idea of the normal practice can be gained, however, from the length of the terms actually served and from the exceptions noted. English tradition had made seven years the approved term but even that appeared to be unsatisfactory, for it was lowered by the Common Council of New York in 1694 to four years, but it was again restored to seven in 1711.[22] Late in the eighteenth century indentures expired when the boy reached twenty-one years of age, and this custom continued into our period for there are cases of service of more than seven years.[23] From five to seven years was the average term noted by Whitney for the period before 1840.[24] In 1826 Horace Greeley's master in Poultney, Vt., cited the usual term as five years.[25]

The National Typographical Society, concerning itself with the conditions of labor in the trade, recommended to its local

---

Press of Chautauqua," in *Centennial History of Chautauqua County*, p. 96. He says the apprentices were paid thirty to forty dollars per year, beginning at thirty, and increasing each year five or ten dollars; usually paid in produce, or by an order on a merchant.

[19] Parton, James, *Life of Horace Greeley*, p. 53; Greeley, Horace, *Recollections of a Busy Life*, pp. 61-62.

[20] Original indenture, cited above.

[21] Whitney, *op. cit.*

[22] Seybolt, *Apprenticeship*, pp. 75-78.

[23] Bogert's was for nine years and five months; and O'Reilly's was for eight years, though he did not serve the full term.

[24] Whitney, *op. cit.*

[25] Parton, *op. cit.*, p. 53.

societies in 1836 that "every apprentice shall serve until he be 21 years of age; and at the time of entering as an apprentice he shall not be more than 15 years of age; and every boy taken as an apprentice shall be bound to his employer in due form of law." [26] The Columbian Typographical Society, a local of Washington, D. C., in adopting these recommendations, however, set the maximum age of beginning the apprenticeship at sixteen years, and shortened the term of apprenticeship from six to five years. [27]

For the purposes of this study it is more important to determine the length of the term actually served than that agreed upon but often left unfulfilled. There were numerous reasons for a shortened period. The boy, having become proficient, might wish to enter business for himself, or he might even be set up in business by his employer and the bond might therefore be terminated voluntarily. [28] The boy, or someone for him, might purchase a release of the bond; or the contract might be abrogated when one of the parties had not lived up to his share of the bargain. Such an abrogation occurred in the case of James Bogert, who was taken away from Thomas and James Swords of New York because the board was not "up to standard." [29] Furthermore, the printer might fail, or move his establishment; and finally, the apprentice might run away, willfully violating his bond.

Although hundreds of printers and papers have been studied, concerning only twenty-four printers were there found data defining their terms of service as apprentices. Four of these served the full term of seven years; seven, a period of six years; four, five years; and the rest, shorter terms. [30] Somewhat fuller information is obtained as to the age at which the boy was indentured. Of thirty-eight printers, eight began at

[26] Stewart, Ethelbert, *Documentary History of Early Organizations of Printers,* pp. 976-977

[27] *Ibid.,* pp. 917-918.

[28] This was often done by James D. Bemis for his boys. *Infra,* chap. iii.

[29] MS sketch of the life of Col. James Bogert by John N. Bogert (1873). This is in the possession of J. N. Bogert of Binghamton, N. Y.

[30] Two for four years; four for three years; three for two years. See biographical data in Appendix.

fourteen years age; seven at thirteen years; six at fifteen; six at sixteen; and five at seventeen. One was bound at the age of eighteen; two at twelve; and one each at eleven, ten, and seven. These figures do not appear conclusive, though the greatest number of cases fall between the ages of thirteen and fifteen. The distribution shows that the higher age was more frequently the case in the second half of the period of this study.[31]

Another approach to this same question is to seek information concerning employers' preferences. For the period of forty years after 1790 more than one hundred advertisements for apprentices, specifying the age desired, were noted. Generally two ages (e.g., "14 to 16") were stipulated. In most cases fourteen was the minimum age and sixteen the most popular maximum. The higher ages were in advertisements dated after the first decade of the nineteenth century; while with three exceptions references to boys of ten to thirteen years were in advertisements earlier than 1810.[32] The tendency to take boys who were somewhat older is noticeable but not very marked for the years between 1810 and 1830.

These advertisements supply other interesting clues to the ideal apprentice. Early notices contain few details, but with the increasing size of the newspapers the advertisements became more descriptive. The prospective apprentice was advised that if he came well recommended, possessed habits of sobriety and industry (sometimes expressed in the negative, or as one put it "free from gross habits"),[33] he would receive "good encouragement." Another went further and stipulated that, "those who love idleness and indulge in disobedience, gambling, sabbath-breaking and rioting in the streets and grog-

---

[31] Of eighteen apprenticed at fifteen years or over, eleven were as late as 1810, or later.

[32] Of 102 advertisements, 63 specified a fourteen-year minimum, only eighteen set fifteen years; and eight mentioned thirteen or sixteen. In setting a maximum, 44 preferred boys of sixteen or younger; fifteen did not want a boy over fourteen; 27 would accept one up to fifteen years, and 12 would go as high as seventeen years. Three who advertised for a boy up to eighteen years, and one for a lad of twelve, may be counted as exceptions.

[33] Goshen *Orange County Patriot,* May 14, 1816.

shops, need not apply." [34] Sometimes it was specified that they
should have a "tolerable education," a "common school education," or should be able to read and spell. Not a few printers,
some of whom were Democrats, desired their apprentices to
come from a "respectable family;" [35] to have "good connections;" [36] or be, as one put it, "of genteel connections." [37]
Another specification not hard to understand was: "one from
the country preferred." [38] Even in that day, apparently, the
town-bred boy was less desirable as a laborer. Occasionally the
nature of the work was suggested, but this was rare. When
the *Lodi Pioneer* asked for an "Active lad, Aged xiv, or xv.
wishing to make a trial at riding post, sawing wood, feeding
pigs, and learning 'to print,' " a contemporary considered it
amusing. [39]

The printer's apprentice, like apprentices of most craftsmen
of the day, was given a variety of duties. They ranged from
the chores common in any home containing a large family, to
the essential work attendant upon printing. The work might
be made easy or hard, depending upon the master and upon
such other circumstances as the size of the establishment, the
number of apprentices or other help, and the age of the lad.
It was the dirty and often obnoxious tasks which gave the apprentice the common appellation of "printer's devil." He must
often have appeared as smutty as a sweep and so thoroughly
begrimed as to create the impression that the condition was
permanent. The very variety of duties, however, made apprenticeship interesting, and if properly and gradually taught to
the aspiring boy each task became a milestone in his professional development. Like the graduate of our schools and colleges of today, the master printer was proud of his training. [40]

[34] Palmyra *Western Farmer*, Mar. 28, 1821.
[35] Cooperstown *Freeman's Journal*, Nov. 20, 1820.
[36] Poughkeepsie *Republican Herald*, Nov. 27, 1822.
[37] Ballston Spa *Saratoga Advertiser*, Dec. 5, 1804.
[38] Newburgh *Political Index*, July 4, 1826; Cf. Brooklyn *Long Island Patriot*,
June 5, 1822, and Poughkeepsie *Republican Herald*, Nov. 27, 1822.
[39] *Newburgh Gazette*, Nov. 24, 1827.
[40] Cf. Isaac Riggs in the Schenectady *Cabinet*, May 28, 1821. "Yes, *Gentlemen*
editors, I am a *typesetter*—I served an apprenticeship of near five years and

First of all the apprentice was the printer's errand boy. In offices where a number of boys were employed this duty fell upon the youngest or last to enter.[41] He delivered the papers to the village subscribers and ran to the post office for mail (if the printer were not postmaster also).[42] In some cases he rode as post boy to deliver papers over the countryside,[43] but this was generally done by a man or boy especially employed for a route.[44] He swept and cleaned the office, kept fires going, washed the forms, and carried water for that purpose and for wetting paper; he was taught to wield the two heavy ink balls, described above, and eventually was required to set type. As soon as he could bear the bodily exertion he might be called upon to act as pressman, too. Horace Greeley recalled that such presswork, "beyond my boyish strength," was required of him while an apprentice in Vermont.[45]

One of the most disagreeable tasks remembered by early apprentices was that of "treading pelts." This was done in preparing the skins to be used on the ink balls. The method has been described by Lewis G. Hoffman:

A Pelt was a dried sheepskin, divested of the wool, immersed in the *slop pail* until well soaked, then taken out, rinsed [wrung] by hand of the surface water, as far as practicable, for *treading*. It was then rolled up in old newspapers and rolled under the foot, changing the papers as was required until every particle of moisture was expunged [expelled] from it, which rendered the skin as pliable and soft as a lady's glove. Then it was in order for a Printer's ball. Treading out a pair of skins

---

a half, to learn the art, trade and mystery of *typesetting* and *presswork;* and I have no objections to your informing your numerous patrons that the 'obscure paper, printed somewhere about Schenectady,' is conducted by a *typesetter*—that he writes his own articles (such as they are), sets up the types and then assists in doing the *press work*."

41 Most offices employed one, two, or more apprentices, although Alden Spooner confessed that he printed the *Suffolk Gazette* at Sag Harbor for two years without the aid of a boy.

42 The printer of the Hudson *Northern Whig,* May 9, 1809, had a controversy with the postmaster who would not give his papers to an apprentice without a written order.

43 See Selkreg, J. H., *Landmarks of Tompkins County,* p. 123, for this service performed by Anson Spencer while he was an apprentice in Ithaca.

44 See chap. vii.

45 Greeley, *Recollections,* p. 63.

was an epoch in a printers devil's life which he will always remember until *odor* is lost in forgetfulness.[46]

There can be no doubt that the boys worked hard. Edwin Scrantom, recounting the events of the day before Dauby's Rochester office was burned out, gave his own experience, which might have been typical:

Until 12 at night, we had been working off the *Gazette* on the first side, and as the issue day was next Tuesday, we were apprehensive that unless we could get the type from that form on Monday to distribute and then set up for the inside, we should be behind time. Master and apprentices had labored hard together, and the task of working off the paper had been accomplished. It was now past midnight and we apprentices were very weary, and leaving the form on the press we prepared for "turning in" to our bunk.[47]

Lewis G. Hoffman, who served his apprenticeship under Jesse Buel at Albany, wrote:

In winter we ate breakfast by candlelight, took dinner at 12 (except publication days), supper at 6, returned to the office, and set type until 9. The "eight hour system" was not then in vogue.[48]

Strict observance of the Sabbath was a matter of public concern. Thus it was a serious charge and a reflection upon the reputation of a printer, if it were said that he obliged his apprentices to work on that day. A misunderstanding arose in Auburn when a political handbill printed in the office of Henry C. Southwick was dated on Sunday. His defense consisted in a published statement, signed by his journeymen and apprentices, denying the imputation that they were ever required to work on Sunday.[49] In another case the charge was direct and explicit:

Timely Notice. If a certain *French Printer,* in Congress Street, by the name of Francis Adancourt does not desist from his practice of tampering with our Journeymen, or of enticing our Apprentices from their

[46] Letter of Lewis G. Hoffman, in a clipping in the annotated copy of Munsell, *Typographical Miscellany,* opposite p. 234. In American Antiquarian Society.
[47] Scrantom, Edwin, in *Rochester Democrat & Chronicle,* Mar. 8, 1871.
[48] Letter of Lewis G. Hoffman, Munsell, *Typographical Miscellany,* annotated copy, opposite p. 234.
[49] Auburn *Advocate of the People,* May 7, 1817.

duty, and *hiring them* to *WORK* in his *Jacobin Office* on the *SAB-BATH DAY,* he will be dealt with according to the Statute in such cases made and provided.

Troy, 7th June, 1808.   *Wright, Goodenow & Stockwell.*[50]

In the eyes of the printer the boy was a laborer and there was no virtue in coddling him. The obligation to supervise the boy's training and education was fulfilled in the printer's own way. Some masters took their responsibility lightly, contending that the work itself was educational, and centered their efforts on the mechanical instruction. Others found time to impart to the boy much of their accumulated store of practical information.

The apprentice's opportunities for a formal education varied, and the results were probably more varied. Erastus Shepard was permitted to attend school during his six years apprenticeship to Ira Merrell, of Utica, but he was not an apt pupil. On being reproached for failure to prepare a declamation, he told his teacher: "I do not expect to become an orator—it is enough for me, if I can make a first rate journeyman printer." [51] Some boys in the larger towns were sent to school, while others obtained most of their education at the "case." William Williams once remarked, "I formed my stiff handwriting at the printing office before I was thirteen." [52] Alden Spooner in 1823 criticized his erstwhile apprentice Samuel A. Seabury, publisher of the *American Eagle,* for his errors in orthography, grammar, and typography. Seabury retorted by laying the blame on his master, whom he said he copied; but Spooner was sure that, even as an apprentice Seabury had never been known to copy anything "correctly." [53] One of the outstanding attempts to provide educational facilities was the establishment of libraries for apprentices. Solomon Southwick, dedicating a library at Albany in 1821, outlined a course of study for apprentices for four or seven years, to which he

---

[50] *Troy Gazette,* June 7, 1808.
[51] Follett, *op. cit.,* p. 16.
[52] Williams, John C., *An Oneida County Printer,* pp. 12-13.
[53] Brooklyn *Long Island Star,* April 17, 24, 1823.

recommended that they should give two hours a day of "unremitted devotion." [54] Such a library was opened in Brooklyn in 1823, but similar facilities, of course, were seldom available to the apprentice in the country office.

Thurlow Weed's experiences as an apprentice throw a flood of light on the master printers of that day. He was bound to Thomas Chittenden Fay, of Onondaga, "a coarse, vulgar man, who used to swear and storm about the office, but, [who] on the whole treated me well, and rather prided himself on making a printer out of such a blockhead. By his wife, who was a patient, industrious, tidy woman, I was treated with great kindness, for which I remember her with gratitude." When Fay disappeared, the bound boy was taken as an apprentice by Royall T. Chamberlin in the office of the *Tocsin* at Union Springs. Of his new master, Weed wrote:

His office was in the old town of Scipio, some nine miles from the Cayuga bridge. We boarded with the editor and publisher's father, who lived on a farm about two miles from the office. We took an early breakfast, brought our dinner with us, and returned to supper in the evening. I enjoyed this very much, especially as it was in peach season and Mr. Chamberlin's father had the fruit in great abundance and perfection.

This idyl was soon terminated, for the editor was a love-sick swain whose unrequited ardor resulted in melancholy and a lapse of business.

In William Williams, of Utica, whose treatment of apprentices is referred to below, Weed found an excellent master, but here his service ended at the outbreak of the War of 1812. After a journey to Sackett's Harbor, he again found an indulgent master in Thomas Walker, of Utica.[55] Subsequently he served as a journeyman for Samuel R. Brown in Auburn, then engaged in writing his history of the late war. His description of this printer's household is an interesting commentary on the environment in which apprentices were trained:

[54] Southwick, Solomon, *Address at the Opening of the Apprentices' Library,* Albany, Jan., 1821, p. 40.
[55] Weed, *Autobiography,* pp. 22-26.

Mr. Brown was an even-tempered, easy going, good-natured man...
Mrs. Brown was placid, emotionless and slipshod. Both were imper-
turbable. Nothing disturbed either. There was no regular hour for
breakfast or dinner, but meals were always under or over done....
The printing sympathized with the housekeeping. We worked at inter-
vals during the day, and while making a pretense of working in the
evening, these hours were generally devoted to blind-man's buff with
two or three neighborhood girls, or to juvenile concerts by Richard
Oliphant, an amateur vocalist and typesetter.[56]

It is evident that the provision for the comfort and well-
being of apprentices varied with the dispositions and the resources of the masters. In some cases boys were admitted to
the comforts of home and the family table; while in others
they were subjected to ill treatment and inferior food. James
Bogert, as an apprentice in New York City in 1802, complained that "many hogs [were] better housed and fed. Often
he had to shake the snow from his bed on retiring and arising,
while rancid butter, mouldy bread, and spoiled meat" were so
frequently placed before him that he revolted.[57] Edwin Scrantom, as apprentice to A. G. Dauby in the early days of that
pioneer in Rochester, remembered distinctly the

rough box, or "bunk," that was rigged up on the floor under one of
the counters, for this was the sleeping room for the apprentices—two of
us—and coming to this scanty provision, as I did, from a bed that my
mother had always in her love provided...the contrast was so great
...that it brought homesickness and sighing and sometimes tears.[58]

But if there were some cases of hardship and illtreatment,
there were other instances of kindness and care on the part of
the master and his wife and of pleasant memories on the part
of the apprentice. Such masters as James D. Bemis, of Canandaigua, and William Williams, of Utica, trained a multitude
of lads and received much praise from their "graduates," not
only for the technical training, but also for fatherly care and

[56] *Ibid.,* pp. 40-41.
[57] MS sketch of James Bogert by John N. Bogert (1873).
[58] Scrantom, Edwin, in *Rochester Democrat & Chronicle,* Feb. 3, 1877.

counsel.[59] Much of the success of the printer's household, especially in the care of apprentices, depended upon the "hard-
working wife, who boarded the hands, and became in many
instances a second mother to the apprentice boys, mending
their clothes, caring for them in sickness, and encouraging
them to read and improve their minds so that they might also
in time be fitted to be editors and publishers." [60]

An interesting commentary on the medical care given is
afforded in an original bill submitted by Dr. Amos G. Hall
to Thomas Walker, of Utica, October 27, 1819, covering a
period of about two years. Extracting teeth, bleeding, emetics,
dressing wounds, dressing a finger, medicine, balsam of honey,
syrup, something "to take the film from the eye," plasters and
professional visits, made a bill of $12.25. From this amount
perhaps fifty cents should be deducted for extracting a tooth
"for Son;" the remainder represented medical care for apprentices.[61]

A well-organized household, in marked contrast with that
of Samuel R. Brown of which Thurlow Weed told, was pre-
sided over by Jesse Buel, while he was the printer of the state
paper at Albany. In later years Lewis G. Hoffman wrote in
tribute to Buel:

Everything was systematized by him. In summer he arose with the sun,
and his boys likewise. Breakfast was taken at 7 o'clock, dinner at 12 and
tea at 6. His boys sat at the same table with him, and his family
and his apprentices in the order of seniority; that is the oldest first,
next to him, and the youngest last. His wife and sister were helped
first. His apprentices in order next, then his children, who were young,
and himself last. When a stranger dined with him the same order was
preserved, and his apprentices have, at different times, set [sic] at the
same table with Martin Van Buren, while Attorney General of the
State; Wm. L. Marcy, Recorder of Troy; Gen. Root of Delaware,
Roger Skinner, and other dignitaries now forgotten. Those were "old

[59] MS letter of L. H. Redfield to Henry O'Reilly, January 30, 1858, a tribute
to James D. Bemis, in O'Reilly Collection. Bagg, M. M., *Pioneers of Utica*, p.
619, gives a remarkable list of notable apprentices to William Williams.

[60] McKinstry, "The Press of Chautauqua," in *Centennial History of Chautauqua County*, pp. 96-99.

[61] Original bill, pasted in one volume of *Columbian Gazette*, Oneida Historical Society.

Fashioned," republican, patriarchal times, and the old Judge apparently took as much pleasure in having us sit with him, as we did. The modern doctrine of "running against the wind, or this or that man's nobility," was not a part of his system of "Parental government," for that feeling he tried to inculcate in his boys, and they *did* believe it and gave him respect for it.[62]

If an apprentice did not benefit from such a paternalistic system, it was his own fault. That, at least, was the doctrine then preached, and at the opening of the Apprentices' Library in Albany Solomon Southwick advised apprentices of their rights and obligations:

The duty which you owe to your master is not an absolute, but a conditional duty. If your master perform his obligations to you, then you are bound by the letter and spirit of your Indentures, and by every tie of honour and gratitude, to be zealously faithful to him.... Your master stands in room of your parent, and you owe him, therefore, filial, as well as covenant or conventional duty; and while on the one hand you ought not to be wronged by him with impunity; you ought not on the other hand, to be over nice in exacting all that you may conceive due you at his hands. Remember that while he learns nothing from you, you learn of him that art which is to support you through life; that he is *bound to sustain you* whilst learning it, in sickness as well as in health; remember, too, that while he shares your labour, you share none of his risk or responsibility.[63]

Although this was excellent advice, it must have sounded trite. Not all apprentices were earnest, capable of advancing in the profession and worthy of their master's trust, and not all masters were capable teachers able to furnish proper instruction. The artificial connection of apprentice and master was more difficult than the relationship of father and son to which it was compared. The necessity for removing conflicts and misunderstandings justified the master in chastising an apprentice, although colonial precedent considered "unreasonable correcting" a valid ground for court action which might result in freeing a boy from his bond. As late as 1833, how-

[62] Letter of Lewis G. Hoffman in Munsell, *Typographical Miscellany*, annotated copy, *loc. cit.*

[63] Southwick, *op. cit.*, pp. 44-45.

ever, a New York master was upheld in "severely whipping" a seventeen-year-old apprentice.[64]

From uncertainties and misunderstandings which caused the boy to believe that apprenticeship was an impossible situation arose the problem of the runaway. Enough has been related above to suggest plausible reasons for this abrupt termination of the contract. In cases which have come to our attention the evidence is both one-sided and exaggerated. Most runaways seem to have proved themselves undesirable before absconding. Some were advertised as having embezzled from the master, as being lazy, drunken, or addicted to liquor; others were characterized as deceitful, mean, ill-favored, base, wicked, dishonest, ungovernable, ungrateful, untrustworthy, and capable of the most offensive crimes. The masters generally disclaimed all responsibility for them, and offered only a nominal reward—six pence, half cent, or, in one case, "an old pelt."

In any event the runaway was a problem for the trade. The printer advertised the offender, not with the hope of recovering his services, but as a means of retaliation. It was unlawful for anyone to employ a runaway, and the advertisement was intended to discourage the practice. Printers were extremely cautious and hesitant about taking a boy who had some knowledge of the trade, unless he could prove his story.[65] In these circumstances many runaways drifted to the cities. With some knowledge of the trade they were inclined to return to it, and as they became older, to set themselves up as journeymen. Thus they formed a class of cheap labor in competition with experienced or regularly trained journeymen.[66]

A number of cases appear to prove that prospects for the faithful and industrious apprentice were very good. At the age of twenty-one, or at the expiration of his indenture, he became a full-fledged journeyman. Now he could work for others at whatever wages he could command, or with a little capital he might establish himself as a master, acquire apprentices,

---

[64] Seybolt, *op. cit.*, pp. 79-80

[65] Thurlow Weed was questioned by William Williams as to why he had not served out his apprenticeship. *Autobiography*, pp. 25-26.

[66] See *infra*, p. 43, for a discussion of "half-way journeymen."

and have his own business, which was a common practice in western New York, where the printer was a pioneer. James D. Bemis set up in business a number of his boys, and other printers followed his example.[67] Much depended upon the ability of the individual apprentice to grasp his opportunity. If he met the test of the business world, his success was assured, but many good craftsmen failed to emerge from the ranks of the journeyman printers.

As a class, journeyman printers obtained a bad name. They were popularly reputed to be vagabonds, drifting from place to place and office to office, unsatisfied, and unwilling to settle down. Likewise, they were said to be unsteady in their habits and especially addicted to excessive use of liquor. Thurlow Weed recorded that of all the journeymen he knew one quarter were habitually intemperate, while another quarter, "though not inebriates, drank enough daily to keep themselves impoverished."[68] He distinguished between the journeymen from Hartford, Boston, and other New England towns, who were temperate and frugal, and those from Baltimore and Philadelphia, who were more often thriftless or dissipated.[69] That the customs of the craft contributed to the intemperate habits of the craftsmen is evident from Weed's comments:

The printing house habits condemned by Dr. Franklin had not been reformed. Journeymen in most offices were required to pay "footing," which meant a treat by the newcomer, all the old journeymen and masters were required to treat the hands whenever signature "o" was put to press. At eleven o'clock A.M. invariably, and too frequently afterwards, journeymen would "jeff" for beer. In this way a large share of their weekly earnings was mortgaged, each journeyman having a formidable "tick" at the grocery to be adjusted on Saturday evenings.[70]

There are a number of individual cases to substantiate these generalizations, although many journeymen, like Weed and Franklin, were able to be temperate in the midst of tempation.

[67] A number of these cases are mentioned, *infra,* pp. 83-84.
[68] Weed, *Autobiography,* p. 44.
[69] *Ibid.,* pp. 58-59.
[70] *Ibid.,* p. 58. See Franklin's *Autobiography* for the prevalence of these customs in English printing offices.

Bemis characterized his first partner, John K. Gould, as "a worthy man, but of habits that killed him." [71] Frederick Follett, historian of the press of western New York, in his generally favorable record notes Seymour Tracy, "a one-legged Tracy," of Genesee County, whose "grossly intemperate habits unfitted him for business"; [72] and he quotes the letter of Lewis H. Redfield regarding John A. Stevens, for twenty years printer of the Canandaigua *Ontario Messenger:*

If I am not mistaken, Mr. S. was not considered a very good printer, but he was esteemed as a most kind and benevolent hearted man. I regret to add, that in after life, adversity overtook him, and yielding to intemperate habits, he finally ended his days in the poor house of this county. I well remember that at the time I was an apprentice, it was a common practice to keep ardent spirits in the *Messenger* office to be drank by those who visited the office on business, and by the hands.[73]

Follett also remarked concerning David M. Day, an apprentice, and later partner, of Stevens: "What printer of Western New York does not mourn his untimely end, and regret the fatal cause." [74] Many proprietors tried to discourage these bad habits, and commended those who earnestly sought to avoid the fatal consequences. Most advertisements for journeymen had a requirement for steadiness, "steady habits," or sobriety. Charles Holt, in writing a letter of recommendation for Ebenezer Mack, called him "a young man of genius, intelligence, *sobriety* [italics mine] and integrity." [75]

The nomadic propensities of the journeyman printer are illustrated by the record of a few whose later prominence saved them from obscurity. Having completed his apprenticeship, Luther Tucker went to Vermont; then he worked as a

[71] Autobiographcal letter of James D. Bemis, dated Nov. 17, 1846, in *Ontario County Times,* June 30, 1897.

[72] Follett (1847 edition), p. 58.

[73] *Ibid.,* p. 7.

[74] *Ibid.,* p. 7.

[75] Treman, E. M., and Pool, M. E., *History of the Treman, Tremaine, Truman Family,* p. 395.

journeyman in Philadelphia, Baltimore, Washington, and New York City. Finally he became a partner with Henry C. Sleight in Jamaica, L. I., and in Rochester, and later settled in Albany.[76] Daniel Munger, after leaving Franklin Cowdery, who taught him his trade, worked with Weed and Martin in Rochester, but he was lured to the road by stories that printers received twenty dollars per week in New Orleans. With another journeyman printer he worked through Erie, Pittsburgh, and Washington, Pa., Louisville, Ky., and New Orleans, La. Later he found jobs in Buffalo and in Detroit, Constantine, and Lansing, Mich.[77] Even more remarkable was the career of William A. Welles, who started with an apprenticeship in New York, and worked for well-known printers and publishers throughout the land. He was in Boston with "Ben" Russell, and then in Andover, whence he went to sea. Later he worked in Portland, Me., Concord, N. H., and Hartford and New Haven, Conn. He was employed by Matthew Carey, of Philadelphia, "Poulson, Mrs. Lydia R. Baily, John Bioren, Duane, 'Billy Fry,' &c." Finally he was connected with papers in Buffalo, Geneva, and Salem, N. Y.[78] His amazing account of his travels leaves no doubt that one printer possessed a restless spirit.

These wanderings of printers can be accounted for in several ways. Jobs were not numerous in most towns. The work was uncertain, and job work might provide temporary employment after which there would be a slack period.[79] Political campaigns gave an unusual impetus to the country printer whose establishment was normally small, and consequently for several months additional jobs for journeymen were available. Advertisements for journeymen held out the prospect of "constant," or "continuous," employment. One stated that the

[76] Howell, G. W., and Tenny, J., eds., *History the County of Albany,* p. 369.
[77] Letter of Daniel Munger from *Detroit Daily Advertiser,* Dec. 12, 1857. Clipping in the scrapbook of Henry O'Reilly. New York Historical Society.
[78] *Littell's Living Age,* Mar. 28, 1846, VII, 626-627. This was a report of the Printers' Festival of that year.
[79] Cf. Wright, Richardson, *Hawkers and Walkers of Early America,* pp. 111-113.

opening was good "for two or three months," while another merely said "a few months." [80] Apparently employment for a matter of months was considered relatively permanent.

A reason later advanced for the wanderings of printers was the unwarranted practice of employing "half-way journeymen," or "two-thirders," boys who had served but a partial apprenticeship, in the place of full-fledged journeymen. This practice was noted especially in the larger offices, and the printers of New York protested:

Under the direful influence of the unwarrantable practices, the professors of the noblest art with which the world is blessed, have become "birds of passage," seeking a livelihood from Georgia to Maine. It is owing to such practices that to acknowledge yourself a printer is to awaken suspicion and cause distrust. It is owing to such practices that the professors of the noble art are sinking in the estimation of the community. [81]

A compensation for this sorry condition of the wandering journeyman, however, was the romantic distinction of his numerous experiences, of which men like Welles were quite proud. Not only was the traveled journeyman a marvel of worldly wisdom to the young apprentice, or even to the young proprietor of a backwoods office, but his varied accomplishments and fund of accumulated information were real assets. His practical deficiencies, so glaring to his employer, have generally colored the recorded estimates of his character.

Since 1776 journeymen printers had been organized for the maintenance of a wage scale. Six dollars per week was the early standard wage; this was raised (1799-1809) to seven dollars for book and job work and eight dollars for newspaper work. [82] A scale for piecework was also fixed, but an investigation by the New York Typographical Society in 1809 showed that in New York compositors were working for twenty cents per one thousand ems, instead of twenty-five cents; "pressmen working at 25 cents per token (240 sheets), and numberless

[80] Kingston *Plebeian*, Aug. 19, 1805; Herkimer *Farmer's Monitor*, Apr. 15, 1806.

[81] Report of the Typographical Society, Dec. 30, 1809, Stewart, *op. cit.*, p. 875.

[82] *Ibid.*, pp. 860-864.

boys at from $4 to $4.50 per week." [83] In 1815 a new price
scale of nine dollars per week, or twenty-seven cents for one
thousand ems, of composition was adopted. In 1816 Philadelphia journeymen pressmen fixed a scale with nine dollars
per week for a ten-hour work day.[84] Although the typographical societies protested against the employment of learners,
runaway apprentices, and half-trained adults, they failed to
enforce rules which were intended to prevent the condition. As
a result runaway apprentices frequently found work in offices
where printers were satisfied with inferior help. The printers'
societies were not slow to point out that this meant inferior
printing, a deteriorating personnel, and the removal of restraint over young boys in the trade which left them subject
to the evils of dissipation and debauchery. Well-trained and
experienced workmen found that their places were taken by
boys and men who would work for what they could get.

Of the number that have completed their apprenticeship to the printing
business within the last five years but few have been able to hold a
position for any length of time, and it is an incontrovertible fact that
nearly one-half that learned the trade are obliged to relinquish it and
follow some other calling for support.[85]

The duties of the journeyman were of course similar to
those of the apprentice, but being a grown man, he was expected to shoulder the heavier tasks, which, of course, meant
presswork. Composition fell to the lot of all, but the pressman
had a large responsibility. It was for him to see that the paper
was properly wetted down the night before, to see that ink was
properly distributed, that the balls were kept in proper order,
and to examine the sheets as they were "pulled." So important
were these duties that Van Winkle believed that in the hands
of a good workman the press itself became a secondary consideration.[86]

[83] *Ibid.,* p. 873.
[84] *Ibid.,* p. 877.
[85] Commons, J. R., and associates, *History of Labour in the United States,* I,
114; Stevens, *op. cit.,* p. 67 *et seq.*
[86] Van Winkle, *op. cit.,* p. 192.

On the other hand the heavy labor took toll of the pressman's physique, as Edwin Scrantom testified when he compared the old "two pull" press with the improved model:

The old press required great and continued muscular strength, so much so that many who worked at the press continually, as I have seen, have become deformed, the right shoulder becoming enlarged, and the wall of the chest being driven against the left shoulder depressed it, and so the body in walking became sidewise, the right arm and shoulder being in advance of the rest of the body. All pressmen, too, had a discrepancy in their feet, for the right foot, always placed on the "step" when the "pull" was made, that foot always became enlarged beyond the other, and the writer is a living example of this discrepancy.[87]

The pressman's lever, like the oar of the galley slave, held the body captive.

The good journeyman, however, might become the real directing head of the establishment. Thurlow Weed was the actual manager of the office of William L. Stone, in Herkimer, in the absence of that budding politician; and David Frothingham, a journeyman employed for eight dollars a week in 1799 on the New York *Argus,* was held responsible for the publication of the "libel" on Alexander Hamilton which appeared in that paper.[88] Advertisements for journeymen held out the prospect that the applicant might become foreman in the office and asked that he be "capable of taking charge of a newspaper establishment in the country"[89] or that he "undertake to instruct five or six apprentices."[90]

The melancholy picture of the journeyman printer is little relieved by a consideration of his prospects. The early printer usually entertained thoughts of being able to open an office of his own either for job work or to run a newspaper. His master was perhaps an editor, as well as a practical printer, and those in the office were given a chance at all branches of the work.

[87] Scrantom, Edwin, in *Rochester Democrat & Chronicle,* Mar. 30, 1871.
[88] Weed, *Autobiography,* pp. 33, 37; *Greenleaf's New York Journal and Patriotic Register,* Dec. 14, 1799. See this case *infra,* chap. vi.
[89] Lansingburgh *Farmer's Register,* Jan. 17, 1804.
[90] Batavia *Republican Advocate,* Sept. 14, 1827, advertisement of a York, U. C., printer.

Ebenezer Mack's recommendation written by Charles Holt, of the New York *Columbian,* stated that he was a "good writer (in verse or prose) and a correct republican." [91] Some succeeded in making the transition from journeyman to editor, but as time went on, the printer-editor was replaced by the publisher, who simply owned the plant and hired his editor as he did his compositors and pressmen. The printer resented the encroachment of this "speculator on the labor of printers" and denounced the "hireling editor." The advent of large capital in the printing business, the use of expensive improved presses, and the change in labor conditions, lessened the opportunities of the journeyman in his profession.[92] Of those journeymen who were his associates in New York in 1817, Weed mentioned a few who rose to higher positions, but "much the largest number remained journeymen through life." [93] While thrifty printers were never numerous, the inducements to practice thrift were steadily decreasing.

[91] Treman and Pool, *op. cit.,* p. 395.

[92] Stewart, *op. cit.,* p. 912. See *infra,* chap. v, for a discussion of the passing of the printer-editor.

[93] Weed, *Autobiography,* p. 58.

III

OUR OWN AFFAIRS

MY BROTHER *had, in 1720 or 1721, begun to print a news-paper. It was called the* New England Courant. *The only one before it was the* Boston News-Letter. *I remember his being dissuaded by some of his friends from the undertaking, as not likely to succeed, one newspaper being, in their judgment, enough for America.*—FRANKLIN, *Autobiography.*

I COMMENCED *the publication under circumstances very flatter-ing, but I have been disappointed in my calculations of success. Those persons who gave me assurances of support have nearly all thrown their weight in the scale against me . . . my subscription list has dwin-dled to a mere trifle—my advertising is reduced to a scanty pittance— and those indebted have been extremely dilatory in making payment. With these prospects before me, after having ruined my health, I am compelled to withdraw from the field, with an expensive family de-pendent upon my labor for support. I have published the paper nearly five years, and have endeavored to maintain the character of an honest and consistent politician, and to render my paper interesting and useful to my subscribers. . . . I now request all those who have heretofore patronized me to give their support to Mr. Cuthbert, editor of the* Re-publican. . . . *I now retire from the turmoil of politics and shall prob-ably never again consent to engage in any political contest. To my subscribers and friends I wish happiness and prosperity.*—SOLOMON BAKER *in the* Schoharie Observer, *Oct. 2, 1823.*

THE *editor of the* Schoharie Republican, *pleading an excuse to his readers, stated that the editor, proprietor, publisher, printer, foreman, and oldest apprentice (TWO in all) were sick, and the whole concerns of the office had been left in charge of the devil.*—Pough-keepsie Journal, *April 8, 1829.*

SINCE printing establishments sprang into being with amazing rapidity in various parts of the state, in frontier settlements as well as older communities, there was naturally much conjecture as to the cause of this development. Was it due to the condition of the printing craft? Facts revealed in the previous pages hardly justify such a belief. Was it the natural concomitant of the opening of new country? Was it due to the peculiar business conditions of the day? Was it to be accounted for only as an expression of the violent partisan interest in politics, and the utilization of the press as a political agency? Or could it be explained as a necessary part of democratic government? An examination of the evidence, including the testimony of contemporaries, may help us to give a tentative if not a definitive answer to these questions.

In 1794 an economic interpretation of the spread of printing offices was advanced by the English traveler Henry Wansey in discussing the opportunity for tradesmen in America. Printers did very well, he said, especially in the back country, "for they are all great newsmongers"; [1] but this was merely begging the question. Another English commentator, less favorably disposed toward American institutions, was Thomas Hamilton, who remarked that the power of the press was great because nine-tenths of the people read newspapers and nothing else. The form of government in America, he believed, was unfavorable to the development of a taste for good literature; hence the preference for newspapers. [2] Alexis de Tocqueville, in his keen analysis of American institutions, held that "the extraordinary subdivision of administrative power has much more to do with the enormous number of American newspapers than the great political freedom of the country and the

[1] Wansey, Henry, *An Excursion to the United States of North America in the Summer of 1794,* p. 80.
[2] Hamilton, Thomas, *Men and Manners in America,* I, 194-199.

absolute liberty of the press."[3] In other words, the fact that voters were expected to participate in local, state, and national elections made them constantly conscious of politics, whereas if their responsibility had been limited to periodic votes for members of Congress, their interest in public affairs would not have been so great. This was a natural comment for a Frenchman, but it seemed less valid when one contrasted America with England. As a matter of fact, national politics figured more prominently than problems of local government in the multiplication of newspapers.

A more convincing explanation came from a German source, Brockhaus's *Konversations Lexikon* (Leipzig, 1848), quoted by Munsell. "The support of so enormous a number of papers is possible in America, aside from the general interest in politics, through their cheapness, through the mass of advertisements they publish, and the freedom of these advertisements from every sort of tax."[4]

An anonymous English writer in the *Penny Magazine* (1841) describes the ease with which a newspaper was started in every newly settled community in America. According to this writer, as soon as a requisite number of people have congregated in a given locality,

some adventurer in the printing line is attracted from a distant and older settlement, aware that the publisher of a newspaper always ranks among the leading characters of a newly-settled district. This person, who probably has never ranked higher than a journeyman typesetter, on account of the universal credit system, finds little difficulty in establishing a weekly paper in some such new locality as above alluded to, which, to a person without capital or friends to assist him, would be out of the question in this country,—whereas in most parts of America it is the easiest thing imaginable, and, for the most part is managed after the manner following.

In the first place it is necessary to have a building erected for a printing office, which some carpenter or other undertakes to do, and as the work is to be performed on one year's credit, thirty or forty percent. more is agreed to be given than if the money were to be forthcoming

[3] Tocqueville, Alexis de, *Democracy in America*, II, 120.
[4] Munsell, *Typographical Miscellany*, p. 198.

on the completion of the job. However, he (the printer) gives the carpenter promissory notes to the amount of the contract, bearing the usual rate of interest; which notes are *traded away,* as the customary phrase is, a dozen times or more before they become due,—not always at the value they bear on their face, but (according to the circumstances) at what parties may be willing to receive them at.

But a printing-office is of no use unless supplied with printing-types; and the necessary amount of old and worn-out types is probably procured (on credit of course), and is forthwith sent to furnish the new printing office. Hence it is that the most of these newly established papers are not only very indifferently gotten up, and abound with almost every variety of typographical error or blunder, but the types are of that character to give the whole a blurred and sorry appearance. The quality of the paper is also of a very inferior description; nor do the subscribers, under the circumstances in which most papers are first published, either desire or expect anything but a cheap article....[5]

There were several ways in which the establishment of a pioneer press was undertaken. First, as suggested above, an enterprising printer might invade virgin territory and by appealing to the inhabitants insure himself of enough support to launch his paper. A second method was that in which the initiative came from a group in the community, who sought out and financed the printer. A third method, similar to the second, was to secure support for the printer from a single patron. The following anecdote, related by Garrett Furman, suggests that the first method was employed successfully by one Long Island newspaper proprietor.

When I was a small boy, while on my way to school one morning, I stopped a few moments in the harvest field where my father, elder brother, and others were at work. While I was standing with my satchel hanging on my arm, we saw a person upon the road alight from a black horse, with saddle bags on, while we all stood wondering; what his business could be no one could say or imagine. He soon approached the party holding in his hand a bundle of folded papers; he advanced, and was received by my father with the usual courtesy of strangers' meeting. ...I thought him to be a sheriff, perhaps. He proved to be a fine looking and well spoken man, whose business was to inform my father

[5] London *Penny Magazine* (1841), X, 243. While written some ten years after the period under review, it probably applies as well to the earlier period. It is given thus fully to show the tenor of the comment.

that he was about establishing a newspaper in Brooklyn, and wished to get subscribers among the farmers and others. Neither said one word about politics, that I recollect of, but he descanted largely on the price current for grain, hay, stock, and all kinds of produce. With this he formed a sheet as a sample of the style that the paper would appear on. The price current seemed to take pretty well with father; but, I recollect very well, he did not like (in those humble times) to incur the expense. The yearly subscription [price] I do not at present recollect; however, after a short hesitation the old gentleman consented to become a subscriber, for which Thomas Kirk, for him [sic] it was, thanked him very politely, and after inquiring of him which of his neighbors was most likely to subscribe to the *Long Island Star,* he bowed and wished all a good morning and soon remounted his black pony and rode off, while father and the rest resumed their labors....[6]

This same practice of canvassing the community enabled Augustine G. Dauby to establish the first paper in Rochester. Edwin Scrantom recalled his advent as follows:

He was a tall, slim man, graceful and easy in every movement, engaging in conversation, fluent in speech, and used choice language.... He was very generally criticized when he first came to Rochester; some saying he was a Frenchman, and others that he was an imitator of French manners and airs. But he was everywhere welcome. Colonel Rochester took him by the hand and encouraged him to get out his newspaper at once. A week prospecting rather discouraged Mr. D. and he was half a mind to go east to Canandaigua or Geneva, or west to Buffalo or Detroit. The principal men of the place rallied around him, [however], and all promised aid and encouragement to the new printer. There were very few papers taken in Rochester at that time. Only two weekly papers came here, one from Albany and one from New York. ...But everybody agreed to take the village newspaper, and the business men to advertise, and large stories were told of what the future would do....After much deliberation Mr. D. concluded to open his printing office.[7]

But even with a promising group of subscribers, some initial capital was necessary for the purchase of press, types, and other supplies, and the enterprising printer might have to obtain additional support. The means for establishing the first

[6] Stiles, H. R., *History of Brooklyn,* III, 927-928.
[7] Edwin Scrantom, in *Rochester Democrat & Chronicle,* Feb. 3, 1877.

press in Chautauqua County were subscribed by individuals contributing "from five to thirty dollars with the expectation of their being refunded." [8] As in many other cases, the hope of a refund was a vain one.[9] More frequently, the local group which supplied the necessary capital was given a lien or mortgage on the materials, and hence came the editorial jibe, that so-and-so's press was not his own. For example, the press and office of David Frothingham, first printer on Long Island, were mortgaged to three men for the sum of thirty pounds sterling, February 1, 1797.[10] When Frothingham was contemplating his project he was offered a house at East Hampton by the Rev. Dr. Buell. He preferred Sag Harbor, however, as the place of greater trade, and called upon its residents to offer equal encouragement. "It is a custom as ancient as the noble art of printing that... a young beginner [who] sets up his business in a country place ... [should] have some premium, such as wood, &c. [supplied for him] as the great expense often strips him of all his cash." [11]

The second method by which a new paper was established, was that in which the leading men of the community, however motivated, sought a printer for their purposes. The *Jamestown Journal* was launched by a group of citizens, who spent several months corresponding in search of a likely printer, only to find that Adolphus Fletcher, trained as a printer in New England and then working on a nearby farm, was just the man desired. He was persuaded to leave the farm and began a successful editorial career in 1826.[12] In Plattsburgh a group of men with political motives met at the house of Peter Sailly and decided to proceed with the publication of the *Plattsburgh Republican*. They chose one of their number, Col. Melancton Smith, as editor; a printer was then obtained, and the first

[8] Follett (1847), p. 21. Letter of H. C. Frisbee from Fredonia, Nov. 30, 1846.
[9] McKinstry, "The Press of Chautauqua," *Centennial History of Chautauqua County*, p. 99.
[10] MS bill in the Pennypacker Long Island Collection.
[11] D. Frothingham to Henry Dering, Feb. 7, 1791. Pennypacker Collection.
[12] Hazeltine, G. W., *The Town of Ellicott*, p. 240.

number was issued April 13, 1811.[13] In many more cases which could be cited, the ownership of the plant fell to a group of persons, even though they were not the prime movers in its establishment. The *Niagara Journal* said, in defense against the charge of monopoly, "It is true, our paper was originally purchased and set in operation by a company of gentlemen, without distinction of party; and who had in view, probably, the benefits resulting to the country from a Press located in this village." [14] The *Orange County Republican* was begun in 1806 with "money ... advanced in equal shares by twenty-four patriotic citizens of this county, consisting chiefly of respectable farmers and mostly inhabitants of the town of Montgomery." As in other cases where there was an association of this sort, there was no secret of the fact, and notices of the meetings of the proprietors were published in the columns of the paper.[15]

The third method by which printers opened new establishments was the promotion of the project by a single patron. A man of some means who had investments in the new country, who was interested in politics, or who was the principal citizen in the growing community, might employ a printer and provide an establishment to serve his purposes. Captain Charles Williamson, one of the promoters of the Genesee country and agent of Sir William Pulteney in the Pulteney Purchase, obtained a press in Northumberland or Sunbury, Pa., in 1796 and was able to establish William Kersey and James Edie as printers and publishers of the *Bath Gazette and Genesee Advertiser*. In the same year Lucius Cary, of Newburgh, was induced by Williamson to give up his office there and to go to Geneva, where a house (worth $2,000) was provided for him, and he was enabled to bring out the *Ontario Gazette and Genesee Advertiser* in April, 1797.[16] In Cooperstown, Otsego County, Judge William Cooper was the patron of the newspapers published by Elihu Phinney in 1795 and by John H.

[13] Hurd, D. H., *History of Clinton and Franklin Counties*, p. 131.
[14] *Black Rock Beacon*, May 15, 1823.
[15] Ruttenber, E. M., *History of Orange County*, p. 187.
[16] Turner, O., *History of the Pioneer Settlement of the Phelps and Gorham Purchase*, pp. 457-458.

Prentiss in 1808.[17] The principal patron of the press in Sag Harbor was Henry T. Dering, Collector of the Port, who handled the negotiations successfully with David Frothingham in 1791, Selleck Osborn, who succeeded him in 1802, and Alden Spooner, who followed Osborn in 1804.[18] Daniel Cruger, of Steuben County, himself a former printer, supplied the funds necessary for the establishment of Benjamin Smead in Bath.[19]

The correspondence of these printers with their patrons reveals in some cases the cost of the materials necessary to start and the amount and kind of help given. Benjamin Smead had published papers at Brattleboro and Bennington, Vt., before enlisting in the war in 1812. Returning to civilian life in New York state, with a wife and six children to support, he worked for a time as a journeyman in Albany for Jesse Buel and for the Hosfords. He then felt that he would like to establish himself in Watertown or Bath, preferably Bath, and so appealed to Mr. Cruger. But let him voice his own proposal:

My pecuniary circumstances are low, but retaining much of the vigor of youth, with my eldest son, who is a printer,[20] I could edit and print a respectable paper. To embark in such an enterprise, at such a distance, I want the loan of 5 or 600 dollars three years without interest, office room one year free of rent, and six months of stock. The stock comprises only paper and ink, and may amount to nearly 200 dolls. per annum. The money is required to furnish printing materials and defray expenses of removal. I have an excellent press and the other material shall be good; all these I will give over as security for the money immediately on my arrival, which will be as soon as possible after its receipt.[21]

This appeal was dated July 28, 1816, and apparently was given a favorable reply, but Cruger limited his loan to $300 as shown by Smead's letter of September 25, 1816.[22] Of the $300 advance, $180 was used for type. That left $120 for all

---

[17] Livermore, S. T., *A Condensed History of Cooperstown*, pp. 105-106; 157-159.

[18] MS correspondence in Pennypacker Long Island Collection.

[19] Clayton, W. W., *History of Steuben County*, pp. 77-78.

[20] Two of his sons, Henry D. and Benjamin F., succeeded him at Bath.

[21] Clayton, *op. cit.*, pp. 77-78. The correspondence is given in full.

[22] *Ibid.*

other expenses, which Smead was sure would come to $150 at the minimum; therefore he appealed for an additional amount: "Sir, to fit my family for the journey, to procure some other necessary articles, and for expenses for them on their way, I shall require 150 dolls., which will make only 30 more than you offer." But this was not all, as the following requests show. "I wish you would send me 3 waggons, with 2 good horses each, cheap as they can be hired; they to bear their own expense. This expense I estimate on an uncertain foundation at 150 dolls." The total advanced then, was $480, for which he maintained that his equipment would be liberal security.[23] In a subsequent letter he assured his patron that blanks, cuts, and other equipment were very necessary; that, desiring economy, he would not contract for more than his own and his family's needs and what the business would require; and that in view of these plans he had relinquished labor in Albany which had been offered to him. He expressed his hope and faith in Mr. Cruger and the latter's faith in him.[24] It was no small matter to carry a press into the new country, and the funds required represented a much greater purchasing power than the same amounts would have today.

The correspondence of Selleck Osborn with Henry P. Dering, of Sag Harbor, shows a similar relationship. Osborn had come from New York, where he had been employed as a journeyman, had looked over the ground and consulted Mr. Dering. He had broached the subject of "what encouragement would be given" in his introductory letter of December 9, 1801, but apparently had not been answered when he wrote in February, 1802, and took up the delicate question:

Are the influential men of Sagg Harbor, and its vicinity willing to assist so far in the establishment of a *good* Newspaper as to advance a sum sufficient for the purchase of a small but decent assortment of materials, payment being secured by the property itself?—

This may be a bold question; but when I consider the frequency of

---

[23] *Ibid.*

[24] *Ibid.* In another place he wrote, "I wish you to engage me a comfortable house and well lighted office, near to each other. The procuring of stands, trough, &c. before my arrival, would facilitate the first publication."

this kind of encouragement given of late to literary exertion, I indulge the pleasing hope that the proposal will not be rejected.[25]

In a subsequent letter he set the amount. "I have deliberated upon the requisite sum for establishing the office; and I calculate that 300 Dollars will be sufficient to commence it on a decent footing." This, of course, did not include the price of a press, for that was mentioned, too. "Young Elliott, formerly apprentice to Mr. Frothingham, is of opinion that the old Press used by him may be repaired so as to render good service. —It may be advisable for me to see it before I contract for any other." [26] Whether he succeeded in getting the full $300 is not revealed. After having obtained some of his materials he wrote the following: "The sum which I mentioned the day I left the Harbour for the purpose of procuring sundry materials, which require ready money, will be necessary as soon as it can be conveniently transmitted—Fifty or Sixty Dollars will be sufficient." [27]

Not every prospective printer was fortunate enough to secure an advance of cash in order to establish his office. Of his early experience in Schenectady, Isaac Riggs wrote:

Instead of being assisted, as more than *four fifths* of the printers have been, both in city and country, when they first commenced, with a considerable sum of money, to be re-imbursed at some future period *without* interest, it has been my lot to pay interest on nearly the whole amount of the first purchase of my establishment.[28]

That several hundred dollars had to be advanced to set up even a small office is evident. Sale prices of establishments with a patronage would, of course, include an additional amount for good will. Thus Thurlow Weed paid $800 for the establishment of John F. Hubbard, of Norwich, although it was as-

[25] Selleck Osborn to H. P. Dering, Feb. 2, 1802, Dec. 9, 1801. This correspondence is in the MSS of the Pennypacker Long Island Collection.
[26] Selleck Osborn to H. P. Dering, Feb. 24, 1802.
[27] Selleck Osborn to H. P. Dering, Apr. 14, 1802.
[28] *Schenectady Cabinet*, Jan. 2, 1828. He preferred his course, however, for it freed him from any control in his editorial career.

serted by his friends that its value was only $350. The transfer of the office also included the agreement that Hubbard would leave the county and not publish a paper in competition with Weed.[29]

In view of the considerable outlay necessary to establish an office, what were the prospects that the printer could repay the loan? What chance was there that the profits would justify the expense? It must have been true in not a few instances that the subsidy had to be continued. Such a situation prevailed in Sag Harbor where the press of Alden Spooner was owned by a group headed by Henry P. Dering. "He informed me," wrote Spooner in an autobiographical sketch, "that the press and types [left by a former printer] were owned by about twenty persons whose names he gave. Some gave five, some ten, and some twenty dollars. If I would furnish each of these my paper for four years, then the materials would be mine." [30] This was, of course, a kind of subsidy. That some of these gentlemen continued their interest, and that the printer was still indebted to them is shown by the following document, executed some seven years later.

Received, Sag Harbor, March 1, 1811, of Messrs. Hugh Gelston, Ebenezer Sage, & Henry P. Dering, Eighty-Dollars, being the amount of the deficiency during the last six months of the *Suffolk Gazette.* Received of them in behalf of the Proprietors of the *Gazette* during that term. Witness my hand.   *Alden Spooner.*[31]

Yet Alden Spooner later became the editor of a New York paper and was prominent and influential in political and community affairs.

One should not conclude, however, that printers were never able to pay off their initial obligations. Lewis H. Redfield was one who overcame this handicap. Several hundred dollars, the first installment of his loan from his former master, James D.

[29] Barnes, T. W., *Memoir of Thurlow Weed,* pp. 9-10.

[30] Quoted by Tooker, W. W., "Early Sag Harbor Printers," *Sag Harbor Express,* Jan. 23, 1902.

[31] MS in the Pennypacker Collection. Spooner at this time printed the paper "For the Proprietors."

Bemis, was paid off at the end of six months. Subsequently the balance was paid, and Redfield, free from his obligation, soon wielded great influence as a prosperous proprietor of a weekly newspaper.[32] After seventeen years he retired with a "respectable competency." [33]

If the printer of a country newspaper put himself deeply in debt, upon what could he rely for an income sufficient to meet his obligations? How could he at the same time meet his operating expenses and eke out a profit so as to make a living for himself and family? Like other questions with regard to his economic status, these questions cannot be answered simply. Printers who discontinued "from want of patronage," as they so frequently said, were candid enough to note several reasons for their failure.[34] Among these may be found: the lack of income from subscriptions, the reluctance of their debtors to pay, the scarcity of cash, the insufficiency of the community's support for a newspaper, the destructive competition of rivals, and, finally, the high cost of living. It is impossible to determine which of these was the most potent. The following details as to income, however, may help to explain the success of some printers and the failure of others.

Of the sources of income the first to come to mind is direct revenue from subscriptions. All printers sought a large subscription list, since it was the measure of success. As a source of income, however, even a long subscription list was seldom sufficient. Few printers could support themselves or stay in business on it alone. Samuel R. Brown in his valedictory in the *Saratoga Patriot* claimed that "its circulation exceeds that of any country paper in the state, perhaps in the union," yet "experience teaches me that the emoluments of the Office are not adequate to the support of my family, even on the most economical plan." [35] Francis Stebbins of Hudson reported at the end of his first year "that the receipts [from subscriptions] for

---

[32] Syracuse *Evening Herald,* July 5, 1882.

[33] Canandaigua *Ontario Repository,* Dec. 21, 1831.

[34] Cf. Sag Harbor *Suffolk Gazette,* Feb. 23, 1811; Jamestown *Chautauqua Republican,* Dec. 31, 1828, regarding the Sandy Hill *Sun.*

[35] Ballston Spa *Saratoga Patriot,* July 20, 1813.

the past year have not amounted to one third of the expenses of the establishment," and "that if each individual was to be punctual, the whole receipts would not more than cover the actual and necessary disbursements." [36] Subscribers did not pay at a uniform rate and were generally in arrears.[37] The editor of the Rochester *Craftsman,* for example, after little more than a year and a half found five thousand dollars in unpaid subscriptions, while Isaac Riggs, of Schenectady, listed one thousand in outstanding accounts within a few months.[38]

The situation, nevertheless, had some advantages which the philosophical or cynical might discern.

> At best, a country newspaper is of little profit to the publisher. Disconnected with other business, it could not support a family. Did politicians fully understand this, especially those who, to manifest their dislike of an editor or his course, sometimes discontinue their subscriptions; did they know that they were inflicting individually an injury of less than *fifty cents per annum,* they would consider it a matter too small for an exhibition of anything like feeling.[39]

Franklin Cowdery, an editor who had plenty of experience with unsuccessful projects, saw a bit of humor in the situation in which, "one printer has received three shillings and another ten, in the course of a week, on newspaper subscriptions, and the facts are published as evidence that the times are improving." [40]

More revenue was to be obtained from advertising than from subscriptions, as printers seemed to realize when they devoted most of their space to business notices. "It is not our fault that the *Patriot* is so crowded with Advertisements—A Printer cannot live without money, tho' a farmer may—We can get no pay for our papers (except for a few persons who are punctual), but for advertisements we sometimes get pay. ... " [41] Others were apologetic when their growing list of

[36] Hudson *Northern Whig,* Dec. 26, 1809.
[37] See *post,* chap. vii.
[38] Rochester *Craftsman,* Nov. 17, 1830; Schenectady *Cabinet,* Sept. 10, 1817.
[39] Saratoga Springs *Saratoga Sentinel,* May 4, 1830.
[40] *Chronicle of Geneva,* Sept. 2, 1829.
[41] Goshen *Orange County Patriot,* July 1, 1810.

advertisers seemed to result in the abbreviation of the news which they were accustomed to present.[42] This apology was one which the printer was glad to make, for his brethren judged his success or failure by the extent to which the people of his community advertised. It was well known that "advertisements always constitute the best, and not infrequently the principal support of a country paper." [43] Advertising, too, was regarded as a fair index to the business prosperity of the community, and with that prosperity the fortunes of the printer were indissolubly linked.[44]

Since advertising was a principal source of support, its lack might be a prime cause of failure. "The county of Otsego," ran the valedictory of the printer in Cherry Valley, "though extensive in boundaries and thickly populated, will not afford that *advertising patronage,* (which is the main support of a weekly journal) to two papers of either party." [45]

The almost universal rate for advertising was one dollar for a square (column width, and as long as wide) for three weeks' insertion, each subsequent insertion being charged at the rate of twenty-five cents, or in some cases eighteen or eighteen and three-fourths cents.[46] It might be stated differently, however, as "Fifty cents for the first insertion—Half price for each continuation per square," or as seventy-five cents for the first insertion and twelve and one-half cents per week for continuations.[47] The *Hudson Balance Advertiser* provided for half-square advertisements pro rata, that is twenty-five cents for the first insertion and twelve and one-half cents for each subsequent insertion.[48] Payment in advance was expected of "stran-

---

[42] *Auburn Gazette,* Apr. 30, 1817.

[43] *Onondaga Register,* Jan. 25, 1826.

[44] *Ibid.,* Aug. 15, 1827 and July 22, 1829. The *Cortland Observer,* Sept. 18, 1829, distinguished between the apparent prosperity of Skaneateles and the lack of it in Homer on this basis.

[45] Cherry Valley *Otsego Republican Press,* Aug. 6, 1813.

[46] Newburgh *Political Index,* Feb. 5, 1811, has the 18¾ subsequent; Herkimer *Honest American,* Sept. 12, 1811—18 cents.

[47] Hudson *Northern Whig,* Jan. 3, 1809; Brooklyn *Long Island Star,* Oct. 23, 1811; Bagg, *Pioneers of Utica,* p. 155, quoting the *Columbian Patriotic Gazette,* 1799-1800.

[48] *Hudson Balance Advertiser,* Jan. 5, 1808.

gers, or persons living at a distance." [49] Regular advertisers
were given special rates for longer terms, one printer fixing the
rate at five dollars for the year per square, but at the same time
he served notice that "all accounts over one year's standing will
be charged 12½ per cent." [50] As a special inducement, one
printer offered advertising six percent cheaper to subscribers
than to non-subscribers.[51] Advertisers of new publications
(books and magazines) hoped to get their advertising in
return for copies of their own publications or an exchange,
with a commission for the printer on subscriptions he obtained.[52]

The difficulty of applying published rates was revealed by
the rules adopted by the proprietors of newspapers in Utica in
1826. "We shall hereafter charge all notices of regimental
orders, and notices of meetings, civil or political, the same price
as for advertisements," and "we shall charge for all insolvent
notices of ten weeks, three dollars, and six weeks, two dollars,
including affidavits." [53] There was apparently a tendency to
take advantage of the printer and to encroach upon his valuable space without making any return. So the Herkimer printer
inserted in his terms, "communications not suiting the views of
the Editor, will be published for 25 cents per square." [54] The
casual observer of many sheets will note that the "square"
tended to become elongated, which would of course shorten
the revenue.

Of the advertising which came to the printer of a country
paper, that classified as "legal" was most remunerative. It
varied with different papers, due to local conditions, but the
printer was usually pleased if this kind of matter crowded his
news and literary columns.[55] It might happen, as in the case of

[49] *Ibid.,* and Hudson *Northern Whig,* Jan. 3, 1809.
[50] *Oswego Palladium,* Dec. 28, 1821.
[51] Advertisement of the *American Eagle* in Sag Harbor *Suffolk County Recorder,* June 7, 1817.
[52] See advertisement of the "Poems" of William Ray in Auburn *Free Press,*
Mar. 9, 1825.
[53] Utica *Western Recorder,* Nov. 21, 1826.
[54] Herkimer *Honest American,* Sept. 12, 1811.
[55] *Glens Falls Observer,* Dec. 3, 1827.

the *Northern Post,* of Salem, that more than three-quarters of the paper was taken up with these legal notices.[56] When the *Onondaga Journal* was offered for sale, one of the chief inducements held out to the prospective purchaser was the fact that "the *advertising,* being chiefly legal, is of course the most lucrative and substantial kind of patronage that can pertain to a country printing office." [57] Strong efforts were made to obtain whatever of this patronage was available. George L. Birch, of the *Long Island Patriot,* a Brooklyn paper, issued an edition for Queens County and designated Joseph Pettit, of Hempstead, as his agent to handle the legal advertisements for that county. His rival in Queens, Henry C. Sleight, assumed that notices for Queens in the *Patriot* would not meet legal requirements and copied them with corrections in his own paper, doubtless expecting to receive the remuneration.[58]

When a paper was discontinued, in order to meet the requirement of the law the notices would have to be transferred to another paper, and publishers often waited impatiently for the passing of a competitor.[59] Eager to avail himself of the advertising belonging to the Glens Falls printer, James Wright, of Sandy Hill, reported inaccuracies in the notices in his rival's publication and wrote to the attorney-general of the state that its publication was not continuous. E. G. Lindsey, printer of the *Glens Falls Observer,* retorted that his paper had been published each week, but that it had been necessary for him to reduce its size to a half sheet for a few weeks.[60] The very lucrative nature of the legal notices caused numerous controversies between printers similar to this quarrel over the patronage of Warren County.

It is impossible to generalize concerning the proportion of the country editor's income which was received from advertis-

---

[56] Salem *Northern Post,* Aug. 2, 1810.
[57] Advertisement in the *Onondaga Register,* Dec. 6, 1826.
[58] Brooklyn *Long Island Patriot,* Dec. 29, 1825, prints the letter of Sleight.
[59] *Plattsburgh Republican,* Apr. 14, 1827.
[60] Jas. Wright to S. A. Tallcott, Feb. 23, 1827; E. G. Lindsey to S. A. Tallcott, Feb. 9, 1827; MSS in the New York State Library; papers from the attorney general's office.

ing. Printers were often poor bookkeepers, and such accounts as they kept are not now available. Their estimates and conclusions have been used as the basis of the preceding paragraphs. Any attempt to figure the financial returns for a given paper by the measurement of space and the application of the rate would be so inaccurate as to be useless. Advertising sometimes produced a substantial revenue, and one upon which the printer placed great reliance.

Another source of income for every printer of a newspaper was the job printing. It sometimes represented the difference between success and failure. Thurlow Weed, upon arriving in Manlius to begin his paper there, was almost without funds and had his family to support. In this exigency an order for fifty handbills advertising a wool-carding machine, for which he received $1.25, was his salvation.[61] But much of the job printing was of a political character and therefore dependent upon the favor of one of the parties. If there were only one paper in the community, however, it might get the patronage of both parties. So Weed, a Republican in politics, assisted his Federalist employer, William L. Stone, in Herkimer, by privately printing the handbills and tickets for the Republicans, even at times, as he said, turning the key on his employer.[62] Some printers, however, tried to be neutral in politics in order to keep the patronage of both parties.[63]

Job printing for the party or local government became in some instances a privilege for a few favored printers. Thus Isaiah Bunce, of Salina, was accustomed to print the village ordinances at his own figure, until an inquiring agent for the trustees discovered that John Durnford, of Syracuse, would do the same work for one-half the price. The agent who revealed this state of affairs concluded that on previous charges the taxpayers had been "shaved one hundred per cent, for the sake of giving their printing to Mr. Bunce." [64] Job printing, in fact, was conceived to be a proper adjunct of the newspaper press.

61 Weed, *Autobiography*, p. 88.
62 *Ibid.*, pp. 31-33.
63 Cf. *infra*, chap. v.
64 *Onondaga Register and Syracuse Gazette*, June 3, 1829.

When this was questioned the editor of the *Monroe Republican* was emphatic in his protest:

A newspaper establishment usually relies upon the accidental job printing for a part of its patronage and support, and is by that means enabled to afford its papers thus cheaply to their [*sic*] subscribers. This is a fair and proper appendage to an establishment of the kind, and without which in the country it will not only cease to be profitable, but will cease to exist.[65]

From all these sources the printer was obliged, of course, to exact his due. There, one might truthfully say, was the rub. With but one exception [66] the printers and the newspapers which have come within the scope of this study made periodic calls for their pay. The printer's dun, the "pay the printer" sign in all its various forms, was such a common thing in country papers that one gets the impression of a profession which was always hard up. Although these duns do not tell the whole story of the printer's financial position, they do reveal the perennial struggle to meet operating expenses. While pleading for cash, the printers were always ready to receive commodity payment. Occasionally they suggested that their wants were urgent; for instance, during severe winters the printers in northern towns, such as Oswego, Troy, and Plattsburgh, sent out their cry for "WOOD! WOOD!" [67] Hubbard of the *Norwich Journal* "wanted immediately 50 *Bushels good Wheat*. One Dollar per bushel will be allowed on account," [68] and an Auburn printer, after suggesting that wood was seasonal, added, "also, wanted Butter, Cheese, Lard, Wheat, Corn, Oats, Rye, Feathers, Flax, Wool, at fair prices—also a little *CASH*." [69] So numerous were the commodities acceptable to the printer that the rural subscriber had little excuse for

---

[65] Rochester *Monroe Republican,* Dec. 27, 1825.

[66] Elihu Phinney of the Cooperstown *Otsego Herald.* He claimed, Nov. 5, 1808, never to have urged payment over a period of fourteen years. He did intimate on occasion that payment was expected, but complemented his subscribers on their punctuality.

[67] Troy *Northern Budget,* Jan. 30, 1821; *Plattsburgh Republican,* Mar. 10, 1827; *Oswego Palladium,* Dec. 6, 1822.

[68] *Norwich Journal,* Sept.-Oct., 1820.

[69] Auburn *Cayuga Republican,* Dec. 26, 1821.

failure to pay for the paper. At times, however, he learned that only cash would satisfy the printer.

The Publisher of this paper wants *money* of those who owe him. If each one who is indebted will pay NOW *without delay,* in MONEY, only *one half* of what they owe, it will be of essential service in the prosecution of his business.[70]

While the problem of collections was serious, the printer often treated it lightly. The following good-humored suggestion includes three alternatives. "The crops, this year, are good, and the fruits fine, especially potatoes. Money is said to be scarce, but law is brisk, and duns to the printer, 'plenty as blackberries.' "[71] People did like to run bills, and the printer had to make earnest efforts to collect. When the time fell due he made personal calls for payment. He accepted notes from subscribers who were unable to pay, and he authorized agents to collect for him.[72] Sometimes the post rider was so authorized, but if he was irresponsible or a minor, an agent was sent to accompany him on the route or the printer himself made the collection tour.[73]

There remained the possibility of bringing pressure to bear on the delinquents. The printer would threaten to put overdue accounts in the hands of the sheriff, but unless he were planning to go out of business or leave the town, he was always too much a seeker after public favor to pursue this course. Even when the printer had given up his former connection, it was recognized that there might be an unfavorable sentiment against his paper. The editors of the Poughkeepsie *Republican Herald* sought to dispel the idea that they were in any way responsible for the "numerous suits... against the old patrons of the *Herald,* by the agent of the administrators of C. C. Adams a former [late] Editor of this paper."[74]

[70] *Ibid.,* Dec. 2, 1829.
[71] *Chronicle of Geneva,* Sept. 2, 1829.
[72] Kingston *Plebeian,* June 28, 1808.
[73] Brooklyn *Long Island Star,* Dec. 6, 1813. Multiplication of references here would not be difficult, as the practice was general.
[74] Poughkeepsie *Republican Herald,* Sept. 13, 1815.

Another form of pressure that received more discussion than actual application was the publication of the names of "Runaway Patrons." Many printers toyed with the idea and reprinted what their brethren said, and a few made up their own lists of delinquents and printed them, sometimes with comment. Pomeroy Tucker, of Palmyra, was one of these. With his pen dipped in gall he produced a list of eleven persons who owed him a total of $30.28. He promised another list shortly, and hoped that this might "check the evil." The following is a sample of his citations:

Mr. S. Cutler (Samuel Cutler, we believe), school-master, author of a new system of Arithmetic, (as he says,) maker of reflectors, pianissimos, &c&c, or, in other words, a sort of "jack of all trades," came to this place, strutted about our streets for some time, contracted many small debts, fell in love with several girls, and finally decamped on the tow path the other day without paying his bill at the office, amounting to about .... $5.00.[75]

The English observer, quoted above,[76] gave an accurate description of the procedure in most country newspaper offices when he wrote:

But it should also be understood that the whole community of advertisers expect to pay in kind (if they ever pay at all) for the insertion of their advertisements; and should some of this class of patrons of a newspaper have nothing to tender in payment that the printer can by possibility make use of himself, he is generally under the necessity of accepting whatever such persons are willing to turn out for him, as they express it, which he has to dispose of in the best way he can. He therefore seldom finds much difficulty in maintaining himself and family, if he have one, for his subscribers and advertising patrons find little difficulty in supplying him with provisions, stores, fuel, and all the necessaries of life; but the great difficulty lies in procuring the amount of cash that is absolutely necessary to carry on business with, for there are but few things in a new settlement that people trade in, that can be converted into cash without considerable loss on the original value of the article, or at a considerable degree of expense and trouble.[77]

[75] Palmyra *Wayne Sentinel,* Aug. 4, 1826. Lists also appeared in the Troy *Northern Budget,* Aug. 18, 1817, and in the *Schenectady Cabinet.* For the latter see the Malone *Franklin Telegraph,* July 20, 1826.

[76] *Supra,* p. 50.

[77] London *Penny Magazine* (1841), X, 244.

Having considered the printer's sources of income, it is logical to inquire as to his operating expenses. It has been intimated that his receipts, or a large part of them, were in the form of commodities not convertible into cash. Nevertheless, unlike the farmer, he needed cash. Labor was partly paid in cash, but journeymen's wages frequently took the form of orders on advertising merchants. Paper, as many printers testified, was a "cash article," and the paper bill might average more than ten dollars a week.[78] A Poughkeepsie paper used weekly "nearly two reams, at *four dollars and fifty cents* a ream." [79] Ink and house rent also had to come from the scant supply of money.[80] Any increase, change, or improvement of equipment was bound, also, to mean an increased outlay of cash. The *Delaware Gazette* informed its readers that it had expended "rising of *one thousand dollars*," in getting press and types for its enlargement, while the *Schenectady Cabinet* proposed an outlay of "about *six hundred dollars*" to get new type and add an extra column to the sheet.[81]

These costs, especially the items in the paper maker's bill, varied with the size of the establishment, and the circulation of the newspaper. To appreciate the significance of the printer's costs one needs to know their relation to total income, but such estimates are difficult to obtain. In 1798 the *Northern Budget,* of Troy, impressed its readers with the statement that its weekly expenses, "tho' an infant establishment," were "at a moderate calculation *thirty dollars*." [82] The Poughkeepsie *Political Barometer* figured that, after taking from the two-dollar-per-year subscription price forty cents for paper, thirty cents for the cost of publishing, and one dollar for delivery by post rider, there was left but thirty cents profit.[83] In percentages this would be 50 percent for delivery, 20 percent for paper, 15 percent for publishing costs, and 15 percent profit.

---

[78] Ballston Spa *Saratoga Patriot,* Mar. 2, 1813.
[79] Poughkeepsie *Independent Republican,* July 20, 1813.
[80] *Ibid.*
[81] Delhi *Delaware Gazette,* Sept. 10, 1828; *Schenectady Cabinet,* Jan. 2, 1828.
[82] Troy *Northern Budget,* Oct. 16, 1798.
[83] Poughkeepsie *Political Barometer,* Jan. 1, 1805.

Added to this estimate was the declaration that the receipts had "not been sufficient to discharge the regular bills of our paper maker." [84]

There is nothing more erroneous than the general opinion in regard to the profits of newspaper printers in this country. Putting advertisements out of view, there are very few, perhaps not a tenth part of the newspapers in the United States, that, under the present state of our currency would clear their expenses. The price of labor is greatly enhanced within a few years; the value of money consequently reduced. This circumstance (which adds to the expenses of newspaper establishments at least twenty per cent on their amount when prices of newspapers are fixed at their present low rate) added to the taxes imposed by the government on paper and postage, operate very oppressively on the printer.[85]

In the period following the War of 1812 prices were going up, and labor, which was scarce, demanded higher wages. No generation is ever satisfied with its living costs, and complaints are bound to be numerous. To persons familiar with present-day price levels, commodity prices of a hundred years ago seem low. But in 1804 Charles Holt, of Hudson, found the cost of his bread and butter excessive.

Flour that was 28 s, is now 56 s. a hundred, and butter is raised from 1 s. to 2 s. 4 d. per lb. Still the twelve shillings for our paper is only an hundred and fifty cents yet, and that won't buy a decent load of wood.[86]

As noted above, prices rose after 1814, but those quoted by Thurlow Weed for 1819 (when the post-war depression must have affected them) were low.[87]

Rent for a small house and garden [in Manlius, where he was then located], one hundred dollars a year; butter, ten cents a pound; beefsteak, eight cents a pound; eggs, six cents a dozen, with other articles

[84] *Ibid.*

[85] Brooklyn *Long Island Star*, Nov. 22, 1815, quoting the New York *Columbian.*

[86] Hudson *Bee*, Nov. 27, 1804. "s." and "d." are here substituted for the symbol /.

[87] He was comparing them with another post-war period, 1869.

produced on farms in proportion,—the whole amounting at the close of the first year, to about five hundred dollars.[88]

These facts should be kept in mind when the costs of materials are considered.

The printer's necessary economies, affecting his standard of living, at times must have lowered his station in the community. Those who set up establishments might be quite impecunious. Thurlow Weed's straits in Manlius have been mentioned.[89] In 1826 he was gaining influence as a politician. "He had been a member of the Assembly a year before. He was one of the poorest and worst dressed men in Rochester. He dwelt in a cheap house in an obscure part of the village.... He sometimes had to borrow clothes to give him an appearance befitting his talents," and on one occasion he had to borrow a shilling from Frederick Whittlesey for bread for his family. "It was rare that one so poor should be so great. Spattered with ink, and with bare arms he pulled at the old hand press of the *Telegraph,* and at a rickety table that would have been dear at fifty cents, he wrote those sparkling paragraphs, which in later years made the *Albany Evening Journal* famous." [90]

At the beginning of his venture in Sag Harbor in 1804 Alden Spooner confessed, "my whole fortune consisted of about five or six dollars in my pocket, and scarcely a decent suit of clothes to my back. My mother and sister were wanting immediate relief, which was the main reason of my going to Sag Harbor." [91]

The high prices in the years after the war found Lewis H. Redfield struggling to pay off the debt contracted with Bemis to set him up in business. The need for economy drove him to cut his expenses by boarding himself and his apprentice in his office, with very little in the way of comfort.[92] Franklin Cowdery, after the failure of one of his many ventures, declared

---

[88] Weed, *Autobiography,* p. 78.
[89] *Ibid.* and *supra,* p. 64.
[90] Stanton, Henry B., *Random Recollections,* p. 19.
[91] Tooker, W. W., *loc. cit.*
[92] Obituary in Syracuse *Evening Herald,* July 15, 1882.

to his subscribers, "our family must and shall be supported." [93]

The family, indeed, played a considerable rôle in the lives of most printers. In one of his editorial jibes at James Bogert, his contemporary in Geneva, Cowdery made a reference to "celibacy." To this Bogert replied, "in the language of a country editor quoted by *Noah*,[94] 'What the d—l has an editor to do with a wife! Writing for glory, and printing on *trust,* they ought to be ashamed of themselves to indulge in such luxuries!!' " [95] But the wife was a very important part of most printing establishments. Not only did she feed, clothe, and care for a large household, including the office help, but she was frequently initiated into the technical processes. Some wives could set type, while others "folded book forms, stitched pamphlets, made selection of copy, and followed the business as closely as her husband." [96] The historian of the press in Chautauqua County has emphasized the economic motivation of the matrimonial ventures of western New York printers.

In truth it was absolutely necessary that the early publisher should marry to get along at all. Matrimony was not a matter of money with him, but was made necessary by the absence of money. Nearly all his subscriptions were paid in farm products. Storekeepers would advertise if they could pay in trade, but not otherwise. Cash was seldom received, (came mostly from legal notices) and must be religiously saved to buy paper and pay for the materials which had been bought on credit. Hence there was very little money for the hands or for the family.[97]

From the marriage notices of scores of printers one learns that many of these young craftsmen married less than six months after the establishment of their first business ventures. A helpmate seemed necessary if the enterprise were to succeed.[98] The printer, like his fellows in other crafts, was pri-

[93] Quoted in the Rochester *Craftsman,* May 11, 1830.
[94] Mordecai M. Noah of the New York *National Advocate.*
[95] *Geneva Gazette,* Feb. 11, 1829.
[96] McKinstry, *loc. cit.,* p. 96.
[97] *Ibid.*
[98] The intimate connection of some wives with the craft is shown in their choosing printer husbands the second time. So Nancy Moffitt, widow of Robert Moffitt (d. 1807), was married in 1810 to Oliver Lyon, the surviving partner of

marily concerned with making a living and finding a way of
life. However noble his early dreams of public service, however idealistic his public utterances, he was a craftsman and
a laborer striving to win profits from his trade.[99]

In contrast with the difficulties of those printers who struggled to keep revenues above expenditures were the fortunate
circumstances of others whose establishments prospered. They
found in the printing of newspapers, together with all the other
enterprises that might be connected with that occupation, an
advantageous and profitable career. Since they were business
men rather than craftsmen, they seem best described by the
business term *entrepreneurs*. They operated establishments
which were a far cry from the one-room printing office.

The dean of this group, although he was still a young man
when he retired, was James D. Bemis, of Canandaigua. Perhaps Bemis caught a vision of the possibilities of a business
empire when he was dispatched by his employers, Backus &
Whiting, booksellers of Albany, to establish a bookstore for
them in York (Toronto), Upper Canada. Their plan to extend
their chain of bookstores to Canada was checked, when Bemis,
detained by impassable roads, opened the bookstore in Canandaigua and then bought a newspaper there.[100] He was at first
more interested in the newspaper (from 1804 to 1810 the
bookstore was run by Myron Holley), but he was soon extensively engaged in the book and stationery business. Before the

---

Moffitt & Lyon, who had continued the paper. After the death of C. C. Adams
in 1812, Mrs. Adams continued the Poughkeepsie *Republican Herald* for a
short time. In 1818 she was married to Richard Nelson, one of the proprietors
of the *Dutchess Observer*.

[99] A different view is expressed by J. E. Klock in Clearwater, A. T., *A
History of Ulster County*, pp. 505-506. "Men did not enter the newspaper business in those days to make money. The motives were a mixture of that strange
vanity which yearns to see its thoughts in print, and that nobler emotion which
leads men to abandon hope of material prosperity in order to advocate the
political and religious principles they hold dear." Facts cited above, as well as
in the following section, will refute this generalization. Printers did have the
hope of success, for some succeeded. And can it be proved that the printer
who failed would not have been as conspicuous a failure in some other field?

[100] An Autobiographical letter of Bemis, printed by Noah T. Clark in the
Ontario County Times, June 30, 1897. Clipping in the scrapbook of the late
C. F. Milliken of Canandaigua.

Erie Canal opened in 1825 he was a sort of wholesaler for the western country. "Instead of procuring articles in either branch of business in New York, as is now the case," wrote Frederick Follett in 1846, "merchants were very generally throughout the West supplied from his establishment, swelling his sales from 20 to $30,000 a year." He was the agent for type founders, press manufacturers, and ink makers (though for many years he made his own ink), and he kept this expanding business for years under his own hand and his supervising eye. "He was thus compelled to work all day—and to keep up the Editorial department of his paper, and his correspondence, write half the night." [101] His interests in western New York grew so rapidly that he became a wealthy man and started many others on the road to financial success. Although he has been called the "pioneer printer," it was as an *entrepreneur* rather than as a craftsman that he made the greatest contribution to the life of his generation.

Here I have lived [he testified], and from time to time spread my business over the country—to set up young men in business from Onondaga to Detroit. In this way fifteen bookstores were sent abroad. I established the first presses and bookstores in Erie, Wayne, Livingston, and Onondaga counties at a pecuniary loss to myself of from $20,000 to $25,000 but with the satisfaction of knowing that I had put a goodly number of young men in active and successful business.[102]

.   .   .

My weakness was [that] I did not value money. I did value the reputation of an honest and independent editor. It was the aliment of my life, and I have allowed its loss to disturb me. During my business career I had ten partners, and I am satisfied that I was not a good judge of character, and my devotion to the pleasure of editing ruined my business experience.... I can only say that I was a faithful apprentice, an efficient and pains-taking journeyman, and indulgent master, yet a sovereign one, with a disposition somewhat spoiled by bringing up about 80 boys with journeymen, clerk girls, and directing outdoor persons. For many years there were from 40 to 60 souls dependent in various ways on the "old establishment." [103]

[101] Follett, *op. cit.*, p. 4.
[102] Autobiographical letter of Bemis, *loc. cit.*
[103] *Ibid.*

Another notable example of the enlargement of a printing office was the Phinney brothers' establishment, in Cooperstown. The *Otsego Herald* was started by Elihu Phinney in 1795, but upon his death in 1813 the responsibility had been assumed by his sons, Henry and Elihu, who devoted themselves particularly to the publishing and book-selling branches. In January, 1821, the newspaper was discontinued, but the other enterprises were advanced in a way that labels the Phinneys not only as *entrepreneurs* of the printing business but as pioneers in the diffusion of literature.

The Messrs. Phinney originated several peculiar methods of business, among which were large wagons ingeniously constructed to serve as locomotive bookstores. They also had a canal boat fitted up as a floating bookstore, which carried a variety beyond that found in ordinary village bookstores, anchoring in winter at one of the largest towns on the Erie canal.... They also stocked and maintained for many years the largest bookstores in Utica, Buffalo, Detroit and other large towns.[104]

Similar large establishments were located in Utica, Auburn, Troy, and later Rochester, Buffalo, and Ithaca.[105] From Utica spread the fame of William Williams under whose paternal care a large number of apprentices received an excellent training.[106] It was no ordinary country printing office which was described by Ebenezer Mack when he offered for sale his half interest in the *"Ithaca Journal* Establishment—Printing office, Bookstore,&c.&c.":

The paper, as may be seen from its columns [a reference to advertising], is well patronized; a more than ordinary share of Job and Book printing is done in the office; the sale of books is considerable and increasing, and the location for publishing extensively is scarcely surpassed; there are some copyright and other valuable privileges, with a share in a Paper Mill....[107]

---

[104] Livermore, *A Condensed History of Cooperstown,* pp. 161-162. These developments occurred over this period and until 1849, when fire destroyed their plant, and its removal to Buffalo followed.

[105] Poughkeepsie and Brooklyn were of course known as printing centers. Other towns can boast of imprints in some number from their respective presses but were not then known as publishing centers.

[106] Williams, J. C., *An Oneida County Printer* (1906); an excellent treatment.

[107] Auburn *Free Press,* Oct. 18, 1826.

The process of entering the ranks of the *entrepreneurs* usually began with the enlargement of the newspaper. One of the first ambitions of the country printer was to brighten his dingy sheet with a "new dress" (new types) and to enlarge its size so as to correspond more nearly to that of the city papers, for which he would need a new press. The "demy" sheet might thus give way to a "royal" or "imperial" size. To do this he would take his subscribers into his confidence and explain to them not only the expense to himself, but the advantage to them, of such an improvement. A larger sheet, and perhaps smaller type, would result in more reading matter and more advertising space in better style; and for all this there would be no increase in price.[108] Nearly every newspaper of any longevity, however, made the attempt at improvement. The *Poughkeepsie Journal* in 1795 proposed to change from "four pages folio" to "eight pages quarto," but this change was not adopted.[109]

An even more evident sign of progress was the issuance by larger establishments of semi-weeklies, and finally of dailies. The idea of printing a semi-weekly paper had been entertained by some of the early country printers. In 1794 the *Lansingburgh Recorder* began as a semi-weekly, but it soon changed to a weekly.[110] The *Ontario Freeman* was published "every *Monday* and *Thursday*" in 1803, but later it became a weekly;[111] while the *Brooklyn Minerva* in 1807, and the West Farms *West Chester Patriot* in 1813, began their brief careers as semi-weeklies.[112] These are not to be classified with the semi-weeklies which were the outgrowth of well established weeklies. Albany had a semi-weekly paper as early as 1788, which her preëminence as the political capital of the state may have justified, but no country establishment felt able to support a

---

[108] Brooklyn *Long Island Star*, May 31, 1810; Canandaigua *Ontario Repository*, Jan. 2, 1816, suggested that enlargement would enable the printer to give more of the proceedings of Congress.

[109] *Poughkeepsie Journal*, Aug. 26, 1795.

[110] See issues of Dec. 26, 1794 and Apr. 28, 1795.

[111] Canandaigua *Ontario Freeman*, Dec. 29, 1803.

[112] *Brooklyn Minerva*, Nov. 7, 1807 (photostat); West Farms *West Chester Patriot*, July 3, 1813.

semi-weekly until the *Utica Patriot and Patrol* came out as a semi-weekly, January 2, 1816. The experiment did not appear to be successful, for it reverted to weekly publication, April 2 of the same year. In 1818 proposals were issued by William L. Stone for a semi-weekly in Troy; [113] yet it was five years before the *Troy Sentinel* began its successful career as a semi-weekly.[114] Utica, wishing to emulate the Trojan success, tried again in 1826 with the semi-weekly *Sentinel and Gazette,* and this time managed to continue until the end of 1828.[115] Editor Redfield, of Onondaga, hailed this *denouement* with the reflection that "it will hereafter be published weekly, like any other decent country paper." [116] The *Buffalo Emporium* also began as a semi-weekly publication, December 11, 1826.

Daily papers were not numerous outside the large cities, and a landmark in American journalism was established when Henry C. Sleight and Luther Tucker brought out the *Rochester Daily Advertiser,* the first daily west of Albany, October 25, 1826. In Brooklyn, Alden Spooner made a three-month experiment with the *Evening Star,* only to abandon it for want of patronage.[117] He was too near the New York dailies to compete.

Another field for expanding establishments was the publication of the religious periodicals, which seemed to be numerous after 1820. In some instances they were sponsored by individual promoters, usually clergymen; but in a number of cases they were backed by the patronage of a district group, church conference, or institution; for example, the *New York Baptist Register* was "published by the New York Baptist State Convention—the profits of this paper sacred to the cause of missions," but printed by D. Bennett and Co., of Utica. Utica was the principal center of this activity,[118] with Auburn also promi-

---

[113] *Troy Post,* Oct. 16, 1818, gives the prospectus.

[114] *Troy Sentinel,* July 15, 1823. The *Budget* came out as the *Troy Budget and City Register* (semiweekly), Jan. 3, 1826.

[115] *Utica Sentinel and Gazette,* June 13, 16, 1826.

[116] *Onondaga Register,* Dec. 24, 1828.

[117] April 2 to June 30, 1827.

[118] In addition to the *Baptist Register* (1824), were the *Utica Christian Magazine* (1813), Presbyterian; *Utica Christian Repository* (1822) succeeded

nent.[119] There were certain printers of Utica, especially Williams, and some of his apprentices, who took a strong interest in this development.[120] Other towns also found themselves in this field. The Troy *Evangelical Restorationist* in 1824 noted the passing of the *Messenger of Peace,* of Hudson, and the *Gospel Inquirer,* of Glens Falls.[121] Buffalo had its *Gospel Advocate* (1822), Watertown its *Herald of Salvation* (1822), and Potsdam its *Day Star* (1827), all Universalist journals.[122] In Schoharie was the *Evangelical Luminary* (1824), Lutheran, followed by the *Lutheran Magazine* (1827).[123] Proposals were issued by printers in Hudson (1816) and Moscow (1817) for religious periodicals, which apparently never materialized.[124] Generally these periodicals were the product of a printing office which was at the same time issuing a weekly paper. Although the printer in some cases was a member of the denomination sponsoring the journal, he regarded the extra work in his office

by the *Western Recorder* (1824) Presbyterian; the *Evangelical Magazine* (1825-1827), Universalist, succeeded by the *Utica Magazine* (1827), and later revived (1829-1830); the *Christian Journal* (1829); and the *Baptist Sunday School Journal* (1828).

[119] See the *Gospel Messenger* (1827), Episcopal; *Gospel Advocate* (1820), Universalist; and proposals issued for the Presbyterian *Evangelical Recorder,* in the *Auburn Gazette,* Aug. 13, 1817.

[120] Cephas Bennett of Utica became the first printer of Burma, entering that country with Adoniram Judson. Ranney, R. W., *A Sketch of the Lives and Missionary Work of Rev. Cephas Bennett, and His Wife, Stella Kneeland Bennett.*

[121] Troy *Evangelical Restorationist,* May 14, 1825. It was followed by the *Troy Review,* (1826). Hudson also had the *Evangelical Witness* (1824), Reformed; followed by the *Christian Statesman.* Ruttenber, *History of Orange County,* pp. 192-193.

[122] French, *Gazetteer of the State of New York,* pp. 281, 352; Munsell, J., *Typographical Miscellany,* p. 14. Dates in parentheses are those of establishment, as nearly as they can be ascertained.

[123] French, *op. cit.,* p. 603; Roscoe, W. H., *History of Schoharie County,* p. 81

[124] Hudson *Northern Whig,* Nov. 26, 1816; Moscow *Genesee Farmer,* Sept. 11, 1817. An interesting variant from these was the periodical devoted to one phase of religious controversy, such as *Plain Truth,* published at Canandaigua (1822-1824), in opposition to foreign missions. Its printer, Thomas B. Barnum, who also issued the Canandaigua *Ontario Republican,* seemed to have a penchant for criticism and aroused several contemporaries by his caustic comments upon clergymen and missionaries. See the Canandaigua *Ontario Repository,* May 21, 1822; *Palmyra Herald,* Oct. 30, 1822, and Nov. 6, 1822; and Palmyra *Wayne Sentinel,* Apr. 7, 1824.

as job printing. With the editors and their policies he was not concerned.[125]

The publishing of books furnished another lucrative field of endeavor. Not only were there volumes of sermons and tracts, but reprints of standard works were numerous. Well known books by foreign authors which were not protected by copyright furnished the copy for profitable ventures in many country printing offices. Thus, in 1796 Mackay Croswell, of Catskill, printed Voltaire's *Philosophical Dictionary;* John P. Reynolds, of Salem, printed *Hume's History of England* in 1806; [126] Tenny and Miller, of Sangerfield, issued proposals for printing by subscription "a new edition of Dr. Scott's *Family Bible*"; [127] while the "first book printed in Western New York" was *Pickering's Letters* printed in the Bemis establishment in 1812.[128] Enough similar instances might be listed to fill a volume, for scarcely a printer in the state failed to undertake some such task.

An even more profitable field was the publication of schoolbooks, such as Webster's *Spelling Book,* for which contracts were made with the proprietor, and from which Seward and Williams, of Utica, made an annual income of two thousand dollars over a period of fourteen years.[129] Webster's *School Dictionary*, Morse's *Geography*, and *Elements,* and the schoolbooks of Walker and Lyman Cobb were the leaders in this period.[130]

More interesting are the works of local writers and those of contemporary importance. Two outstanding publishing events

[125] Since the editors of these religious periodicals were neither printers nor journalists, they need not be included in this study. They have been listed, however, among "editors" in the Appendix.

[126] Hill, W. H., *The Press of Washington, Saratoga, and Warren Counties,* p. 125 ff.

[127] Onondaga *Gazette and Onondaga Advertiser,* June 5, 1816.

[128] L. H. Redfield to Henry O'Reilly, Mar. 10, 1858. O'Reilly presented a copy to the New York Historical Society.

[129] Bagg, *Pioneers of Utica,* pp. 162-163.

[130] Jedidiah Morse MSS and Noah Webster MSS in New York Public Library. Wright, Goodenow, and Stockwell to Noah Webster, Jan. 23, Feb. 9, 1807. Bemis & Ward to Noah Webster, Jan. 16, 1833. Mack and Andrus, Ithaca, were the publishers of Cobb's works.

occurred in western New York in this period. The first was the printing of William Morgan's revelation of Masonry in the office of David C. Miller, in Batavia (1826), which, with attendant events, profoundly influenced the development of the press within the state.[131] The second was the publication of the *Book of Mormon* or "Golden Bible" of Joseph Smith by E. B. Grandin, of Palmyra (1830). For this he received three thousand dollars for five thousand copies, binding included. Grandin was the proprietor of the *Wayne Sentinel*.[132] It is interesting to note that Thurlow Weed, when a newspaper proprietor in Rochester, was offered the printing of both of these works.[133]

The printing of sermons for local divines was common, for sermons were an important part of the literary diet. While at Sag Harbor, Alden Spooner printed those of Lyman Beecher and of D. S. Bogart, of Southampton, but his supply of type was so meager that he had to work nights to run them off so that he might use the same type in his newspaper.[134] Nearly every community, however, could offer a volume of sermons to the printer.

Ira Merrell, of Utica, issued a Welsh hymn book in 1808, and followed it with a catechism in Welsh for the local clergy.[135] This is an interesting example of printing in a foreign language for a local need. As noted above, Mack and Andrus, of Ithaca, possessed musical type with which they published *The Musical Monitor; or, New York Collection of Devotional Church Music*.[136]

Another type of publishing for which there seems to have been a demand was the yearly almanac, and some establishments became well known for their almanacs. *Phinney's Calendar,* long issued from Cooperstown; Ashbel Stoddard's *Columbian Almanac,* begun in 1795; and *Beer's Western Cal-*

---

[131] Batavia *Republican Advocate,* Aug. 18-25, 1826, Miller's paper.
[132] Follett, p. 42.
[133] Weed, *Autobiography,* pp. 212-213; 359.
[134] Tooker, W. W., *loc. cit.*
[135] Bagg, *Pioneers of Utica,* p. 161.
[136] This went through at least eight editions, 1822-1833.

endar; or, Southwick's Almanack, for the vicinity of Auburn, are examples.[137] This publication had the advantage of a distinctly local clientele and a periodic revision, not to mention the advertising included.

That publishing sometimes bulked large in the activities of the printing office is evident from the fact that William Williams was taunted with "reaping a rich harvest from the *printing* and *selling* of Anti-Masonick books." [138] One printer was so frank as to tell his subscribers that due to business in another county, "and also having engaged to complete a large quantity of book work, we are, for the present, obliged to make our paper a secondary consideration" and to issue it in reduced size.[139]

Local interest in a public event sometimes gave the printer an opportunity for a timely publication. This was true of many executions for murder; the "confessions" of the murderer, his last words, and a description of the dire event, being highly valued for their didactic influence, appeared in pamphlet form. It needs no vivid imagination in this day to suppose that they sold like "hot cakes," and to appreciate why printers quarreled as to which had the prior right of publication.[140] They were sometimes sold on the day of, and at the scene of, the event and were distributed by post riders along with the newspapers.[141] Like our modern "yellow journals," these accounts exalted the importance of the criminal, and, in spite of the warnings against crime which they were supposed to contain, they were clearly cases of mercenary exploitation by the printer.

The bookstore and printing office were sometimes combined,

---

[137] Livermore, *op. cit.;* Munsell, *Typographical Miscellany,* p. 146; *Auburn Gazette,* Nov. 15, 1818.

[138] Utica *Oneida Observer,* Feb. 23, 1830.

[139] Morrisville *Madison County Gazette,* Apr. 12, 1818.

[140] Such a quarrel took place between Tiffany, of Lansingburgh, and Barber, of Albany, over the "Writings of Whiting Sweeting," Lansingburgh *American Spy,* Sept. 2, 1791.

[141] See Poughkeepsie *Political Barometer,* Aug. 6, 1805, for an advertisement of "The Confessions of Peter Shaver, Respecting the *Murder* of His Sister."

and the printer frequently distributed not only his own publications but those of his brethren and works imported from the
cities. Lists of titles are common in advertisements in country
papers, and they give a clue to the reading habits of the community, or possibly to those of the printer, whose self-education
was forwarded by the variety of his stock. Salisbury's Buffalo
Bookstore issued one list containing "seventeen books on law,
fourteen on medicine, fifty-four on religious subjects, fifty-four
on history, poetry and philosophy, and only eleven novels." [142]
Just as the secular books circulated by Benjamin Franklin
broadened the outlook of the people of Philadelphia,[143] so did
those circulated by the stores of his emulators affect the towns-
folk of New York.

A bookstore was usually considered an asset, but Francis
Stebbins in offering his office for sale commented that it was
"unencumbered by the annexation of a stock of old and unsale-
able books, as is so often the case in the sale of such establishments." [144] For the printer, however, an advantage of the
bookstore was the possibility of paying off some of his debts
in books or stationery.

The bookseller felt his business threatened, then as now, by
unfair competition when the practice of selling "books in numbers" was disclosed. This meant pamphlet publication of the
Bible in "160 numbers" at twelve and one-half cents per number; or "Josephus in 95 nos. at 12½ cents per No." It was
pointed out that this made the total cost excessive as compared with the price in book form and gave an enormous profit
to the promoter. Serious, too, was the fact that it undermined
the market of the ordinary bookseller who carried a stock.[145]

The bookstore then, like the drugstore today, seems to have
been the container of a host of articles and the dispenser of
varied services. It was but a short step to the opening of a
reading room. There the literary minded might avail them-

[142] Johnson, Crisfield, *History of Erie County*, p. 195.
[143] Cook, Elizabeth C., in *Cambridge History of American Literature*, I, 116.
[144] Hudson *Northern Whig*, Aug. 22, 1811.
[145] *Troy Sentinel*, Apr. 22, 1825.

selves of the editor's "exchanges," and the subscribers to the movement might provide the means by which a larger selection of books and periodicals could be maintained. The reading room at Saratoga Springs was to have "most of the important daily, semi-weekly, and weekly newspapers of our country," and the same establishment projected a circulating library.[146] The *Rochester Telegraph* reading room received a generous contribution of twenty dollars from J. Wadsworth, Esq., of Geneseo, no small encouragement to its projectors.[147] The Auburn circulating library contained eight hundred volumes, and its terms were $3 for one year; $2 for a half year; $1.25 a quarter; $.62 for a month; or by the volume, 6 cents for a duodecimo or smaller and 12½ cents for an octavo.[148]

Another service naturally pertaining to the bookstore was that of subscription agent for books, magazines, or newspapers. Wright, Goodenow and Stockwell, of Troy, listed the following for which they were agents:

> *New York Evening Post, N. Y. Herald,* the *Balance* (which papers need no recommendation in this state)—the *United States Gazette*—the *Repertory* (which are two of the best papers on the continent, the former published at Philadelphia and the latter at Boston)—*Litchfield Monitor, Albany Centinel, Lansingburgh Gazette,* the *Churchman's Magazine,* printed at New Haven (Conn.), and the *Monthly Anthology and Boston Review,* a meritorious work of rising reputation, and of which a more full account and character will be soon given.[149]

This was, of course, a Federalist list, and a different set of publications would have been carried by a Republican printer.

Lottery tickets were commonly sold by the printer, and his name also appeared as an agent for patent medicines.[150] Redfield, of Onondaga, sold fire insurance and was the agent for nurseries in Flushing supplying all kinds of shrubs and rose-

---

[146] Saratoga Springs *Saratoga Sentinel,* May 16, 1819.

[147] *Ithaca Journal,* May 3, 17, 1826.

[148] Auburn *Advocate of the People,* Dec. 4, 1816.

[149] *Troy Gazette,* Sept. 17, 1805.

[150] Pomeroy Tucker of Palmyra was the agent for the "New York State Lottery." See Palmyra *Wayne Sentinel,* Dec. 31, 1823. Many others could be listed.

bushes.[151] John H. Prentiss, of Cooperstown, advertised the patent rights for any town (except Otsego) for Hackley's "perpetual steam still and water boiler," on the merits of which he promised to discourse.[152] In fact, the printer found his calling such as to exclude him from very few activities from politics to peddling.

The extension of his influence both as politician and as business man was the dominant desire of the *entrepreneur,* and in no way was this better done than by setting up newspaper presses in neighboring towns and counties where there was as yet no paper of his political persuasion. For this proceeding there was the precedent of Franklin who was a partner with Thomas Whitemarsh in setting up the Charleston *South Carolina Gazette* in 1731.[153] Thus Bemis, the dean of the Western New York printers, set up in business his apprentices Smith H. and Hezekiah A. Salisbury as proprietors of the *Buffalo Gazette* (1811), the first paper in Erie County; sent Oran Follett, another of his printers, and Rosswell Haskins, a bookbinder, to Rochester to manage the bookstore of A. G. Dauby's printing office, whence Follett went to Batavia where he established the *Spirit of the Times* in 1819;[154] encouraged Lewis H. Redfield, another of his boys, to begin publishing the *Onondaga Register* in 1814; and in 1821 backed Chauncey Morse, who had been a journeyman for him and Redfield, in establishing the *Livingston Journal* in Geneseo. In 1822 Orsamus Turner, who had also been apprenticed to Bemis, founded the *Lockport Observatory.*

These printers and proprietors of newspapers, trained in the technical and political school of the master, were expected to show through their respective prints the thoroughness of their preparation. Sometimes they drifted a bit, as in the case

[151] *Onondaga Register,* files 1814-1827.

[152] *Cooperstown Federalist,* June 8, 1811.

[153] Cook, Elizabeth C., in *Cambridge History of American Literature,* I, 116-117.

[154] Sellstedt, L. G., "Rosswell Willson Haskins," Buffalo Historical Society *Publications,* IV, 262-264. Later Oran Follett was a partner of Haskins in Buffalo.

of the Salisburys, from the strict Federalism they learned in Canandaigua, but the political prominence of Bemis due to these connections is undeniable.[155] He kept his eye on these protégés, either to commend or reprove. On one occasion he wrote, "There is no *federal* paper now published at Buffalo—the *Gazette* having gotten entirely into anti-federal hands." [156] The Salisbury brothers had dissolved their partnership, and William A. Carpenter had formed a new partnership with Hezekiah. It was contrary to the political code to sell a newspaper to one of the opposition.

While publishing the *Otsego Herald* at Cooperstown Elihu Phinney was a partner in setting up the *Olive Branch* at Sherburne, Chenango County, in 1806, while George Gordon Phinney, another of his family, established the *Herkimer Herald* in 1808.[157] At Herkimer, too, the Federalist rival of Phinney, John H. Prentiss, of Cooperstown, aided his brother Henry and his apprentice William L. Stone to publish the Herkimer *American*.[158] Other efforts of this sort were those of James Bogert, of Geneva, who helped to found at Ovid in 1827 the *Seneca Republican,* printed by Michael Hayes; [159] an earlier, though less successful, venture at Ovid by Samuel R. Brown, of Auburn, the *Seneca Patriot,* printed by George Lewis in 1815; [160] and the establishment of Richard Corss in Catskill with the *Middle District Gazette* while his partner, William L. Stone, was printing the *Northern Whig* in Hudson.[161] The *Political Barometer* office in Poughkeepsie, begun by Mitchell and Buel in 1802, was the next year extended to include the *Plebeian* in Kingston, which in 1805 was given over wholly to Jesse Buel, while Isaac Mitchell continued to conduct

---

[155] He did not care for office, and in later years ill health marred his political activity. He retired from his paper in 1830.

[156] Canandaigua *Ontario Repository,* Mar. 3, 1818.

[157] Sherburne *Olive Branch,* May 21, 1806; *Herkimer Herald,* June 26, 1808. Later G. G. Phinney printed in Herkimer the *Bunker Hill* (1809-1810) and the *Honest American* (1811-1812).

[158] Herkimer *American,* Jan. 4, 1810.

[159] *History of Seneca County* (1876), p. 54.

[160] Auburn *Advocate of the People,* June 8, 1817, a letter of George Lewis.

[161] Hudson *Northern Whig,* July 30, 1816; Mar. 11, 1817.

the *Barometer*.[162] In 1813 Buel went to a more active field in Albany.

The expansion of the newspaper field was also carried on by James Swords of New York, who set up Oliver Easton as printer of the *Western Centinel* (1794) at Whitestown;[163] and by William L. Stone, who in 1830 when editor of the *Commercial Advertiser* in New York, sent a printer with a press to publish the *Northern Spectator* at Malone.[164] The plunge taken in 1826 by Henry C. Sleight, of Jamaica, in starting the *Rochester Daily Advertiser* has been described. Its success was so marked that he and his partner, Luther Tucker, invested still more and gobbled up competing papers with the avidity of a Hearst or a Munsey.

As a result of the establishment of the *Daily Advertiser* and the publication in connection [with it], of the *Monroe Republican,* a weekly paper, nearly every paper published in the county at the time of our commencement sold out their establishments to us—I furnishing the funds necessary for their purchase, and their subscription lists were added to our own.[165]

It is evident that the propagation of newspaper presses throughout the state cannot be attributed solely either to the drifting printer or to the venturesome pioneer. Such printers there were, however, and statistics concerning them reveal the mobility of the craft during the generation after the Revolutionary War. An examination of the data available for New York yields some interesting conclusions. Of eighty-five printers whose birthplaces are known, thirty-five were born in New York state, twenty-three in Connecticut, thirteen in Massachusetts, seven in Vermont, and one in New Hampshire; a total of forty-four in New England.[166] Of ninety-one printers

[162] Poughkeepsie *Political Barometer,* June 8, 1802; Kingston *Plebeian,* Feb. 8, 1804.

[163] *Utica Directory* of 1828.

[164] Hough, F. B., *History of St. Lawrence and Franklin Counties,* pp. 535-536.

[165] Henry C. Sleight to Henry O'Reilly, Mar. 20, 1873. O'Reilly Collection in the Rochester Historical Society.

[166] Two in Pennsylvania, two in Ireland, and one each in England and France. By including figures collected on editors, not practical printers, twenty-seven would be added to the New England births, and only eight to those of New York.

whose places of apprenticeship are known, seventy-one learned their trade in New York, ten in Connecticut, seven in Vermont, and five in Massachusetts. This is corroborative of the drift of population from New England. These twenty-two printers who received their training in New England were graduated for the most part before 1810; although five were graduated in the decade 1810-1820, none was later. Thus literary New England became the typographical parent of the rural press in New York.

Of the printers who operated newspapers before coming to New York state, twenty were in New England, four in the West, and twelve were scattered from Pennsylvania and New Jersey southward. Of printers who operated newspapers after leaving New York state, we find the following classification: twenty in Western states, nine in New England, six in Pennsylvania, and nine scattered.[167] The drift westward was somewhat qualified by the tendency to return to New England origins or to move into neighboring Eastern states. Ohio and Michigan were the states most favored in the Western movement.

An index to the contribution of New York to journalism in the West is furnished by an analysis of the list of biographies of Wisconsin printers made by Albert H. Allen.[168] Although he gives 203 names, many are mere citations, so it is best to follow the method used above. Of the thirty-six Wisconsin journalists whose birthplaces are listed, thirty-two were born in New York before 1830. Apprenticeships of twenty-three are noted, fifteen of whom were trained in New York, nine before 1830. This preponderance of New Yorkers who worked upon the Wisconsin newspapers of a later period is not without significance.

The westward movement of the pioneer printer is illustrated by the establishment of presses in New York state before 1810.[169] This spread of printing offices followed the routes of

---

[167] Two came from Canada to set up in New York, and four went to Canada from here.

[168] McMurtrie, Douglas C., *Early Printing in Wisconsin* (1931).

[169] See accompanying map.

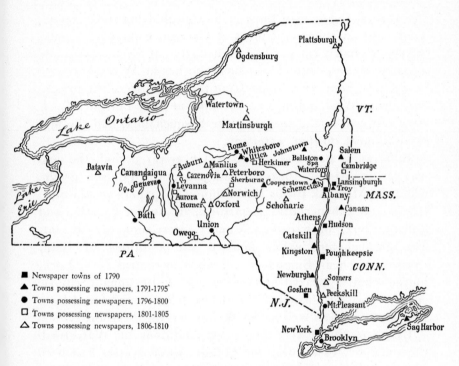

THE SPREAD OF THE NEWSPAPER PRESS IN NEW YORK STATE, 1790-1810

Newspapers at Athens, Aurora, Cambridge, Canaan, Levanna, Mt. Pleasant, Somers, and Union were not permanent. Transfers were made from Whitesboro to Utica; Sherburne to Norwich; Martinsburgh to Watertown; Union to Owego; and Lansingburgh to Troy.

trade and commerce. The Hudson River towns Poughkeepsie, Hudson, and Albany possessed newspapers in 1785, while in 1790 the number of towns having newspapers was augmented by Lansingburgh and by Goshen, a bit back from the river in Orange County. Within the next five years these early establishments were joined by those in Newburgh, Kingston, Catskill, Troy, and an ephemeral press at Canaan, Columbia County. On the Mohawk a paper had been started at Schenectady, and a venturesome printer had issued another at Whitesborough, near Utica. Somewhat apart from the others were the presses at Salem, Washington County, and at Sag Harbor, L. I. Cooperstown, at the source of the Susquehanna, had the first establishment on that waterway.

In 1800, at the close of the next five-year period, the field was larger. Mount Pleasant had joined the Hudson group, while the Mohawk towns which supported papers were Rome, Utica, and Schenectady. Johnstown, in Fulton County, and Ballston Spa, in Saratoga County, were not far distant. The Susquehanna valley boasted the additions of Bath, and Union (near Binghamton) ; while in central New York, journals had appeared at Geneva and at Levanna (Scipio), on the shore of Cayuga Lake. Long Island was served by a Brooklyn press as well as by the one at Sag Harbor.

By 1805 there were important additions at Waterford, Canandaigua, Herkimer, and Owego, while presses had been operated for a short time at Aurora, in Cayuga County, Athens, in Greene County, Cambridge, in Washington County, and Sherburne, in Chenango County.

Batavia furnished a new western outpost in 1810, while the northern counties had presses in Watertown, Ogdensburg, and Plattsburgh. The older groups also had additions, the development in the central part of the state being notable, with Auburn, Manlius, Cazenovia, and Peterboro; Homer, Norwich, and Oxford were part of the expansion in the Susquehanna valley.

The presses established during the next decade have not been indicated on the map, for it seemed impossible to add all the new printing offices without blurring the graphic representation of the earlier development. Soon Buffalo and Rochester entered the list of newspaper towns, the former in 1811, the latter in 1816. In the next year there was a press in Fredonia, Chautauqua County, marking a new advance to the westward; and by 1820 most sections of the state were served by local printers. Starting with those in the Hudson valley, the establishment of newspaper presses was effected in a group of towns along the Mohawk, in a few towns on the banks of the Susquehanna River, and in a third group clustered in the Finger Lakes region. Beyond these the development spread north and west until the newspaper frontier entirely disappeared from the state.[170]

From the story of the expansion of the newspaper press with its pioneers and *entrepreneurs,* one can readily see that this generation was one of "rugged individualism," wherein men succeeded or failed largely as a result of their own exertions. Fortune may have favored a few, but the opportunities of the growing country and the equally adolescent profession were numerous and open to all. It is not surprising, then, to discover that co-operation among competitors was infrequent. What little there was is noted below.[171]

The rates for advertising and subscriptions, which were a source of general dissatisfaction, were the sole subjects upon which country printers co-operated in this period. As early as 1798 a Troy printer, noting the action of Boston newspaper publishers in passing resolutions to raise rates and to demand prompt payment from subscribers and post riders, expressed his approval.[172] While three Albany offices reached an agreement

---

[170] Material in the foregoing section appeared in a paper by the author, "The Spread of the Newspaper Press in New York before 1830," *New York History,* Apr., 1933.

[171] Unions of printers, typographical societies, were formed in this period in Albany and in New York city, but had little influence upon the country printers (although Henry C. Southwick and Thurlow Weed were members of the New York society while they were working there). These societies are fully treated in the works of Ethelbert Stewart and George A. Stevens cited above.

[172] Troy *Northern Budget,* Oct. 16, 1798.

on rates in 1813, the country printers did not follow suit until the following year.[173] Then two establishments at Pough-keepsie, Rudd and Stockholm, of the *Republican Herald,* and Paraclete Potter, of the *Journal,* printed joint resolutions advancing the price of their papers and agreeing on terms as well as on rates of advertising.[174] Ten years later in Poughkeepsie three publishers, "with a view to produce uniformity in their charges, and at the same time to secure to themselves a fair compensation for their services," agreed to a list of prices for newspapers and advertisements, which they insisted, were "substantially the same . . . as charged for the last twenty years." [175] Five Utica establishments united in 1826 to fix rates for insolvent notices and to agree upon regular rates for notices for political meetings and regimental orders.[176] The co-operation of the Buffalo printers in 1828 was for a different purpose, as is shown in the following quotation:

subscribers . . . will, from this time, be required, *unconditionally,* to settle their subscription accounts at the close of each twelve months. . . . A compliance with these terms is not asked as a favour; *it is demanded as a right.* The resolution which we have taken is one founded in justice, and will be rigidly enforced by each one of us.[177]

Similar objectives were favored by those who proposed a printers' convention. Although the project held out many possibilities, real and fantastic, to the dissatisfied members of the craft, to others it promised little capable of realization. In 1822 Isaac Riggs, an inveterate seeker after public favors, proposed a *"Convention of Master Printers—*I mean those who have been regularly bred to the business—and particularly editors of newspapers," to devise ways and means of having the state printing patronage divided and put into the hands of regular printers.[178] Riggs maintained that his object in the

---

[173] Munsell, *Typographical Miscellany,* pp. 120-121.
[174] Poughkeepsie *Republican Herald,* Dec. 28, 1814.
[175] Poughkeepsie *Dutchess Observer,* Oct. 13, 1824.
[176] Utica *Western Recorder,* Nov. 21, 1826.
[177] *Buffalo Journal,* July 10, 1828.
[178] Schenectady *Cabinet,* Apr. 3, 1822. Riggs was anxious for some of the printing patronage, and he especially disliked Cantine & Leake, who were not

proposed congress was not to raise the price of papers but merely to combat governmental discrimination. A different purpose was quite apparent in the clarion call sent out by the printer of the *Geneva Palladium* in 1825. City printers were making revenues amounting to thousands of dollars, he said, and contrasted their fortunes with the plight of his country brethren:

we are confident there are not a few of our profession, who do not perceive the great benefits which might be derived from some general understanding or system universally adopted, which would go to place the publishers of *country* papers, on something like a footing with their brethren of the city—and which would enable them to enjoy some of the advantages possessed by every other trade and mechanical business.... We can see no reason why Printers, more than any other class of mechanics, should labor for nothing—why they should, with immense exertion of both mind and body, produce a weekly paper for the amusement and instruction of *others,* and receive little or no compensation for *themselves*—nor why New York Editors should, by their manoeuvres, deprive them of a very great share of patronage now left them.

There is a remedy for these things—we have it in our power to apply this remedy and by acting in concert to redress our flagrant grievances.

It is a fact, which cannot be controverted, that the publishers of country newspapers do not enjoy the advantages possessed by the poorest mechanics. If the latter labor with industry, they have their reward, in a corresponding advance toward independence. But if the poor Devils of PRINTERS labor *forever,* waste the *midnight oil* and *crack* their *sinews,* with exertion, what reward have they? NONE.

Better that the price of Newspapers should be reduced *one half,* and receive *prompt payment,* than that things should remain as they now are; and that *others* should reap the benefit of *our* labors.

These disadvantages are not universal. The Printers of the city of New York have formed themselves into a society for protection and benefit—and those of the *country* have certainly the same right.

Let, then, the PRINTERS of the *Western District*—of every county west of *Utica,* deputise one or more of their numbers, to meet in CONVENTION, in *Canandaigua* or Geneva (either of which is central enough), at some no very distant period, then and there, to adopt such measures, as shall be most conducive to the general welfare—and thus

---

practical printers, and who had succeeded Jesse Buel as State Printer. Cf. *infra,* chap. iv, on state printing.

place themselves on a footing with other professions—namely, that of receiving *an equivalent* for their labors.[179]

The Black Rock printer scoffed at the idea, and, while there was considerable notice of Riggs's proposal, there is no evidence that a meeting took place.[180] In 1828 another proposal was printed, this time in the *Ontario Chronicle,* Geneva, for "a state Convention of *Printers* at Auburn, on the 25th of September next for the purpose of adopting some effectual method of securing *pay* for papers, &c." [181] The Onondaga printer granted its desirability but doubted that rules would be adhered to or that printers could be secure until all men became honest.[182] It is probable that the cool reception accorded this proposal was due in part to the general opinion that its promoter, Franklin Cowdery, was poorly qualified to speak for the printers. His Geneva venture had been but recently launched, and he had complained constantly about the public patronage and his own meager support.[183]

No association of country printers was formed during this period, and no state convention was held until the Printers' Festivals of the forties which were instituted to celebrate the birthday of Benjamin Franklin.[184] These, too, were social and fraternal rather than commercial in their intent. Thus the country printer remained an individualist in managing his business concerns.

[179] Quoted in the *Black Rock Gazette,* Apr. 12, 1825. By the "manoeuvres" of city editors he probably referred to the practice of issuing a weekly or semi-weekly edition "for the country," begun by Noah Webster in 1794. See Bleyer, *op. cit.,* p. 115, and *infra,* chap. vii.

[180] *Black Rock Gazette, loc. cit.*

[181] *Onondaga Register,* Aug. 20, 1828.

[182] *Ibid.*

[183] Cowdery became the editor of the *Ontario Chronicle,* Feb., 1828.

[184] Follett's *History of the Press of Western New York,* frequently quoted, was issued as a result of the Festival at Rochester, Jan. 18, 1847. One was held the previous year, also, *viz.,* a letter of William A. Welles in *Littell's Living Age,* VIII, 626-627, Mar. 28, 1846; but little is known about others. See the Preface by Wilberforce Eames in the 1920 reprint of Follett's *History.*

IV
CORRECT PRINCIPLES

NEWSPAPERS *are to political parties in this country what work-ing tools are to the operative mechanic.*—JABEZ D. HAMMOND, History of Political Parties in the State of New York, *I, 279.*

PROFESSIONS *of impartiality I shall make none. They are al-ways useless, and are besides perfect nonsense, when used by a newsmonger: for, he that does not relate news as he finds it, is something worse than partial; and as to other articles that help to compose a paper, he that does not exercise his own judgment, either in admitting or rejecting what is sent him, is a poor passive tool, and not an editor. For my part, I feel the strongest partiality for the cause of order and good government, such as we live under, and against everything that is opposed to it....I wish my paper to be a rallying point for the friends of government.*—WILLIAM COBBETT, Porcupine's Works, *V, 3-7.*

THE *design of this paper is to diffuse among the people correct information of all interesting subjects; to inculcate just prin-ciples in religion, morals, and politics; and to cultivate a taste for sound literature.*—Prospectus of the Evening Post, *Nov. 16, 1801.*

FROM the days of the earliest newspapers in America, printers have been unable to escape political connections. While the first presses were employed in producing such printing as the authorities needed, the first newspapers sedulously avoided giving offense to those in power. The *Boston News-Letter,* the first periodical print in America (1704), carried prominently under its head, "Published by Authority." This was to forestall the fate which befell Benjamin Harris's attempt at circulating the news in 1690. His *Publick Occurrences Bothe Foreign and Domestick* was suppressed after its first issue. John Campbell, printer of the *News-Letter,* justified his authorization by "waiting on His Excellency or Secretary for approbation of what [news] is Collected." [1]

With the appearance of James Franklin's *New England Courant* in 1721 came the first opposition paper, for the *Boston Gazette* of William Brooker, of which Franklin had been printer, was a mere chronicle of the news. Franklin, however, aided by a group of abler writers, made an issue of many problems of the day and frankly took sides. His criticism of those in authority caused him to be thrown into prison and finally called forth a prohibition of his paper. Since the language of the order for prohibiting his publishing activities was, "That James Franklin, the Printer and Publisher thereof, be strictly forbidden by this Court to Print or Publish the New-England Courant, or any Pamphlet or paper of the like Nature, except it be supervised by the Secretary of the Province..." he continued to print it under the name of his brother and apprentice, Benjamin. [2] The paper still gave offense, however, and James Franklin was again imprisoned when he ad-

[1] Bleyer, Willard Grosvenor, *Main Currents in the History of American Journalism,* pp. 44-47.
[2] *Ibid.,* pp. 51-59.

mitted being the publisher. Further efforts were made to stop his obnoxious press before he left Boston in 1726.[3]

Benjamin Franklin, as is well known, ran away from his brother and established himself as a printer in Philadelphia. There in his *Pennsylvania Gazette* he continued the publication of original material, which he had begun to write in secret for his brother's paper, and charted his course during the difficult times of the struggle with England. In Philadelphia, also, Andrew Bradford started the *American Weekly Mercury,* in which he vigorously opposed the action taken against Franklin in Boston, on the basis of law and justice. He, too, had felt the reproving hand of a colonial government.[4]

In New York the first newspaper was William Bradford's *New York Gazette,* begun in 1725 as the official newspaper of the colony. The appearance of an opposition print, the *New York Weekly Journal* of John Peter Zenger, led to controversy and a celebrated libel suit. To this paper, according to Bleyer, "belongs the distinction of being the first newspaper established in America by a political faction as a means of carrying on political controversy." [5] Zenger's strictures on the unpopular Governor Cosby and his council provoked replies in Bradford's paper and eventually led to the arrest of Zenger, who was charged with printing "seditious Libels." [6] The trial and triumphant vindication of the printer was a victory for freedom of the press and an outstanding achievement in the cause of colonial journalism.

With such a background of political activity and fearless opposition to authority, the colonial press became the principal agency of governmental controversy. The struggle over taxation and in behalf of colonial rights, the resistance to the Stamp Act, the issuance of effective political pamphlets from the pens of James Otis, Samuel Adams, and John Dickinson,

---

[3] *Ibid.,* pp. 59-60; Hudson, Frederic, *Journalism in the United States,* pp. 66-71.

[4] Bleyer, *op. cit.,* pp. 61-62.

[5] *Ibid.,* pp. 62-64.

[6] *Ibid.,* pp. 64-65; Hudson, *op. cit.,* pp. 81-93; Rutherford, Livingston, *John Peter Zenger, His Press, and a Bibliography of Zenger Imprints,* pp. 28-29.

and the multiplication of the stirring appeals of Tom Paine, testify to the political importance in this era of the printing press. Colonial newspapers and their counterparts from the same presses (the pamphlets) played an essential part in the separation from England. Of importance, too, in this connection were the Tory printers, whose papers gave no little aid to the British.[7]

With the end of the struggle there was no decline in journalistic activity—in fact, conditions were in some respects conducive to greater activity, since the times were not normal. During the troubled years of the "critical period" the newspapers were filled with spirited arguments over political principles. It is true that constitution-making was better done in secret, more forwarded by private letters than by public pronouncements, but controversy was eventually forced into the open. The framing of state constitutions and the campaigns for their adoption gave plenty of exercise to the choppers of political logic.[8]

The struggle over the ratification of the Constitution of the United States, with its attendant campaign of education in which *The Federalist* of Hamilton, Madison, and Jay was challenged by the vigorous writings of Richard Henry Lee and Elbridge Gerry, further illustrated the importance of the press and its value in gaining political ends. The propertied interests, who sponsored the new government, were conscious of the rôle of the newspapers in their success, whereas the disorganized opposition was learning from experience.

When the opponents of the Constitution, the Anti-Federalists, emerged as a political party, it became apparent that government in the United States was to be an affair of partisans. Hamilton and Jefferson, heading the rival schools of thought, introduced as journalists John Fenno and Philip Freneau, respectively. These editors (they were not printers)

---

[7] Bleyer, *op. cit.,* chap. iii, "The Press during the Struggle between the Colonies and England."

[8] Nevins, Allan, *The American States during and after the Revolution, 1775-1789,* p. 121, *et seq.* See also Spaulding, E. Wilder, *New York in the Critical Period, 1783-1789,* chap. v, *et seq.*

guided the destinies of the *Gazette of the United States* and the *National Gazette,* their respective party organs in Philadelphia. The former was supported financially by Hamilton and by contributions from his pen, and so it was recognized as the official paper. Freneau was subsidized by Jefferson in receiving the office of translator in the State Department. Jefferson averred that he contributed nothing to Freneau's columns, though the attack upon the policies of Hamilton won his commendation.[9] Hamilton also financially assisted other editors, such as Noah Webster with his *American Minerva* in New York, and William Cobbett, the celebrated "Peter Porcupine." Finally in 1800 he established the New York *Evening Post* under the editorship of William Coleman.[10] In the meantime the Jeffersonian group had raised a crop of democratic, or Anti-Federal, editors whose fulminations were so violent and effective that Hamilton's ministrations seemed the only recourse for the powers behind the administration. Thomas Paine, James T. Callender, Philip Freneau, and Benjamin Franklin Bache were setting a pace and adopting a tone which was to color journalism in America for a generation.[11]

From the innocuous beginnings of the colonial era the press had developed into a social force which was potent in controlling the political fortunes of the nation. Some saw this force as a mighty engine pumping the lifeblood of a growing democratic government, while others felt that in the hands of demagogues and pernicious office seekers it was spraying a foul poison over the tender growth of free institutions. In either case it was a great power, which caused men to rejoice or shudder as they watched. Important factors in this development were the country papers, each with its own party connection. Their increasing numbers helped to make up the party's strength in the nation, to mold its opinions, and to fashion its

---

[9] Bleyer, *op. cit.,* pp. 105-111.

[10] Nevins, Allan, *The Evening Post, a Century of Journalism,* p. 13; see also the same author's introductory essay in *American Press Opinion, Washington to Coolidge,* Pt. I.

[11] Nevins, *Evening Post,* pp. 12-13. See also Faÿ, *The Two Franklins, Fathers of American Democracy,* a biography of Bache.

destiny. They were quite as ardent, too, in their support of its principles.

Violently partisan as were the printers of political sheets, they did not always air their own prejudices in articles and editorials. Some papers were almost devoid of original matter, and some printers scarcely wrote a line. They clipped the writings of "Camillus" and "Aristides" from their favorite city papers, republished public documents and legislative records, and thus served as a sounding board for the voices of the party leaders.[12] The efforts of these party leaders were directed toward partisan indoctrination and defense of party measures. Enlightenment of the electorate on matters of public concern was not conceived as their duty.[13] Consequently, the printer became a mere link in the chain of party organization. He found many duties and some privileges accruing to him from this connection, and, subordinate though he was, he considered himself a "politician."[14] Some printers developed, it is true, into capable editors, who wrote their own editorials, but until late in this period, the common run contented themselves with what was supplied.[15]

The rôle of the printer-politician appeared simple, but was sometimes quite difficult. Parties were in a state of flux. New York presented a complicated mixture of national politics, state issues, and social and family rivalries. The state's leaders, divided by the struggle over the Constitution and Hamilton's financial measures, fell to bitter quarreling, in which the issues were obscured by personal ambitions.

The staunch, aristocratic Federalists, such as Hamilton and Jay, lost much of their influence, while the numerous Clintons and Livingstons gained. They placed Aaron Burr in the vice-presidency, but he lost followers as a result of his

---

[12] *Infra,* chap. v.

[13] Cf. Adams, Henry, *History of the United States,* I, 120.

[14] The word "politician" did not possess the present day connotation. The obituary of C. C. Adams of Poughkeepsie read, "As a politician he was firm, decided, and consistent..." Poughkeepsie *Republican Herald,* Apr. 13, 1814.

[15] Note percentage of editorial in statistical analysis of newspaper content, *infra,* chap. v, Table I, pp. 311-312.

devious course when the election of 1800 was thrown into the
House of Representatives. Burr's attempt to become governor
in 1804 produced a three-cornered fight in which the Livingstons ran Morgan Lewis, who received many Federalist
votes, and defeated the Clintonians. Burr dropped from the
picture with the death of Hamilton, but Lewisites and Clintonians continued their battles, while the Federalists waited
for an opportunity to collect their scattered adherents.[16]

The unpopularity of the embargo gave new vitality to the
Federalists, who had become so weak that they ran no state
ticket in 1804 or 1807. Their revival in 1810 was signalized
by the nomination of Jonas Platt for governor. They had kept
their strength chiefly in certain Hudson River counties and in
the new settlements to the westward populated by immigrants
from New England. Here the leading landholders dominated
politics, and, often through their aid, Federalist newspapers
occupied the field.[17] From Hudson, Columbia County, a Federalist stronghold, Harry Croswell, printer of the *Balance,*
was removed to Albany in 1809 to use his editorial talents in
the cause.[18]

Republican printers had not been slow in appearing, and in
the principal towns and counties a "democratic" sheet was to
be found.[19] They were generally less favored with financial
support, and were constantly referred to as "dingy democratic" prints, although in some cases they were as ably edited
as their more respectable rivals. Two examples might be cited,
the Hudson *Bee* of Charles Holt, a Connecticut printer who
had been imprisoned under the sedition law of 1798, and the
Farmer's Register of Francis Adancourt, a Frenchman of

[16] Fox, Dixon Ryan, *Decline of the Aristocracy in the Politics of New York,*
p. 61, *et seq.*

[17] *Ibid.,* p. 50, and chap. vi; Bemis, of Canandaigua, Williams, of Utica,
Phinney and later Prentiss, of Cooperstown, and Bogert, of Geneva, were outstanding Federalist printers.

[18] Hammond, Jabez D., *History of Political Parties in the State of New
York,* I, 278.

[19] See the list of newspapers, and political connections, for 1810 in Thomas,
Isaiah, *History of Printing in America,* II, 519-520. As early as 1803 Federals
were calling their opponents "democrats" in place of "jacobin"; and began to
prefer the name of Federal Republican. Fox, *op. cit.,* p. 87.

Lansingburgh, and later of Troy. These papers were conducted with as much skill and partisan intensity as those of Bache or Callender.

The Republicans were split when Governor Lewis and De Witt Clinton clashed over the charter of the Merchant's Bank, opposed by Clinton and favored by the Federalists. Clinton received the valued support of James Cheetham's *American Citizen* in New York and of the *Albany Register*. Lewis was upheld by two Poughkeepsie papers and the *Plebeian* of Jesse Buel at Kingston. In 1807 the Clintonians, as they were called, put up for governor Daniel D. Tompkins, who was elected over Lewis in spite of the Federalist votes.[20] A new party alignment had been made.

Two important issues were to have much to do with party fortunes, and therefore with political printers, in the following years. These were the proposal for a canal across the state, and the war with England. De Witt Clinton had become steadily more acceptable to the Federalists, and when he advocated a canal which would be beneficial to both the commercial element in New York and Federalist speculators or landed squires in the western country, they were ready to follow him.[21] Clinton therefore soon broke with Governor Tompkins, who was reëlected. A number of his Republican friends felt that he went too far in his nursing of his Federalist followers.[22] Tompkins prosecuted the war with the New York militia, while a large portion of the old Federalists were outspoken in their opposition. Thus it was not surprising that Clinton's presidential ambitions for 1816 came to naught, and that Tompkins, whose reputation was enhanced as a result of the war, became Vice President under Monroe.

The effects of these changes upon the editors of newspapers

---

[20] Hammond, *op. cit.*, I, 219-247. He is in error, however, in connecting Isaac Mitchell of the *Political Barometer* with the Poughkeepsie *Journal*. See Poughkeepsie *Political Barometer*, Sept. 9, 1806, for details of the propagation of Clintonian papers. Allusion was made to a "27,000$ fund." The Newburgh *Recorder* was now purchased and converted into the *Political Index*, Clintonian. Poughkeepsie *Political Barometer*, Apr. 8, 1806.

[21] Fox, *op. cit.*, pp. 153-159.

[22] *Ibid.*, pp. 169-172.

were obviously very disconcerting. Which way were they to turn? Everyone sought to be considered consistent, and yet to play politics is to be inconsistent, to watch the main chance rather than to act upon principle. Although there was public condemnation for a "trimmer," country printers had to alter their courses to meet the changing currents. A few instances will suffice to show how some editors behaved.

Elihu Phinney, of Cooperstown, had moved to Otsego, under the aegis of the Federalist squire of that region, Judge William Cooper. In 1807, however, he was supporting the embargo, which made him anathema to the unbending judge. As a result another press was set up by Judge Cooper, and the *Cooperstown Federalist* left no uncertainty as to its stand. Phinney, in spite of this opposition, had difficulty in convincing brother editors of his Republicanism, and Isaac Mitchell called him to terms for deserting Lewis:

> The pseudo federal paper called the *Otsego Herald,* published at Otsego, by the cidevant Judge Phinney, came out, at a pretty early period, warmly and decidedly in favor of Gov. Lewis, and so continued for some time after I published the *Crisis* in this City; once, on the margin of his paper, which he exchanged for the *Crisis,* was written— *"Mr. Mitchell, I am your friend; I wish you knew me"*—The plain construction of which must be that he was friendly to the cause I was advocating. Soon after this he relinquished his vindication of the Governor and his anathemas against "the faction," began to whiffle about, advised the people to support Tompkins for Governor and Storm for Lieut. Governor, and finally came out a confirmed Clintonian.[23]

Phinney printed this in order to justify himself, but except for remonstrating against "this querulous mode of 'silly' warfare," he did little more than to accuse Mitchell of being a hireling of Judge Cooper.[24] In Sherburne, with the aid of John F. Fairchild, Phinney established the *Olive Branch* which the redoubtable Charles Holt of Hudson declared, "would be moderately Federal, if it dare." This imputation on the Republican sympathies of the proprietor was stoutly denied:

[23] Cooperstown *Otsego Herald,* June 25, 1807, quoting the Albany *Republican Crisis.*
[24] *Ibid.*

"The charge of *federalism* (modern, spurious federalism) or *quidism,* is a burden too galling to be borne by the person who superintends this paper." [25]

On the other hand, James Bogert, of Geneva, who stated that he had formerly printed a neutral paper, came out strongly Federalist in 1809:

America is threatened, and no doubts remain in the minds of the Editors of this paper that there exists a formidable French party in this country, whose object is the destruction of our happy constitution, the subversion of our liberties, and the annihilation of the political principles of *Washington.* Impressed with the force of these opinions ... they now unequivocally declare that the politics of this paper will be *Federal Republican.*[26]

Nevertheless, he supported the war policy in 1812 and finally enlisted.[27] In 1813 divisions within the Republican ranks in Albany resulted in the establishment of the *Argus,* which endeavored to counteract the influence of Solomon Southwick, editor of the *Albany Register,* who had deserted Governor Tompkins. Under the editorial guidance of Jesse Buel, former editor of the Kingston *Plebeian,* the *Argus* soon became one of the principal political journals in the state.[28] When De Witt Clinton was expelled from the mayoralty of New York in 1815, he seemed to be politically forsaken, but two years later he was elected governor without opposition.[29] He was not the leader of a united party, however, and his enemies in the Tammany Society, as well as some disgruntled Federalists, formed the "Bucktail" party, which took its name from the Tammany insignia of the deer's tail which was worn on the hat on certain occasions.[30] Clinton's policies, notably the advocacy of the canal, found the Bucktails in opposition, aided by such localities and interests as could see no advantage for themselves in the internal improvements.

[25] Sherburne *Olive Branch,* June 11, 1806.
[26] Geneva *Expositor,* Apr. 26, 1809.
[27] *Geneva Gazette,* 1812-1814.
[28] Hammond, *op. cit.,* I, 358.
[29] *Ibid.,* I, 399, 445.
[30] *Ibid.,* I, 450-451.

On this issue, too, newspapers took sides and carried on political warfare. In Chenango County Thurlow Weed, an ardent Clintonian, clashed with John F. Hubbard, of Norwich, whose press he had earlier purchased. Norwich was not especially benefited by the "Grand Canal project," and Hubbard became a Bucktail, though he later advocated the Chenango Canal. When the Bucktails carried Chenango in 1819, Weed discovered that his opposition paper was doomed in the county.[31]

Bucktail papers increased elsewhere, as the Ithaca *American Journal* noted, but not more than one-fifth of "the old standard republican papers" were opposed to Clinton.[32] In 1820 a Clintonian paper was established in Orange County to counteract the influence of the Bucktail *Patriot,* while in Ulster County the Kingston *Craftsman* was started to support Clinton's policies.[33] In Cayuga the partisan quarrel was complicated by the presence of the *Advocate of the People,* supporting the "Low Salary Party," which shared patronage with the Clintonian *Republican* and the Bucktail *Patriot.*[34] A professed Bucktail in 1822, seeking aid for a newspaper in Sag Harbor, felt that his being a nephew of Alden Spooner, a Clintonian, undermined his chances.[35] The Clintonians were so enraged at the effective journalism of Azariah C. Flagg's *Plattsburgh Republican,* that in 1822 they set up the *Northern Intelligencer* to oppose him.[36] The *Elmira Gazette* turned Bucktail in 1828 and so irritated a group of its patrons who were Clintonians that they set out to get an opposition press to represent them. They founded the *Elmira Whig* in that year.[37] At that time there were, according to the *Argus,* forty-nine Bucktail papers in the state.[38]

[31] Weed, *Autobiography,* pp. 76-78; 85.

[32] Ithaca *American Journal,* Nov. 3, 1820.

[33] Goshen *Orange County Patriot,* Feb. 7, 1820; Sylvester, *History of Ulster County,* pp. 145-146.

[34] Auburn *Cayuga Republican,* Mar. 24, 1819; Follett, *op. cit.,* p. 50.

[35] Thomas Miller to Henry P. Dering, June 19, 1822. Pennypacker Long Island Collection.

[36] *Plattsburgh Republican,* Apr. 6, 13, 20, 27, May 4, 1822.

[37] Article by Rev. James Durham in the *Elmira Gazette,* July 14, 1853.

[38] *Argus,* Mar. 10, 1828, quoted by Fox, *op. cit.,* p. 316.

The constitutional convention of 1821, while a major event in the political development of the state, did not produce party divisions so much as it marked the death of the aristocracy and therefore of Federalism.[39] After this the chief effort of all politicians was to avoid the appellation of "Federalist" or "aristocrat," and to seek the support of "the People" or to become "The People's Party." [40]

From the welter of men and issues, both national and state, which complicated the politics of the early twenties, there emerged a remarkable group, headed by Martin Van Buren and William L. Marcy, who became known as the "Albany Regency." Their solidarity and power stirred the opposition, and their efficiency in serving party ends gave them a national reputation. That they realized and utilized the power of the press is indicated, by the fact that two of their members, Azariah C. Flagg of the *Plattsburgh Republican,* and Edwin Croswell, then editor of the *Argus,* were printer-editors.[41] The latter, who had been writing pungent paragraphs for the *Recorder* in Catskill, became the state printer, but his chief service consisted in writing effective editorials, which revealed his genuine literary ability.[42] He made his paper a national power as well as a state power.[43] In the presidential contest of 1824 the Regency undertook to carry New York for William H. Crawford, but the Clintonians went to the support of John Quincy Adams. Clinton came back to the governorship that year with an overwhelming vote, and he was reëlected two years later.[44]

State politics, especially as they affected the newspaper

[39] Officially declared dead in 1820 by the "fifty-one high-minded gentlemen." —Hammond, *op. cit.,* I, 228-230; Fox, *op. cit.,* chap. viii, "Property or People."

[40] Fox, *op. cit.,* pp. 272-273.

[41] *Ibid.,* pp. 281-284.

[42] The Catskill (Greene County Historical Society) file of the *Catskill Recorder,* (1818-1819) has a number of articles labeled with the pen, "Ed," or "Edwin." In these years his father, Mackay Croswell, founder of the paper, was his partner.

[43] Hammond, *op. cit.,* II, 121-123; 524.

[44] *Ibid.,* II, 173-175. After two terms (1817-1822), he had been succeeded by Joseph C. Yates. The constitution of 1821 substituted a two year term for the former three year term.

press, were now profoundly stirred by the "Morgan excitement," which had followed the abduction of William Morgan
in 1826, after his attempted revelation of Freemasonry. In-
censed by what he regarded as unwarranted proscription by
the Masons because he had linked "overzealous members of
the fraternity" with the crime, Thurlow Weed became the
organizer of the Anti-Masonic party.[45] With David C.
Miller's *Republican Advocate* in Batavia and Weed's *Anti-
Masonic Enquirer* in Rochester as a nucleus, an enormous
growth of Anti-Masonic newspapers spread over the state
to fan the embers of the feeling against the secret organization and its supposed insidious influence. Although the older
journals were in some cases inclined to scoff and treat lightly
the political movement, other papers vigorously defended
Masonry.[46] In a few communities newspapers were established
with the avowed purpose of defending the Order; for example, the *Craftsman,* at Rochester, edited by Elijah J. Roberts,
who was assisted for a time by James G. Brooks, the
poet.[47]

The backers of the *Craftsman* overreached themselves, and
in 1830 a committee appealed for a loan of $3,000 in sub-
scriptions of "from 25 to 100 dollars each," as well as for
additional subscriptions for the paper, to lift it from the finan-

[45] Upon learning of the outrage, Weed wrote a paragraph in the *Rochester
Telegraph,* in which he stated: "The persons engaged in this violation of the
law must have been overzealous members of the fraternity. It is incumbent,
however, upon the better informed Freemasons to take the laboring oar in dis-
covering the whereabouts of the absent man, and in restoring him to his
liberty." His partner, Robert Martin, was a Mason, and when Weed's paragraph caused a number of Masons to discontinue subscriptions and advertisements, Weed turned over his share of the establishment, and sought employment elsewhere. At both Utica and Troy where he applied for editorial
positions, his obnoxious comment had preceded him, and he was unable to
find a place. Thereupon, with a few local backers, he procured an old Ramage
press in Rochester and set up his Anti-Masonic newspaper.—*Autobiography,*
pp. 213-215.

[46] The Cooperstown *Freeman's Journal,* later to oppose Anti-Masonry, expressed confidence in the "morgan" committee on which were Weed and Whittlesey, both boys from Otsego. Quoted in the Rochester *Daily Telegraph,* Nov.
5, 1827.

[47] *Craftsman,* 1829-1830. The *Chautauqua Republican* of Jamestown was also
set up for this purpose. Hazeltine, G. W., *The Town of Ellicott,* p. 244.

cial straits into which it had been thrust by circumstances.[48] Not all Masons, however, were sympathetic with the tactics of Roberts, and the Jacksonian (Regency) party began to consider him such a liability that it publicly repudiated him.[49]

During the campaign of 1828 Clinton, who personally had always been hostile to Adams, declared for Jackson but was unable to take his party with him.[50] One party writer in reply to the claim of the *Argus* that the Clintonians were lining up for the General, stated:

The opinions of Mr. Clinton's friends with regard to the Presidency can only be ascertained by the complexion of the papers they support. ... The *Albany Daily Advertiser* [italics supplied for titles] has been again and again stigmatized as the mouth piece of Mr. Clinton and denounced as often in the *Argus* and its kindred prints, as having for its object the destruction of "the Republican party." This paper, it is well known, is a strenuous asserter of the claims of Mr. Adams for the Presidency. The *Troy Sentinel,* a leading Clintonian paper, gives an undivided support to Mr. Adams. The Utica *Sentinel and Gazette,* one of the most active papers in this region, in support of Mr. Clinton, is not less decided for Mr. Adams. The Rochester *Telegraph,* the *Ontario Repository,* the *Buffalo Journal,* and every paper of importance in the state (with a single exception), which has supported Mr. Clinton, also supports Mr. Adams.[51]

The exception was the *Evening Post* of New York.[52] The Anti-Masonic group favored Adams for the presidency but were unable to co-operate with Adams men for a state ticket, and, in spite of the efforts of Weed, they ran a forlorn hope

[48] *Ithaca Chronicle,* Aug. 11, 1830, printed the circular appeal which it said was "confidential" and "finds its way to us in the *Western Emigrant,* published at Ann Arbor, Michigan territory."

[49] Henry O'Reilly to A. C. Flagg, Nov. 11, 1829 (Flagg MSS): "I was compelled in self defense to come out upon that paper and expose the character of its management. It is a thorn in the side of the party, although all our friends here (except friend Griffin) lose no opportunity of disclaiming all connection with it politically."

[50] Fox, *op. cit.,* pp. 314-315.

[51] *Onondaga Register,* Aug. 1, 1827.

[52] Fox, *op. cit.,* pp. 315-316. See also Nevins, *The Evening Post.* Governor Clinton died suddenly in February, 1828.

in Solomon Southwick, another printer-editor.[53] The party did so well in the election, however, that it gained in strength in the following year. Weed, who for a time was denounced for his efforts to merge the state ticket of the Adams party with that of the Anti-Masons, now shared its direction with Francis Granger, William H. Seward, Myron Holley, Albert Tracy, William H. Maynard, Henry Dana Ward, and Frederick Whittlesey.[54] The last three named were also conductors of newspapers. In 1830 Weed was sent to Albany as editor (at $750 a year) of the *Evening Journal,* the new official organ of the party.[55]

These divisions endured until after 1830, the Anti-Masonic party even running a presidential candidate in 1832. They eventually combined with the other opponents of Jackson in the new Whig party, in whose counsels Weed and Seward were to find new opportunities and to give new proof of their political acumen.

These main currents in politics were not the only outlets for partisan zeal. The shifting forces which compelled political leaders to organize "Young Men's" meetings, and a "People's Party," made it imperative to appeal to laborers and mechanics, whom the old-school politician held in disdain. Many workingmen, or "Workies," as they were called, doubted the sincerity of such appeals. They began to organize for independent political action, and of necessity they sought a press to give voice to their program.[56] Their demands were:

Equal universal education, abolishment of imprisonment for debt, abolition of all licensed monopolies, an entire revision or abolition of the present militia system, a less expensive law system, equal taxation of property, an effective lien law for laborers on buildings, a district system of elections, no legislation on religion.[57]

[53] McCarthy, C., "The Anti-Masonic Party," *Annual Report* of the American Historical Association for 1902, pp. 375-380.

[54] *Ibid.,* pp. 384-385. Maynard formerly edited the *Utica Patriot,* Ward conducted the *Le Roy Gazette* (1828-1830), and Whittlesey, the Rochester *Monroe Republican* (1827).

[55] Weed, *Autobiography,* pp. 360-362.

[56] Fox, *op. cit.,* pp. 355-357.

[57] Commons, J. R., and associates, *History of Labour in the United States,* I, 275.

This program was kept at the head of the New York *Working Man's Advocate,* the principal organ of the "Workies," beginning with the first issue in 1829.[58] In other parts of the state the movement had newspaper support, notably from the *Mechanic's Free Press* in Utica [59] and the *Farmer's Register and Mechanics' and Manufacturer's Journal* in Troy.[60] In Rochester *The Spirit of the Age* came out at the beginning of 1830, as a semi-monthly publication by Thomas B. Barnum, formerly a Canandaigua printer, and Charles F. Ames, who had edited a paper in Hudson. The first number had articles on the "Militia System," the "Lien Law," "Imprisonment for Debt," and "Capital Punishments." [61]

Although the average country paper contained little local news, occasionally its columns were enlivened by spirited arguments over local issues. In the early days of settlement the very name of the village might be a subject of controversy. The earliest paper in Manlius, the *Derne Gazette,* sought to change the name of the town to "Derne"; [62] and because of Phinney's feeling against Judge Cooper, his *Otsego Herald* led in the movement to call the village "Otsego" instead of "Cooperstown." [63]

Another matter which agitated the pioneer journalists was the location of the courthouse, for of course it was advantageous for any printer to be in the county seat. With unselfish concern for the best interests of Onondaga County, Lewis H. Redfield, of the *Onondaga Register,* advocated the selection of Syracuse as the seat of county government rather than Onondaga Hollow, where his own office was located, because he recognized the commercial advantages of the little village on the canal.[64] In Seneca County, too, the location of the court-

[58] *Ibid.*
[59] Nov. 14, 1829.
[60] Dec. 18, 1827.
[61] Rochester *Craftsman,* Dec. 29, 1829. Abolition of capital punishment was later added to the demands of the *Working Man's Advocate,* Commons, *et al., op. cit.,* I, 275.
[62] Clark, J. H. V., *Onondaga,* II, 221-222.
[63] Cooperstown *Otsego Herald,* Apr. 3, 1807-July 17, 1813.
[64] *Onondaga Register,* Jan. 2, 23, 1828.

house was an issue, and the *Ovid Gazette* had as one of its purposes getting the courts to sit in Ovid half the time.[65]

The development of the west and the growth of its population produced another much mooted question, that is, the division of the larger counties into smaller political units. Opinions differed quite naturally as to the advisability of changes and as to the resulting effect upon personal, local, or party fortunes. Ontario was one of the older counties so divided, and the newspapers were often filled with opinions concerning the procedure to be followed in making the division.[66]

The Canal created a newspaper war in Erie County, where the advocates of Black Rock as the terminus for the canal, led by General Peter B. Porter, employed the *Black Rock Beacon* to set their claims before the world.[67] The inhabitants of Buffalo were just as eager to have the terminus there, and the advantages and disadvantages of each village were well aired in the press. Hoffman, the Black Rock printer, said that he had no intention of maligning his neighboring town, but he did point out that five ships had run aground on the sand bar.[68] After some investigation by the state authorities, the issue was decided in favor of Buffalo.[69] In Oswego, too, a canal question was important, and rival printers carried on a prolonged controversy over the construction of the Oswego Canal.[70]

The reader will have observed that the establishing of newspapers by political groups for political ends was not uncommon. While the printer, on occasion, initiated the enterprise, he soon found himself in a state of dependence—upon patrons who had advanced the money for his materials; upon the papermaker and others who had given him credit; and upon the good faith of debtors who took their own time and mode of payment. If his dependence was likewise upon a political

[65] Follett, *op. cit.*, p. 51.

[66] *Palmyra Register*, Dec. 6, 1820. This issue contains a long article considering various proposals for the division.

[67] Salisbury, Guy H., "The Press of Erie," in Buffalo Historical Society *Publications*, II, 215-216.

[68] *Black Rock Beacon*, Jan. 9, 1823, *et seq.*

[69] Salisbury, Guy H., *loc. cit.*

[70] *Oswego Palladium*, Apr. 30, 1825, *et seq.*

group, he was under another sort of obligation. Having ascertained the views of his patrons he agreed that he would be steadfast in his support of their political principles and would submit to their guidance in determining editorial policies. Meetings of the proprietors were regularly held, and when the group became too numerous to attend to the task, a few members were delegated to supervise the paper. A meeting of the proprietors of the *Plattsburgh Republican* was called for July 23, 1814,—"for the purpose of choosing the annual Superintending Committee, and for transacting such other business as may be deemed expedient." [71] Judge Cooper once averred that he was not only the "sole owner of the press and types," but "one of the committee for examining pieces offered for publication in the [Cooperstown] *Impartial Observer.*" [72]

Although the proprietors rarely put their names before the people, in many cases the public were told that he whose name was on the imprint acted "For the Proprietors." In other cases in which the proprietors were as actively engaged, the attempt was made to give the printer the sole responsibility. In this event it became the aim and purpose of the rival editor to tear away the mask and to reveal the true editor. Thus John C. Spencer was reputedly the "editor" and also the financial backer of the *Ontario Messenger* of John A. Stevens; other newspapers constantly asserted that this was true, but Stevens repeatedly denied that Spencer either wrote for or owned the paper. Even when Spencer purchased the establishment for $360 at a sheriff's sale, the paper remained under the name of John A. Stevens. [73]

The charge of being a "hireling" editor, a "mere typesetter," one who worked for pay and not for principle, was an

---

[71] *Plattsburgh Republican,* July 16, 1814. The *Orange County Republican's* proprietors also met frequently, after public notice, *viz.,* Sept. 11, 1806.

[72] Cooperstown *Otsego Herald,* Mar. 18, 1809.

[73] *Geneva Palladium,* Aug. 23, 1820; see also Weed's references to Spencer in the Rochester *Telegraph,* May 27, 1823; and the Auburn *Cayuga Patriot,* Oct. 6, 1824. See *Black Rock Beacon,* Apr. 17, 1823, for affidavit of Lewis G. Hoffman, its printer, that General Peter B. Porter had never contributed to its columns, although he was commonly ascribed as its backer, and was the leader of the harbor interests.

imputation that all printers resented. Such a charge was made so frequently by rival editors, however, as to raise the suspicion that it was often not unfounded. Occasionally one admitted a connection capable of this interpretation. The following confession of Hiram Leavenworth of the *Waterloo Gazette* was intended to clear himself of the charge of such control, though it appears to incriminate him with regard to an earlier period.

> Five or six months after [the establishment of the paper by George Lewis, in May, 1817], the present editor [Leavenworth] purchased the establishment of Mr. Lewis. Shortly after Judge M'Lean came to this place, he entered into an agreement with the editor (for a certain length of time) to pay him a stipulated sum of money per week, and to receive, as a consideration therefor, the avails of the newspaper, and the privilege of editing it. His name was attached to the *Gazette,* during his editorial connection with it, as is well known to every one of its patrons. That contract has long since expired, and with it every particle of Judge M'Lean's dictation of the editorial department.[74]

No mention is made of any change in the newspaper's political position, but the printer left that matter entirely in the hands of his financial supporter.

Of another sort was the case of Morgan Bates, who had been opposed to Masonry and Jackson, but who agreed to edit a Jacksonian, Masonic paper in Jamestown, after "sufficient inducements" were offered him to leave his establishment in Warren, Pa.[75] He supported the cause of his employers without a murmur, but when he failed to get adequate compensation he left town. He was engaged subsequently in newspaper work in New York with Horace Greeley and finally rose to high political position in Michigan.[76]

Quite different was the attitude of Thurlow Weed, who refused to compromise, even in the years when he was a struggling and impecunious printer. In a letter from Manlius, September 23, 1821, where he had just established the *Onondaga Republican,* he wrote, "A Bucktail paper was of-

74 *Waterloo Gazette,* June 9, 1819.
75 Hazeltine, *The Town of Ellicott,* p. 244.
76 *Ibid.*

fered to me. It is much better supported than this, but I could not take it. It would be palpably inconsistent with my former course, although a liberal overture." [77] Timothy C. Strong, of Palmyra, however, dallied with the proposals of the Bucktails and admitted that his final refusal of their overtures was dictated by expediency rather than by principle:

At that time, before our political views were changed, *entirely and effectually* changed, we were repeatedly urged by certain bucktail characters to "come out with our paper." We objected, and honestly explained to our solicitors, the grounds of our objections. We were sensible that our success in business depended very much upon the patronage that our paper might receive. We also well knew that there were but a few bucktails within the sphere of its circulation, which was then (& now is still more so) [*sic*] pretty extensive, and that the principal part of these were in indigent circumstances. We were therefore unwilling to sacrifice interest at the shrine of party.[78]

In further justification of himself and his position, Strong revealed how some of the party resources were used to subsidize printers. He had intimated that if he were to advocate the Bucktail cause, he would expect some financial assistance to indemnify him for possible losses.

Assistance was accordingly offered [he wrote]. A letter was addressed to one of the monied leaders of the party, requesting the loan of 600 dollars, for this purpose. We saw the letter—we also saw the answer to it, which stated *that his funds were already exhausted by granting similar requests; but that he would immediately call on his friends, and that no time should be lost in procuring the amount.*[79]

The financial dependence resulting from such subsidies might lead the printer into the position of a mere tool of the politicians. Not only did he abandon his freedom as a critic, but his continuation in business was determined by the success of the party. Politicians were unscrupulous, too, in discarding a refractory tool or in breaking their promises. So David Holt, of Herkimer, having split with his supporters over the Mer-

[77] Barnes, T. W., *Memoir of Thurlow Weed*, p. 19.
[78] *Palmyra Register*, Feb. 9, 1820.
[79] *Ibid.*

chant's Bank issue, found his establishment literally destroyed by the tactics of his former patrons. They set up an opposition press, forced him from his quarters in the courthouse, caused his official patronage to be withdrawn, and allowed his press and types to be sold by the sheriff.[80]

That the practices of the day were responsible for a cynical attitude toward the integrity of printers is revealed by a letter of Oran Follett, long a printer in Batavia and Buffalo, who in 1832 sought to counteract the influence of the *Albany Argus* and the "Regency."

But how can such an influence be created at Albany, and how maintained? "God said let there be light and there was light," "The vox populi" &c. The voice of the people is the voice of God. And who is it gives voice to the will of the people? It is the humble man of types and paper, who is himself controlled by cash. Plant deep "the root of all evil," and good will spring from it. We have but to will it and it is done—apply the talisman and a genius springs forth that will pervade the whole State, shedding light and giving life and vigor in all directions, and to all our actions.[81]

This facetious view of the printer's corruptibility was followed by a plan for raising a fund to be used in party warfare. It was to fill a party chest by contributions from all parts of the state; the whole to be devoted to subsidizing a newspaper in Albany.

To purchase an established paper for the purpose of changing its political character was viewed as a heinous act by the brethren of the type. It savored of pressure on the former owner, however much he may have desired to relinquish his business, and it was most disconcerting in changing the political line-up of the community. The printer could not but be apprehensive of the effect upon his own business.[82] His unfavorable reaction was, of course, heightened if he knew that

[80] Herkimer *Farmer's Monitor*, May 19, 1807.
[81] Oran Follett to Joseph Hoxie, Feb. 6, 1832. Follett Correspondence in the *Quarterly Publication* of the Historical and Philosophical Society of Ohio, V, 52.
[82] See *infra*, chap. vii. The printer of the *Northern Whig* in Hudson offered his establishment for sale to "A young man of enterprise, and of *Sound Federal Principles* who can be well recommended..." *Northern Whig*, Jan. 24, 1815.

the opposition forces were to be strengthened. The following paragraph well illustrates this attitude:

A political renegade, supplied with funds for the purpose by the Albany Regency, purchased the establishment of the *Buffalo and Black Rock Gazette* and has converted it into an organ of the Combination— a humble echo of the will of Pope Martin the First. Noah, who very often "takes a cloud for a comet," pompously and formally announces this change of masters and doctrines of that paper, as "A Sign in the West." [83]

In some ways, however, it was preferable to have the new interest acquire an existing press rather than establish a new one. Such action would not increase the number of establishments bidding for support. The Anti-Masonic papers were perhaps the best example of this process of political infiltration.

The [Herkimer] *Free Press* was established soon after the commencement of the present year. It came into existence, like most of the other anti-masonic papers, because there was no paper in that county that dared to tell the truth respecting the principles and acts of the Masonic Institution.... They [the people of the county] resolved to have a press. They formed an association of stock holders for the purpose. They entrusted the primary management of its affairs to a committee who were well worthy of its confidence. To prevent any man from saying that they crowded their way in when there was already a sufficient number of papers in that county, they purchased one of the offices which was then in use there. The purchase was in negotiation for a number of days, and that fact was well understood throughout the village, together with the terms on which it was finally made. [84]

In Buffalo, when those interested in the Anti-Masonic movement desired an organ, they approached both S. H. and H. A. Salisbury in an effort to acquire one of their papers. The latter, publishing the *Buffalo Patriot*, realized that his acceptance of this support meant the loss of the sheriff's patronage, and he requested that an additional consideration be added to the

[83] *Buffalo Emporium*, Apr. 17, 1828. "Noah" was Mordecai M. Noah of the New York *National Advocate*.
[84] Utica *Elucidator*, June 8, 1830. This press sustained violence from its enemies, nevertheless. See *infra*, chap. vi, for cases of violence.

proposal to cover this sacrifice. What he received for taking
the step it is impossible to determine from the conflicting and
biased testimony of contemporaries, yet he succumbed to the
"inducement." [85]

There was much controversy, too, over the supposed "pur-
chase" of the *Rochester Daily Advertiser* by Martin Van
Buren in 1828. This paper, as noted above, was founded by
Henry C. Sleight, of Sag Harbor, in partnership with Luther
Tucker, his foreman, who set up the office in Rochester. Henry
O'Reilly was employed as editor. In September, 1828, Tucker
sought the permission of Sleight to come out in support of Van
Buren. Sleight would not support the "Regency" politician for
any office, whereupon he was asked if he would sell his interest,
and for what terms.

> I [Sleight] immediately named my price which was promptly agreed
> to, and several of Mr. Van Buren's political friends endorsed Mr.
> Tucker's note for fifteen hundred dollars, twelve months from date,
> which, after being endorsed by Mr. Van Buren and Mr. Van Ben-
> thuysen of the *Albany Argus,* was discounted at one of the Albany
> Banks, and the amount remitted to me by Mr. Tucker. The remainder
> of the purchase [price] he retained as a loan from me and afterward
> amply repaid.[86]

News of this note reached the rivals of Tucker, who attached
to it a sinister significance. Weed saw it as a design of the
Masons in an attack upon Anti-Masonry, to which Mr. Sleight
was supposed to have objected.[87] It was shown, however, that
the note was merely for the purpose of enabling Tucker to
purchase his partner's interest.[88]

In 1829 the Anti-Masonic group in Ithaca felt that there
was need of a "free press" in Tompkins County, and they advertised for a printer in the following notice:

[85] *Buffalo Emporium,* Nov. 26-Dec. 17, 1827. See also the reference to the
"arrangement" in a letter of Albert H. Tracy to Thurlow Weed. Barnes,
T. W., *Memoir,* p. 31.

[86] H. C. Sleight to Henry O'Reilly, Mar. 20, 1873. O'Reilly Collection.

[87] Rochester *Anti-Masonic Enquirer,* Oct. 21, 1828; see also *Onondaga Register,* Oct. 29, 1828. It also involved Weed in a libel suit with Tucker, *q.v. infra*
chap. vi.

[88] Rochester *Anti-Masonic Enquirer,* Oct. 27, 1828.

Any gentleman of competent abilities to conduct a press, would receive from 500 to 1,000 subscribers, with a portion of Advertising. Communications on the subject may be made to either of the subscribers [of which there were five, the Corresponding Committee], or to a convention of delegates from the several towns in the County, which is to hold a meeting on the subject of establishing a press, in the village of Ithaca, on the second Wednesday of January next.[89]

A somewhat similar method of obtaining anti-Clintonian sheets had been attempted by Noah of the *National Advocate* in 1818 when this advertisement appeared, copied in several papers throughout the state:

To PRINTERS. *Three* Newspaper Establishments are wanted to purchase in any town in the counties of Ontario, Oneida, Cayuga, Washington, Saratoga, and Montgomery. Printers of Republican papers, who are desirous of disposing of their establishments will acquaint the proprietor of the National Advocate of the situation, the quantity and quality of the type, and the condition of the press, the number of subscribers, and the terms of sale. None need apply unless they are residents of the aforementioned counties.[90]

It is apparent that the publication of a newspaper was often a service to a political party; and there were other partisan services for which the printer received rewards. The English writer, whom we have previously quoted, was much impressed by the political activities of the country printer.

Politics being a leading feature in all American journals (the annual elections and other movements creating a constant political excitement), the editor or conductor of a newspaper, of the very lowest order, is looked upon, in the little sphere in which his paper circulates, as a leader of one or other political sect or party; and if he be fortunate enough to advocate the cause of the successful candidates for office, it is understood that this advocacy entitles him to the consideration of the successful party, and that he is fairly entitled to some place or office to which a salary is attached, as binding him to his party, and by thus

[89] Batavia *Republican Advocate,* Dec. 25, 1829; notice dated Dec. 19, 1829. Needless to say, Ithaca gained her Anti-Masonic press, the *Ithaca Chronicle,* in 1830.

[90] Schenectady *Cabinet,* Sept. 16, 1818; also noted in *Auburn Gazette,* Sept. 23, 1818; and Canandaigua *Ontario Repository,* Munsell, *Typographical Miscellany,* p. 137.

extending his means, putting him in a situation of effecting still more in future party struggles.[91]

It was a day when the least move on the part of a politician was construed as possessing political significance, often far beyond the actual facts. When Martin Van Buren endorsed a printer's note, it was widely published as an instance of political control, another attempt to "improve the condition of the press." [92] To some, Thurlow Weed was not just a partisan printer, but a kind of political errand boy whose journeys about the state were shrouded in mystery. If he journeyed to Albany in mid-winter to urge upon Governor Clinton the appointment of a sheriff for Chenango; [93] or visited Washington, perhaps to get the ear of Henry Clay and the administration for Anti-Masonic ambitions; [94] or went to Vermont to bring back Elisha Adams, a witness in the Morgan trials, and to New Hampshire in search of Orson Parkhurst for the same purpose; [95] he went not as an official, but as a secret agent, expenses paid, in whom officials or party leaders placed confidence. To opponents and neighbors he was just a journeyman; and yet, according to H. B. Stanton he wielded at that time as much "power, perhaps, as at any subsequent period in his life." [96]

Few printers could be politicians in the sense that Weed was. If they were not powers in themselves, however, they were constantly present in party counsels. They were often secretaries of conventions or political clubs; they were members of corresponding committees, or of committees of organization. They kept in touch with those high in party counsels, suggesting appointments and other acts in their localities and reporting upon the prospects for approaching elections. Printers and editors were the antennae by which the

[91] London *Penny Magazine,* June 26, 1841, X, 244.
[92] *Onondaga Register,* Oct. 29, 1828.
[93] Weed, *Autobiography,* p. 78.
[94] *Rochester Daily Advertiser,* Apr. 10, June 30, 1828.
[95] Canandaigua *Ontario Repository,* May 7, 1828; Utica *Oneida Observer,* May 25, 1830.
[96] Stanton, H. B., *Random Recollections,* p. 19.

party leaders sensed the cross currents of political life, enabling them, if they were wise enough, to steer a safe course. They furnished the signals of approaching danger, pointed out mistakes, though in their own ambitious servitude, they may have been overzealous.[97]

So Augustine G. Dauby of the *Oneida Observer* was denominated as "one of those who early won for Utica its political prominence. *He distributed prizes; he did not seek them.* He set up men, and put them down; he assisted in constructing policies and parties. He was an ally to be sought and an adversary to be feared." [98] In a letter to Flagg of the "Albany Regency" in 1829, he withdrew his approval of Jay Hinman for appointment as Clerk in Equity, although he had signed his petition. He had been under the impression that the office was inconsequential; "but I have since learned that the situation is lucrative and important," so he suggested another nominee.[99]

Henry O'Reilly wrote Flagg of a successful election when the Anti-Masons had only 600 votes "against us." He then suggested the party's course in Rochester.

By continuing the exposures which I have commenced, of the *extravagance* of the Anti-Masonic rulers, &c&c, touching on their inroads on the Jury system as well as on the one sided administration of Justice, I think much good may be accomplished in this county. The less said about *Masonry* the better. It will be my aim to turn attention *now* as much as possible on national politics, &c.[100]

He also condemned the activity of Roberts and the *Craftsman*.[101] This was not mere bigoted partisan talk but a report and a suggestion to be followed with a view to party advantage.

A result of this political activity, if not the motive for it, was the rewarding of the printer with some of the party spoils.

[97] See A. C. Flagg MSS in New York Public Library. Especially letters of V. W. Smith (Syracuse), O. Follett (Buffalo), Ch. G. DeWitt (Kingston), A. G. Dauby (Utica), and H. O'Reilly (Rochester).
[98] Bagg, *Pioneers of Utica*, pp. 541-542.
[99] A. G. Dauby to A. C. Flagg, Oct. 4, 1829. A. C. Flagg MSS.
[100] Henry O'Reilly to A. C. Flagg, Nov. 11, 1829. A. C. Flagg MSS.
[101] *Supra*, p. ooo.

A survey of offices held by printers shows what a wide range this parceling of offices sometimes covered. There were some who obtained elective office, and their ranks increased after the change in the state constitution of 1821, but a larger number secured appointive posts. The latter ranged from the office of commissioner to take the acknowledgment of deeds, to sheriffs, judges, and county clerks; coroners, jailers, clerks of court, marshals, assessors, constables, district attorneys, school clerks, surrogates, justices of the peace, supervisors, census officers, military officers, and canal collectors were numerous. Printers found the most suitable elective office to be that of assemblyman in the state legislature, although a few went to Congress. The appointive office which seemed most appropriate as a political reward for the printer was that of postmaster. Benjamin Franklin's long postal service was a hallowed precedent. The position had its distinct advantages for the printer-editor. In the early days the postmasters possessed the franking privilege, and were thus able to circulate their papers free of charge.[102] They had first access to such news as came through the mails and were well situated both to receive exchanges and to forward their own papers. Possession of a printing office was helpful in providing space for a post office. The number of printer-postmasters for this period is not great, partly due to the variety of other offices; but the office of postmaster does rank as the political position most commonly filled by printers.[103]

Party divisions in the state, as well as in the nation, were responsible for removals or dismissals from office, actions which rarely failed to excite spirited comment. The Clintonian defection caused a number of removals, while the overturn of

---

[102] Salmon, Lucy M., *The Newspaper and the Historian*, p. 87. It has been suggested, too, that in colonial times the newspaper was the sideline of the postmaster, "a pleasant little speculation of no vital importance to his fortunes"; the combination was so frequently noticeable that "indeed the first outcome of a new postoffice appointment was likely to be a new weekly." Cook, E. C., *Literary Influences in Colonial Newspapers*, pp. 9-10.

[103] There were thirteen among those whose data are known, before 1830; four whose reward came later, making a total of seventeen. Nine more could be added, if editors, not printers, were included.

1829, when the Jacksonian party came in, was notorious. Van Buren and the "Regency" were held responsible for the "proscription" of Daniel Cruger, of Bath, Stephen B. Leonard, of Owego, and other postmasters (who were not printers), at Norwich and Brooklyn. The reputed reason was their recent support of Clinton.[104] At about the same time David Holt, of Herkimer, and Solomon Southwick, of Albany, were removed from their offices because of unsatisfactory accounts.[105]

Appointment of printers to post-office vacancies, too, was hailed by rivals as significant. In 1829 this occurred more frequently than in any previous year, for the Jackson party relied heavily upon the press. Dauby, the Utica printer-politician, came into his own, although his predecessor of the other party had barely warmed the place and complained bitterly.[106] Lewis H. Redfield of Onondaga protested against the haste in his case, for he resigned to take effect June 30, but he was not permitted to serve out the month.[107] Sag Harbor and Sandy Hill printers were given their rewards at this time, as was a newly established editor in Brooklyn.[108]

There were small perquisites in the hands of the postmaster, which made the office more desirable. It was customary to advertise in the newspapers lists of letters in the post office. The proprietors of the *Dutchess Intelligencer* complained that this privilege had been taken from them, thus depriving them of "patronage worth about *three dollars and fifty cents per year!*" The comment that "the work goes bravely on," was a cynical reference to the small amount involved.[109] Thus was the printer's political allegiance kept forever before him.

Several minor appointive offices were coveted by the impe-

[104] Schenectady *Cabinet,* May 22, June 2, 1822; *Poughkeepsie Journal,* May 31, 1820; *Norwich Journal,* Aug. 9, 1820; Brooklyn *Long Island Patriot,* Jan. 2, 1822.

[105] Poughkeepsie *Dutchess Observer,* Jan. 31, Feb. 7, 1821; Southwick was not a country printer, but see *A.S.P.* Vol. I, 21st Cong. 1st S. No. 94, p. 247; *Norwich Journal,* Feb. 13, 1822.

[106] Bagg, *Pioneers of Utica,* p. 541.

[107] *Onondaga Register and Syracuse Gazette,* June 10, 1829.

[108] Saratoga Springs *Saratoga Sentinel,* June 30, 1829; Brooklyn *Long Island Star,* July 31, 1829; Utica *Oneida Observer,* June 23, 1829.

[109] Poughkeepsie *Dutchess Intelligencer,* July 15, 1829.

cunious printers. As justice of the peace, commissioner to acknowledge deeds, coroner, or village clerk, his fees were not likely to be large, but they were perhaps the mite which turned the scale in his stinted economy.[110] As commissioner, Thurlow Weed found the two or three dollars per week a welcome aid in the support of his family while he struggled to maintain his newspaper in Norwich.[111] If a printer were so lucky as to be made sheriff, not only was he more amply rewarded by fees, but he had also for his paper the regular printing patronage of the office. The added prestige of one who held an office in the local government was not to be ignored by such a seeker after favor as the printer of a newspaper.

Few printers found these rewards showered upon them without solicitation.[112] Usually many earnest and urgent representations had to be made to the governor or Council of Appointment. An inveterate applicant was William Ray, an editor in Essex, Onondaga, and Ontario counties, whose long epistles to Governor Tompkins requesting various appointments recited his public and party services, sufferings in the Tripolitan war, the inefficiency, not to mention moral incapacity, of his rivals, and, most important of all, the destitution of himself and his family.[113] Being a poet, he was not averse to appealing to the governor in rhyme:

My situation is truly distressing. I cannot possibly hold out much longer,

Sunk in self consuming anguish
Can the poor heart always ache?
No—the tortur'd nerve must languish
Or the strings of life must break.[114]

The principal trouble with Ray seemed to be that he protested too much. He met all the supposed charges of his

---

[110] There were four printers and five editors who were justices of the peace in this period. Two printers served as coroner, and three were commissioners of deeds. Three were village clerks. Three printers (Elihu Phinney, David Holt, and Jesse Buel) were appointed judges, while running their country papers.

[111] Weed, *Autobiography*, p. 78.

[112] Thurlow Weed's one appointive office was an exception. *Ibid.*

[113] Quoted in Brown, George L., *Pleasant Valley*, pp. 233-247.

[114] *Ibid.*

enemies and for good measure denounced their personal characters. His one virtue as an office seeker was that he was frank and made the issue quite clear. He considered himself more worthy than the county clerk and sought his job.

I now have the editing of a paper here, but without pay, perquisites or emolument of any kind, and you may judge gentlemen with what spirit and feelings I can persist in devoting my exertions to the present measures of the administration. Should a man literally stall fed by it and pronounced by the public voice unworthy of the station be continued in office or any other man except myself be appointed to the office of County Clerk.[115]

Or again, six days later:

I now edit a Republican paper without any fee or reward. Give me the office and I will continue to do it—shall continue to foster and support the establishment without which I fear it must fail.[116]

Rebuffed for one appointment, Ray maintained his hopes with his injured feelings, and, while proposing to publish a pamphlet to justify his rights and character, he bethought himself that with the outbreak of war some office of a military character might yield him support. In fact, he begged of the governor:

My family is in a state of absolute starvation, and if your Excellency should feel disposed to send me some trifling pecuniary aid until a situation could be procured for me I should feel thankful. Perhaps the office of Barrack master in or about Albany might be obtained for me or a deputy commissar of provision stores or some such sedentary employment—or if I could obtain a place as Editor of a government paper like the Albany Republican, or even have money advanced to continue the Editor of a paper here it might relieve my distress. But if there is no help for me, if I am forever abandoned by your Excellency do for Heaven's sake let me know it without delay.[117]

The governor apparently could resist no longer, and Ray was made Brigade Quartermaster with the pay and rank of

---

[115] *Ibid.,* pp. 240-241. Letter dated May 12, 1812.
[116] *Ibid.,* p. 241. Letter dated May 18, 1812.
[117] *Ibid.,* pp. 246-247. Letter of June 29, 1812.

major.[118] He was, in fact, rewarded on several occasions. He became a justice of the peace in Essex in 1809, and in Onondaga County in 1816 he was made a magistrate and a commissioner in the courts of record.[119] Later he went to Geneva and was there "nominated by the judges of Ontario County for justice of the peace." [120]

One editor with a long career of service in important partisan journals was Charles Holt, who in 1818 found himself beset by adversity and appealed to Jabez D. Hammond of the Council of Appointment.

After employment of twenty years of his life as a republican editor, through all the vicissitudes of prosecution, fine, imprisonment, personal contest, and other events of political warfare (in behalf of his principles and his party)—your petitioner finds himself, from a series of adverse circumstances, destitute of property, with a large family (of eight young children, and in part, two other dependents) under the necessity of applying to the honorable Council of Appointment for the first time, for public employment in a civil office....[121]

Statements of partisans, in which liberties with facts and figures were frequently taken, have to be accepted with reservations, yet the reports which editors were led to publish are illuminating. Henry C. Frisbee of the *Fredonia Censor* learned that his rival, Harvey Newcomb of the Westfield *Chautauqua Phenix,* was leaving for Buffalo, "where he is to receive $250 per ann. for editing the *Patriot,* and the same amount for his services as deputy county clerk. Now, *if* he can get this, we are not surprised at his desire to leave the *Phenix;* the instinct the same as rats leaving a rotten ship." [122]

Elective office was also within the gift of the party, or at least was more easily attained with party backing. After 1821 some of the offices mentioned above, such as justice of the

---

[118] Ray, William, *Poems...to Which Is Added a Brief Sketch of the Author's Life,...Written by Himself.* (1821), p. 250.

[119] *Ibid.,* p. 251.

[120] *Onondaga Register,* Mar. 5, 1823.

[121] Charles Holt to Jabez D. Hammond, Apr. 7, 1818; MS in New York Public Library.

[122] *Fredonia Censor,* Mar. 25, 1829. Newcomb edited the *Buffalo Patriot* from Apr., 1829, to Jan., 1830, and was deputy county clerk.

peace and county clerk, were transferred to the elective category. If this made the printer less servile to the governor and
Council of Appointment, nevertheless he remained a politician.
His strategy in seeking office now included the questionable
practice of self-nomination. While any politician could present
his name to the voters, the printer found it easy to set up his
own candidacy in the editorial column. Some, it is true, abused
this advantage and offered themselves when there was little
other backing.[123] The ever-hopeful Franklin Cowdery reasoned
his way thus:

NOMINATION. presuming that the present incumbent of the Clerkship of this county will be nominated, and probably re-elected to the
Assembly; and consequently be unwilling to have his name run for two
offices at one and the same election; I consider myself to be on justifiable as well as republican ground, in offering to come before the people
of the county of Allegany, as a candidate, on the first Monday in
November next, for the office of *Clerk of the Court of Common Pleas.*
Angelica, April 20, 1822.   *Franklin Cowdery.*[124]

Successful officeholders, too, with varying degrees of reluctance, kept their names before the readers of their papers.
Said D. C. Miller in 1831,

A combination of circumstances, personal, pecuniary, and political, which,
at this time, it is unnecessary to detail, have induced me at this juncture
to do that which I had never intended to have done. It is to appeal to
you for your suffrages for the clerkship of the county, for one term more,
and one term only.[125]

To the insatiable Isaac Riggs, of Schenectady, always hunger-
ing for some of the party fruits, self-nomination was a boon;
this did not escape the satire of one of his brethren of the type.
In view of his perennial appeals to the electorate, the following
notice was a palpable hit.[126]

[123] S. S. Freer ran for Congress, a forlorn hope, in 1826. Brooklyn *Long Island Patriot,* Aug. 31, 1826.

[124] Moscow *Livingston Gazette,* May 9, 1822.

[125] Batavia *Republican Advocate,* Oct. 28, 1831.

[126] Canadaigua *Ontario Repository,* Nov. 11, 1823.

At the request of Isaac Riggs, I do, as one of his friends, offer him as a candidate at the ensuing election for the offices of Clerk, Sheriff, Assemblyman and Coroner.

Schenectady, Aug. 2, 1825.   George Ritchie, Jun.[127]

An interesting comment, to the effect that printers were generally poor candidates for elective office, was made by D. D. Spencer of the *Ithaca Chronicle*. Since he proved the point by his own as well as by his rival's experience, the partisan tone of the remarks need not cause them to be discounted.

We have sometime seen the remark that editors do not make popular candidates. The evidence of this is not so much in the fact that they are sometimes defeated with a defeated party, as in the fact that they sometimes run *behind* the candidates on the same ticket. We refer to two or three particulars in confirmation of the remark.

In 1825, Ebenezer Mack, editor of the *Ithaca Journal,* and a masonic High Priest withal, was a candidate for Member of Assembly, and he *lost his election* by a majority of *three hundred and forty*. At the recent election the editor of the *Ithaca Chronicle* [i.e., the writer], being a candidate for the same office, was *defeated* by a majority of *something less than a hundred*.

In 1829, the same *Ebenezer Mack* was again a candidate, and run sixty-one votes behind the highest, and twenty behind the lowest on the same assembly ticket. At the recent election, the editor [the writer] has run *forty-four* votes *behind* the highest and 17 behind the lowest on the same ticket.

Now all this seems to corroborate the remark to which we have referred in the commencement of this article. And it seems to prove, also, that in this instance the editor is about *half as unpopular* as Ebenezer Mack! Which is certainly very humiliating.[128]

---

[127] Schenectady *Mohawk Sentinel,* Aug. 4, 1825. Ritchie was the printer of this paper.

[128] *Ithaca Chronicle,* Nov. 16, 1831. The available statistics are not conclusive on this point. There were eleven country printers member of assembly before 1830; seven who were after 1830. One printer reached the state senate before 1830, and one got to Congress. Four others entered Congress after 1830. Some printers were elected county clerk and village clerk after the constitutional revision of 1821. Data on the unsuccessful candidacies of printers are too fragmentary for generalization. In this period, too, four editors (not printers) were elected to the assembly, two to the senate, and three to Congress. Five, three, and four, respectively, reached these positions after 1830. One, Preston King, became a United States Senator.

As has been suggested, one highly appropriate method of rewarding a loyal partisan in the printing business was to name him government printer or to award him job-printing contracts for various governmental agencies. From the very beginning printers enjoying these perquisites were regarded as recipients of political favor. Although frequently criticized by their jealous rivals, they clung tenaciously to the remunerative connection. Many presses were established with little other thought than that they would serve the local government.

For the period under review, during which the practice of naming a state printer was well established, a principal objective of ambitious printers was to qualify for the office. The custom of giving preference to the New York or Albany printers did not deter country printers from entering the field. By a law passed February 25, 1805, provision was made for the immediate printing in the newspapers of the laws passed by the legislature, before their formal publication by the state printer. This publication was to be in the paper of the state printer in Albany and in newspapers designated in four districts of the state. These were Cheetham's *American Citizen,* of New York, in the Southern District; the Kingston *Plebeian* of Jesse Buel, in the Middle District; the *Washington Register* of J. P. Reynolds, of Salem, in the Eastern District; and the *Columbian Gazette* of Thomas Walker, of Whitestown, in the Western District. The act stipulated that these printers should be paid for this service "a sum not exceeding two hundred dollars." [129] In 1809 the legislature ended this system by which country printers received some of the patronage in the printing of the laws, and henceforth statutes were officially printed only in the paper of the state printer.[130]

Assurance that he would receive the state patronage was undoubtedly a principal motive for the removal of Jesse Buel to Albany in 1813 and for his establishment of the *Albany Argus.* He was urged to take the step by Judge Spencer and

[129] *Laws of the State of New York* (1806) IV, 19-20.
[130] *Laws of the State of New York* (1809), p. 524. The Act was passed Mar. 29, 1809.

some others, whose influence gained him the appointment of state printer in 1815, a position he held until 1820. His successors in this period were all inhabitants of Albany, although Edwin Croswell, mentioned above as the newspaper voice of the Albany Regency, had been a printer in Catskill.

The hue and cry over the fact that the office was thus monopolized did not escape the attention of the country printer. As a partisan, if for no other reason, he upheld or denounced the situation existing at the capital. Of the protestants none was more voluble than the aforementioned Isaac Riggs, of Schenectady, whose criticism was whetted by his own candidacy. He scored the appointment of Messrs. Cantine and Leake, who had purchased the *Argus* in 1820, and succeeded Buel as state printer, apparently by prior arrangement, although a lower bid was presented by E. & E. Hosfords. It pained him, too, that Cantine and Leake were not practical printers but lawyers and politicians.[131] The award, however, was hotly defended by certain Bucktail papers which denounced the lower bid as an attempt to cheapen the work of printers, since it would be less than cost.[132] Riggs anticipated a change as soon as the new constitution became effective, and he presented elaborate proposals, estimates, and samples, in support of his application.[133] With his usual frankness he linked his political pretensions and their success with the continuance of his paper. "The fate of my *intended* application to the Legislature, for the office of Printer to the State, will decide whether I continue the publication of the *Cabinet* or not." [134]

Country papers throughout the state clamored for a more general publication of the laws at public expense. The many advantages of such a procedure were set forth by the *Saratoga Sentinel* as follows:

[131] *Schenectady Cabinet,* Feb. 28, 1821.
[132] *Norwich Journal,* Apr. 11, 1821; and Kingston *Craftsman,* Mar. 18, 1822. See also views of *Albany Daily Advertiser,* Nov. 25, Dec. 4, 18, 1822, copied in Munsell, *Typographical Collections* (MS Vol.), VI, 42-62.
[133] Munsell, MS, *loc. cit.,* VI, 57-59.
[134] *Schenectady Cabinet,* Jan. 1, 1823.

The plan of publishing all the public acts of a state in its newspapers is not novel. It has been practised for years in most of the eastern states, and with the happiest effects. Their inhabitants in this respect, are more enlightened, and less liable to encounter litigation. Law suits are less frequent—a better state of society exists—and a greater degree of prosperity and happiness is attendant upon industry.[135]

Several editors considered the publication of the statutes in newspapers so desirable that they proposed to publish them without remuneration. The *Corrector* of Sag Harbor even enlarged its sheet and added fifty cents to the price, so confident was it of public support in this project. In addition, however, it intended "at the end of each year (say sometime in May, which will be *six* or *eight months sooner* than the laws are *now* received by the public officers) gratuitously [to] present each of our subscribers with a pamphlet (exclusive of the paper) containing the general laws of the state for the preceding session; together with the *local* laws of the counties of Suffolk and Queens."[136] The *Onondaga Register* cited the failure of an act to provide general newspaper publication of the laws but promised that "the most important will be inserted gratuitously in this paper as we find room."[137]

Proposed plans for the publication usually were based upon the assumption that various newspapers would receive payment on the same scale as that granted the state paper. In 1817 Barnum and Nelson, printers of Poughkeepsie, in writing to Alden Spooner, who had just begun the publication of the *Columbian,* stated their desires frankly.

We wish to have something done this winter by the Republicans, to distribute the printing of the state laws more generally among the printers of this state; the patronage of the state printer is enormous. We suggested a plan to Mr. Irvine [former printer of the *Columbian*],

[135] Saratoga Springs *Saratoga Sentinel,* Dec. 16, 1823.
[136] Sag Harbor *Corrector,* Mar. 29, 1823.
[137] *Onondaga Register,* Dec. 19, 1827. Another such law was introduced in the assembly the following year by Mr. Tallmadge of Dutchess. Delhi *Delaware Gazette,* Apr. 9, 1828.

which he said he approved of. We will write you on this subject in a few days.[138]

Although such a proposal had considerable support from the printers, objectors were not wanting, and they appear to have carried the day. Thurlow Weed viewed it not only as a dangerous extension of the patronage in the hands of his opponents but also as a useless multiplication of printed matter which would not be read. This last point is interesting, for most printers held the opposite view, and it indicates that at this early date Weed favored the inclusion of more interesting material in the newspapers. The reasons for his opposition were set forth with his accustomed vigor:

Governor Van Buren's *pressing* recommendation to the Legislature, to provide for the newspaper publication of the Revised Laws, is among the most designing and unprincipled acts of his political career. The object is a base one; and the effect of it will be pernicious beyond all former example. His object is to commit and pension at least one venal press in every county in the state. By creating this immense amount of patronage, he will be enabled to hold out a bribe that too seldom fails of tempting either the poverty or the avarice of those to whom it is offered. Thus subsidized, the Press, which ought to be as free as air and fearless as virtue, becomes the muzzled organ of faction and the tamed beast of burden to demagogues. And this is what Gov. Van Buren calls "improving the condition of the press."

The publication, in so many newspapers, of this vast amount of law lumber, would cost the people an immense sum of money, for no valuable purpose. Not one twentieth part of the people could ever see the particular newspapers in which they would appear, and of the fraction who did see the papers, not one tenth part would ever read such tomes of law. The expenditure, therefore, would be an utterly worthless one. But the evil does not stop there. The money is not merely squandered. It goes to advance schemes positively bad. The people are made to pay by stealth, for supporting Mr. Van Buren's *"improving presses,"* and to furnish the sinews for carrying on his political campaigns.[139]

[138] Letter dated Oct. 29, 1817, Poughkeepsie *Dutchess Observer,* Nov. 12, 1817. The letter was intended to be confidential but was intercepted, opened, and published by Noah, concerning whom there were some disparaging remarks, in the *National Advocate!* It was then published with explanation by the writers.

[139] Rochester *Anti-Masonic Enquirer,* Feb. 10, 1829. This practice was adopted by the state in 1845, when a statute was enacted for the publishing of

The country printer's interest in state patronage went beyond his concern over the printing of legislative enactments.[140] There were notices of insolvency and of mortgage sales which could not be monopolized by the state printer, since the law generally required publication in the counties in which the parties affected by such legal actions resided. The income of the state printer from legal notices alone was estimated in 1830 at $5,000 annually.[141] Returns to the local printer were, of course, commensurately smaller, but they were to him an important item. The records of the state Attorney-General's office contain information concerning the remuneration which country printers received for publishing notices of foreclosure sales. The items range from a charge of $3.50, one dollar of which was for posting the notice on the courthouse door,[142] to a bill for $85.50, which must have included numerous notices.[143] In 1822 Thomas Walker, of Utica, claimed that the state owed him $247.22 "for advertising sundry state mortgages" and asked that the sum be deposited to his credit in one of the banks of Albany.[144] This was an exceptional account, most of the printers having received only small sums in any one year.

The printing of notices of insolvency was not always controlled by state officials. In certain circumstances some local politician became the dispenser of this form of patronage. In Auburn the *Cayuga Patriot* complained that Judge Miller was sending notices of insolvency to the *Free Press,* in which the judge had an interest.[145] Doubleday, of the *Patriot,* proposed to enlighten the public on this subject:

---

the laws in two newspapers in each county, to be chosen by the local board of supervisors. *Laws of the State of New York* (1845), pp. 305-306.

[140] There is much interesting material on the subject of the emoluments of the state printer, which has never been thoroughly treated, but it does not pertain to this study.

[141] Oxford *Chenango Republican,* Oct. 20, 1830, quoting *Albany Evening Journal,* Jan. 13, 1830. See also Poughkeepsie *Dutchess Intelligencer,* Oct. 20, 1830.

[142] Samuel Talcott to G. M. Davison, Dec. 25, 1823. MSS in New York State Library.

[143] Jno. G. Stower to Jas. Dexter, Esq., Dec. 18, 1823.

[144] Thomas Walker to S. A. Tallcott, Att'y Gen., Feb. 23, 1822.

[145] Auburn *Cayuga Patriot,* Sept. 29, 1824.

As the law has not fixed the compensation of the country printers on publishing insolvent notices, the people may be curious to know whether it costs any more to have them published in the *Patriot* than in the Federal papers? We can inform them that it does not. We do not shrink from investigation. We know that we have not only been accommodating in our terms of payment, but have invariably charged *one third less* for publishing insolvent notices, than neighbor Skinner did, when Judge Miller gave HIM the *exclusive privilege* of doing that business. For what purpose then have the Federal lawyers entered into a combination against us? [146]

Several years earlier Henry C. Southwick, of Auburn, had complained that the lawyers, being of the opposing party, had discriminated against him in this matter of patronage.[147] In Chenango County it was charged that General Obadiah German swore not to permit Hubbard of the *Norwich Journal* to "publish another notice of insolvency, and that he actually *compelled* a man to carry a notice to Oxford to be published." [148] The insolvent notice was, therefore, both a "reward" and a punishment.

The sheriff of the county controlled much of this patronage, and it behooved the printer, if possible, to be in his favor. In Delaware County the sheriff, Roger Case, noticed that the under sheriff had inserted a legal advertisement in the *Republican*. He thereupon gave public notice as follows:

It being my intention to give to the *Gazette,* the printing that may be required in performing the duties of the office of Sheriff, I conceive it expedient in this public manner, to advise all my Deputies that I shall expect them to have inserted in the last mentioned paper, all such notices and advertisements as shall in the exercise of their office, require publication in one of the Newspapers of this County.[149]

The practice of awarding the patronage of the sheriff's office to the victorious faction was so well established that the *Poughkeepsie Journal* could felicitate its rival on its prospective good fortune:

[146] *Ibid.*
[147] Auburn *Advocate of the People,* Mar. 5, 1817.
[148] *Norwich Journal,* May 28, 1818.
[149] Delhi *Delaware Gazette,* Jan. 29, 1823.

We congratulate our neighbor of the *Herald* on the prospect of approaching patronage, which the installation of the new sheriff affords. As our late *Clintonian* sheriff gave all his patronage to the *Observer,* of course on account of the zealous support that paper has steadily rendered the administration, the *Herald,* which has been uniformly adverse, has surely undisputed claims to the patronage of the present Bucktail incumbent.[150]

The loss of the sheriff's patronage in Manlius was the cause of Thurlow Weed's stopping the publication of the *Onondaga Republican.*[151] Other cases of sheriff's patronage might be cited, the papers themselves being the best evidence. In Troy it was alleged that the patronage of the Recorder's office was so important as a subsidy for the *Farmer's Register,* that the office had been filled recently with the sole purpose of providing for the printer.[152] The political value of his paper was thus confirmed.

By an act of 1818 the rate for legal advertisements was fixed at fifty cents "per folio" (72 words) for the first insertion, and twenty-five cents for each subsequent insertion. An act of 1821 fixed the rate for insolvent notices at $1.67 for six weeks, and $2.00 for ten weeks.[153] In the same year an investigation by a committee of the senate into the charges made by the state printer, did not find them excessive, although those for insolvent notices formed the major portion of his remuneration.[154]

Regulation of printing rates, even of the rates charged by the state printer, was resented by the country printer. The embattled Isaac Riggs again asserted himself:

It may be asked, how the business of the state printing can affect other printers? I answer—the charges of the state printer will give a tone to public sentiment as to the charges of other printers, and if they (other printers) refuse to receive the same as the state printer, the legislature

---

150 *Poughkeepsie Journal,* Feb. 28, 1821.
151 Weed, *Autobiography,* p. 90.
152 Troy *Northern Budget,* May 26, Dec. 15, 1818.
153 *Revised Statutes of the State of New York* (1829), II, 648-649.
154 Poughkeepsie *Dutchess Observer,* Mar. 21, 1821. The committee felt that these notices would diminish, due to a recent court decision. There is no clue to the nature of the latter.

have the same right to lay their hands upon them (particularly as to their legal business, which is all or nearly all many of them have to do) as they have upon the state printer.

To be more explicit, if the legislature have the right (which I shall not dispute) and the disposition, too, to cut down the state printer from $2.50 to $1.00, for publishing insolvent notices, they have the same right to cut down other printers in the same proportion, for publishing sales by virtue of mortgages; sheriff's sales; surrogate's, probate's, and insolvent notices, &c. If this should be the case, more than one half of the printers of this state had better kick their types and presses out of doors, than attempt to print another newspaper.[155]

In addition to the state and local patronage, a few printers were favored by that of the Federal Government. An act of Congress, approved March 2, 1799, directed the Secretary of State to have the laws passed by that body "published at least in one of the public newspapers, printed within each state: and whenever . . . the aforesaid publication shall be found not sufficiently extensive for the promulgation thereof . . . in a greater number of newspapers . . . not exceeding three in any state." [156]

For a time the necessary publication in New York seems to have been confined to the cities of New York and Albany. Beginning in 1810, however, a country printer was among the favored three. From 1810 to 1820 John A. Stevens, of Canandaigua, received this patronage; from 1821 to 1825 Oran Follett, of Batavia; and from 1826 to 1828, the Rochester paper successively published by L. W. Sibley, Edwin Scrantom, and Luther Tucker, was the beneficiary.[157]

The remuneration received by the printer who was thus enabled to denominate himself "Printer of the Laws of the United States," was one dollar per page, which amounted to approximately one hundred dollars annually. Data for the early years are not available, but a report of Secretary of State Henry Clay for the years 1823-24 and 1824-25 gave the

[155] Schenectady *Cabinet,* Mar. 17, 1819.
[156] *Statutes of the United States,* 1799 (Folwell Edition), p. 488.
[157] Canandaigua *Ontario Messenger,* 1810-1820; Batavia *Spirit of the Times,* 1821-1825; Rochester *Monroe Republican,* Jan. 10, 1826. Cf. also subsequent references. Files of the first two in the Library of Congress are those addressed to the Secretary of State as proof of publication.

amount paid to each paper as $123.25 and $104.00, respectively.[158] This was no inconsiderable item in the budget of the country printer, and any change in awarding this patronage was liable to result in a flurry of partisan charges. When the Federal patronage was taken away from the *Monroe Republican,* a Jackson paper, it was intimated that Thurlow Weed's visit to Washington in 1828 was responsible for this "vindictive spirit of the reigning powers." [159]

From its meager funds the party occasionally rewarded the partisan printer. Whenever possible the jobs of printing handbills, ballots, pamphlets, and other party literature were given to him.[160] It was looked upon as party service, as well as patronage. There were drawbacks to this situation, as the following complaint intimates. At that time, as well as today, party funds were not always adequate for the expenditures deemed politically necessary.

During the last three years the Editors of the *Herald* have printed almost every paper, handbill, pamphlet, or circular (and the number has not been small) that have appeared on the republican side of the house in Dutchess.

Committees of election have regularly been appointed, whose business it ought to have been, to have raised a fund for the defraying of these necessary expenses. They, however, have invariably neglected this part of their duty, and bills to the amount of hundreds of dollars are now due us for these services.

The whole amount of monies received by us for defraying the above mentioned expenses, during the period above specified, does not exceed forty dollars, the principal part of which has been paid by two individuals. If the Republicans of Dutchess believe it to be our duty to defray the expenses of their elections, they ought to say so—and give us the credit of supporting the party....

We are very willing to bear our portion of the burden, but not the whole.[161]

Being a beacon of correct principles, shedding light upon the electorate, had its disadvantages as well as its advantages.

[158] H. Ex. Doc. No. 41, 19th Cong. 1st S., pp. 5-8.
[159] *Rochester Daily Advertiser,* Jan. 18, 21, 1828.
[160] Cf. Thurlow Weed's experience, *Autobiography,* pp. 39, 90.
[161] Poughkeepsie *Republican Herald,* Mar. 19, 1817.

V

THE HERALD OF A NOISY WORLD

THE *Herald of a noisy world,*
  News from all quarters lumbering at his back.
                      Quoted by FOLLETT.

THE *Printer's Boy will ne'er refuse,*
  To bring you papers fresh with news,
From ev'ry country, ev'ry where,
Whate'er is wonderful and rare,
From Georgia to the northern Maine,
Who fought, who fell and who was slain,
Who nab'd a horse, and who hath stole—
Who broke into or out of gaol.
Beside ten thousand other things,
From blackguards up to dukes and kings.
All marriages we shall relate,
As well as great affairs of state,
In fact our columns shall abound,
With all things rare that can be found.
CARRIER'S ADDRESS, in Cayuga Republican, Jan. 8, 1820.

AT *last the floundering carrier bore*
  The village paper to our door.
Lo! broadening outward as we read,
To warmer zones the horizon spread;
In panoramic length unrolled
We saw the marvels that it told.
Before us passed the painted Creeks,
  And daft McGregor on his raids
  In Costa Rica's everglades.
And up Taygetos winding slow
Rode Ypsilanti's Mainote Greeks,
A Turk's head at each saddle-bow!
Welcome to us its week-old news,
Its corner for the rustic Muse,
  Its monthly gauge of snow and rain,
Its record, mingling in a breath
The wedding bell and dirge of death;
Jest, anecdote, and love-lorn tale,
The latest culprit sent to jail;
Its hue and cry of stolen and lost,
Its vendue sales and goods at cost,
  And traffic calling loud for gain.
                  WHITTIER, "Snow-Bound."

ALTHOUGH essentially a newspaper, the country print of a hundred years ago was much different from that of today. The first observation one is led to make in reading these papers is that they were almost devoid of local news, a fact quite disconcerting to the local historian. Apparently the editor's definition of his function included neither the purveying of neighborhood gossip nor the describing of outstanding happenings in the immediate vicinity. Such efforts as he did make to record local events proved that he was not always well informed. He had no faith in the idea that his readers would pay for information which they could secure by word of mouth from their neighbors.

The newspaper was political, in the broad sense of the word. The affairs of governments, of Congress, and of state and Federal officials were given at length, and wars and elections were staples of the news. This was a time when political concerns were uppermost, and the country paper was its reader's contact with the world outside. This fact must be kept in mind to understand the content and the character of the news columns. Even local elections of political consequence might receive only a subordinate position.[1] Failing his usual supply of what he considered news, the printer would apologize and fill his paper with miscellaneous matter.

In one field, however, that of marriages and deaths, the printer sought to give local news. A considerable list was often found under the head of "Hymeneal," though frequently this section was made up of cullings from the exchanges, far and near. There was no attempt to separate the local events from items of general concern in this department nor from curiosi-

[1] Johnson, C., *History of Erie County*, p. 224, comments upon the uncertainty displayed by the *Buffalo Gazette* as to whether there was an election in Willink and Concord. Cf. Hooker, Richard, *The Story of an Independent Newspaper*, ch. iii, pp. 14-21, for a discussion of the weekly newspaper in 1824, the *Springfield Republican*.

ties of names and circumstances which struck the editor's fancy.[2] In recording deaths, likewise, the printer often failed to distinguish between the obituary notice of an outstanding local citizen and that of a national figure or foreign celebrity.

In reporting marriages and deaths the printer's gullibility or lack of acquaintance with local affairs frequently got him into trouble. Occasionally he had to apologize for an account of a wedding which had not occurred. Then, he would announce his intention to exact vouchers for, or insist upon proof of, the correctness of such items in the future.[3] The *Long Island Star,* referring to the value of its vital statistics, remarked, "emigrants from Long Island in the Western Country look with interest to our marriages and deaths."[4] In the days of restricted communication such reliance upon the newspaper was explainable.

Faulty reporting was also evident in erroneous death notices. The *Onondaga Register* was forced to correct its statements on at least two occasions. It will be recalled that such a circumstance much later elicited the famous remark of Mark Twain, that reports of his death had been "exaggerated." The following shows how easily the printer might be misled and then mislead the public:

> Our last paper, which was published in the absence of the editor, noticed the death of Judge Munro, of Camillus. It is a mistake, although the information was derived from a source, which at the time could not be doubted. We are happy to state that the Judge is in usual good health, and we hope he may yet live many years, and continue to be, as he has been, a blessing to his numerous connexions and friends.[5]

Of some local importance, too, was the business information, prices current, bank-note tables, and marine list. The latter was found, of course, only in towns situated upon some

---

[2] *Ibid.,* pp. 197-198.

[3] For example, Ithaca *Republican Chronicle,* Oct. 12, 1825; Troy *Northern Budget,* Dec. 4, 1821, and Sept. 30, 1823; *Lansingburgh Gazette,* June 24, July 1, 1806; *Saratoga Sentinel,* Sept. 20, 1820; *Plattsburgh Republican,* Sept. 29, Oct. 6, 1821.

[4] Brooklyn *Long Island Star,* Mar. 6, 1816.

[5] *Onondaga Register,* Mar. 4, 1829; also one July 9, 1817.

waterway; the Hudson River sloops, the arrivals on the Erie Canal, and the Delaware and Hudson Canal, and boats on the lakes, touching Oswego, Buffalo, Plattsburgh, or even Ithaca on Cayuga lake, were thus recorded.[6]

During the period under survey there was a noticeable tendency to include more items of local interest, but as late as 1828 a representative paper, the *Onondaga Register,* printed only 102.5 inches of county news in one year, little more than one half of one per cent of its total space.[7] A statistical study has been made of the contents of certain country papers, in which all printed matter has been divided into seven categories. Periodic comparisons of the various type of material have been made, based upon measurement of the space in the newspapers. The results, in percentage of content, are given in Table I, pages 311-313.

Domestic news, originating in or concerned with the United States, reached a maximum for any year in 1828 when the Cooperstown *Freeman's Journal* devoted 23.32 per cent of its space to that category. The minimum of 4.69 per cent appeared in the Hudson *Northern Whig* in 1809, the earliest year taken for comparison. The average was approximately thirteen per cent.

Foreign news received more space than domestic news in 1809, but in 1812, with American war preparations to the fore, it was distinctly subordinated, and remained so in subsequent years. An increase in the amount of foreign news is noted for 1823. This is a category which the modern reader finds hard to understand in a country paper.[8] During the first year of the century proclamations of Napoleon and his generals were given *in extenso* and those of the chancelleries of other powers were frequently printed throughout the period. Matters of little apparent concern for an inland community were

---

[6] *Ithaca Journal,* Oct. 8, 1828; Kingston *Ulster Sentinel,* Oct. 8, 1828. See also Oswego, Buffalo, Black Rock, and Plattsburgh papers.

[7] The percentage is 0.56, advertising being included in the total space. For this reason, news of local affairs was not given a category in the statistical study.

[8] Cf. Johnson, *op. cit.,* pp. 197-198.

copied with great assiduity. An era of European peace was a difficult one for the harassed printer in search of news.

One editor in humorous vein explained his difficulties:

No news! says the printer. No news sure enough reiterates the reader —in truth there is the most "plentiful scarcity of marvelous events," at the present moment, we commonly meet with—all has been said that can be about the crops—about the weather—the earth, the atmosphere, and the ocean—Since Jackson has done fighting the Spaniards—and the Georgians have left off murdering the Indians—since there is not much chance of the sable Haytians getting together by the ears,—since the sea snake has become an old story, the mail and bank robberies are cleverly over; and the Bunker Hill battles are all fought out, there is absolutely nothing on the carpet to make the common people stare! A dish of your common everyday occurrences becomes insufferably insipid, unless served up with battles and murders; outrage and violence, with a dessert of earthquakes, explosions and tornadoes. But since the times are thus, perhaps people will become reconciled, one of these days, with such miserable fare, as health, peace, individual happiness, and national prosperity.[9]

The journalists of the day, in fact, seemed deplorably remiss in getting the news value out of domestic events, yet the bareness of the report sometimes gave it power. What could be more crushing than the deliberate relation of the following:

Northampton, Dec. 3. We hear from Westfield that on Sunday night last, a mill, which was also the residence of a family, was consumed by fire:—What renders this circumstance peculiarly distressing is, a man, his wife and three children perished in the flames.[10]

The editor of the *Onondaga Register* gave many details of the "Great Fire at Mobile," commenting on the number of houses destroyed and the amount of insurance, while in the same issue, he noted in his finest type, a conflagration in his own community, two weeks after the event, in one sentence:

[9] *Onondaga Register,* Oct. 21, 1818. Copied from another paper.
[10] Poughkeepsie *Political Barometer,* Mar. 4, 1806. Another, in New York, read: "The house of Mr. Elizur Hinsdale, of Le Roy, Genesee Co. was consumed by fire on the night of the 23d ult. The wife of Mr. H. and two of his children perished in the flames." *Onondaga Register,* Dec. 5, 1827.

We have omitted to mention that the Store-house of Mr. John Rogers, at Syracuse, was destroyed by fire on the 6th inst. Mr. R.'s loss, we are sorry to add, is very considerable.[11]

This attitude toward local affairs is further emphasized by the tardy inclusion of a local department in country journals. In 1827 the *Cayuga Patriot* was exceptionally progressive, when it announced that "a portion of our paper will, whenever expedient, be devoted to the local concerns and interests of this village." [12] The first regular "local department" of the Cooperstown *Freeman's Journal* made its appearance in 1851, while in the next decade the *Lyons Republican* initiated its "country correspondents," a feature of the country paper familiar to all present day readers.[13]

Sensationalism, so common now, was occasionally displayed, as, for example, when the public mind was agitated over a murder or public execution. The space devoted to the subject, rather than the size of the type, is the criterion. However, in 1806, the Poughkeepsie *Farmer* displayed in three-fourth inch capitals the "Trial of Jesse Wood for the Murder of his Son." The story occupied four of the five columns of the first page, and half of page two.[14] The *Catskill Packet* tried to satiate the public demand with a "List of Horribles," a column and a half of fourteen murders or accidental deaths, with all the harrowing details. These were collected from Ulster County, Poughkeepsie, Vermont, Connecticut, Massachusetts, Dartmouth, N. H., Pittsburgh, and Philadelphia. One which happened "last July" was still news in September.[15]

Another feature, considered indispensable by the country printer, was the inclusion of Government documents. Heading this list was the annual message of the President, which might crowd out all other matter except advertising and on some

[11] *Ibid.,* Nov. 21, 1827.
[12] Auburn *Cayuga Patriot,* Apr. 4, 1827.
[13] Shaw, S. M., *History of Cooperstown.* Chronology. Shaw was then the editor of the paper. Facts in regard to the starting of the "Country Correspondents" by William T. Tinsley, nicknamed "Tinsley's Old Maid Column," submitted by Mr. E. S. Kelley of the *Lyons Republican.*
[14] *Farmer,* Dec. 10, 1806.
[15] *Catskill Packet,* Sept. 3, 1792.

occasions was carried in an "extra." The governor's annual message, too, found its regular place, along with significant executive documents and correspondence. Those who craved political fare considered these morsels of the highest quality. No doubt they were thoroughly digested by the reading public. Mention has already been made of the practice of printing the laws as passed, either by contract or voluntarily, and of the salutary effect of this upon the public.[16] Notable speeches in Congress or the legislature were sometimes given in full, when obtained through the favor of a Congressman or political patron.

This category, as seen in the statistical tabulation, often in the earlier years totaled in the neighborhood of ten per cent of the newspaper's content. The largest amount appeared in the Hudson *Northern Whig* in 1812, when many proclamations and reports of the Government regarding the war were included. This paper, by the way, was a Federalist organ and was critical of the war. There is noticeable, also, a considerable decrease in the percentage in this category for the years 1823 and 1828. By that time many of the papers had been enlarged, and the necessary documentary material encroached less upon their space. Furthermore, as speedy publication of executive messages became the sign of an enterprising newspaper, such documents were frequently circulated in "extras."[17]

While news and documents often reflected the political complexion of the paper, or might be regarded as political events, there is justification for another category, designated as "Political." Partisan controversy, especially on the eve of elections or during campaigns, was liable to monopolize the attention of the newspaper reader. The party organ, carrying on the struggle for its principles, held its columns open for partisan communications and for the fulminations of the party's national and local leaders. Extensive reports and resolutions of political meetings comprised another form of political propaganda.

---

[16] *Supra,* chap. iv.
[17] See *infra,* chap. vii, for reference to enterprise in obtaining the message.

The percentage of such matter might be as high as twenty, but was usually around ten in the earlier years. With the coming of the "era of good feeling," in 1818 and 1823 (years in which there was no national election), there was a considerable decline in the political material (five per cent was the highest, and one paper contained less than one per cent), but the percentage went back to as high as twenty in the election year of 1828.

As to the desirability of a large quantity of controversial matter there were differing opinions. Some of the early pioneer printers felt that they must abstain from partisan propaganda if they were to keep all of their clientele satisfied. A few of them opened their columns to politicians of both parties, the Manlius *Herald of the Times* heading page 2, "Republican Department," and page 3, "Federal Department." [18] The *American Constellation,* of Union, Broome County, gave each of the two parties two columns of the third page, which was captioned "Political Pie." [19] Thus the reader could take his choice of opposing doctrines. The "great press of political matter" and the importance of the approaching election were urged by one printer as justification for this neglect of other departments.[20] "The political campaign being over, we shall resume our usual variety of matter," said another.[21] The *Western Spectator and Anti-Masonic Star,* of Palmyra, discovered that as a party journal it had more space for nonpolitical matter than when it tried to present both sides of public questions.[22] Yet the *Otsego Herald* found that too much partisanship was a drawback.

As experience has taught us that the insertion of violent party productions, to the exclusion of more interesting and useful subjects, has lessened the circulation of the *Herald,* formerly, and as the numbers have constantly increased, since we have adopted a milder regimen, the *Herald*

---

[18] *Herald of the Times,* July 19, 1808.
[19] *American Constellation,* Nov. 22, 1800; *Orange County Patriot,* Dec. 24, 1811, also had "Republican" and "Federal" departments.
[20] Kingston *People's Advocate,* Oct. 13, 1824.
[21] *Onondaga Register,* Nov. 5, 1828.
[22] *Western Spectator and Anti-Masonic Star,* June 14, 1831.

will continue to circulate such information, only, as in our judgment, will promote the general good.[23]

Impinging on the political field was the editorial, which slowly found its place in the country paper. The amount of what might be called editorial material varied with the ability, or originality, of the conductor of the press. Some printers were mechanics rather than writers and rarely ventured an original composition. Others, slowly at first, developed their talent and became able journalists. Many of the former were freely denominated "editors."

The duty of an editor...consists very much in the task of judicious selection; and from the ample materials that are spread before him, he can generally furnish a weekly repast that shall prove acceptable to his readers, even in these peaceful times.[24]

Not only were some printers incapable of editorial writing, but even those disposed to try original composition found that their time was too much occupied with other concerns. Of Benjamin Franklin, with his many-sided interests, it has been said that he rarely found time to "edit or collate the chance medley of stale items which passed for news" in his *Pennsylvania Gazette*.[25] On several occasions printers explained to their readers that they had been unable to give enough attention to the editorial department.[26] Editor Curtis of the *Chautauque Eagle* printed an article by "Camillus" of whose sentiments he did not approve, "but as the Editor will for some time have nearly all of the mechanical work of the office to perform, he cannot say anything that would give rise to a controversy with Camillus."[27]

One resource for the busy printer was to get some sympathetic citizen of the community to wield the pen—usually without remuneration other than the satisfaction of authorship

---

[23] *Otsego Herald,* Sept. 19, 1805.

[24] *Onondaga Register,* Aug. 9, 1826.

[25] Cook, Elizabeth C., in *Cambridge History of American Literature,* I, 115-116.

[26] Cooperstown *Impartial Observer,* Apr. 1, 1809; *Catskill Recorder,* May 14, 1804.

[27] Mayville *Chautauque Eagle,* Aug. 24, 1819.

—and thus anonymously to fill the editorial column. In his prospectus for the *Recorder* Mackay Croswell, of Catskill, noted that he had "received promises of assistance from several gentlemen in this village." [28] The *Cayuga Republican*, whose printer, Thomas M. Skinner, was no writer, obtained "the assistance of a gentleman whose leisure and talents, we doubt not, will enable him to furnish something in addition to the usual variety of our columns." [29] These anonymous contributors were often the subject of dispute, when rival editors charged the paper with being the mere mouthpiece of a politician, the "real editor." So John C. Spencer was said to be the editor of the *Ontario Messenger* and the *Ontario Freeman*, Peter B. Porter of the *Black Rock Beacon*, "Mr. H. [olley]" of the Canandaigua *Western Repository*, and James Tallmadge of the *Dutchess Observer;* but all of these connections were emphatically denied.[30] Such denials, apparently, were not believed. The principal argument usually was that the poor printers were incapable of such literary efforts, and this led to wholly reckless allegations as to the identity of the writer.

Yet successful printers were frequently men of literary competence. The New York *Courier and Enquirer* gave a favorable, or at least charitable, view:

Country Editors in our State are generally printers by occupation— the slender remuneration they receive where every county has at least two weekly papers, will not warrant the employment of established and cultivated talent. Nevertheless the country Editor who puts forth no pretensions, and claims no exclusive merit or influence, is by no means deficient in intelligence, discretion and useful talent. There are many of them placed by capricious fortune in humble situations, who possess vigorous intellect, capacious minds, taste and intelligence. If, therefore,

[28] *Catskill Recorder,* May 14, 1804.

[29] Auburn *Cayuga Republican,* July 16, 1828. See also the amusing incident related by Beman Brockway, *Fifty Years in Journalism,* pp. 25-27, of his purchase of the *Oswego Palladium* in 1845. George H. McWhorter, collector of the customs house, had edited the paper for fifteen years for Mr. Carpenter, its publisher, and presumed that he would continue to do so under its new owner. He almost felt a proprietary right, which embarrassed the young journalist.

[30] Rochester *Telegraph,* May 27, June 3, 1823; *Black Rock Beacon,* Apr. 17, 1823; Canandaigua *Western Repository,* Oct. 25, 1803; Poughkeepsie *Dutchess Observer,* Sept. 25, 1816.

we are not always presented with the evidence of these acquirements, the fruits of these native plants, in every country newspaper we open, let us remember that the country editor in many instances, not only selects and culls the news and important items from other journals, but is frequently under the necessity of combining in his own person the offices of editor, compositor, pressman, and sometimes carrier of his own paper, and is happy to receive in payment, whatever his patrons may have to offer, in the way of indispensable objects of life.[31]

The predicament of the printer was more facetiously put by another as follows:

A country editor is one who reads newspapers, selects miscellany, writes articles on all subjects, sets type, reads proof, works at press, folds papers and sometimes carries them, prints jobs, runs on errands, cuts and saws wood, works in the garden, talks to all his patrons who call, patiently receives blame for a thousand things that never were and never can be done, gets little money, has scarce time or materials to satisfy his hunger or enjoy the quiet of "nature's grand restorer," and esteems himself peculiarly happy, if he is not assaulted and battered by some unprincipled demagogue.[32]

The printer's debut as an editor was likely to be in the form of brief political comment, or in controversy with his rivals. He was fortunate if he did not have one or more brother editors hunting his literary scalp, and he seldom refrained from retaliating. Some of these recriminations were harmless sparrings, while others resulted in the litigation mentioned above. The chief wonder is that the public tolerated, if it did not enjoy, so much in the way of personalities. Isaac Mitchell, of the Poughkeepsie *Political Barometer,* who was not a practical printer, in one number took flings at Cheetham, of the *American Citizen,* Charles Holt, of the Hudson *Bee,* Solomon Southwick, of Albany, Thomas Walker, of Utica, and copied an attack on David Holt, of the Herkimer *Monitor.* Then, since he must be away for a time, he suggested to "adversary editors and writers, the propriety of a truce, until he returns to his post, of which they shall have due notice." [33]

[31] Quoted by Rochester *Anti-Masonic Enquirer,* Dec. 21, 1830.

[32] Cooperstown *Freeman's Journal,* May 10, 1830, quoting the editor of the Williamstown *Advocate.*

[33] *Political Barometer,* Dec. 17, 1805.

Two weeks later he gave notice "to friends and foes" that he had returned sooner than he had expected.[34] Perhaps the truce had not been observed by all parties.

Francis Adancourt, of the Troy *Farmer's Register*, complained that original articles of his were copied in the *National Intelligencer* and the *Pittsfield Sun* without credit being given to him.[35] His spirited editorials were both well written and voluminous. Several country editors could be named whose work would stand comparison with the best of that time. William Williams, of Utica, well known for his mastery of the mechanical side of the art and his training of others, covered a wide range in his choice of subjects. He wrote on the colonization of free blacks in Haiti, upon the utility of railroads, and upon canal tolls.[36] At the same time he did not keep out of controversy.

David Denniston, of the Newburgh *Mirror* and *Rights of Man*, achieved notoriety for his radical ideas on both religion and politics. A disciple of Tom Paine and an ardent Republican, he advanced to the editorship of the *American Citizen*, and its semi-weekly, the *Republican Watch Tower*, in New York City, a position which he held until his death in 1803.[37] Elijah J. Roberts, of the Kingston *Craftsman*, became associated with M. M. Noah on the *National Advocate* in the metropolis, while William L. Stone, a most trenchant partisan as well as a cultured man and a scholar, found an outlet for his many talents on the *Commercial Advertiser*.[38] It is hardly necessary in this connection to suggest the breadth of editorial view developed by Jesse Buel, a champion of improved agriculture, and Luther Tucker, later associated with him; by Thurlow Weed, whose devious political activity has served to eclipse his broad sympathies and sensible comment; and by

[34] *Ibid.,* Dec. 31, 1805.

[35] *Farmer's Register,* Apr. 4, 18, 1815. Several mistakes in giving credit for copied material were noted in *Ontario Repository,* July 30, 1822.

[36] Williams, J. C., *An Oneida County Printer,* pp. 110-111.

[37] Ruttenber, E. M., *History of Orange County,* p. 193. See *Rights of Man,* Sept. 12, 1803, for Denniston's refusal to declare his belief in a supreme being, in being sworn before the Court of Common Pleas.

[38] Kingston *People's Advocate,* Oct. 13, 1824.

Edwin Croswell, of the *Argus,* long considered a Nestor of the New York press.[39]

The paid editor, usually a lawyer hired for the purpose, began to replace the printer-editor in the latter period of this study. It was alleged in 1825, that the Poughkeepsie *Republican Telegraph* had imported its editor from Hartford, "to scribble for it at a salary of *eight hundred* dollars a year." [40] Orville L. Holley was hired in 1823 to edit the new semiweekly *Troy Sentinel.* A year later he "voluntarily relinquished the fixed stipend upon which he first engaged to conduct it, and has become interested in its profits." [41] J. T. Buckingham, the Boston editor, while speaking in 1848 before the Franklin Typographical Society in that city, referred to this "innovation" of hiring an editor as having been started in 1811 by the *Massachusetts Mercury.* When he was young, he said, it was a disgrace for a printer not to edit his own paper. At this time (1848) he believed that he was the "only individual living in Boston, if not in the Commonwealth, who unites the printer and editor in one man." [42]

Such a change was quite naturally resented by printereditors. Isaac Riggs gloried in the fact that he was a "typesetter," when one of his contemporaries used the term to reproach him. He enumerated the great editors of the days of his apprenticeship, who were also "typesetters." Then he spoke of the change:

...the *gentlemen* editors (not type setters) who conduct many of the public Journals of this time, viz. the editor of the National Advocate is not a *typesetter*—the editor of The American, I believe, is a *lawyer*—the editor of the (Ulster Co.) Craftsman is a *lawyer*—the late editor of the (Hudson) Bee was a *typesetter,* but for being independent, he has been obliged to abandon his establishment, and the paper

[39] These and many other outstanding editors of the state in the period about 1830 (John H. Prentiss, U. F. Doubleday, A. G. Dauby, A. C. Flagg, V. W. Smith, Ebenezer Mack, Henry C. Frisbee, and Frederick Follett), are reviewed in an appreciative chapter in Brockway, Beman, *Fifty Years in Journalism,* pp. 418-422.

[40] Poughkeepsie *Dutchess Observer,* Jan. 12, 1825.

[41] *Troy Sentinel,* July 15, 1823; July 13, 1824.

[42] Stewart, *Documentary History of Early Organizations of Printers,* p. 912 n.

is now, I believe, edited by a *lawyer*—the Argus is edited by one lawyer, and not a *typesetter*—the editor of the Northern Budget is a lawyer—the Sandy Hill Times is edited by a *lawyer*—the editor of the Geneva Palladium, I believe, is a lawyer. I might add more but enough is shown to satisfy the veriest skeptic who they are that give tone to public sentiment.[43]

Most printers recognized their obligation to supply miscellaneous literary matter for their readers. Since the country paper was virtually the only literature in many homes, such content, indeed, was essential. The prospectus of a new paper, usually long and effusive with protestations of impartiality, justice, and good will, held out the promise of a rich literary fare. When it changed its form, the Hudson *Balance* outlined its new plan. "The last page of each number will be devoted to literary and miscellaneous matter. It will be reserved for the favors of our correspondents, either in verse or prose; and deficiencies, when any happen, will generally be supplied by selections from new and approved works." [44]

The "Poet's Corner," "Bower," or "The Muse," as it was variously styled, was a common feature, and might be filled with effusions of local versifiers and wits, with doggerel from the pen of the editor, or with selections from Byron, Thomas More, or Mrs. Hemans. Two editors of country papers, William Ray and Selleck Osborn, became well known as poets, were widely copied by their contemporaries, and published collections of their verses.[45] As might be expected, the quality of the verses in the newspaper was very uneven.

Another opportunity for budding poets was the annual Carrier's (or Post Boy's) Address, which was a feature of the first issue of the new year. In addition to florid and sentimental couplets suitable to the season, there were often clever satirical

---

[43] Schenectady *Cabinet,* Mar. 28, 1821. Significant, too, was an advertisement of "a gentleman, at present disengaged, (formerly editor of a Public Paper) [who] wishes to obtain a similar situation."—*Ithaca Journal,* Oct. 13, 1824.

[44] Hudson *Balance,* Jan. 5, 1808.

[45] Ray, William, *Poems,* Auburn (1821), Troy (1826); Osborn, Selleck, *Poems,* Boston (1823). See the Appendix for data on the lives of these. James G. Brooks, a poet under the pseudonym of "Florio," was also a country editor for a short time.

jibes on political affairs and contemporary events, and they were worth reading for these thrusts, rather than for any poetic quality.[46] When the editor or his friends felt unequal to the task of such composition, a premium was offered in the hope of securing an appropriate poem. One printer offered a volume, not exceeding five dollars in value, from his bookstore as a prize for the best New Year's Address submitted by one of his subscribers.[47]

Moral essays, didactic anecdotes, and curiosities of literature and science were freely translated to the paper from exchanges, books, and even from encyclopedias. Narratives of considerable length might be continued in successive issues. Isaac Mitchell, editor of the *Political Barometer,* was the author of a romance entitled, "Alonzo and Melissa," a story which ran through several numbers of that paper, was later published in book form, and which gave him some reputation as a writer.[48] The counterpart of the modern "woman's page" is discernible in these selections, and the printer did not disdain a direct appeal to female patronage. The prospectus of the *Balance,* for example, promised to present "strictures on female education and manners: the virtues and foibles of women will occasionally be pointed out, and their character scanned with a *brother's* eye." [49]

Religious matter comes under this same category, but in most newspapers it was subordinate to more general ethical disquisitions or was omitted as more suitable for the denominational periodical.[50] One printer who was compelled to include much religious material on account of his obligation to his financial backers, discovered that his subscribers complained and stopped subscribing. This particular brand of preaching,

[46] A collection of the best of these addresses would be a valuable commentary on the times.

[47] Canandaigua *Ontario Repository,* Dec. 15, 1824.

[48] Poughkeepsie *Political Barometer,* June 5-Oct. 30, 1804; later published as *The Asylum; or, Alonzo and Melissa; an American Tale Founded on Fact,* by I. Mitchell, Poughkeepsie (1811). See the letter by Professor Edward Bliss Reed in New York *Nation,* Feb. 25, 1909.

[49] Hudson *Balance and Columbian Repository,* Jan. 5, 1802.

[50] *Supra,* chap. iii.

at least, seemed inappropriate in the columns of a country paper.[51]

Agricultural information was another field which the editor might emphasize with the hope of appealing to his predominantly farming clientele.[52] Many country papers made a pretense of serving the interests of the farmer—the *Farmer's Gazette* (1816-1817) and *Farmer's Advocate* (1820-1821), of Bath; the *Saratoga Farmer* (1820-1821), of Ballston Spa; the *Orange Farmer* (1820-1825), of Goshen; the *Madison Farmer* (1828-1829), of Hamilton; the *Farmer's Monitor* (1805-1807) and the *Republican Farmer's Free Press* (1830-1832), of Herkimer; the *Farmer's Journal* (1812-1813), of Homer; the *Long Island Farmer* (1821-1826), of Jamaica; the *Farmer's Register* (1792-1793), of Kingston; the *Farmer's Oracle* (1796-1798) and *Farmer's Register* (1803-1832), of Lansingburgh and Troy; the *Republican Agriculturist* (1818-1820), of Norwich; the *Genesee Farmer* (1817-1824), of Moscow; the *American Farmer* (1803-1814), of Owego; the *Western Farmer* (1821-1822), of Palmyra; the *Country Journal* (1785-1789), the *American Farmer* (1798-1800), and the *Farmer* (1806-1807), of Poughkeepsie; the Waterford *Agriculturist* (1820-1821); and the *Seneca Farmer* (1823-1831), of Waterloo.

This list is a formidable one, but few of the papers justified their names. The agricultural journal was a later venture, in which Jesse Buel and Luther Tucker were pioneers.[53] Agricultural information, however, was obtained for the miscellany in several ways. The editor of the *Oswego Palladium* made his own observations.

The Season.—Having occasion to ride about the country, a few days since, we took pains to examine the fields near the road, to learn the

---

[51] See case of Samuel A. Seabury, *infra,* chap. vi; quotation from the *Suffolk County Recorder.*

[52] One printer in 1797 estimated that 700 of his 1,000 subscribers were farmers—from whom he sought "country produce" in payment. *Poughkeepsie Journal,* Sept. 12, 1797.

[53] Rochester *Genesee Farmer* (1831-1839), Luther Tucker's journal, was united with Buel's *Cultivator* at Albany in 1839. Solomon Southwick's *Plough Boy,* Albany (1819-1823) by "Henry Homespun," was an earlier attempt.

agricultural prospects of the farmer. From what was discernible, we have the pleasure to state, that in no season do we recollect to have seen all kinds of vegetables look so remarkably fine as the present. English grain is very good; Indian corn never promised a more abundant harvest; potatoes, though fine, are not quite as large as expected.[54]

Agricultural societies were forming in many communities, and the proceedings of their meetings were frequently given in full in the newspaper. This was a community affair over which the editors did not lock horns. "With the aid of Mr. Lappon, Editor of the *Freeman's Journal*," wrote a rival editor in Cooperstown, "we are enabled to present our readers with the outlines of the proceedings of our second annual cattle show." [55]

Literary and miscellaneous magazine material in quantitive measurement ranged from 16 per cent in some papers to less than 3 per cent in others. Except for the early years of the nineteenth century, the mean seems to have been around 9 or 10 per cent. Later, enlarged sheets with smaller type were able to carry more material on a greater variety of themes without a pronounced change in the percentage. The large percentage in the Cazenovia *Pilot* in 1809 might have been due more to the scarcity of other matter than to literary inclination, for its printer, Oran E. Baker, was not a writer—which was evident from the paucity of editorials. Yet those printers who possessed a talent for original composition might for that very reason diminish their miscellany—casting aside the scissors for the pen.

Advertising as a source of the printer's income has been discussed in Chapter III. As an important part of the newspaper's content, it deserves further attention. Like Mr. Dooley, who resented the encroachment of reading matter upon the space of his favorite magazine advertisements, the reader of a century ago no doubt gave a thorough perusal to the commercial notices in his *Gazette*. To the antiquarian and student of today they are no less interesting. In their quaint

---

[54] *Oswego Palladium*, Aug. 17, 1820.
[55] *Otsego Herald*, Oct. 12, 1808.

appeals, often rich in human interest, may be found much valuable data for the social history of the community. The variety of these advertisements, as well as the flavor of their content, is suggested by the sprightly verses of William Ray, composed for a rhymed prospectus.

Retailers here may advertise
Their goods, and wares, and merchandize,
With—'Just receiv'd, and now for sale,
'By piece, by pattern, yard, or nail,
'Fresh goods, of latest importation,
'From ev'ry kingdom, port, and nation—
'Brandy, tobacco, rum, and wine,—
'Tea, sugar, broadcloths, superfine—
'Coffee, and pepper, and molasses,
'Mugs, pitchers, teapots, looking glasses—
'Callicoes, muslins, ladies' feathers,
'For them to fly with, thro' all weathers;
'Shawls, flannels, ribbons, tapes, and laces,
'And veils to cloud their pretty faces;
'Horse whips, for such as want them most,
'(And such as want them, what a host!)
'All which we paid for, in our notes,
'And offer cheap, for corn and oats—
'Wheat, rye, or barley, butter, cheese,
'Credit, or money, if you please,
'Though specie scarcer is, by far,
'Than tories were in time of war.'
Lawyers and sheriffs, often troublish,
Fi, Fa's and mortgages may publish,
And sell the debtors goods and chattels,
For costs and int'rest—toys and rattles;
And when all other sources fail,
Pack off his body to a jail;
Although they sometimes, paring thin,
The carcase leave, but take the skin.

To escape from too much work or flogging,
Should your apprentices be jogging;
Should horses, cattle, sheep, or swine,
Half starv'd at home, walk out to dine—
(Meeting some unforeseen disaster,
Never return to "serve their master;")

Here you may spread the news around,
And find them—landed in a pound.
Or should your kind and loving spouse,
Desert your bed, and board, and house
(For naught on earth, as you can tell,
But being lov'd by you too well)—
Ramble and tattle, scold and fret,
And run you, head and ears, in debt;
Here you may all your reasons muster,
And warn the public not to trust her,
Who basely has your head cornuted,
On pain of being prosecuted.
Here, too, the woman may defend
Her character, from head to end,
And swear by all that's great and good,
No lady ever since the flood,
Not even Bonaparte's old queen,
Was so abus'd as she has been;
Whose very life was rendered risky,
By that nefarious son of—whiskey;
While neighbors prove to one another
That one's as much to blame as t'other.[56]

As is indicated in Chapter IV, legal notices might form a large part of the advertising space, depending, of course, upon the character of the printer's political connections and the abundance or scarcity of his commercial matter. In a new venture business notices might be extremely scarce. In quantity, as shown by Table I, pages 311-313, advertising frequently occupied one-half the total space; and there were issues which had three out of four pages thus set up.[57] In the several years taken for analysis, it will be noted that there was less variation in this category than in others. The first and last pages were preferred for the advertising matter, and whenever possible advertisements were allowed to stand in type from week to week. The printer's file of a paper, where it has been preserved, shows at times his notations as to the length of time

[56] Olean *Hamilton Recorder,* June 11, 1819, originally in *Onondaga Gazette* (1816), Ray's *Poems* (1821), pp. 89-95.
[57] *Plattsburgh Republican,* Nov. 27, 1819. A previous issue, May 8, 1819, apologized for so much space being devoted to advertising.

the notices were to run, when they were to be taken out, and, perhaps, when paid for. The English observer, so frequently quoted above, noted the practice of advertisers with his usual acidity.

Most persons dealing largely in advertising, agree with the Editor for so much by the year; hence it is no uncommon thing to find some of these people's advertisements standing in type from one end of the year to the other, which is a saving of time to the compositor. Some of the advertisements—in order probably, to attract more notice—are placed upside down, while others are placed lengthwise in the columns; and in order to make them look as imposing as possible, small wood engravings, wretchedly executed, of men, dogs, cattle, houses, &c., are inserted wherever there seems a chance of their not being notoriously out of place.[58]

A full discussion of newspaper advertising of this period is beyond the scope of this work, but a few comments may serve to indicate its chief characteristics. As a rule advertisements were column width, but two columns and larger advertisements were not unusual.[59] In the early days these would have been a heavy tax upon the printer's space. The forms of the notices did not vary greatly, being limited by the printer's supply of type. Legal notices, of course, were set solid, and commercial ones frequently followed suit, with only a single line of larger, or bolder, face at the top. Any variety had to be in content, rather than in form. A few rude wood cuts of hats, ships, carriages, and other significant symbols (the runaway boy, and the absconding wife, for example), were set in the corners of these squares. As such cuts became more numerous the general effect was as monotonous as that of the matter set in solid type. Yet every advertiser felt himself slighted if such a display was not accorded his notice. By 1825 printers began to complain of the larger cuts. The printer of the *Troy Sentinel*, following the cue of a New York paper, resolved to enforce a rule for smaller cuts, and explained his reasons.

[58] *Penny Magazine*, (1841), X, 244.
[59] A quarter-page advertisement, with a cut of a boat "CHEAP" four inches high, appeared in the Schenectady *Cabinet*, Feb. 11, 1818.

It is obvious, upon a moment's reflection, [he wrote] that the advantage of a cut, in the columns of a newspaper, depends not on the absolute, but on the relative size of it; and therefore, a small cut is as conspicuous, where all the cuts are small, as a large one, where all are large. Besides—large cuts are a serious inconvenience in the press, from the difficulty in inking and working them neatly; and on that account, as well as on account of their undue size, they injure the mechanical beauty of the paper.... The small hat and the small steamboat are as effectual, as signals to the eye, as the large ones, and the exclusion of the latter would give us room for several advertisements.[60]

Later in this period, when cuts were more easily obtained, papers were less likely to be particular in this regard.

One might suppose that the notices of merchants, manufacturers, and small tradesmen would supply the bulk of the advertising; but in this respect the early newspapers differed from those of today. The use of much space to list a great variety of wares had not become a common practice. The advertiser was often content to suggest the nature of his business, the quality of his merchandise, and to note plainly the location of his store or shop. In the *Troy Budget* an entire section was eventually devoted to business "cards," a kind of classified directory of business men, which justified its subtitle, *City Register*.[61] Personals, casual wants, and offers for sale vied for space with the regular advertisements. Many notices of occupations and trades which have now disappeared form an interesting commentary on the times. The hatter, cooper, miller, tailor, shoemaker, blacksmith, and carriagemaker were frequent advertisers. Lists or descriptions of commodities, too, give an idea of the commercial life as well as the material comforts of the country population. The exotic and unusual make the most prosaic description of these advertising pages appear like exaggeration and distortion; yet in dealing with the art which achieves its ends by its efforts to attract attention, a recital of unusual practices is not out of place.

The various kinds of advertising, some now obsolete, and

---

[60] *Troy Sentinel,* June 14, 1825. In his next volume the printer was successful in excluding the larger cuts.

[61] *Troy Budget and City Register,* Jan. 3, 1826.

the efforts to be unique, are of interest today. Lotteries were then prominent, and were frequently held for the benefit of colleges and charitable institutions. The "Union College Lottery," the "Medical Science Lottery," and the "New Jersey College Lottery," are examples. The lottery office might be named a "Temple of Fortune," and the printer was often glad to note himself as an agent. A maiden with an overflowing cornucopia was sometimes the symbol for the cut illustrating this notice, although a classical temple was also used. The patent medicine advertisement had its inducements for the country printer then as today, and the claims and testimonials for "remedies" and "cures" have a modern ring.[62]

Numerous "personals" gave spice to the sheet not always found in the news columns. The runaway apprentice was described in far-from-flattering adjectives. One apprentice who was thus advertised retaliated, perhaps with the connivance of the printer, by announcing that his erstwhile "boss" had lost his knowledge of his trade, and by soliciting the public's favor for himself.[63] Of a like sort, unfamiliar to us today, were the warnings concerning runaway slaves and absconding wives. Offers of negroes for sale, and a "want ad" to purchase were found in the same issue in 1809.[64]

FOR SALE. About three years' time of a smart *Negro Wench, 24 years* old. She is offered for sale for no other reason than having a child. Enquire at this office.[65]

This was revolting to some, and a good Quaker protested as early as 1795.

Friend Power. As (contrary to thy wishes, I hope) thy paper is obliged to be the channel through which those unfeeling mortals dare advertise their fellow beings for sale,—(and mark, "for no fault,") and when done, withhold their names and hide behind "Enquire of

---

[62] See Jones, Pomroy, *Annals of Oneida County,* p. 522, for the patent medicine activities of Obadiah Ballou in the Utica area.

[63] Newburgh *Political Index,* Aug. 13, 1811.

[64] Hudson *Northern Whig,* Jan. 24, 1809.

[65] *Ibid.*

the Printer," willing I suppose to be known only to their brethren of like principles who are willing to traffic in human flesh—Thou art desired to give the following [argument not given here] place in thy journal, and oblige.   *A Correspondent, Friend & Customer.*[66]

In beginning the *Suffolk County Herald* at Sag Harbor, Selleck Osborn showed a similar distaste. In discussing the heading of his paper, he wrote:

He might also have quoted some very quaint motto, from Shakespere, or Milton, from Cicero, Junius, or Washington: but he observed a newspaper some time ago, with a dashing motto concerning *freedom,* and the *rights of man* (which are subjects too serious for burlesque) while the first words in the very first column were as follows: *"For Sale, a strong, healthy, negro woman in the prime of life, with a pair of infant twin children; to be sold in one lot or either of them separately, at the option of the purchaser or purchasers. Enquire of the Printer."* This was enough to destroy the Editor's relish for mottos.[67]

The usual advertisement giving warning of a runaway wife was occasionally varied by the wife's advertising the husband; or by one individual's frankly stating that the woman, whom he named as passing herself as his wife, had never been lawfully married to him.[68] At last one chivalrous editor resented the whole system and refused to print the notice of an aggrieved husband.

We received by Monday's mail, a request from a man in New Paltz to publish his runaway wife. For the honour of that good old town, we committed it to the flames. Our gallantry may, perhaps, carry us too far, but, really, we are of the opinion that in nine cases out of ten, the blame ought to be laid at the door of the lord instead of the lady. We are convinced, moreover, that the women of New Paltz love their husbands too well, to desert them "without just cause." [69]

[66] *Poughkeepsie Journal,* Sept. 23, 1795. Nicholas Power was the printer.
[67] Quoted from *Suffolk County Herald* in Poughkeepsie *Political Barometer,* Aug. 5, 1802.
[68] Cooperstown *Freeman's Journal,* May 1, 8, 1826; Schenectady *Cabinet,* Jan. 13, 1813.
[69] Kingston *Ulster Sentinel,* June 2, 1826. As a variation, one lonesome swain inserted his notice for "A Wife Wanted," and gave his specifications.

Similarly interesting are the advertisements for services, or offering services. A school teacher offered his services and explained that he could "teach the higher branches of education, including the French language." [70] Indicative of the manners and customs of the time were those headed, "Wet Nurse Wanted," with the details of the employment, and a demand for "a woman of good reputation." [71] A barber's notice began, *"I'll Shave You Directly. Look Here!!"* [72] Another referred to his establishment in the grandiose terms of a "Proclamation" as his "Ducal Palace." [73]

Another type of notice was that found most frequently in the town of Poughkeepsie. Here "Stands for Horses" was carried as a supplement to the *Poughkeepsie Journal*. A rude cut of a stallion with the name, for example, "Real Club," "Sourkrout," or "Young Cub," was a feature of these notices, the "extra" at one time carrying as many as thirteen. It was a seasonal affair, the supplement being continued for but eight weeks. [74]

In fact, to quote again from our English critic,

...everyone that has got anything, no matter what, to trade in, notifies (to make use of an Americanism) the public thereof through the columns of the newspaper. The parties advertising are rarely satisfied with telling their tale in a simple and straightforward way, but appear to consider it necessary to puff egregiously, and to make use of bombast and rhodomontade upon the most ordinary occasions. Should there happen to be two or three small stores kept in the neighborhood, the rival storekeepers are continually advertising goods that they have (or profess to have) from some distant city or place of import, or else informing their customers and others that they are in want of oats, flour, wool, butter, boards, poultry, &c. The first in the field is sure to be outdone by the second, and the second by the third, for if one advertise a hundred pieces of Manchester goods as just received, his neighbor next week will advertise the arrival of a thousand pieces at his store, while a third party will follow at the next opportunity, and probably assert

[70] Kingston *Craftsman*, Jan. 2, 1822.
[71] Kingston *Plebeian*, Nov. 15, 1805; Feb. 21, 1806; *Manlius Times*, May 15, 1810.
[72] Newburgh *Political Index*, Mar. 5, 1822.
[73] Hudson *Northern Whig*, Jan. 11, 1810.
[74] *Poughkeepsie Journal*, Mar. 5, 1799; Extras Mar. 19 and May 7, 1799.

that he has received one hundred thousand pieces, though in fact not one of the whole triumvirate ever had fifty pieces in his store at one time.[75]

Thus the variety, as well as the use for which the advertisement was employed, present a constant fascination. The creditor advertised for his debtors to pay him. There were no professional advertising men in those days, nor had "psychology" been invented, yet Yankee ingenuity sometimes found vent in such novelties as the following:

THE WAR. All persons indebted to the subscriber, are requested to run away, enlist in the army, take the benefit of the insolvent act, pay their debts by the fifteenth of February next, or receive a visit from the *Constable!* G. Needham.[76]

One advertiser, probably in need of cash, fell into the vernacular and asked the most natural question in large type, "WHO WANTS A WAGGON." [77] Sometimes, too, political opinions got into the notice, as in the case of the following:

Reuben Morton, jr. Caulker. Informs the public, friends in particular, that since the mysterious, unexampled, incomprehensible, philosophical scheme, the *Embargo,* is partially raised, his employers may be accommodated with his work, with fidelity and dispatch, and the smallest favor gratefully acknowledged. N.B. Wanted, the oil of Washington's administration, it being a sovereign antidote against rust accumulating on mechanic's tools.[78]

The printer himself often made considerable contributions to his advertising columns. His business concerns, agencies, books for sales, duns to debtors, and appeals for help or commodities might round out the supply of notices in time of deficiency, or form a surfeit of unprofitable advertising. Not all such insertions were concerned with printing and bookselling, however, and many an interesting fact has come to

[75] *Penny Magazine* (1841), X, 243-244. The American penchant for exaggeration and bombast, noted here, was mentioned by other English travelers. See Nevins, Allan, ed., *American Social History as Recorded by British Travellers* (1923).

[76] *Onondaga Register,* Feb. 22, 1815.

[77] *Troy Gazette,* Dec. 14, 1805.

[78] Hudson *Northern Whig,* Mar. 7, 1809.

light through his ready recourse to advertisement. Elihu Phinney little anticipated the interest of posterity in an amusing incident in his early career which he frankly described in the following notice:

Two small shoats a sow and a Barrow came to the door of the subscriber some time the fore part of this Summer, in a starving condition, the sow has lately had a litter of pigs since which they have been fed.— The owner is desired to prove property, pay charges and take them away. Canaan, September 18, 1794.   *E. Phinney.*[79]

Thus it is not hard to understand why the advertisements of these country newspapers—with their crop of quaint and informing personals, their light upon social and business customs, their directness, and their variety—have become a mine of information for historian and antiquarian. Through them pulsed the activities of growing communities, and in them there is a reality which cannot be concealed by crude cuts and blurred print on yellowed paper.

The news, or "intelligence," with which the readers of a country journal were regaled, was generally quite "stale"; nor was it likely to be accurate. There was no system of news-gathering for the country printer, and he had to be content with items found in exchanges or obtained through travelers, acquaintances, and chance correspondence. It was desirable for the printer to receive regularly a newspaper from the center of government, or from Philadelphia, New York, Albany, or Boston; the *National Intelligencer, Aurora, Evening Post, Argus,* and *Columbian* were frequently quoted. These papers he hoped to secure in return for his own sheet or with a payment of the difference in their subscription rates. He would send his paper to a city editor with the request, "Please to exchange." The *Orange County Patriot* protested the remissness of the city editors in responding, stating that, "It is well known to the readers of newspapers, that the publishers derive their news principally from other papers with which they exchange."[80] A Schenectady printer wrote on a copy sent to the

[79] Canaan *Columbian Mercury,* Oct. 1, 1794.
[80] Goshen *Orange County Patriot,* June 11, 1827.

Independent Chronicle of Boston, "Be so good as to send yours[;] at least [the] evening [of] your election." [81] Mackay Croswell, of Catskill, renewing his publication after a brief suspension, apologized for the paucity of matter in his first issue. "It must, however, appear this week under some disadvantages, as the suspension of its publication has broken the communication with other presses in different parts of the union, which divests it of a regular source of information." [82]

The variety of references to other newspapers is no criterion of the printer's exchange list, for he often recopied the second-hand material in other papers. Thus, a reference to the Paris *Moniteur,* or to London, Liverpool, and Edinburgh papers meant no such wealth of reading matter in the country printing office. The quantity of copied matter in a given paper, however, is significant, and such a category, therefore, has been included in our statistical tabulation. No very comprehensive generalization can be made from this data, though it shows that from one-fifth to one-fourth of the total space in the country papers was filled with material from other periodicals. Since advertising is excluded from this category, perhaps 40 or 50 per cent of the reading matter was taken from other papers. This is a conservative estimate, indeed, for credit was not always given when it was due.

This reliance upon secondhand information did not insure a high degree of accuracy, a fact which was recognized by some printers, who tried to supplement their exchanges with more detailed information taken from private letters and from accounts furnished by respectable travelers. None of these sources was reliable.

With respect to the extracts of letters, not one in ten is true. The printer of a daily paper endeavors to produce the earliest news. The multiplication of business frequently leaves no time to reflect upon the improbability of the information, or to compare it with other accounts, or dates. Besides, this precious news is fabricated to answer party pur-

---

[81] Schenectady *Western Budget,* Jan. 30, 1810, copy of the American Antiquarian Society. Many "exchanges" are in this collection, the nucleus being those sent to Isaiah Thomas for his *Massachusetts Spy.*
[82] Catskill *Packet,* Mar. 9, 1799.

poses, and it must find admission, at all events. But this is nothing compared with those printers, who make news in their closets.[83]

This lament of a pioneer printer is reinforced by the complaint of a neighbor as to spurious accounts of foreign events which he had to correct.

Some mischievous Captains of vessels and passengers, have lately been extremely fond of hoaxing the coffee-house loungers in the seaports —palming upon them news which never existed; metamorphosing trifling skirmishes into splendid victories, and transforming the capturing of an outpost into the destruction of an army! In consequence of which, it is generally several mails after news arrives, before we obtain correct intelligence.

As we always insert foreign accounts, *as they are*, we are not responsible for their correctness.[84]

An example of this kind of hoax was the startling story which appeared in a Palmyra paper, October 3, 1821:

The King of England SHOT!! A handbill has been politely furnished us, dated Manlius, Sept. 26th, which says that "a gentleman in this morning's stage, direct from New York, states that just before he left that place, a news boat came up from the Hook with intelligence from a vessel direct from Liverpool, that George IV WAS SHOT IN THE CITY OF DUBLIN, BY AN IRISH GENTLEMAN.[85]

The editor then commented at length upon the wrongs of Ireland, the treatment of Queen Caroline, the fate of monarchs (including Bonaparte), and the succession of the Duke of York. The following week he was unable to add anything to the report. In the issue of October 17, however, he quoted the New York *Statesman* to the effect that the report was a hoax, "manufactured at some place on this side of Sandy Hook. The last advices from Ireland left his majesty in good health and spirits, busily engaged in holding levees, and drinking bumpers of whiskey punch." [86]

---

[83] *Aurora Gazette,* July 17, 1805.

[84] Canandaigua *Ontario Repository,* Oct. 10, 1809. In the local field, too, there were hoaxes upon the printer. The *Auburn Gazette,* Aug. 12, 1818, corrected such a deception as to a murder in the town of Junius, resenting it with some warmth.

[85] Palmyra *Western Farmer,* Oct. 3, 1821.

[86] *Ibid.* and Oct. 10, 17, 1821.

Foreign news, too, was bound to be extremely "cold" by the time it got into the country paper. In 1792 it required at least two months for Paris dispatches to get to points on the Hudson.[87] The trial of Louis XVI, a Paris event dated December 26, 1792, was fresh news the following March 18 in the Catskill paper.[88] In this case it took eighty-nine days, or nearly three months. Accounts of English events, of course, were not so long delayed; a swift trip of thirty days from Bristol in 1803 brought London news which was printed in Canandaigua seventeen days later.[89]

In the war years from 1812 to 1815 the public was eager for news from abroad, as well as from the field of battle at home. The celebrated engagement of the "Constitution" and the "Guerriere" was announced in Boston ten days after the event and was in a Hudson paper eight days later.[90] Napoleon's return from Elba, an event which electrified the world, was not known in New York until April 26, thirty-seven days after the landing at Cannes. A week later Onondaga learned the news from an Albany handbill dated April 28.[91] This was considered rapid transmission. A letter from New York exclaimed: "We truly live in an age of wonders—Since the departure of the Steam Boat, the schooner Sine Qua Non, has arrived in 26 days from France bringing the important news of Bonaparte's having entered Paris. . . ."[92] Forty-four days after Waterloo, Napoleon's defeat was announced in a Hartford newspaper, but another week had elapsed before news of the battle was received in Cazenovia.[93] In 1830 the flight of Charles X was published in New York and Westchester thirty-six days after the event.[94]

---

[87] *Catskill Packet*, Nov. 19, 1792.
[88] *Ibid.*, Mar. 18, 1793.
[89] Canandaigua *Western Repository*, Nov. 19, 1803.
[90] Hudson *Northern Whig*, Sept. 7, 1812.
[91] *Onondaga Register*, May 3, 1815. Published on Wednesday, the paper acknowledged "the politeness of a gentleman in last Monday's stage from Albany," for the handbill.
[92] *Ibid.*
[93] Cazenovia *Pilot*, Aug. 9, 1815.
[94] Peekskill *Westchester and Putnam Sentinel*, Sept. 9, 1830.

As all students of history know, the news of the Treaty of Ghent was so delayed that the battle of New Orleans was fought after the treaty had been signed. The first report of the cessation of hostilities (December 24, 1814) came to America with the British sloop of war "Favorite," which left Plymouth January 2, 1815, and reached New York, February 11. It was published in the New York papers the next day and in central New York on the fifteenth.[95] The news was then fifty-three days from Ghent.

Of more direct concern to the country printer were the efforts for expeditious transmission of domestic news. Most important was the publication of the President's annual message. Metropolitan papers made great exertions to "beat" each other in the first publication of the message, while the country printer could only take advantage of their enterprise.[96] In 1811 the message was rushed by "express" to New York in twenty hours from Washington, and on the same day was printed, in part, by the *Long Island Star* in Brooklyn.[97] Hudson River towns usually got the message by stage or boat, but central and western towns had to wait for the uncertain delivery of mail, or put up with the mid-winter schedule of the stages. The printer did not always receive it in time for his paper and so was forced to get it out first in an "extra."[98] In 1830 the Ithaca printer detailed the whole process of publishing the important document:

The President's Message. Was communicated to both houses of Congress on Tuesday, the 7th, at 12 o'clock. It was received at the office of the *New York Enquirer* at half past three o'clock P.M. on Wednesday—having been brought by express from Washington to Baltimore, from Baltimore to Philadelphia by Steam Boat; and from Philadelphia to New York by the express of the *Enquirer* Office in *six hours and twelve minutes.* We received a copy of the *Enquirer* of Thursday morn-

[95] *Pilot,* Feb. 15, 1815; *Ontario Repository,* Feb. 21, 1815, printed an "extra" on the 15th. Adams, Henry, *History of the United States,* IX, 52-59.
[96] Weed, *Autobiography,* pp. 369-370, tells of his race with Van Benthuysen of the *Argus* to get the message from New York to Albany in 1830.
[97] *Long Island Star,* Nov. 13, 1811.
[98] *Ontario Repository,* Dec. 12, 1809; *Onondaga Register,* Nov. 25, 1818; and Dec. 16, 1829; *Auburn Gazette,* Dec. 16, 1816.

ing, and also the *Morning Herald,* which contained the Message, and are thus enabled to publish it some time in advance of the usual publication. We are also indebted to the hon. Th. Maxwell, our representative in Congress, for a copy in pamphlet form which we received this (Tuesday) morning. By this copy, we are enabled to correct our proof sheet, and thus more fully avoid the numerous errors of the New York impressions, which were occasioned by the great haste at which the message was put to press in that city.[99]

One of the obstacles with which the printer had to contend was the irregularity of the mails which brought him his exchanges. Partisan postmasters were charged with having intercepted, or purposely delayed, the mail to discomfit the printer; and mistakes and negligence were apparently common, not to mention unavoidable delays caused by weather or road conditions.[100] The Cazenovia printer found his *Albany Register* "detained for a number of weeks" around election time.[101] Postmasters at Lansingburgh and Utica were charged with discrimination, allowing mail to pass through which should have been detained, opening papers and delaying to send them on, and permitting "boys" carelessly to handle the mail against regulations.[102] The Oswego printer noted on Friday morning at 10 o'clock, "Our Wednesday mail not having arrived, (and the day of publication having passed,) we are of course under the necessity of issuing our paper, destitute of any official information. . . ."[103]

Under these circumstances, the more enterprising made it their business to get verbal reports from travelers.[104] Hudson Valley papers frequently asserted that they obtained their information from arrivals on "the Steam Boat."[105] Those

[99] *Ithaca Journal,* Dec. 15, 1830.

[100] *Plattsburgh Republican,* May 7, 1813. *Ibid.,* Dec. 29, 1821, and *Saratoga Sentinel,* July 11, 1821, for difficulties of the northern mail. *Poughkeepsie Journal,* Mar. 18, 1818.

[101] *Pilot,* Mar. 4, 1810.

[102] Troy *Farmer's Oracle,* May 16, 1798; Utica *Oneida Observer,* July 6, Sept. 21, 1830; and *Saratoga Sentinel,* Jan. 23, 1826.

[103] *Oswego Palladium,* Jan. 20, 1820.

[104] *Ibid.* Also *Buffalo Gazette,* June 1, 1813; *Oxford Gazette,* June 7, 14, 1814.

[105] Hudson *Bee,* July 18, 1809; *Dutchess Observer,* Nov. 22, 1820.

further inland depended upon travelers by stage. "We were informed yesterday by the passengers in the eastern stage that when they passed through Auburn the State Prison was on fire," noted the *Geneva Palladium*.[106] In Herkimer William L. Stone would stay up the greater part of the night at the stage office to meet the stage, whereupon he would question the passengers as the drivers changed horses. Thus he got material for his "extras" of war news.[107]

More important was the beginning of the modern practice of special correspondence. Most country printers could not hope for this advantage, but when Harry Croswell made improvements in the *Balance* in 1807 and took in a partner, he was able to add:

I have also concluded to spend a portion of each week, during the sitting of the legislature, at Albany, which being the seat of government and the most commanding political ground of the state, will afford me an opportunity (exclusive of the attention which I may bestow on a paper in that city) of conveying to my readers, through the medium of the *Balance,* the earliest and most authentic information relating to affairs of state.[108]

William L. Stone, in his prospectus of the *State Gazette,* of Troy, (a newspaper which never materialized), said, "The Editor has engaged able correspondents at Washington during the approaching session of Congress; and he will attend personally at the capitol and sketch the proceedings of our state legislature." [109] Far better was the position of Charles G. De Witt, editor of the *Ulster Sentinel,* who was elected a Jacksonian member of Congress in 1828 and sent weekly letters to his paper relating his observations and experiences.[110] The state constitutional convention in 1821 was an important topic in the press, and the *Saratoga Sentinel* carried a series of let-

---

[106] Quoted in Kingston *Craftsman,* Oct. 17, 1821.
[107] Stone, W. L., *The Life and Times of Sa-go-ye-wat-ka, or Red Jacket* (1866), Memoir of the author by his son, p. 15.
[108] Hudson *Balance,* Nov. 17, 1807.
[109] *Troy Post,* Oct. 13, 1818.
[110] Kingston *Ulster Sentinel,* Dec. 1829-Jan. 1830.

ters "From Our Correspondent." [111] Thus did some of the country journals overcome their difficulties.

The country newspaper of this era was more than a medium for local merchants, pettifogging lawyers, and rural politicians. The rural *Gazette* had a broad outlook; it embraced the whole world outside, and brought to its limited circle of readers the passing show of great events and personages. It was indeed "the herald of a noisy world."

[111] *Saratoga Sentinel,* Sept. 5, 1821.

VI

A FREE PRESS

THE *liberty of the Press is indeed essential to the nature of a free state; but this consists in laying no* previous *restraints upon publication, and not in freedom from censure for criminal matter when published. Every free man has an undoubted right to lay whatever sentiments he pleases before the public: to forbid this is to destroy freedom of the Press; but if he publishes what is improper, mischievous, or illegal, he must take the consequences of his own temerity.*—BLACKSTONE.

THE *Liberty of the Press consists in the right to publish with Impunity, Truth with good motives for justifiable Ends, tho reflecting on Government, Magistracy, or Individuals.*—ALEXANDER HAMILTON, in "Trial of Croswell," 1804.

READER, *it has given me much pain to write such a string of lies as I have presented you in this number. If it has been such a task for me to fill one little paper with them, how the devil does Holt get along with such a piece of work from year to year. Perhaps by being accustomed to it. However, I despair of acquiring the habit; and therefore must give up the idea of becoming a democrat.*—H. CROSWELL, The Wasp, January, 1803.

> THAT *Editor who wills to please*
> *Must humbly crawl upon his knees,*
> *And kiss the hand that beats him;*
> *Or if he dares presume to walk,*
> *Must toe the mark that others chalk,*
> *And cringe to all who meet him.*
> Lansingburgh Gazette, July 28, 1829.

IN SPITE of what has already been related concerning the venality and mercenary motives of some printers, it is true that in this period there were many who either from strong party affiliations and prejudices or from a resolute conviction of truth and principle defied authority and invited prosecution at law. It was a time of excesses in defamation and violent personal criticism. Partisanship in politics was so virulent that few party editors could pursue a course of moderation. To quibble or extenuate was to incur the despised reputation of a "trimmer." Party service often degenerated into personal abuse which in turn brought attacks upon the freedom of the press.

These excesses were certainly to be deprecated; but the other extreme, regulation and suppression by authority, is in a democratic country more to be feared. The extent to which printers were, or had the opportunity to be, independent critics is pertinent to this study. Mere excessive criticism or abuse, however, is not the measure of a writer's independence. It may, on the contrary, be an evidence of the utmost subservience to those who, unwilling themselves to enter the lists, can persuade or hire others to assume responsibility for them. To what extent, then, was the country printer subservient and servile? Were the authorities oppressive? And how much credit is due the printer as an independent critic?

Freedom of the press became a stirring issue in colonial times, as has been indicated, and the cases of Franklin and Zenger exalted the printer as a champion of free expression. Royal instructions to colonial governors from 1686 to 1730 required that nothing should be printed "without your especial leave and license first obtained." [1] This was the sort of curb upon printing contemplated by Blackstone in his frequently quoted statement, that freedom of the press consisted in "lay-

[1] Duniway, C. A., *The Development of Freedom of the Press in Massachusetts* pp. 64-65.

ing no previous restraints" upon publication, and did not imply the irresponsibility of the printer for the consequences.[2] There was no censorship, however, no "previous restraints" on printing in later colonial times, and control was limited to prosecution for "seditious libel" under the common law.[3] Most of the colonial cases involved the right to criticize the authorities of the Government, and arose when printers were prosecuted for such criticism. In this category came the Zenger prosecution.

Political dissension, and the partisanship of the Revolution, engendered violence and an abuse of the liberty of printing which was carried over into the nineteenth century. A generation of journalists had been trained in a school which admitted no temporizing or impartial spirit. Under these conditions the party in power, accustomed to think of its opponents as disloyal and dangerous, spread on the statutes the first general law for curbing free expression.[4] The Sedition Act of 1798, a wartime measure in anticipation of a struggle with France, mentioned in quite vague and general terms several kinds of "sedition" which were then common. A more liberal view of the doctrine of "seditious libels" was gaining favor, and the new law was an effort to check this tendency. It stipulated punishments and handed prosecution over to the Federal courts.[5]

The Alien and Sedition Acts of 1798 were directed against foreign-born Republican editors and others who were notorious for their vituperative attacks on the leaders of the Government. Obviously partisan laws sponsored by the Federalists, they expired with the Adams administration in 1801. Few country printers were prosecuted under these laws, as they were intended primarily for bigger game, the editors of such

[2] Chafee, Zechariah, *Freedom of Speech*, pp. 19-20.
[3] *Ibid*. See also Duniway, *op. cit.*, p. 89.
[4] Duniway, *op. cit.*, pp. 143-144.
[5] Prosecutions of printers under the common law, by Federal authorities, had already begun in 1798, before this enactment. Many of the so-called Sedition Act prosecutions were partly or wholly based on the common law. Anderson, F. M., "The Enforcement of the Alien and Sedition Laws," in the *Annual Report* of the American Historical Association for 1912, p. 118.

leading Republican papers as the Philadelphia *Aurora,* the New York *Argus,* and the *Richmond Examiner.*[6] William Durell, printer of the *Mount Pleasant Register,* was an exception. He was convicted and sentenced to four months' imprisonment, with a fine of fifty dollars, April 3, 1800.[7] Two other New York country printers, not then serving in that capacity, were convicted and imprisoned. They were Charles Holt, of the New London, Connecticut, *Bee* (later printer of the Hudson *Bee*),[8] and David Frothingham, a former printer of the first paper on Long Island, who was convicted of publishing a libelous assertion with regard to Alexander Hamilton in the New York *Argus,* which he printed for Mrs. Greenleaf. Three and four months' imprisonment, respectively, was sufficient to terminate the newspaper connection of each.[9]

It was natural that the type of journalism which had provoked the Alien and Sedition Acts should not cease with the change of administration, and soon Jefferson became as uncomfortable in the face of Federalist jibes and slanders, as Washington and Adams had been when attacked by Republicans. He even concluded that, "It is a melancholy truth, that a suppression of the press could not more compleatly deprive the nation of its benefits, than is done by its abandoned prostitution to falsehood. Nothing can now be believed which is seen in a newspaper." [10]

Although the Republicans were content to leave prosecutions

---

[6] Bleyer, *op. cit.,* pp. 120-121.

[7] New York *American Citizen,* Apr. 18, 1800. This is included by Bleyer as a prosecution under the Sedition Law, but it was noted in the *Citizen* that it was for libel and not for sedition. Cf. also Anderson, *loc. cit.,* p. 121, and references. Anderson notes that Durell was later pardoned by President Adams.

[8] *Otsego Herald,* Oct. 10, 1799, May 1, 1800; and Troy *Northern Budget,* April 30, 1800, reprint news of the Holt trial.

[9] *New York Greenleaf's Patriotic Register,* Nov. 13, Dec. 7, 14, 1799. Bleyer, *op. cit.,* p. 121, includes this case of Frothingham with others as "attacked directly or indirectly through the Sedition Law." It was not caused by an attack upon the government of the United States or its officers, however, and was prosecuted in the state court of Oyer and Terminer, and the sentence was to Bridewell. Cf. Hudson, *Journalism in the United States,* pp. 215-216. The case is not mentioned in Anderson, *loc. cit.*

[10] Ford, P. L., ed., *Writings of Thomas Jefferson,* IX, 72, quoted by Bleyer, *op. cit.*

for libelous assertions to the states under the common law, they were able to curb country papers in much the same fashion as had their opponents. Perhaps the most notable prosecution was that in 1804 of Harry Croswell, of the Hudson *Balance,* the leading Federalist organ outside New York City. With the appearance in Hudson of Charles Holt's *Bee,* Croswell had also issued a frankly scurrilous sheet called *The Wasp.*[11] In this appeared the following attack upon Jefferson, for which suit was brought against the publisher.

Holt says, the burden of the Federal song is, that Mr. Jefferson paid Callender for writing against the late administration. This is wholly false. The charge is explicitly this: Jefferson paid Callender for calling Washington a traitor, a robber, and a perjurer—For calling Adams a hoary headed incendiary; and for grossly slandering the private character of men, who, he well knew, were virtuous. These charges, not a democratic editor has yet dared, or ever will dare, to meet in an open manly discussion.[12]

Croswell had not written this paragraph, but assumed responsibility for it. The state attorney-general, Ambrose Spencer, who was a stout partisan, procured an indictment charging a libel on President Jefferson.[13] Alexander Hamilton was retained as counsel for the defense and made a careful and reasoned argument, one of the last of his career, of which the notes only are extant. In his argument before the supreme court of the state Hamilton discussed the entire law of libel, the result being a change in the law of the state permitting the giving of truth in evidence. Thus the case became one of the outstanding libel trials of the time.[14] Croswell, however, was for several

[11] Cf. *infra* pp. 187-188.

[12] Hudson *Wasp,* No. 7, Sept. 9, 1802.

[13] MS note of Harry Croswell in the file of the *Wasp,* New York Historical Society. He states that it was penned by Thomas P. Grosvenor, a young lawyer (brother-in-law of Elisha Williams), whose name he did not wish to expose. This contradicts the statement in Bleyer, *op. cit.,* p. 137, that it was reprinted from the *Evening Post.* This work also has a variant reading of the paragraph, which is taken from *The Intimate Life of Alexander Hamilton,* by A. McL. Hamilton. See further discussion of this case *infra* p. 197.

[14] MS volume in the handwriting of Justice James Kent, *Croswell* ads. *People.* New York Public Library.

years persecuted by a series of libel suits, some of them at the instance of Spencer.[15]

At this time, too, Hamilton argued a case for a Federalist printer who was charged with contempt. Samuel S. Freer, of the *Ulster Gazette,* was indicted, as he put it, "for daring to complain that truth is a libel." [16] He had criticized the court which was then sitting in the Croswell case. Being much worried over the possibility of imprisonment, Freer appealed to the famous leader of his party. Hamilton in a patronizing manner is said to have reassured him.

Well, my good fellow (that being Hamilton's usual salutation), we don't know what can be done [do not know what we can do] for you. If the [court] should imprison you, that will have to be borne by you alone: we cannot suffer in your stead; but, should they fine you, the money will be forthcoming. As regards counsel, I am with you, heart and hand, and will plead your case [cause].[17]

Freer was let off with the nominal fine of ten dollars after Hamilton had made an impassioned plea for the freedom of the press.[18]

These suits were all instances of prosecution for attacks upon the Government or its officials. So far as partisan tactics were concerned, much the same result could be obtained through private libel suits. These, too, often were akin to persecution, and unless the printer had strong support from his own party he felt weak and helpless. Mackay Croswell, of Catskill, expressed his fears as well as his resolute independence, when suit was brought against him by De Witt Clinton.

Why a little country paper whose circulation is extremely limited, should be selected by the Mayor of New York, or his tools, as an object at which to aim his vengeance, is impossible to tell. Let them, however,

---

[15] *Lansingburgh Gazette,* July 24, 1804. Also Croswell MS, *loc. cit.*

[16] *Lansingburgh Gazette,* Jan. 3, 1804.

[17] Sylvester, N. B., *History of Ulster County,* p. 144; and Schoonmaker, M., *History of Kingston,* pp. 418-419. These vary as to details of the story, indicated by brackets in the above quotation, and their sources have not been located. The story is not improbable.

[18] *Ibid.* and *Lansingburgh Gazette,* Feb. 21, 1804. Official report is in Caines, I, 484, 518.

go on. We trust that we are to answer before an impartial jury of our country. All we ask is, that De Witt will suffer his suit to proceed in the ordinary channel—that he will not step out of the ordinary course, either to *strike or to pack* a jury. If he will do this, though the editor is but a poor printer, and his antagonist is clothed with all the power of a triumphant family, he fears not the issue.[19]

If the consciousness that the party leaders were back of him led the printer to be reckless in his publications, it also led him to expect financial assistance in case he were prosecuted and convicted. It is hard to believe that some printers could continue in the face of frequent prosecutions without aid from "the fund," [20] but Francis Adancourt, of Troy, asserted that the party backing was not always forthcoming when a trial had ended in a fine. He was fined $800 in 1809, and Cheetham editorially expressed the hope that it would be made good to him; to which he replied, "Thank you, good captain, for your good wishes; but they don't pay printer's fines here so readily as they do in New York." [21]

In 1820 Adancourt commented on the $200 fine imposed on his contemporary Zephaniah Clark, of the *Northern Budget*. "Mr. Clark was only a nominal defendant. We hope those who have led him into the scrape will behave less shabbily towards Mr. Clark, than some of the same gentry did towards us on a similar occasion, some years ago. Printers ought not to fight and pay, too." [22] Evidence that Adancourt wrote libelous matter at the direction of his backers, and that his fines were paid by them, was presented by the above mentioned Clark, in a case where Adancourt charged John C. Wright, another printer, with perjury.[23] This subservience of the printer-editor to those for whom he labored was more apparent than real, for in many instances his partisan pronouncements were in accord with his own convictions. In a letter written after his

---

[19] *Catskill Recorder,* July 23, 1804.

[20] Poughkeepsie *Political Barometer,* Oct. 28, 1806, referring to Cheetham's double fine of five hundred dollars, added, "These are heavy calls upon the fund."

[21] Troy *Farmer's Register,* Dec. 12, 1809.

[22] *Ibid.,* Dec. 25, 1820.

[23] Troy *Northern Budget,* June 9, 1818.

establishment in Manlius, Thurlow Weed stated that he could not consistently take a Bucktail paper, but he confessed that his political views might be determined by the situation in which he found himself.

"If I am so fortunate as to be prudent and discreet," he wrote, "I think I can acquire a little influence. But politics are strangely entangled. I hardly know what to touch. What is to become of the schism in New York? I feel partial to the new lights." [24]

The first paper in Manlius, by the way, had come to a bad end because it had insisted upon an attitude of rank partisanship, and made attacks "scandalizing respectable candidates for office." Its proprietor, Abraham Romeyn, became involved in libel suits and soon was in bad repute.[25] Where there was but one paper in the community, moderation in party matters was the course of wisdom. The proposals of Thomas Kirk marked him an independent man. He admitted that his was to be a party paper, but

Disdaining all servile attachment to any man, or set of men whatever, his support will be afforded only to those whose conduct he conceives entitle them to his approbation and esteem.

Neither the promise of official patronage on the one hand, nor the subsidiary aids of private or party contribution on the other, is pledged to guarantee the risque [sic], or defray the necessary expenses of this undertaking.[26]

It is difficult to determine how constant the average printer was in his devotion to such professions of independence. The conflicting views of various editors throw little light on the question. Much must be implied, and the keen student will read between the lines in such opinions as the following, relating to the establishment of the *People's Press* in Batavia.

It is not unknown to the patrons of the *Press* generally, that it was established in 1825 from necessity, arising from the unprecedented treachery and insufferable insolence and duplicity of the manager of the *Advocate;* and from its commencement, a most savage warfare has been

[24] Barnes, *Memoir of Thurlow Weed,* p. 19.
[25] Clark, J. H. V., *Onondaga,* II, 221-222.
[26] Brooklyn *Long Island Star,* June 8, 1809.

prosecuted against it by that infamous paper, and its equally *infamous* immediate supporters; that they have constantly predicted the downfall of the *Press,* and left no means unessayed to produce that effect.[27]

In reply to this the printer of the *Advocate* made a statement which indicates that he was courageously maintaining his independence against a strong combination in the county.

The only *necessity* for establishing the *Press,* was that the then editor of the *Advocate* would not go into the measures of a set of juntocrats, who had combined together for the purpose of monopolizing all the offices in the town or county. This combination was composed of all the existing parties of the day. Republicans and Federals, Clintonians and Bucktails, were all amalgamated, without distinction. This, and this alone, rendered the establishment of the *Press* necessary.[28]

That the independent printer was not always able to maintain his position is revealed by the difficulties of Silvester Tiffany, who refused to print in the *Ontario Freeman* an account of the local convention of 1804 submitted to him by Augustus Porter. Porter then suggested that a definite policy of the paper should be established, and submitted the following proposals:

That he [Tiffany] should fill his paper merely with *nominations for the Republican candidates, and statements of facts*—or, that he should occupy half his paper with nominations, communications, statements of facts, &c. furnished him in favor of Mr. Lewis; and the other half of it, with those furnished him in favor of Col. Burr;—and that if neither of these propositions were agreeable to him, he should conduct his paper as he thought most conducive to his interest.[29]

The meaning of the last alternative may be implied from the fact that Porter was soon compelled to reply to the accusation that he had "by threats and other coercive means, obliged Mr. Tiffany to stop the publication of the *Ontario Freeman*." [30]

A most interesting case was that of Samuel A. Seabury, who was beholden to several gentlemen for the wherewithal to start

[27] Batavia *Republican Advocate*, Sept. 4, 1829.
[28] *Ibid.* See also statement in the issue of Oct. 1, 1830.
[29] Canandaigua *Western Repository*, Apr. 17, 1804.
[30] *Ibid.*

the *Suffolk County Recorder* in Sag Harbor. In order to get this aid he signed the following:

I hereby agree that Messrs. W., G., and P. or either of them, as they may agree, shall have the sole direction of the paper of which I am the editor; and engage that nothing, excepting advertisements, shall be printed in its columns without their consent.

[Signed] *Samuel A. Seabury.*[31]

Let Seabury describe his position:

When this obligation was presented to me to sign, I felt myself placed in a very difficult situation; to sign it, was not my wish, and my sensibility led me to be fearful of the consequences of not signing it.

In this state of dilemma (the Rev. Mr. Gardiner, and H. P. Dering, Esq., being present), I observed that "I would sign and abide by it, as long as I found it for my interest," they unanimously agreed that it would not be expected for me to abide by it any longer; with this reply I took up my pen and signed my name. And I did, in conformity with my verbal, and the spirit and meaning of the written obligation, conscientiously abide by it. But when my subscribers called at the office, and informed me, that my inserting in the paper so much religious matter to the exclusion of all other, was displeasing to them, that they expected such domestic, political and foreign news as was common for newspapers to make known—others from the same cause called and without ceremony erased their names as patrons of my paper, unless I refuse to publish so much religious matter. Thus circumstanced, I considered myself honorably released from my verbal, and the spirit and meaning of the written obligation; as it was no longer to my interest, but much against it, to adhere to it. . . .[32]

After reciting more of the woes resulting from the foregoing agreement, Seabury heroically observed:

But, Rev. Sir, I must inform you, altho' I am poor in purse, I am independent in spirit; and although I cannot boast of riches, I can boast of heroic ancestors, who fought and bled & died for the liberty you now enjoy.[33]

While some printers imagined themselves perpetually embattled in the cause of righteousness, others assumed the martyr's

[31] Sag Harbor *Suffolk County Recorder,* Aug. 9, 1917.

[32] *Ibid.* Also Cf. *Supra* pp. 53-55, ownership by group; and *supra,* chap. v, religious matter in newspaper content.

[33] *Ibid.*

rôle with ease. The following hyperbole from the pen of Henry C. Southwick, of Auburn, was a part of his defense of that professional martyr, William Ray, who had been dismissed as editor in Onondaga County.

But Mr. Ray was too independent, for a little nest of officeholders in that county, whose object and whim is to muzzle the press, and make the printer subservient to their views. This fact is not confined to Onondaga solely, but the system was adopted throughout the state two or three years ago; and every printer or editor who would not surrender his independence into the holykeeping of this *Inquisition of Office-Holders,* a general cry of *Crucify him! Crucify him!* was issued against him—public patronage was withdrawn, and a system of persecution set up against him, as black and as infamous, considering the relative situation of the two countries, as ever disgraced the annals of Old Spain.

Mr. R. dared to be honest, and furnished the readers with truths—sound, good, and wholesome truths—too unpalatable, however, for these gentry to swallow—for they would sooner smother truth, and hunt every spark of public virtue out of existence, rather than have anything published, which might expose their masters at the Capitol, and jeopardize their offices. For this independence in Mr. R. he has been deprived of his situation as Editor of the *Gazette;* and that paper, we presume, will now be managed to suit the views of this little junto, and keep the public still longer ignorant of these abominable measures which have been practised upon them, by the general and state governments. We regret that Mr. Morse, the proprietor of the office, would have listened for the moment to these creatures, and given away his independence, to subserve the views of these designing demagogues.[34]

In a subsequent issue Southwick was much harsher on Morse, "the typesetter to the little nest of Officeholders, and High Salarymen in Onondaga county," and was more convinced of their designs on the press of the state.

We knew months ago that the Robespierre cabal were conspiring to oust Mr. R.—we were told so in Albany, long before we left that city. Nay more, we had it from one of their own mouths. Ray was too independent—Morse pliant, and capable of being moulded into anything—just such creatures as the demagogues want, and just such ones as are wanted throughout the state, to *set types* for them, and publish such articles *only* as they may dictate, and nothing more.[35]

[34] Auburn *Advocate of the People,* Oct. 30, 1816.
[35] *Ibid.,* Nov. 13, 1816.

Southwick was not unique in his ability to detect insidious plots against the liberty of the independent printer. Many newspaper proprietors magnified trivial incidents into widespread conspiracies. Some of them labored under a persecution complex, which prevented them from distinguishing between accidental delays in the delivery of their papers and a scheme to drive them out of business. The mere fact that the weeklies in Rochester were "publishing (not *simultaneously,* but) on *successive days,* so as to make a sort of daily paper," convinced the printer of the *Daily Telegraph* that he was the victim of persecution.[36] Some of the most bitter controversies in the press could be traced to this feeling on the part of newspaper publishers that they were suffering from unfair competition. Their resentment found frequent expression in scurrilous attacks upon those whom they regarded as their oppressors. The bitterness of political controversy and the desire of editors to furnish their readers with "lively amusement" were not the only factors responsible for the resort to personal abuse in the press.[37] Personalities and resort to doubtful charges frequently leading to litigation, degraded the press, and explain the prevalence of anonymous publication and the employment by reputable persons of others to bear the brunt of their battles.

There is no standard by which to measure scurrility in the press, unless it be the quantity of the output. The question as to whether one period was worse than another, therefore, is largely a matter of opinion. According to James Melvin Lee:

The darkest period in the history of American journalism was that which began at the close of the second war with England, a time truthfully characterized as the "period of black journalism," when a greater depth of degradation was reached than was ever touched in the so called "yellow" period of recent times. Those who look over the papers of this era will find that all the customary courtesies of life were put aside; that the papers of both parties employed the vilest, grossest epithets in the English language; that the newspapers advanced the most atrocious

[36] *Rochester Daily Telegraph,* May 2, 1827.
[37] "The newspapers continued to find in personal abuse the most lively amusement they could furnish their readers." Adams, Henry, *History of the United States,* III, 208.

charges against those holding public office and even so forgot themselves as to attack wives and sisters in their disgraceful accounts of the personal activities of officeholders.[38]

It is difficult to see that the standards of American journalism immediately after 1814 were worse than those of an earlier period, say before 1805, in which flourished Bache, Duane, Cheetham, Cobbett, and Callender. In reading the country papers of New York state, such a division did not occur to the writer, nor does it seem fair. The Clintonian split, and more especially the Anti-Masonic flurry produced some bitter personalities; and of course the Jackson campaign of 1828 was notorious. These stand out as intense spasms of party rancor and journalistic degradation, but they hardly justify the belief that the general tone of journalism from 1814 to 1830 was more scurrilous than it had been during the preceding twenty years.[39]

A few specimens of personalities may not be edifying, but they illustrate the temper of the times. The following from Herkimer shows how epithets flew in 1810.

A Mean Blackguard,—Captain *Consequence,* or in other words, *Charley* Holt, has been pleased, if he ever was pleased, to *daub* in his paper the following ridiculous paragraph against the editor of the *Honest American:* "A Dishonest American—The foolish rascal in Herkimer, who to the disgrace of the name of an editor, is the lickspittle of the *Public Advertiser,* cannot expect further newspaper notice, but will be silenced without disturbing our readers with so pitiful a subject."

Capt. *Charley* talks of "silencing us," but the captain is informed that he nor all the *men* he could raise while a captain in Hudson, will be able to silence us. Capt. *Charley* says we cannot expect further "newspaper notice." God grant we may not receive any further notice from so mean a scoundrel. This "pitiful subject" wishes not to "disturb" his "readers." It is well known that as far as Capt. Charley's influence extends, he has done more to disturb the republican party than any other editor in the

[38] Lee, James Melvin, *History of American Journalism,* p. 143.

[39] Professor Allan Nevins considers the period 1793-1805 the blackest before the Civil War; and rates that after 1865 the worst we have known. Claude G. Bowers, also trained as a journalist, who has written of several periods, considers the venality of William Cobbett, and the period before 1801, the worst of all that he has observed.—Letters to the author.

state. An eternal good-bye to you, Capt. *Charley,* unless you plan to take further notice of us than that of "newspaper." [40]

Even humor was made malicious.

How now, moon-calf!—As a friend I would advise Mackay,[41] the *Catskill Recorder* man, to stick close to his *beer pots,* his *decanters,* his *billiards,* and his *cardtable,* and let the *Whig* alone. Be advised, Mackay. You are no editor. Your own concerns are more than you can manage: Let those of your neighbors pass. Billiards and Beer, Mackay, are your element—but 'ware criticism! It won't do. Ne sutor ultra crepidum. Throw up your hand, Mackay—ten to one you'll get loo'd![42]

The Federalists liked to characterize their Republican rivals as common members of the rabble, given over to vicious habits, as is evident from the following couplet and note printed in 1812.

—the fell tribe who compose the wise club,
Where Dayton presides and holds forth to his mob.*
* A Club or knot of politicians who hold their sittings in a room annexed to the Democratic printing office in this city, of which a man by the name of Dayton is the standing President; who is judge of the inferior court of this County and a Just-ass of the Peace,—a very wise man you may suppose; as he ought to be, to preside [over] a knot of politicians who edit so intelligent a paper as the *Bee.*[43]

An account of a man's conduct in such a light as below—a part of a furious editorial campaign conducted by Francis Adancourt against James Dole—was dangerous and likely to produce more than mere words. The writer in this case was a Republican.

... This recalls to my mind a transaction which took place in this village about two years ago, and shews that *Dole's* idea of *expense* differs from that generally understood by honest men.
Dole procured to be published in the *Northern Budget* several foul and infamous slanders against the character of Capt. G. D. Young, accompanied with a promise to Mr. *Lyon,* the editor of the *Budget,* that

[40] Quoted from the Herkimer *Honest American* in Benton, Nathaniel S., *History of Herkimer County,* pp. 221-222.
[41] Mackay Croswell.
[42] Hudson *Northern Whig,* June 13, 1815.
[43] *Ibid.,* Jan. 6, 1812.

he would be paid for publishing it.—Mr. Lyon published the pieces (I believe there were several) as he was directed, and after fulfilling his part of the contract presented his bill to Mr. Dole for payment—Mr. Dole denied the debt—Mr. Lyon sued him, and an independent jury awarded to Mr. Lyon the amount of the bill. . . .

Dole also declared publicly in Mr. Moulton's bar-room that he was not the author of a libel on several gentlemen in this village (and which appeared in the *Troy Gazette*) signed *Auracolis,* but that he received it from Mr. *David Allen,* of Lansingburgh, who requested him to hand it to Doctor Lewis for publication—however, the Doctor declares unequivocally before the Grand Jury, that *James Dole* was the author, and Mr. Allen peremptorily declared that he had no knowledge of the article. . . .[44]

The "lie" was frequently hurled in various forms.

If Clark, Mr. Croswell's former under-devil, will assert, or sanction an assertion that either of the gentlemen to whom his *drivers* have thought proper to allude in the last wigwam journal, or any other person, have ever written a single paragraph for the editorial department of this paper, since it has been under my control, I shall pronounce him, and publish him to the world as an INFAMOUS AND VILLAINOUS LIAR.[45]

Equally plain was the meaning of the editor of the *Otsego Herald.*

Poor crazy Dowse and his English organ, have told a lie!! Gov. Clinton never suspended the editor of the *Otsego Herald,* and Gov. Jay, being convinced that he had been deceived by such fellows as Dowse, about nine months after the supersedeas appointed him to higher offices, which commissions were held by the editor under Gov. Jay, until his term expired in 1801.

Another Lie!—They lie in saying that he aided in the appointment of the Postmaster. This last may be termed a *white lie;* but it is a *lie!* [46]

Sometimes an offensive publication was put in the form of a handbill in order that the newspaper might avoid responsibility. Such was the procedure in the case described by John F. Hub-

[44] Troy *Farmer's Register,* Feb. 12, 1811. Printers referred to were Oliver Lyon and Eldad Lewis.
[45] Hudson *Northern Whig,* June 27, 1815.
[46] *Otsego Herald,* Mar. 18, 1809.

bard, of Norwich, which, by the way, was in the later period of the Clintonian defection.

> *Correction.* A handbill issued from my office, written by myself, in reply to an abusive one issued from the *Agriculturalist* [*sic*] office.[47] It implicated the *political* conduct of *A. Cook,* Esq. It was written under the impression that he was the author of the one printed at the *Agriculturalist* office. It is due him to state, that he solemnly avers that he had no hand in that slanderous publication. He handed me an article in reply, which at first I told him I would publish in my paper. But on mature reflection, as it implicated men who had nothing to do with the handbill which I published, I concluded it would produce a personal warfare, not very interesting to my readers, and I thought best not to give it publication. I, however, offered Mr. Cook to publish it in a handbill free of expense. This course would at least put him on a par with me.[48]

If the use of the handbill demonstrates a tendency to scatter abusive matter indiscriminately, touching whom it might, there is at least some regard for the dignity and responsibility of the newspaper. Thurlow Weed, then printing the *Republican Agriculturist,* sought to check the worst effects of personal warfare, just as he later endeavored to suppress the "coffin handbill" of the Jackson campaign in Western New York.[49]

Another method of circulating slanderous attacks without filling the newspaper to the exclusion of other material, was the small, scurrilous publication, of which the *Wasp* of Harry Croswell was a good example. While the nominal editor was "Robert Rusticoat, Esquire," it was "Printed at the Balance Office By Harry Croswell, For the Editor." Even the heading was made to declare its character, when there was substituted, *"Printed For the Editor* In Defiance of the DEVIL And the Whole Host of Democrats."[50] In addition to the libelous attack upon Jefferson for which Croswell was prosecuted, there

[47] Hubbard always insisted upon spelling the name of Weed's paper, the *Republican Agriculturist,* with an extra syllable.

[48] *Norwich Journal,* Apr. 11, 1821. Hubbard was guilty of inserting in his newspaper, however, some rather rank insinuation regarding Weed. See *Norwich Journal,* Sept. 20, 1820.

[49] Weed, *Autobiography,* pp. 307-308.

[50] *The Wasp,* Vol. I, Nos. 1-12, July 7, 1802-Jan. 1803. Complete file is in the New York Historical Society.

were others directed against the president, which were quite as bad. The following quotation is from a communication entitled, "A Few 'Squally' Facts."

Mr. Jefferson wrote a letter to Mazzei, in which he plainly declared he detested our constitution and that he and his friends would break its "Lilliputian ties." Mr. Jefferson was too weak in his nerves openly to stem the popular current, setting so strongly in favor of the constitution, he therefore insidiously, determined to gratify his hatred, by endeavoring covertly to undermine it.—For this purpose:

1st He employed Freneau and paid him, for writing the grossest lies and most scandalous calumnies against all its friends and supporters.

2d He covertly encouraged every other, who would prostitute his pen, in an attempt to destroy the character and influence of Washington and his associates—Witness the friendly invitation to Tom Paine, immediately after that infidel had written his villainous libel on our beloved Washington—Witness his encouragement and even writing in that sink of filth, the *Aurora*—witness, in short, his whole conduct and policy.[51]

Thus the *Wasp* was strongly political in its motivation, although at first it gave considerable space to the personalities of rival editors: to Holt, of the *Bee,* and to Isaac Mitchell, of the Poughkeepsie *Political Barometer,* its principal Republican contemporaries.

Of a similar complexion was the *Switch,* also Federalist, "By Anthony Switchem, Esq. & Co.," at Cooperstown. It proceeded from the office of the new *Impartial Observer,* in reply to the avowed purpose of Phinney, of the *Otsego Herald,* to discourage the circulation of his rival. Phinney so successfully gave the *Impartial Observer* the nickname, "the Imp," that the name was changed to the *Cooperstown Federalist.* The *Switch* contained the following to indicate its character.

> To seek, to find, the kennel'd pack,
> And lacerate the Rascals back,
> Detect their crimes, expose their pranks,
> And put to flight their ragged ranks.

[51] *Ibid.,* Aug. 12, 1802.

The Editors confidently assure the public that no exertions shall be wanting on their part to render the *Switch* interesting to their feelings.[52]

Judge Cooper, who owned the *Impartial Observer,* declared himself not pleased with the *Switch,* and eventually it was suppressed.[53] The motive of the sponsor of the *Switch* was a vindictive one in the competition of editors. No copies of this paper are now extant.

Some later scurrilous sheets seemed to be less purely political and more like attempts to capitalize on pointed personalities and daring wit. Perhaps these were the progenitors of some of our modern scandal sheets, though they were certainly on a higher moral plane. Northern New York in 1823 was bothered by the *Scribbler,* "made up of scandal, criticism, ribald personalities, and amorous verse." Starting his paper in Montreal, Samuel Hall Wilcocke, under the pseudonym of "Lewis Luke Mucallow," was driven out of that city, and resumed publication in Burlington, Vermont. Thence in December, 1823, he carried his press to Rouse's Point, where he also began the *Harbinger.* Later he went to Plattsburgh. His strictures not only aroused the Canadian authorities, but the citizens of Plattsburgh, and he was indicted by the Grand Jury. He then gave it up, and he subsequently moved to Canada.[54]

In Auburn James M. Miller began the printing of the *Castigator* by "Captain Caleb Cudgel, Esquire and Company." [55] By 1823 it had been removed to Ithaca, where with some interruptions several series were issued. Its title, as well as some of its contents, testify to its caustic quality. By its own statement it was "calculated to 'shoot at folly,' expose hypocrisy, and 'lash the rascals naked through the world.' " [56] Controversy naturally arose, and finally Captain Cudgel came in for some

[52] Prospectus in the Cooperstown *Impartial Observer,* Mar. 4, 1809. *Otsego Herald,* Mar. 18, 1809.

[53] *Otsego Herald,* Mar. 18, 1809, contains the letter of Judge Metcalf, describing the interview of Cooper and Phinney. See also Livermore, *History of Cooperstown,* p. 106.

[54] Hurd, D. H., *History of Clinton and Franklin Counties,* p. 132.

[55] Auburn *Castigator,* June 23, 1819.

[56] Ithaca *Castigator,* Jan. 1, 1823, *et seq.*

cudgeling himself, which caused an interruption in publication.[57]

Not less scurrilous, if a bit more sprightly, was the sheet entitled *Paul Pry,* which was issued in Rochester. This bearer of tales seems to have been popular, for it was soon printing four hundred copies [58] and was turning down communications, *viz.*

We are literally smothered with communications this week; some of them will be found in our columns; some in our next; some at a more convenient season; and some never.[59]

Almost any statement might contain a sly dig.

Since our first page was printed we have concluded to receive subscriptions for half the time of our intended publication (that is, for *two months*), from gentlemen whose business will not allow them to remain longer in the village.[!] [60]

Specimens of its censorious paragraphs and satirical humor may have their value as illustrations.

Mr. Pry—Sir, There is a young gentleman in this village learning a trade in Buffalo street, who cuts a great swell in the fashionable world, wears cloth at $8, per yard &c, and if I am correctly informed his salary amounts to only $40 per year; I would like to inquire through the medium of your useful paper, whether this hopeful youth is not considerably in arrears with his Boss, and if so how long a time at the present rate it will take to get through with his apprenticeship, if he should be honest and stay with his master until the Dr. and Cr. side of the leaf are equal?   *Decency.*[61]

The following crack at a brother editor must have shown all, who did not know, the direction from which these shots were fired.

There is a rumor afloat, which we fear is too well founded, viz: that when O'Reilley disclosed to the President, the object of his mission

[57] Ithaca *Museum and Independent Corrector,* Apr. 16, 1824.
[58] Rochester *Paul Pry,* May 9, 1829.
[59] *Ibid.,* May 22, 1828.
[60] *Ibid.,* May 9, 1829.
[61] *Ibid.,* May 22, 1828.

to Washington, the old veteran, with a contemptuous look, advised him to "tarry at Jerico till his beard be grown,"—an insult which the little gentleman took in a high dudgeon.[62]

Another journal of this class was the *Reflector,* published at Palmyra beginning in 1828 by "O. Dogberry Jr." [63] In Troy there appeared in 1824 *The Fowler,* by "Gilbert Gunflint Esq.," which in some respects, also, belonged in this category.[64]

Not only was the possibility of legal action involved in such personalities and attacks, but physical violence was not unknown. These were the days when political enemies were real enemies who sometimes put their convictions into action. So the Federalists of Hudson were little inclined to tolerate some of the tirades of Charles Holt. When an article in the *Bee* was directed at Elisha Williams, that high-toned aristocrat, with an escort of his political supporters whom he concealed in a nearby cellar of an unfinished building, ambushed Holt and knocked him down as he came from his office. The outstanding position of Williams in the community was enough to arouse a great excitement over the escapade, which almost resulted in physical combat between opposing partisans.[65]

There were many who felt that chastisement was the only punishment fit for printers who publicized scandal and resorted to personal abuse. The following notice, however, indicates that at least one attempt was made to impose an "affair of honor" in which the printer was not "honorable."

To the Public. On Tuesday last I received a Written Challenge demanding satisfaction for either real or supposed insult offered to Mr. *W. W. Wands,* which having immediately accepted, and he, tho' the Challenger, now declining to give me a meeting, I must take the liberty of declaring Mr. W. W. Wands a Rascal and a Poltroon. Troy, April 27, 1797.   *John Weller.*[66]

[62] *Ibid.,* Aug. 8, 1829.
[63] Follett, *op. cit.,* pp. 40-41.
[64] Troy *Fowler,* May 11, 1824.
[65] Miller, S. B., *Sketches of Hudson,* p. 60. For the character of Williams see Fox, *op. cit.* pp. 41-43.
[66] Troy *Farmer's Oracle,* May 2, 1797.

Wands was the printer of the Lansingburgh *American Spy.*
Shortly after this, however, he left that city and went to
Philadelphia.[67]

Later in Hudson a Federalist printer took notice of a threat.
Francis Stebbins was a combative politician and would not let
such a hint pass.

A Card. It has been stated to the editor of this paper, from a pretty
correct source, that *Moses I. Cantine,* Esq., the District Attorney, in a
public conversation in this city, during the last week, declared that *the
Editor of the Northern Whig ought* to be TARRED AND FEATH-
ERED, *and that he* (the District Attorney!) *would himself go any
length for the purpose of accomplishing it.* The editor of the Whig, by a
previous arrangement, leaves the town this day, on a journey to the
eastward, he will return next week; until which time Mr. Cantine
will be allowed the privilege of refuting this charge; if untrue; but in
case of its not being denied, the Editor will then proceed to dispose of
the *District Attorney,* in such a way as shall then be deemed expedient
and proper.[68]

Reports of an editor's encounter with the irate victim of his
newspaper attacks were sometimes highly colored, especially if
they appeared in an opposition print. In the following account
John F. Hubbard gloated over the supposed discomfiture of
his rival:

Summary Justice. Thurlow Weed, Editor of the *Agriculturalist* [sic]
having several times in his paper attacked *L. Clark* Esq. in a scurrilous
and base manner, departing from truth, all rules of decency and political
warfare; and in the last week, in an article headed "A Card," having
made a charge against him which was malignant and false, he was called
on by Mr. Clark, with a statement from Mr. Steere (who knew) of
its *falsity.* He handed him a refutation to sign. Mr. Weed refused to
do him that justice, and Mr. Clark gave him, what he *richly merited—
a cowhiding.*[69]

It appears that Weed wrenched the whip from Clark and used
it in his own defense, although the extent to which either was
chastised is hard to determine.[70]

---

[67] *Ibid.,* June 6, 1797.
[68] Hudson *Northern Whig,* Oct. 12, 1813.
[69] Norwich *Journal,* Nov. 9, 1819.
[70] *Ibid.,* Nov. 16, 1819. Hubbard contended that Weed struck *"one* or *two*
blows; but...that his blows 'sung innocent,' and 'spent their force in empty

The Anti-Masonic frenzy, or "Morgan excitement" as its opponents called it, produced strong enmities, and printers were from the first in the thick of it. In the beginning David C. Miller, of Batavia, printer for Morgan, was subjected to rough treatment. At the time of Morgan's disappearance Miller's printing office was set on fire, endangering the lives of his employees. The following night he was seized by a mob and roughly carried to the neighboring village of Le Roy, where he was turned over to a magistrate; but since no charge was made against him he was released.[71]

Such attacks on Anti-Masonic editors and their presses provided a martyrdom on which their cause thrived. The censure of Dr. Jesse Fifield, of Waterloo, by William Child, of the *Seneca Farmer,* "for some of his masonic acts," caused the doctor to start litigation against the printer and finally to enter his office and assault him with a club.[72] C. S. McConnell, of the Geneva *Republican Phalanx,* who had opposed the Anti-Masons, was brutally beaten in his office by Robert S. Rose, a candidate for Congress;[73] and Simeon Francis, editor and printer of the *Buffalo Emporium,* was attacked in the street "in a most dastardly manner," by Ebenezer F. Norton, a recent candidate for the assembly, whom he had provoked by articles in his paper.[74] In two of these instances legal action was taken by the printers, and Rose was convicted and fined.[75]

Equally serious in the eyes of the printer was the attack upon his press, the very means of his subsistence, which was

---

air.'" Weed did not mention this incident in his *Autobiography,* but his side was given in the Norwich *Anti-Masonic Telegraph,* Feb. 24, 1830. In the *Memoir* by T. W. Barnes, p. 15, a resident of Norwich recounted that Weed "seized the Whip and applied it to Mr. Clark to his satisfaction."

[71] Batavia *Republican Advocate,* Sept. 15, 1826. This paper was dated on Friday, the first outrage being committed Monday. As Miller was incapacitated by the experience, his son Charles W. Miller, wrote of the incidents. Three men, found guilty of this assault, were sentenced to be imprisoned for three months, six months, and one year, respectively. *Buffalo Emporium,* April 19, 1827.

[72] *Republican Advocate,* Oct. 30, 1829.

[73] *Geneva Gazette,* Nov. 5, 1828.

[74] *Buffalo Emporium,* Nov. 5, 1827; *Buffalo Journal,* Nov. 6, 1827.

[75] Rochester *Craftsman,* Oct. 13, 1829.

quite naturally regarded by his enemies as the engine of libelous publication. Asa Child, of the *Montgomery Republican,*
suffered such an attack from his political enemies, the report
of which was given in later years by his daughter.

I well remember the time when politics were running so high in
Governor Clinton's day. The Democrats [Bucktails] had no press in
Johnstown at that time, and were obliged to get their printing done
at my father's office. And one night they went in and demolished the
form that was ready for the press in the morning, and scattered the
type in every direction. The excitement was so great we trembled
for my father's life.[76]

The efforts of the *Anti-Masonic Free Press,* of Oswego,
apparently aroused the antipathy of some of the more strenuous citizens of that village, whose retaliation is graphically
described in the following item.

On Saturday the 27th last, we were surprised to witness a tragedy,
or a battle, we know not what to call it, between the printers of the
Free Press office and the members, or part of the members, of the fire
company, who, it appears were determined (to use their own expression) to "cleanse the Anti-Masonic office." The report, it appears, had
been in circulation ever since the appearance of an article which cau-
tioned the fire company as respects discipline, etc. The engine was taken
to the dock, filled with water, and discharged on one of the buildings on
the wharf—it was then proposed by some of the members to go up and
"Cleanse the anti-masonic printing office." The attack was commenced
by pouring a sheet of water into the windows, to the great annoyance
of the Anti-masonic compositors, who it appears repelled the attack by
a sudden discharge of a brace of pistols through the windows for the
purpose of frightening them away. The assailants charged upon the
office—They rushed headlong upstairs, collared the editor [Mr. Oli-
phant], knocked down the cases and made pi of everything that appeared
in the way.

"Let us throw the d—d anti-masonic press out the window," roared
the Stentorian voice of one of the rioters—who, it appears, when on
taking hold of it found it was rather too heavy to be tossed out of the
window very easy. "Knock down that d—d little anti-masonic editor,
throw him out of the window and stamp him in the mud," roared another,—but it appeared, one of the journeymen stepped forth in defense

[76] Child, Elias, *Genealogy of the Child, Childs, and Childe Families,* p. 137.
Cf. the case of the *Lansingburgh Gazette; Buffalo Emporium,* June 18, 1827.

of Mr. Oliphant, presented a pistol, and told them if they laid hands on him (the editor) he should protect him.

The rioters were at length quelled by arresting Mr. O. together with his journeymen, for an assault with attempt to kill, when by the by, the fire company were the assailants. The trial lasted until the next Tuesday, when the "prisoners" were all discharged but one, who is bound over, in bonds for four hundred dollars, to appear at court. We forbear making further remarks until after the trial, when we hope the prisoners will be released, and the press, the ark of our public safety, be permitted to stand unimpaired by the hand of violence.[77]

An earlier instance of violent seizure of printing materials and press was the case of the *Waterloo Gazette* in 1817. This paper was first started at Ovid in 1815 as the *Seneca Patriot* by Samuel R. Brown, of Auburn, who sent his journeyman, James G. Hathaway, as a partner, and obtained another printer, George Lewis, of Manlius. At the close of the first year there seemed to be some confusion as to the division of the proceeds and also as to the relative shares of Hathaway and Lewis. After some negotiation, however, the establishment came into the hands of Lewis. He took the paper to Waterloo and published it as the *Waterloo Gazette*. Although Hathaway still maintained that he possessed an interest, which on two occasions he sold to other printers, he was unable to make good his title. Lewis then sold to Hiram Leavenworth, who employed Hathaway as a journeyman.[78] In the meantime the paper had become implicated in the struggle over the location of the county courts. It had offended the former sheriff, who now was inclined to make use of the disappointed and aggrieved Hathaway. So on November 6, 1817, Leavenworth was decoyed away from his office, leaving Hathaway at work, and in his absence the press and types were loaded on a wagon and carried off. The press was found near an inn owned by the ex-sheriff, but the type had been "distributed" through the town. Hathaway was then apprehended and lodged in prison, from whence he bemoaned the "injustice" done him. The

[77] *Watertown Censor,* Apr. 13, 1830.
[78] Auburn *Advocate of the People,* Nov. 26, Dec. 10, 1817; letters of Hathaway and Lewis, respectively.

crudeness of this attempt not only caused the legal penalty to be employed but antagonized most of the printers of the district.[79]

With such a prevailing spirit of violence and abuse, the resort to law was regarded as the logical means of maintaining order and respectability. It was also the ready recourse of the politician in checking the overzealous attacks of his opponents in the press. In considering these incursions upon the freedom of the press, therefore, it is necessary to examine the law of libel as it was then applied.

Libel suits were generally instituted under the procedure of the English common law, and lawyers followed the usual English practice. There the traditional doctrine was "the greater the truth, the greater the libel," which even Andrew Hamilton was unable to circumvent in the trial of Zenger. In this famous case the prosecution also contended that only the fact of the publication could be determined by the jury, while the court must determine the law and whether the publication were libelous. In a masterful speech in favor of speaking and writing the truth Hamilton persuaded the jury to judge of both the law and the fact and secured the acquittal of Zenger, a resounding victory for the freedom of the press. These early, colonial cases were all for seditious or criminal libel; i.e., for written defamation, which was considered a cause of disorder and a crime against the state. Civil libel, originally verbal defamation, directed against a private individual was prosecuted under the common law. Truth was admissible in civil libel to procure a mitigation of damages, but was considered irrelevant in cases of criminal libel.[80]

An outstanding gain was made in connection with the notorious Sedition Act of 1798. Section 3 of this statute included the provision that:

---

[79] *Ibid.*, Dec. 10, 1817; see also *Ontario Repository*, Nov. 18, 1817.

[80] Hudson, Frederic, *Journalism in the United States,* pp. 85-90; Rutherford, Livingston, *John Peter Zenger,* pp. 63-124. See Bacon, Matthew, *A New Abridgement of the Law,* 3d ed., London (1768), III, 495.

...it shall be lawful for the defendant, upon the trial of the cause, to give in evidence in his defence, the truth of the matter contained in the publication charged as a libel. And the jury who shall try the cause, shall have a right to determine the law and the fact, under the direction of the court, as in other cases.[81]

It was not a permanent gain, however, for the act expired with the Adams administration, March 3, 1801. Subsequent cases were therefore subject to the same ancient interpretations, pending action by the state legislatures. In New York this legislation was hastened by the trial of Harry Croswell for a libel on President Jefferson. Alexander Hamilton was the counsel for Croswell when the case was argued before the supreme court of the state, and the same ruling as in the Zenger case prevailed, that the jury should determine only the fact of publication, the libelous character being a question for the court.[82] The right of a new trial was denied, and while Croswell was not acquitted the case was allowed to drop. Hamilton's argument that the truth should be admitted in evidence and that the jury should determine the law and the fact convinced Justice Kent, and in the following year a statute was enacted in accordance with his plea.[83]

Hamilton's argument, as recorded by Kent, was that the giving of truth in evidence had been admitted under Roman law, and that its exclusion had come from "a polluted source, the Court of Star Chamber." For this reason it should "deserve to be considered in no better light than as a *malus usus* which ought to be abolished." [84] He also reasoned that a case of libel was one in which the law and the fact were "always blended," and therefore that the jury should be given the power to decide both.[85] The influence of this speech was the greater because Kent, who was greatly impressed, and other

[81] *U. S. Statutes at Large,* I, 596-597.

[82] People vs. Croswell, 3 Johnson, 337; Cooper, Thomas, *Treatise on the Law of Libel,* pp. 78-81.

[83] *Laws of the State of New York* (1805), IV, 232-233.

[84] Kent MS, *Croswell ads. People,* pp. 67-68. MS is in New York Public Library.

[85] *Ibid.,* pp. 69-71.

judges of the court were on the Council of Revision which passed upon the measure finally enacted April 6, 1805.[86]

This law specifically permitted the jury to judge and determine "the law and the fact," and did not compel it to convict on proof merely of the fact of publication of the matter charged as libelous. It permitted the defendant to give the truth in evidence, although not allowing such evidence as justification, unless it could be proved that it was published "with good motives and for justifiable ends." The punishment for a person convicted of publishing criminal libel was not to exceed eighteen months' imprisonment, or a fine of five thousand dollars. Prosecution "by information" was declared unlawful.[87]

The securing in the law of these elements of fairness and justice was not sufficient, however, to mitigate the dangers into which printers were constantly running, through the supposedly legitimate exercise of publication. As one put it:

> I know that the doctrine of libels occupies so broad a field that, in political controversy, it is difficult for Editors of political papers to avoid them, even in defending the principles the most correct. Libels are of two kinds, *express* and *implied;* the first class consists of bold and slanderous attacks on personal character, and justly merits a severe punishment; the second is extremely diffuse and almost uncircumscribable; thus to ridicule the talents, to question the designs, and (tho' we have no sedition law) even critically to investigate the conduct of a public officer, may, in nice construction on common law points, be so defined; hence suits on this principle, might be justified every day, though like Cheetham's pamphlets they should be
> "Born for an hour, perhaps, then squeak and die."[88]

In civil suits it has been notoriously difficult for the legal profession to define a libel. Andrew Hamilton in his speech

---

[86] *Ibid.*, pp. 153-157. Kent records the meeting of the council, including Gov. Lewis, Chancellor Lansing, Judges Thompson, Spencer, and Kent, who met Nov. 3, 1804, and considered objections to the bill.

[87] *Laws of the State of New York* (1805), *loc. cit.* While an English statute, Fox's Libel Act of 1792 (Geo. III, c. 60 § 1), permitted the jury to acquit the accused, even though he had published the document upon which prosecution was based (and therefore enabled the jury to consider the truth of the libel), justification by truth in criminal libel was not provided for specifically in England before 1843 (Lord Campbell's Libel Act).

[88] Poughkeepsie *Political Barometer*, Feb. 11, 1806. Editorial by Isaac Mitchell.

for Zenger condemned and ridiculed the so-called libel of "innuendo," but many such were prosecuted with success. As a result of changes in the law, justification by proof of the assertion became generally recognized, although such justification might be qualified by evidence of malicious intent.

Printers felt themselves protected if they could reveal the name of the author of an offensive publication, but this did not deter the prosecutor from bringing suit, nor the courts from holding them liable. In 1805 the publishers of the *Poughkeepsie Journal* complained of the suit against them after they had given the name of the author. As Federalists they were not concerned with the factional contests among Republicans, in connection with which the communication appeared. "We presume that the instance is unheard of," they stated, "that the printers of a paper have been prosecuted for a publication after giving up the name of the author." [89]

It was not so unheard of as they imagined for the printer to be held responsible for what he did not write. A few years later Oliver Lyon of the Troy *Northern Budget* was convicted and a judgment of $150 sustained in a case where the author's name appeared in the original publication.[90] In 1799 David Frothingham was severely punished and fined one hundred dollars for reprinting from another paper a statement which was considered libelous. He was not the proprietor of the newspaper, the New York *Argus,* which had been printed by him for Mrs. Greenleaf since the death of her husband. He received from her for his services "a salary of eight dollars per week, and no more." [91]

More doubtful in many respects was the suit in which Alden Spooner was convicted for publishing a paid advertisement, which sought the whereabouts of one Christopher Scanlan, who was suspected of stealing a trunk while steward on a boat

[89] *Poughkeepsie Journal,* Oct. 8, 1805.

[90] Dole vs. Lyon, 10 Johnson, 447. The publication was: "I now, sir, publish you to the world as a man destitute of honor destitute of courage, and destitute of every moral principle and feeling which renders a man valuable to society. Troy, 15th November, 1808, *G. D. Young."*

[91] *Greenleaf's New York Journal & Patriotic Register,* Dec. 14, 1799.

on the Mississippi. As a result of the advertisement, Scanlan was seized in Brooklyn and imprisoned, but the case against him was not sustained, and it appeared later that he was innocent, another having been found guilty of the crime. In spite of the good intentions of Spooner, and the lack of malice, he was compelled to pay three hundred dollars.[92] Thus the printer was not entirely safe, even when he inserted an advertisement.

Some idea of the application of the law can be obtained from a review of the libel cases which occurred early in the nineteenth century as they were reported in the press. While a list of some size is thus obtained (Table II, pages 315-316), it is quite apparent that it is not complete. Many cases were not given sufficient publicity to preserve them for posterity, and the details of some were suppressed. This is fairly clear from the case of Francis Stebbins, of the Hudson *Northern Whig*. In his valedictory he mentioned his libel suits of six years' editorship, all of which had been settled favorably to him without trial, except one which he won, and one brought by Martin Van Buren, not then pressed.[93]

The prevalence of suits in the earlier period is shown by the statement of John Woodworth, for the first decade of the century. "This State of Things grew no better as Time wore on, for some years later Most of the Printers in the State, and not a few of the Lawyers, were under Prosecution for Libel." [94] In 1827 libel suits had become so common that their absence in a court session was noted, and some reason for the unusual condition was sought.

The editor of the *Sandy Hill Herald* mentions it as a little remarkable, that the grand Jury in the county of Warren, at the late terms of the General Sessions of the Peace, should have been discharged without finding a general bill of Indictment. It is not so remarkable as Mr. Wright may imagine. The same thing has occurred before; but not lately.

[92] Munsell, *Typographical Collections* (MS vol), II, 303-304; Brooklyn *Long Island Star,* July 31, 1823.
[93] Hudson *Northern Whig,* Dec. 27, 1814. The last only appears in the list herewith.
[94] Woodworth, John, *Reminiscences of Troy,* (2d edition, 1860), p. 43.

Mr. Wright can easily account for the fact, why Warren county has been for the last two years troubled with libel suits, and indictments for libels, when he reflects, that the handbill out of which most of the prosecutions have grown, was written in Washington county, and printed by himself, and sent into Warren county to set our citizens by the ears for the amusement of our neighbors in adjoining counties.[95]

The results of thirty-nine of the sixty-five cases listed are known, although not completely in every instance. Damages were assessed in twenty cases as follows: five under $50, three from $50 to $100, eleven between $100 and $500, and three over $500. In three cases of criminal libel or contempt which are listed, fines were from $10 to $50. The tendency, then, was to make the damages reasonable, or within the ability of the defendant or his backers to pay.[96] Of thirteen more it was reported that settlements were reached out of court, or some other disposition was made of the case. Six of these resulted in a retraction being printed by the newspaper. Four were dropped by the plaintiff, while there were two cases of outright acquittal, and one was dismissed by the court.[97] The remaining twenty-six may likewise have been dropped or settled, for the available papers are silent as to these. Printers were not always eager to publish details of their own cases in court, and an ignominious settlement was almost sure to go unrecorded. The chronological distribution of these cases shows little, but the bitterness of the Anti-Masonic agitation engendered a number of cases for the years 1827-1830.

As to the assessment of damages the following cases, with the newspaper comment, will prove illuminating. In 1818 Daniel Penfield was awarded a verdict of $8,000 against S. H. and H. A. Salisbury, printers of Buffalo, for printing a pamphlet, *An investigation of the title of Hon. William Dickson, Esq. to the township of Dumfries, in the district of Gore, U.*

[95] *Glens Falls Observer,* Oct. 27, 1827.

[96] As noted *supra,* chap. iv, there was a kind of understanding that when printers suffered suits and received fines, as a result of too ardent party service, the costs should be met by the party backers.

[97] To which, perhaps, should be added the case won by Stebbins, *supra,* p. 200, but not listed. On the thirteenth of these the jury did not agree and the case was dismissed.

C. containing an exposition of the conduct of the pretended claimants to said township.... The pamphlet accused Mr. Penfield of claiming the township under a forged deed, which he knew to be forged. The printers tried to justify their assertions as true, but their defense failed.[98] This unusually large verdict was explained by a fellow printer.

In giving the above verdict, the jury acted on the presumption that the printers were indemnified by Dickson, the writer of the pamphlet, who resides in Upper Canada, and beyond the reach of our laws. It appears to us proper to state this, because, though the verdict was fully warranted by the libel, the odium should not necessarily attach to the defendants in this case, to that degree which the trial would seem to indicate. *Ne scutica dignum horribli sectere flagello.*[99]

Were the printers, however, able to collect $8,000 from their Canadian customer?

The disparity between the means of the printer and those of his prosecutor might suggest leniency in the fine. Abraham H. Bennett, of the *Penn Yan Herald,* was tried for libel upon Col. Troup, the agent for the Pulteney estate, whom he had charged with spending three or four thousand dollars in the election against the Republicans. Bennett discovered that he was misinformed and pleaded guilty.

Under these circumstances, Col. Troup...prayed the court to consider the ends of public justice satisfied, and therefore to inflict a nominal punishment on Mr. Bennett. The court thereupon proceeded to admonish Mr. Bennett.... The admonition ended in complying with the prayer of Col. Troup for a nominal punishment; which was no more than ten dollars.[100]

Frequent settlement of libel suits out of court, after they had been instituted, shows the trivial nature of the offenses and the readiness of politicians and others to resort to this legal action for justification, rather than for an award of damages.

[98] *Ontario Repository,* June 30, 1818.
[99] *Ibid.*
[100] *Lansingburgh Gazette,* July 17, 1821, quoting the *Geneva Gazette.*

A gross assertion, an implied charge, or innuendo,[101] against the character of a man, would be followed by a demand of the printer that he disclose the name of the writer. Sometimes this was done, but even when the offending writing was by another, the printer might refuse to give up the name and might assume the burden of proof himself.[102] Whereupon the plaintiff filed his case against the printer, and the latter was notified by legal summons. At this point the matter might rest if the case were not pressed by the plaintiff, and many suits were thus allowed to lapse. At this stage, too, the defendant might repent and give the proper apology, and the suit would be dropped. Mere institution of suit, therefore, was sometimes sufficient to salve the wounded honor of the plaintiff.

Retractions, when printed, often show a complete lack of responsibility on the part of the printer for the libels published. He was misled or under the impression that the facts were as he had stated them. He believed charges readily, because he had implicit faith in the source of his information or in the character of his informant. He could not, however, shift responsibility to his informers unless they were the actual authors.

The tone of the retraction varied greatly. It might show that there was really no feeling of rancor between the parties to the suit, who had been acting only as political partisans; or it might be phrased with such "weasel words" as to make the situation no better, even though complying with the demand of the plaintiff. The former sort is illustrated in the following explanation of the suits by John C. Spencer against James Bogert, of the *Geneva Gazette,* which were "honorably and amicably adjusted."

These suits were commenced by Mr. Spencer, under the impression that in certain communications that formerly appeared in this paper, our object had been to injure his private character. But as political considera-

---

[101] H. A. Reed of Rochester prosecuted the proprietors of the *People's Press* of Batavia for this paragraph: "Hung be the Heavens in black! Iscariot Reed has lost his nomination for Assembly which he was promised after being crowded off the Senatorial race-course." *Anti-Masonic Enquirer,* Nov. 3, 1829.

[102] As in the case of Harry Croswell, *supra,* p. 176 and note.

tions were our sole object, and the author of these communications, as well as ourselves, not having intended to asperse his private reputation, there was no difficulty in settling these suits on an explanation taking place.[103]

It was generally the intention of the plaintiff, in securing a settlement, to make the defendant eat his words. One wonders, in view of its tone, whether the following retraction of Thurlow Weed was satisfactory.

The Libel suits growing out of the $1500 note endorsed last fall, by Gov. Van Buren, were settled, some months since, by the payment of costs, and the execution of the following paper, which was to be published in the *Enquirer*. On Saturday evening, *luther tucker* [sic] demanded its publication in this week's paper....

In this affair, the whole sin lies at *our* door. It was, however, an offense of the head, and not of the heart. We received two letters from highly respectable gentlemen in Albany, informing us that a note made by the leading politicians of this county, and endorsed by the candidate for Governor, had been negotiated in that city. These gentlemen inferred, as we did, that the money was raised for electioneering purposes. We still think, that the fact, unexplained, justified such an inference. Under this impression, we wrote the handbill, in the style of which, it must be confessed, we took counsel, rather of our feelings, than our judgment. Explanations followed which satisfied us that the $1500 was used to buy out a partner in the *Rochester Republican* and *Daily Advertiser* Establishment who was opposed to Gen. Jackson and Gov. Van Buren.[104]

In other instances the printer was made to grovel and humiliate himself, or did so in fear of his prosecutors. Commenting on the retraction published by the printer of the Oxford *President,* a Cooperstown editor remarked that his contemporary, "valuing *money* more than a *fair reputation* ... has proclaimed himself a *Liar* and hopes that it will satisfy..." The retraction follows:

The Editor, disclaiming any, the least [sic] intention to vilify the reputation of any respectable person whomsoever, and with a view to render, as far as in his power, full and complete justice to the character

[103] *Geneva Gazette,* Nov. 24, 1813.
[104] Rochester *Anti-Masonic Enquirer,* Oct. 27, 1829.

of *Stephen O. Runyan, Esq.,* hereby retracts the libellous aspersions upon the character of Mr. Runyan contained in a late communication republished in this paper from the "Olive Branch" on the 16th instant—a conviction of the falsity of the said aspersions, as well as the impropriety of my comments thereupon by way of interrogation, has led to this public avowal of the impropriety of said publication, and which it is hoped, will furnish a sufficient apology both to Mr. Runyan and the public.[105]

In retracting statements it was common to assert that they had been uttered or printed in the heat of a political campaign, thus accounting for their inaccuracy. James Comstock of the *People's Watch Tower,* of Ballston Spa, conceived it his duty,

to correct the inadvertent, erroneous statements, made or said to be made by me, on several occasions, to several of the electors of this county last spring, made under peculiar excitements, before and during a contested election, at which James Thompson, Esq. was a candidate for member of Congress....[106]

David M. Day, of Buffalo, printed articles written by Oliver Forward, a former state senator, which were considered libels upon Peter B. Porter. When the latter brought suit, Forward and Day offered a money settlement. Since money was not wanted, but a rectification of the wrong, this paved the way for the publication of Day's retraction in the *Buffalo Journal.*[107] Settlements and retractions not only emphasize the reckless partisanship of the times, but also show some printers as weak reeds swayed by the storms of political passion.

A few cases of contempt are noted. In this category falls the above-mentioned case of Samuel S. Freer, who was defended by Alexander Hamilton. His offense was commenting upon the court which tried Harry Croswell in 1804. The court found him guilty as charged but let him off with the light fine of ten dollars.[108] Another was that of George L. Birch, editor of the *Long Island Patriot,* who was guilty of holding "up to derision

[105] Cooperstown *Impartial Observer,* Dec. 10, 1808. "Olive Branch" refers to the Sherburne-Norwich *Olive Branch.*
[106] *Saratoga Sentinel,* Nov. 3, 1828.
[107] *Black Rock Gazette,* Sept. 13, 1825.
[108] *Supra,* p. 177. See also New York *Evening Post,* Feb. 24, 1804.

three magistrates of the county of Kings," before whom three of his apprentices had made application to be released from their indentures. Birch made no attempt to justify the truth of his publication but based his plea on "the unshackled freedom of the press, and that slight encroachment upon the character of individuals should rather be winked at than its liberty curtailed." The judge, however, in submitting the case to the jury, "animadverted in very pointed language upon the character of the libel, and its evil tendency in society, and particularly submitted to them that if a person erring in the performance of his judicial duties, should be liable to reprehension in a public journal; or if upon every supposed error, he was to be arraigned before the public and libelled or ridiculed, no person would consent to act in the capacity of a magistrate." The jury found the defendant guilty, but the fine was made only twenty-five dollars in view of the circumstances of the defendant and his publication of an apology.[109] The suit in cases of contempt, therefore, served more as a reprimand, and the court was content to admonish the publishers.

The frequency of libel suits and the threat of prosecution did not act as deterrents in modifying the scurrility and license exercised by the press. Far from living in fear, some printers courted suits and challenged their opponents to prosecute. There was the possibility of lenient punishment, if found guilty, and even the hope that others would pay the fine. There was in addition a litigious spirit abroad among those who brought suit, which used the smallest bit of satire or innuendo as a pretext; and there was a prevalent feeling that "honor" should not permit abusive or derisive language in the press to go unchallenged. Vindication of wounded character could only be obtained in court. Perhaps the political-mindedness of all public personages induced such a preoccupation with libel. It certainly did not proceed from mercenary motives.

In retrospect the era is not made attractive by these conditions, and yet it had its measure of virtue. Freedom of the press is conceded to be a most necessary attribute of political

[109] Brooklyn *Long Island Star*, June 14, 1827.

liberty, and, save for one brief interlude, the press was then free. If, in comparison with the press of today we conceive the conditions regarding libels to have been worse, there are certain differences to be noted. Political or governmental control was then the only possible restraint upon too great license, whereas we have now developed a number of other controls which are stronger than political control. The nation's press was then young (particularly that of the country), and it sought fully to exercise its great powers. The result was some abuse of those powers. It was beginning to learn that, as a great public institution it possessed responsibilities not to be held lightly. As one judge put it:

The press was not put into the hands of editors to enable them to wreak upon individuals their private resentment. In its proper exercise, it was a valuable and powerful auxiliary in the support of free government, but when it transcended its legitimate purposes, and broke out into licentious abuse, it became necessary for a jury to interpose, and curb it by salutary restraints of law.[110]

This was a testing time for political institutions. Not to have permitted free criticism would have been to sacrifice the most valuable fruits of national experience. Political and ethical codes were in the process of formation. Not to have permitted free criticism of public servants would have led to the sanction of evil practices. Printers and editors may not have been individually powerful, but collectively they were a power. While blaming or pitying the printers for their lapses and their incapacity, we should warmly commend them for a courageous exercise of freedom of expression.

[110] Clark, L. H., *Report of the Trial...of Silvanus Miller, Esq....against Mordecai M. Noah* (1823). The quotation is from the charge of Judge Betts to the jury.

VII
THE ENLIGHTENED PUBLIC

O'ER *rugged hills and vallies wide*
  He never yet has failed to trudge-it:
As steady as the flowing tide,
He hands about the Northern Budget.

AARON OLIVER, *Post-Rider,*
Troy Northern Budget (1798).

SAYS *Thomas, our neighbors have wrote to the printer*
  To stop sending news-papers during the winter;
For living is hard and provisions are dear,
And there's seldom much news at this time of the year:
But in summer the papers more news will contain
And then, or in spring we may take them again.
Says John, neighbor Thomas, your scheme makes me smile;
But how is the printer to live the mean while?
If times are so hard as you do not deny
The printer, unless he's supported, must die—
The summer or spring he can never survive,
Unless through the winter you keep him alive,
And if you once starve him it will be in vain
To expect that he ever will serve you again.
Says Thomas, indeed, we did none of us think
That printers could feel, or could want meat or drink.
Or like other people, would cloathing require
Or wood for the warming themselves by the fire.
And if none of these wants any trouble could cause,
They might live as bears do—by sucking their paws.

Schenectady Cabinet, October 23, 1816.

INCONSEQUENTIAL as the printer often seemed as an individual, the fact that the sheets from his press entered the homes and offices of hundreds of his fellow citizens, made it difficult to dismiss him with a wave of the hand. Though the educated may look today with contempt upon the sensation mongers of the press, the yellow journals and the "pulp" magazines, their extensive circulation is a fact not to be considered lightly. It has its importance in our cultural history and in the structure of our civilization.

To determine the influence of the country printer one might multiply the weekly output, as characterized in Chapter V, by the newspaper's circulation, for in that day the newspaper was perused from its head to the last advertisement in the last column. Reading matter was scarce in most homes, and in many the newspaper and the Bible had to fill the want. An editor of Poughkeepsie complained in 1802 that two-thirds of the families along the post routes did not get either of the Poughkeepsie papers. "And it is a melancholy trait in the history of our country, that there are yet many families of property who do not receive, or read any periodical paper.... No family in the United States ought to be destitute of a Bible and a newspaper."[1] Under these circumstances the printer became the evangel of education and literacy, as well as of liberty and political justice.

It must be noted, too, that circulation statistics do not tell the whole story, since every copy of a paper was likely to be read by several persons. Those who could not pay, or would not subscribe, were not averse to borrowing. This practice, of course, annoyed the printer, who occasionally paid his respects to the "borrowing fraternity."[2] The high valuation which many a subscriber placed upon his weekly newspaper is happily evidenced in the well preserved files which have found their

[1] Poughkeepsie *Political Barometer,* June 8, 1802.
[2] *Rochester Daily Advertiser,* Jan. 26, 1827.

way into our libraries, to the immense advantage of students of history.

What, then, was the circulation of the country newspaper? Calculating the newspapers of the state to be fifty-four in 1806, the *Troy Gazette* suggested "700 as the average number struck off at each press, at a publication—which (as the editor of the *Political Barometer* has remarked) is below the real number." [3] Since the fifty-four included seven dailies (of New York city), three semi-weeklies, and three which were issued "thrice a week," the figure was no doubt high for the country paper.

Papers came into existence with as few as one hundred subscribers, and some which had but two to four hundred were making a respectable start.[4] David Frothingham was encouraged to settle in Sag Harbor by the promise of three hundred and fifty subscribers.[5] At the same town in 1817, Samuel A. Seabury set four hundred subscribers as his goal before beginning the *American Eagle*.[6] The *Geneva Palladium* had issued but thirty-seven numbers when its printer died. At that time its subscription list of four hundred, which was reported to be increasing, was cited as proof of the opportunity thus afforded a new printer.[7] Our acidulous English observer found that there was "little difficulty in filling up a list with two or three hundred subscribers' names, for probably in no other country where newspapers exist do the subscribers trouble themselves less about finding the means of paying their newspaper subscriptions when due, than they do in the United States." [8] A list of five hundred subscribers was considered very respectable. Such was the list of the *Black Rock Gazette* in 1827, when it was offered for sale with the statement that it was conducted in an able manner and that "its mechanical style is not inferior to any other paper in the state." [9]

[3] *Troy Gazette*, Dec. 16, 1806.
[4] Batavia *Genesee Intelligencer*, in 1808, Follett, *op. cit.*, p. 56.
[5] D. Frothingham to Henry Dering, Feb. 7, 1791. Pennypacker Collection.
[6] Sag Harbor *Suffolk County Recorder*, June 7, 1817.
[7] *Geneva Palladium*, Sept. 25, 1816.
[8] *Penny Magazine*, X, 243.
[9] *Onondaga Register*, Nov. 7, 1827.

In 1801, Noah Webster sent out a questionnaire to newspaper proprietors in various parts of the country, seeking information on the state of the press. Among other things he asked for the number of papers printed by each establishment, but with what result, unfortunately, we do not know. Some of this correspondence, however, is available.[10] Harry Croswell of the Hudson *Balance* reported that he printed about four hundred and fifty weekly, although his paper had been issued then but six weeks. "We have a prospect, however, of a very liberal support." [11] At the same time the *Hudson Gazette,* which was then an establishment of sixteen years' standing, reported that it issued six hundred and fifty.[12] The *Balance* fulfilled its promise, for in 1803 it claimed a "subscription list, honored with near *seventeen hundred names.*" [13]

A list of a thousand or more names meant a relatively large establishment, one which reached beyond the confines of its own locality and raised the printer to a man of importance. While the larger towns were more likely to support such papers, there were some country papers which had impressive subscription lists. The Hudson *Bee* with eight hundred to one thousand in 1802; the Kingston *Plebeian* with eight hundred, the *Troy Gazette* with nine hundred in 1806, and the *Orange County Republican* with one thousand in 1806, were, of course, located in important centers of the older settled area.[14] But before the end of its first year the rural *Otsego Herald* was reaching "nearly eight hundred ... every week, and distributed in the counties of Otsego, Herkemer [*sic*], Onondago [*sic*], Ontario, Montgomery and Schohary [*sic*], and sent regularly to all the most capital towns in the United States." [15] In 1795,

---

[10] Noah Webster MSS, New York Public Library.

[11] *Ibid.,* Harry Croswell to Noah Webster, June 27, 1801.

[12] Ashbel Stoddard to Noah Webster, June 27, 1801.

[13] Hudson *Balance,* June 28, 1803. At the beginning of his fifth volume, Croswell claimed that "his weekly impression falls little short of two thousand."—Dec. 31, 1805.

[14] Munsell, *Typographical Miscellany,* p. 148; and Miller, *Sketches of Hudson,* pp. 64-65, for the *Bee; Plebeian,* Nov. 12, Dec. 12, 1806; Poughkeepsie *Political Barometer,* Aug. 19, 1806; *Troy Gazette,* Sept. 2, 1806.

[15] *Otsego Herald,* June 26, 1795.

when this section of the state was being laid out by settlers, the *Herald* was a pioneer press and the size of its list is therefore remarkable. The countryside must have been similarly well represented in the list of four or five hundred "dispersed" by the *Bath Gazette* and the one thousand of the *Ontario Gazette* in 1798.[16] In this class, too, might be placed the "enlightened public" of eight hundred and fifty which patronized the Herkimer *American* in 1810, the eight hundred who supported the Cazenovia *Pilot* in 1808, and the one thousand on the list of Bemis's *Ontario Repository*.[17]

In a later period it was natural that with the growth of population some papers would further enlarge their circulation. The *Saratoga Patriot,* a paper considered by its printer to be one of the best patronized in the state, claimed in 1813 that it "weekly published more than 1200."[18] In 1823 the *Dutchess Observer* claimed a circulation of twelve hundred, and announced that for a period of three years it had not fallen below one thousand.[19] Yet such a paper as the Cooperstown *Freeman's Journal,* with two thousand in 1828, was quite unusual.[20] The Poughkeepsie *Republican Telegraph and Observer,* a merger of two establishments, in 1830 issued sixteen hundred and sixty-eight.[21]

An increasing subscription list, of course, was a sure test of expanding influence. The *Buffalo Emporium,* which began in 1824 with only two hundred and fifty-nine subscribers, boasted of seven hundred at the beginning of its second volume, and seven hundred and fifty at the end of its second year. Of the latter number one hundred and fifty were taken in the village of Buffalo.[22] As good a face as possible was presented whenever such figures were quoted by printers, and so the testimony

[16] O'Callaghan, E. B., *Documentary History of the State of New York,* II, 1152.
[17] Herkimer *American,* Feb. 8, 1810; Cazenovia *Pilot,* Nov. 2, 1808; Follett, *op. cit.,* p. 5.
[18] *Saratoga Patriot,* Mar. 2, 1813.
[19] Poughkeepsie *Dutchess Observer,* Sept. 3, 1823.
[20] *Freeman's Journal,* Sept. 22, 1828.
[21] *Republican Telegraph and Observer,* Mar. 10, 1830.
[22] *Buffalo Emporium,* Sept. 3, 1825, Oct. 7, 1826.

given would tend to err in the direction of a large list. Frederick Follett, a printer of wide experience through this period, mentioned approvingly the subscription lists of four papers printed in Chautauqua in 1847, as being 500, 600, and 1,000, respectively. He added, "If they are paying subscribers, this is very well—if, as is too often the case, they are mere men of straw, taking the paper without ever intending to pay, the number is altogether too large." [23]

When a few hundreds made up the total subscription list, the loss or addition of twenty or thirty subscribers might mean the difference between success and failure. Francis Adancourt was undoubtedly gratified by his expanding list during the campaign of 1824, but he was unable to supply his new patrons promptly.

We owe an apology to several of our editorial brethren for not sending them our paper regularly, for several weeks past. The failure has been owing to frequent extra calls for the *Register,* and an unusual influx of new subscribers, whose names generally come in after our form is taken off the press and partly distributed. We have several times endeavored to meet these calls by wetting down more paper; but even this precaution has been found unavailing. On Thursday last we received a list of 19 subscribers, which we could not supply, all our edition being previously disposed of, although we had printed 2 quires more paper than the week previous.[24]

These accessions usually came in the midst of a presidential campaign. So the Jacksonian editor of the *Troy Budget,* in 1828, reported:

During the month of August just passed, we find on looking over our books, that 63 persons have become subscribers. Three persons have discontinued their papers, one because he was moving from the county, one because he had not the time to read it, and one because he was an Adams man, or rather because we were not.[25]

An abrupt change in political allegiance, or an outspoken declaration by one previously neutral, might provoke some to

[23] Follett, *op. cit.,* p. 35.
[24] Troy *Farmer's Register,* Sept. 7, 1824.
[25] *Troy Budget,* Sept. 2, 1828.

drop and others to take the paper. This was most noticeable as the lines were drawn in regard to Masonry after the disappearance of Morgan. After taking its stand with the Anti-Masons, the *Jamestown Journal* claimed an addition of nearly 200 names, with the loss of only ten.[26] On the other hand a Palmyra paper gave up its neutral course to favor Anti-Masonry and lost fifty subscribers, "some avowing their adherence to Masonry as the reason, others declaring their unwillingness to have anything to do with politics, not even so much as to take a political paper." [27]

An attack upon the newspaper's circulation, then as now, was bound to produce a vigorous reaction. The printer's subscription list was a sore point.

The columns of a newspaper are fair game; and we never shall object to decent remarks or manly criticism. But when rivals descend to the dishonorable and contemptible employment, of going about the streets, into grog-shops and bar rooms, stating that the *Emporium* is not read, that it has no circulation, and advising our friends not to take it or advertise in its columns, we shall not hesitate to express the contempt we feel for such fellows. That such remarks are frequently made and such advice given, by those who would wish to be considered honorable men, we have abundant testimony.[28]

Subscribers usually received their papers from the post rider, who made a weekly journey through the country, dispensing newspapers, carrying mail in the absence of a regular mail service, and performing sundry errands for the people on his route. This work might be performed by a boy, a man engaged by the printer, or by the printer himself. Anson Spencer, as an apprentice to his brother, D. D. Spencer, carried his newspapers from Ithaca, sometimes using a one-horse wagon, but in bad weather going horseback.[29] The latter was the common method.

Not the least interesting part of the "Repository" establishment was the post riding, or mode of distribution, which affords an amusing con-

[26] *Jamestown Journal,* Jan. 16, 1828.
[27] *Western Spectator,* Apr. 19, 1831.
[28] *Buffalo Emporium,* Oct. 7, 1826.
[29] Selkreg, John H., *Landmarks of Tompkins County,* p. 123.

trast to the present lightning way of doing things. The most important route was the western, and he who supplied it was, in those days, of as great consequence as is now the superintendent of a railroad. Imagine a small, hump-back, cross-eyed, deaf, old man—and you may see honest Ezra Metcalf, who was as trustworthy as he was ugly—mounted on a skunk horse, and you have the post-rider. And now for his business: In an old-fashioned pair of saddle bags, were stowed from 150 to 200 papers. On top of this was a small portmanteau, containing the United States Mail, with a padlock; but whether the key was intrusted to the rider, as it might safely have been, is not remembered. Thus mounted, with tin horn in hand, which he blew when he got in the saddle, he set off....

The arrival and departure of "old Uncle Ezra," was an event, and caused a gathering of divers citizens, who felt as much anxiety about it, and what he carried and fetched, as do our citizens for the movement of the railroad cars. Errands were sent by him, and he always had some word from our neighbors who lived thirty or a hundred miles off. Once in three months he would bring from the postmaster at Fort Niagara, Lewiston, Buffalo, Batavia, and other settlements, lists of letters to be published.[30]

The best example of a printer, who was also a post rider, was Samuel S. Freer, of Kingston. He would edit, compose, and print his paper in the first half of the week, and then set out on Wednesday or Thursday morning with his saddlebags filled with copies of the *Ulster Gazette,* the traveling apostle of Federalism. He is pictured as having enjoyed the opportunity of dispensing verbal doses of Federalist doctrines at firesides and in public places along his route.[31] This advantage, perhaps, compensated for his distributing, on the same journey, the pernicious doctrines of his rivals, for he also carried the *Ulster Plebeian* and the *Craftsman.*[32] Some of Mr. Freer's editorial remarks elicited the following retort in the *Craftsman:*

As respects the "utter dereliction of principle" with which he is pleased to debit the Republican party.... This much can be taken for granted, that no saddlebags ever mounted over the top of the

[30] Follett, *op. cit.,* p. 5, quoting James D. Bemis.
[31] Schoonmaker, M., *History of Kingston,* p. 418. Another example of a printer who was his own post rider was Stephen B. Leonard, of Owego. Pierce and Hurd, *History of Tioga, Chemung, Tompkins and Schuyler Counties,* p. 103.
[32] Kingston *Craftsman,* Jan. 10, 1821, advertisement of Freer.

Kikeuyt hill upon the back of a galled jade, filled with more "utter dereliction of principle"; than the venerable and glossy pair which for years past, have mounted that hill, choked with Gazettes, under the hardened breech of the Editor. Good morning, Mr. Freer.[33]

The average post rider was a serious problem for the printer. He was often irresponsible and seldom cared to serve long on one route. Some even turned out to be rascals, as in the case of two post riders in Poughkeepsie, who collected what was due their three employers and decamped with their families and baggage.[34] In Erie County the "constable for Willink, and carrier of the news ... 'cleared out for Canada,' taking two horses, eight or ten watches, and other property."[35]

Then there were frequent complaints that the post rider was discriminating in favor of one paper, that the editor who hired him forbade the carrying of other newspapers, or unduly influenced the rider against his political rival.[36] Adancourt, of Troy, suggested to his subscribers that, due to the discrimination of the post rider on one route, they should make other arrangements for receiving their papers.[37] The printers of the Herkimer *American* had to repudiate the charge that their post riders were "restricted in a penalty of two or three hundred dollars from circulating democratic newspapers."[38]

There were two methods of employing post riders. The one probably first adopted was an arrangement whereby the printer would hire the rider for a fixed sum to deliver his papers regularly. Nicholas Power, of the *Poughkeepsie Journal*, informed the public in 1802 "that the different Postriders from his office, now take all the newspapers carried by them on their own account; they become accountable to him; and subscribers to them;"[39] which suggests that another plan had been followed previously. Julius C. Frary carried the Hudson *Bee*

---

[33] *Ibid.*, Mar. 22, 1822.
[34] Poughkeepsie *Dutchess Observer*, Oct. 1, 1817.
[35] Johnson, *History of Erie County*, p. 199.
[36] *Dutchess Observer*, Sept. 25, 1826; Auburn *Advocate of the People*, July 9, 1817; Batavia *Republican Advocate*, Nov. 27, 1829.
[37] Troy *Farmer's Register*, Mar. 12, 1811.
[38] Herkimer *American*, Feb. 8, 1810.
[39] *Poughkeepsie Journal*, Mar. 6, 1802.

"on account of the Editor, to whom each subscriber must be responsible for the papers he receives. To prevent mistakes during the continuance of the present arrangement, the Editor's *printed receipt* will be forwarded to each subscriber quarterly."[40] In addition, the rider was required to give security to the printer.

This arrangement seems not to have worked well, and that of making the rider responsible for all the papers he took was generally followed. The former method, of course, still had to be used if the post boy were a minor. One printer offered the prospective rider a choice of the two plans.

He will either pay the Rider Thirty Dollars a quarter, or he may take the *Plebeian* at a specific price, supply his own customers, they to be liable to him and he to me. Should he in having the papers as his own property elect to take the tour of the whole of Ulster County or take routes [*sic*] for the purpose of distributing them, of which the subscriber may have no idea yet he can have no reasonable objection.[41]

If the post boy adopted the latter method, as most of them did, it was necessary to have a route which would probably occupy him for several days. Printers' appeals for post riders held out the possibility of enlarging the subscription list and thus increasing the rider's income. The bundle of papers for his route was given to the rider at half price, and then he attempted to collect from his patrons quarterly. In 1825 such an arrangement was advertised for a route which could be traveled in three days from Kingston, and upon which "it is supposed at least 400 newspapers might weekly be circulated ... 400 papers weekly, at $2 each year, would amount to $800 per annum, whereof the Post would have the half for carrying and distributing them."[42]

---

[40] Hudson *Bee,* June 25, 1816.

[41] Kingston *Plebeian,* June 27, 1815.

[42] *Ulster Plebeian,* Feb. 2, 1825. Numerous notices for post riders are found in nearly every file. Those cited are only the more explicit. The Newburgh *Orange Telegraph,* July 2, 1829, made a similar statement which was less alluring, if more accurate. Three hundred papers could be distributed on a route which "need not occupy more than three days," and on which "a person of enterprise and energy may clear $150 or $200 per year."

The prospect of $400 a year for working three days in the week was alluring. There was a possibility, too, of small fees for other services. Yet the rider, like the printer, was plagued by the existence of many delinquent customers. Duns from the post rider, "Pay the Post," were as numerous as duns from the printer. Some were insistent, some jocular, and some contained the threat of giving up the route.

The Printer must have his money, and unless all those indebted to me for the last two quarters for papers immediately leave the money at the place where their papers are left, I shall not be able to pay the printer, or to serve them with papers any longer. *James Lester,* Gallatin, Sept. 3, 1812.[43]

One found himself "in danger of a *squeeze* from the printers." [44] Another went further, saying that if his customers did not pay, he must sell his property to pay the printers, or resort to law "to collect his thousand small and scattering debts." [45] Rufus Moss, of Onondaga, who had carried the *Register* for more than ten years paid his respects as follows:

The subscriber would inform his particular friend, the public, that wheat is selling in the New York Market at thirteen shillings, that Adams will be elected President in November, and that the paper printed on the 15th inst. completes the space of six months in which he has served the people faithfully, and for which he expects his thanks and his dues.[46]

As Adams was defeated, and the post rider died the following February at the age of 60, one wonders whether he received his "dues." [47]

The area covered by these riders was, of course, important. Few communities were like Sag Harbor, which its printer considered "well situated for the conveyance of News Papers without the assistance of a post." [48] Towns in the central part of

---

[43] Hudson *Northern Whig,* Sept. 14, 1812.
[44] Cooperstown *Otsego Herald,* Feb. 16, 1815.
[45] *Lansingburgh Gazette,* Apr. 18, 1799.
[46] *Onondaga Register,* Oct. 1, 1828.
[47] *Ibid.,* Feb. 11, 1829.
[48] *Frothingham's Long Island Herald,* Dec. 13, 1792.

the state were naturally interested in their own counties and those adjacent, but they were glad to have their post riders cross their boundaries or even state lines. The Ulster County papers were carried by their riders into Pennsylvania; [49] those of Lansingburgh, Troy, and Plattsburgh into Vermont. [50] The possibilities for an extensive circulation may be realized from the following acknowledgment, though allowance must be made for editorial exaggeration:

The liberal encouragement we receive in Champlaine, Plattsburgh, Chesterfield, Essex C. H. and some other towns in Clinton and Essex counties, in the State, merits our warmest thanks. Nor can we be less grateful to our patrons at Union College, in Schenectady; to those in Pompey, Manlius, Oxford, Niagara & other parts of the Western District in this State—to those at Williams College and in Williamstown, Lenox, &c. in Massachusetts—to those in Bennington, Arlington, Tinmouth, Middlebury, Vergennes, New Haven, Williston Charlotte, St. Albans, and various towns in Vermont; Albany, Waterford, Watervliet, Granville, Ballston, and Saratoga Springs, &c. in this State—and also to all those in this and other states who receive their papers from the various post-riders. [51]

Obviously some of these subscribers were served through the mails. Occasionally a post route became unprofitable because of slender patronage and had to be discontinued. In announcing the discontinuance of one route, the editor of the *Plebeian* gave the following argument:

As we wish the papers to be read throughout our own county, and also in Sullivan, especially as long as the two counties are identified in the interest of the elective franchise, we take the liberty to recommend to our Patrons in those places to form clubs where practicable, to procure the papers either from the office or the nearest Post Office. The greatest number of papers we circulate on the above mentioned route, are between this village and William Sypher's in Wawarsing, a distance of about thirty miles; in the whole of which there is no Post Office. Mr. Sypher lives about twelve miles from the Post Office in Bloomingburgh, Sullivan County. We therefore presume that a number of our Patrons south of Mr. Sypher's and in Sullivan may conveniently get

---

[49] Kingston *Ulster Sentinel,* Feb. 11, 1829.
[50] Troy *Northern Budget,* May 22, 1798.
[51] *Troy Gazette,* Sept. 2, 1806.

papers at that office.... The fact is we have paid at the rate of $182 per annum for carrying 175 *Plebeians* on that route, when better than two thirds of those papers were left between this and Mr. Sypher's.... We are constrained to declare we cannot afford the incidental expenses of that post rider.[52]

Some idea of the remoteness of many subscribers is thus afforded, and it can be seen why at least half of the subscription price went for distribution. In spite of these exertions, it was often incumbent upon the subscriber to journey some distance for his paper. A vignette of this distribution comes from the reminiscences of an old resident of Otsego.

In 1797-8-9, the *Otsego Herald* was generally brought by a post rider, who left our paper each Saturday afternoon at a neighbor's about a mile off, and it was my business to run through the woods over a hill, (often before breakfast,) after the paper, and I generally read the part containing the news, before reaching home. The escape and sailing of the French fleet from Toulon in 1798, with the army for the Egyptian expedition; the pursuit of Nelson in search of it, created a deep sensation in this country, for several months before hearing of the landing in Egypt, and the destruction of the French fleet at the battle of the Nile.[53]

The alternative to the post rider, as suggested by Editor Tappen of the *Plebeian,* was the distribution by "clubs," "companies," or "classes." The printer of the *Olive Branch,* in Sherburne, declared that it was his experience that distribution by post riders yielded him no profit;

but on the contrary, has, in some instances, turned to his serious disadvantage, in consequence of the irregularity of some in distributing the paper, and the improper mode of collection adopted by others, without the knowledge or consent of the editor. The practice, too, of taking the paper in classes, is becoming general, and has, in every instance, been productive of entire satisfaction to the subscribers. Taking these things into consideration, the editor has thought it advisable not to employ any post riders, for the ensuing winter.[54]

[52] *Ulster Plebeian,* Mar. 28, 1815, quoted in Schoonmaker, *History of Kingston,* pp. 416-417.
[53] Beardsley, Levi, *Reminiscences* (1852), pp. 65-66.
[54] Sherburne *Olive Branch,* Nov. 14, 1807.

This plan was, in brief, that a group of at least ten persons, living in one vicinity, should serve themselves by taking turns at going to the printing office for the papers for the group. Thirteen was a desirable number, for then each subscriber would make but one trip each quarter. This also reduced the cost of the subscription and relieved the printer of much responsibility. A much larger group, too, might get papers in this way.

For instance—one class in Exeter, takes fifty-five papers, and each in their [*sic*] turn, must procure them at 2d. each—of course when a person has taken his turn, he has the papers delivered to him for one year, and 3 weeks, and so will each class proportion their turns by their numbers. The person whose turn it is to procure the next packet will find his name and a note thereof, on his paper, so that with a little attention, there will be no mistake.[55]

Even such a system was not without its occasional failures, which caused one editor to supplement it with a new rule— "that when anyone fails in doing his duty in the above respect, and does not send or call for the papers as early as Saturday noon, in the week in which it is his turn, the publisher may procure a person who shall carry the papers for him, to the three places to which branches are directed, and charge said delinquent 37½ cents for the service." [56]

Moreover, there was at least one instance of pressure salesmanship in composing a group. "A person from Brutus informed us that a society had been formed in that town to take the 'Free Press' for one year, and advance the money for the benefit of the Editor—that he had been hurried into the measure by putting down his name by some of his officious neighbors, before he understood the political character of the paper, and that he regretted that he had done so." [57]

From the establishment of post routes by the printers of newspapers, the step to official mail lines was but a short one.

[55] Cooperstown *Otsego Herald,* Dec. 5, 1807.
[56] *Sangerfield Intelligencer,* Oct. 10, 1823; regarding its subscribers in Augusta.
[57] Auburn *Cayuga Patriot,* July 14, 1824; a complaint of a competitor.

From early times in this country the printer had been associated with the post office. He had occasionally occupied the office of postmaster, as has been noted above. He had found it necessary to distribute some of his papers through the mails, and he depended upon the mails for his exchanges and for letters containing news. Probably more than any person in the community, his interests were bound up with the post office. The post rider, as noted above, carried letters, parcels, and messages, in the absence of a mail route. Officials were slow in recognizing the need, and the initiative fell to private individuals—that is, to the printers.

The publishers of the *Albany Gazette* established a line to Niagara, and were so obliging as to deliver Letters through their Post Riders to all Places where there were no Mails, without Charge. These Messengers traversed the Country, which was then in a comparative wilderness state, in every Direction, on Horseback, and meeting at stated Points, interchanged Letters and Papers; and in some Cases, where the Business was not sufficient to support them, Subscriptions were raised for the Purpose among Merchants and others interested in their Continuance.[58]

In Utica the work of establishing new routes was taken up by Thomas Walker, printer of the *Columbian Gazette*. Much of the country to the northward, in Lewis and Jefferson counties, was virgin territory for the circulation of newspapers but needed the establishment of regular routes. Walker obtained from Postmaster General Gideon Granger the authority to establish mail routes wherever they could be self-sustaining. Commissions were then made out in blank and sent to him, and he and Silas Stowe, of Lewis County, were clothed with authority to designate postmasters and to contract for the conveyance of the mails.[59]

Stephen B. Leonard of the *Owego Gazette*, a postmaster

[58] Woodworth, John, *Reminiscences of Troy*, p. 51.
[59] Bagg, *Pioneers of Utica*, pp. 155-156. See original contract between Thomas Walker and the Postmaster General, for carrying the mails from Rome to Sackett's Harbor for $50 per quarter, signed by the assistant Postmaster General, bound in Vol. IX of the *Columbian Gazette* (1811), in Oneida Historical Society.

himself, established post routes from Owego to Norwich, Binghamton, Penn Yan, and Bath, and then obtained government contracts for the mail service by the post riders.[60] Thus the work of establishing postal routes was built upon the necessities of the printer.

In 1790 the postal system of the United States extended along the coast with seventy-five offices, but New York City was the only office in this state until the following year. By 1794 some routes had been established, and Postmaster General Pickering advertised for "proposals" to carry the mail westward to Whitestown and Cooperstown, and on to Canandaigua.[61] It was in that very year that a paper was begun in Whitestown, and in the following year that one was started in Cooperstown. Presses continued to be closely allied with the mails.

A mail route was officially established from Canandaigua to Buffalo in 1797, and shortly after to Niagara. Mail was carried by a single rider until 1808, when a stage route was in operation.[62] Other routes were soon established radiating from Buffalo into neighboring counties.[63] Here again the close relationship with newspaper presses is illustrated. As early as 1807 a newspaper appeared in Batavia on the Buffalo route, and the first press in Buffalo in 1811 was that of a Canandaigua printer.[64]

As late as 1826 the *Freeman's Journal,* of Cooperstown, took the lead in agitation for a new post route from that village to Chenango Point following the course of the Susquehanna and connecting with points to the southward. Petitions, circulated and sent to Washington, failed to influence the officials, who felt that the existing service was sufficient.[65]

[60] Peirce and Hurd, *History of Tioga, Chemung, Tompkins and Schuyler Counties,* p. 103.

[61] Hall, N. K., and Blossom, Thomas, "The Postal Service of the United States in Connection with the Local History of Buffalo," *Publications* of the Buffalo Historical Society, IV, 308-309.

[62] *Ibid.,* pp. 310-311.

[63] *Ibid.,* pp. 312-313.

[64] *Supra,* chap. iv. Follett, *op. cit.,* p. 56, is authority for the first Batavia press.

[65] Cooperstown *Freeman's Journal,* Apr. 17, 1826.

Postal service was greatly expedited by the lines of stage coaches which soon began to ply over the roads from east to west, and later in other directions. Supplying conveyance for travelers as well as communication with distant points, they bade fair to replace the post rider in carrying the mails on main routes. When better roads were broken through the wilderness, there was greater regularity in the service and quicker transmission of mail to and from printing offices.

The printers were glad to hail each new effort in improving the service, as a boon to mankind and as a proof of the progress of the country. So, in 1814, Geneva rejoiced because of its *"Daily Stage.—Summer Establishment.—*This week the Stage commences running every day from *Geneva* to *Utica* and Canandaigua. The *Mail* continues (for the present) as heretofore, to be carried three times a week." [66] The next summer the following appeared in the Onondaga paper:

Expedition. The line of Stages from Albany to Manlius, via Cherry Valley, is again extended to Canandaigua, and performs the whole distance, 200 miles, in two days, arriving at Canandaigua 3 times a week.

The *old main line* via Utica will perform the route from Albany to Geneva in two days. [67]

By 1828 there was an express coach service from west to east across the state. The people of Buffalo were advised of its existence in the following notice.

SIX PASSENGERS Only! Buffalo to Albany.—The New Coach Line TELEGRAPH, leaves Buffalo every evening at ½ past 6 o'clock, —arrives at Auburn the first day, Schenectady the second, and New York by Steamboat from Albany the third. [68]

Regarding the above advertisement, the editor commented, "such exertions to anticipate the wants of the traveling Publick,

---

[66] *Geneva Gazette,* May 18, 1814. The first stage from Canandaigua to Buffalo (1808) was only required by its chartering law to make the trip once a week. As late as 1824 the official regulations required the mails to be transported over this route but three times a week. Hall and Blossom, *loc. cit.,* pp. 311-313.

[67] *Onondaga Register,* Aug. 9, 1815.

[68] *Buffalo Journal,* June 3, 1828.

should not pass unrewarded." [69] Other stage lines in other directions did much to extend communications over the state, but they cannot be enumerated here. Suggestive, however, is the note from Geneva in 1816:

A STAGE has commenced running from this village through Benton and Wayne, to Bath in Steuben county. It is contemplated shortly to extend it to the headwaters of the Allegany. [70]

Much was expected from these lines by the country printer, but his disappointment was great. He printed a multitude of complaints concerning the service. Mails were mishandled and misdirected at the distributing centers; and, at times, a malicious spirit was detected in the system.

The northern mail, which should have reached Plattsburgh three times a week in 1821, was the cause of much complaint. Sometimes the carriers missed a trip; or again they came in with empty bags. The printer was irritated by the occasional change of the route, up the east side of the lake to Charlotte, Vermont. He had a real grievance, too, when an *Albany Argus* was eight days in reaching him, while the stage from Albany made the trip in two. "But the conveyance of the mail," he protested, "seems to be farmed out with reference to accommodating the contractor, instead of the public." [71]

The condition of the roads was a plausible, but not always satisfactory, excuse for delays. "Lest the badness of the roads should be urged as an apology for this tardiness," wrote a Poughkeepsie printer, "we state, that the heavy stage coach of Messrs. Kelsey & Co., which left New York two or three hours *after* the mail, arrived here full of passengers and baggage, nearly twenty-four hours *before it*." [72] If the Poughkeepsie printer felt that this was the most important route in the Union, the people up-state, even more dependent upon the mails, were equally emphatic in their protests. The printer at Geneva put this poser:

[69] *Ibid.* Cf. the New York to Buffalo mail schedule for 1820-1824, given by Hall and Blossom, *loc. cit.*, pp. 312-313.
[70] *Geneva Gazette*, Dec. 11, 1816.
[71] *Plattsburgh Republican*, Dec. 29, 1821; Apr. 13, 1822; Jan. 28, 1826.
[72] *Poughkeepsie Journal*, Mar. 18, 1818.

Whence does it often happen, that intelligence is copied from the Washington into the New York papers, and from the New York into the Albany papers, and, through the latter channels, is received at Geneva sometimes several days before the original papers arrive, although the Washington and New York papers are mailed at the same time for Geneva that they are for New York and Albany? Whence arises this defect, and on whom should the censure rest?[73]

In Cooperstown it was felt that there was a "reasonable cause for complaint in the fact, that our mails, from New York, via Cherry Valley, too often taken the Buffalo route." Thus the printer was left without the means of making his paper interesting and valuable through its regular exchanges.[74] There were also innumerable complaints of the incapacity of local postmasters. The printer of the *Oswego Palladium* was unable for a time to serve his subscribers properly through the Hannibal post office; since the papers were incorrectly routed for distant points. He, like others, blamed the postmaster.[75] Indeed, there were few communities in which the postmaster escaped criticism. He was suspected of opening, delaying, misdirecting, or suppressing mail; was charged with incompetence, ignorance, and with being the tool of politicians. These complaints, so freely aired in the papers, were eventually carried to his superiors in the postal service.[76] Finally, in 1826 the Postmaster General sent out the following circular to all postmasters regarding the handling of newspapers:

Sir: Complaints have been lately made of the delay and sometimes loss of Newspapers sent by mail. These may be attributable in some cases to the careless manner in which the papers are prepared for mail, but in others they are believed to arise from the inattention of the Postmasters. It is feared that some of them are so forgetful of their duty, as to consult

[73] *Geneva Gazette,* Mar. 10, 1819. For further complaint of the delivery of the mails to the westward, see *Buffalo Gazette,* Jan. 7, 1812; Fredonia *New York Censor,* Feb. 25, 1824; and *Rochester Daily Advertiser,* Apr. 2, 1827.

[74] *Freeman's Journal,* May 29, 1826.

[75] *Oswego Palladium,* Mar. 8, Apr. 5, 1822.

[76] *Geneva Gazette,* July 9, 1817; *Oneida Observer,* July 6, Sept. 21, 1830; *Saratoga Sentinel,* Jan. 24, 1821. See, especially, *ibid.,* Jan. 3, 1826, containing a letter from Postmaster General John McLean to Isaiah Bunce, Postmaster, reiterating the causes of his removal and the charges against him. Little was forgotten in this list.

the convenience of contractors on horse-route, by retaining a part of the packets when the mail is so large that the usual number of bags cannot contain it. Others, it is said, being more culpable, retain the newspapers to read them. A moment's reflection must convince every Post Master, guilty of either of these charges, that he trifles with the obligations imposed by his oath of office, and should be held responsible for such gross violation of duty.[77]

With such admonition, it was hoped that such incidents might be averted, or their number greatly diminished.

As already noted above, a list of "exchanges" was an important part of the printer's resources in making up his paper.[78] On the other hand, such a list of any size compelled him to make a larger number of impressions and increased his circulation without augmenting his income. There was no surety that the exchange which he received would be valuable, and it was often an extremely one-sided arrangement. Yet it was not only desirable for the country printer to get the Albany and New York papers—many of his most valued selections being clipped from their pages, but he hoped by sending them his sheet to attract the attention of the great and powerful in his party. Along with the isolated farmer and the petty merchant, these editorial brethren made up his "public," to whom his best original efforts were addressed.

It was disconcerting when his exchanges failed to come regularly. The delay might be caused by some sinister political plot. The printer of the *Long Island Patriot* suspected something of a "dusky hue" when he failed to get the Sag Harbor *Corrector* for four weeks. Through another paper he found that Col. Henry W. Hunt, proprietor of the *Corrector* was "a stump candidate for member of Assembly." "It looks bad, Colonel, when a man is ashamed that his deeds should be brought to light."[79] The *Black Rock Beacon* demanded that "Isaac Riggs, Esquire, member of assembly, chairman of the printing committee—and so forth, inform us his reason for

[77] Circular dated May 28, 1826, *Onondaga Register,* June 14, 1826. Lewis H. Redfield, printer of the *Register,* was at this time postmaster of Onondaga.
[78] *Supra,* chap. v.
[79] Brooklyn *Long Island Patriot,* Sept. 9, 1824.

sending an exchange only when he abuses the state printers—
we should like a regular exchange, or none." [80]

Croswell's Hudson *Balance,* gaining in circulation and influence, decided to reduce its exchange list. "Our means will not
support a tax of upwards of an hundred papers per week,
especially when a great portion of those received in exchange
are little obscure democratic prints, or papers which copy our
original productions without giving credit for them—or,
papers of which we get scarcely twenty in a year." [81] An
Auburn printer complained in 1823 that the *Argus* was no
longer sent to him in exchange, although the former state
printers had always kept him on their exchange lists. He urged
a return to the policy of Jesse Buel, who had made it a rule
while he was state printer to exchange papers with every
printer in the state, in order that state affairs might receive
proper attention in the county weeklies. [82]

In addition to his paid circulation and the copies which went
to other newspaper offices, the partisan editor often distributed
his paper for electioneering purposes. Under the head of "The
Jackson Fund," the *Long Island Star* charged in the fall of
1828 that many copies of the *Long Island Patriot* were being
circulated gratuitously. "Who pays the printer?" [83] Earlier in
the year it was asserted in the *Hudson Gazette* that both the
National Intelligencer, franked by a member of Congress, and
the *Dutchess Intelligencer* were being "circulated in this
county as free as water, without money and without price."
This was stoutly denied by the editor of the latter, who scouted
the whole story. As to the Congressman, "we know it to have
been his uniform practice, for many years, occasionally to
frank the *National Intelligencer,* containing the debates in
Congress, to such of his friends as he pleased, without asking

[80] *Black Rock Beacon,* July 15, 1824. See complaint of this same paper against
T. C. Strong of the *Palmyra Herald,* on account of irregular exchanges. *Ibid.,*
Sept. 4, 1823.
[81] Hudson *Balance,* Dec. 24, 1805.
[82] Auburn *Cayuga Republican,* Sept. 10, 1823.
[83] Brooklyn *Long Island Star,* Aug. 21, 1828.

the permission of Mr. Wilbur, the Recorder, or any one else." [84]

The use of the franking privilege and circulation by congressmen, were probably more general than this statement would imply. In establishing his paper in Bath, Benjamin Smead sought that kind of aid from his patron, Daniel Cruger, then a member of Congress. The logic by which it was justified can be seen in an excerpt from Smead's letter to Cruger.

I transmit them [subscription papers] in separate packets, because I understand I can frank only half an ounce—and as this pursuit is for the *public* benefits, the *public* will not be defrauded,—and therefore (as members of Congress have told me similar invasions are deemed and practiced by them as honorable) I consider it no fraud. If there be any tax, I will pay it for you.[85]

That the free circulation of newspapers was a recognized practice among partisans can be implied from the charge that Bache, of the Philadelphia *Aurora,* was paid by the French minister to send one hundred subscriptions to France and to distribute eight hundred gratis in the United States.[86] When the Government refused to continue six subscriptions to the *Aurora* for American diplomats in Europe, Bache sent them on at his own expense.[87] It is probable that this sort of circulation of country newspapers was not large, but occasionally it provided a part of the printer's public.

The price of newspapers has been suggested as a deterrent to their general circulation. It undoubtedly was in some instances, and yet the rates hardly appear to be prohibitive. For the period of this study the conventional price was two dollars for the year; and when the post rider did the deliv-

[84] Poughkeepsie *Dutchess Intelligencer,* June 25, 1828. There were, also, 75 copies of the *National Intelligencer* distributed at the expense of the government to "Printers of the Laws of the United States," H. Ex. Doc., No. 41, 19th Cong. 1st S. pp. 5-8. See *supra,* chap. iv.

[85] Clayton, W. W., *History of Steuben County,* p. 78, letter of Smead, dated Albany, Oct. 2, 1816.

[86] Faÿ, Bernard, *The Two Franklins, Fathers of American Democracy,* p. 271.

[87] *Ibid.*

ering, as noted above, he received half. A lower rate, usually $1.50, was extended to those who took the paper in
groups ("clubs," "classes," or "companies"), and looked after
the delivery themselves. Village subscribers who took their
papers at the office got a similar concession, as did also mail
subscribers who paid their subscriptions in advance, and who
also paid the postage. It must be apparent that those who received the papers by post, in groups, or in any other way except
by mail, rarely paid in advance. In some instances, however, a
special rate was made for payment in advance; while, at a
later date, advance payment became customary.[88]

Shortly after the turn of the century many papers found the
price of $1.50 the most desirable. The printers of the *Orange
County Gazette,* of Goshen, in its second number, reached this
conclusion. "When the Editors issued out proposals for the
Gazette they conceived that *Two Dollars* per annum would be
as low as they could afford to print it—but not finding sufficient
encouragement, they have concluded to publish it for *One
Dollar and Fifty Cents."* [89] Others undoubtedly found this
cheaper rate more successful in the starting of an establishment.

Beginning with the war years 1812-1815, however, there
was a general tendency to raise the price of subscriptions in
keeping with other commodities. Two dollars was the minimum considered for this period.[90] In June, 1813, the *Buffalo
Gazette* raised the subscription price to $3.00, $2.50 at the
office singly, and $2.00 in groups of 13 or over. The reaction
to this increase was such, however, that in the next month they

[88] Hudson *Balance,* 1801. In this case payment was to be quarterly in advance. Hudson *Bee,* Feb. 19, 1805, charged city subscribers and mail subscribers the same amount, $2.00. Hewett, D., *Traveller and Monthly Gazetteer*
(1828), listing the papers of the United States, mentioned that it was "an almost
unexceptionable custom in the United States, to require the amount in advance
for yearly subscriptions."

[89] Goshen *Orange County Gazette,* May 29, 1805. In that case, those who got
papers in groups might obtain them for $1.25. *Cambridge Gazette,* Mar. 21,
1804. Others who set the price at $1.50 were Newburgh *Recorder of the Times,*
June 6, 1805, and *Goshen Repository and Weekly Intelligencer,* Apr. 28, 1789.

[90] Prospectus of the *Onondaga Register,* July, 1814, a separate sheet for
signatures.

went back to the old price for mail and post subscriptions.[91]
In 1814 Riggs, of Schenectady, "in consequence of the cheapness of money," raised his price twenty-five cents.[92] In the same
year the Poughkeepsie printers, uniting on prices, and citing
the increased costs of materials and labor and the fact that
printers elsewhere had increased their prices (the Albany
printers "One Dollar per annum"), published a new scale:

To Village Subscribers, *Two Dollars and Fifty cents* per annum,
payable quarterly.
To subscribers who receive their papers by mail, *Two Dollars per
annum,* payable in advance.
To Companies who take their papers from the Office, *Two Dollars
per annum,* payable quarterly—Or *One Dollar and Seventy-five Cents,*
if paid in advance.
To subscribers who receive their papers by the *Post Riders, Two Dollars and Fifty Cents* payable quarterly—or *Two Dollars and Twenty-
Five Cents* if paid in advance.[93]

Ten years later, as a result of the economic slump following
the war, the Poughkeepsie printers agreed to put their prices
back at the old level—two dollars for village subscribers, "payable half yearly," and other rates in proportion.[94] Some effort
was now being made to cater to mail subscribers, and for their
benefit the terms were, $1.50 for those who pay in advance and
$2.00 if not paid in advance.[95] One editor put this proposal
convincingly:

We propose to forward this paper for subscribers to any post office in
this country, at *one dollar and fifty cents* a year payable at the expiration
thereof exclusive of postage, and as the postage cannot, in any such case,
exceed fifty cents on each paper a year, being the same price as if it were
transmitted by the post.
To persons living in the immediate vicinity of the post office it must

---

[91] *Buffalo Gazette,* June 29, July 20, 1813.
[92] Schenectady *Cabinet,* June 29, 1814.
[93] Poughkeepsie *Republican Herald,* Dec. 28, 1814. The same action was
taken by the *Saratoga Journal,* Apr. 5, 1814; Hudson *Bee,* Jan. 17, 1815; Hudson *Northern Whig,* Dec. 31, 1816, all with an explanation for the reasons for
their course.
[94] Poughkeepsie *Dutchess Observer,* Oct. 13, 1824.
[95] *Ibid.*

be immaterial whether they get it by either the one or the other mode of conveyance. And as the generality of persons in a town find it necessary occasionally to visit the Post Office, for their letters and papers, friends may in many cases so far accommodate each other in bringing papers from the Post Office as to make it equally convenient for them to receive their newspapers in that way, as by carrier, who is inevitably confined to his road, it not being expected that he would carry them to every person's door on a country route. . . .

Postmasters procuring subscribers for our paper or exercising any agency for us, will, as usual be furnished with the *Plebeian* gratis.[96]

This was the beginning of our dependence upon the mails for the distribution of all but local periodicals. In the light of the present systematic handling of these matters, the vicissitudes of the country printer are striking.

The printer's relationship with his public varied with changing conditions. As newspapers multiplied the patronage of the community was divided, and the profits of the individual printer declined. When every large village had its press, the far-flung circulation enjoyed by the pioneer was unlikely. The increase of population, of course, was some justification for the increased number of presses, but it was not sufficient to maintain the well-being of a rapidly growing craft. The *Massachusetts Spy* pointed this out and that the indirect costs were the principal obstacle to the profitable operation of a printing establishment. The cost of printing five hundred or five thousand newspapers (except for the paper on which they were printed) was approximately the same. While a list of five hundred subscribers might not support a press profitably, twelve hundred or fifteen hundred would be quite satisfactory. When papers were established so rapidly that none could secure sufficient patronage, the printer lacked any incentive to produce a valuable and interesting sheet.[97]

We have been led to these remarks, from observing the multitude of new papers which have sprung up within the last year, in all directions, far exceeding the increased wants of the community. Some of these wear the sickly aspect which betokens approaching dissolution, while others

[96] Kingston *Ulster Plebeian,* Feb. 2, 1825.
[97] Quoted in the *Long Island Patriot,* Dec. 27, 1827.

of a little longer standing, have closed their career. Many of these publications are located in places where neither the concentration of business, nor the means of acquiring information, affords the facilities necessary to justify the undertaking. In the outset, perhaps, by great exertion and solicitation a considerable subscription is obtained, but it is soon found, that when personal subscriptions are remitted, the subscription diminishes, and the circulation if kept up, must be a forced and unnatural one. The truth becomes manifest that names alone will not maintain a paper; the fair promises of support, given in the outset, are forgotten, some subscribers prove unable, and others unwilling to pay. The consequence is, that, it is either suspended, or dwindles along, with just enough vitality to injure others, and without enough to be of any advantage to itself or proprietors.[98]

This condition was perceived by the printers when rivals appeared in their vicinity, and they quite naturally resented it. They were prone to argue that they had vested rights based upon pioneer service to the community. Elihu Phinney declared in 1809 that he considered the *Impartial Observer* "an obtruder on him," and said that he would do all that he could to discourage its circulation.[99] "We admit a legal, but not an equitable, power of supplanting the *Herald*—It was a favorite *bantling* in 1795; and has surmounted numerous and powerful obstacles. . . ."[100]

In 1807 Mackay Croswell was equally sure of the intentions of the backers of the *American Eagle* in Catskill. "We can, say they, by forcing an extensive circulation for our paper, make it an object for merchants and others to give us their advertising support, as we are sensible that two presses cannot succeed here, his downfall and our rise must be the consequence."[101] When the other paper appeared he urged his prior claims, based on fourteen years of service, to the support of the community. "Our paper was established in the infancy of this town—'We have grown with its growth, and strengthened with its strength.'"[102] In Poughkeepsie in 1795, Nicholas

---

[98] *Ibid.*
[99] Cooperstown *Otsego Herald,* Mar. 18, 1809.
[100] *Ibid.,* June 18, 1808.
[101] *Catskill Recorder,* Jan. 5, 1807.
[102] *Ibid.,* Jan. 12, 1807.

Power made a similar plea. He had served the County of Dutchess for ten years. Another paper would mean "that one or both must fall," and he believed the *Poughkeepsie Journal* was deserving of support.[103]

In 1820 the printers of the two newspapers in Goshen were alarmed by the appearance of a third. Its justification was the lack of a purely Clintonian organ. The printer of the *Patriot* merely said that he did not know the two young men who printed the new paper and therefore could not recommend them to the public. "Besides, the prosperity of that paper, might not comport with our own interests in the 'pounds, shillings & pence' department, which . . . is no mean consideration with us." [104]

Alden Spooner's valedictory in Sag Harbor did not mention local competition, for there was none, but stated that his departure was caused by the inadequate support which the community afforded.

Our insular position—our scanty population—the very economical habits of the country, and the difficulty of receiving and dissseminating intelligence before the County would be supplied thro other channels, are insurmountable obstacles. . . . This County has many enlightened and patriotic citizens whose friendship I shall long remember; but they are indeed, too few, for the support of a newspaper.[105]

Printers had hailed with delight the improvements in communication, which assisted them in getting exchanges and the latest news, but these very improvements operated in the long run to the disadvantage of the country papers. In 1827 an editor in Goshen foresaw the ultimate result when he wrote:

It is well known that post roads and post offices have increased rapidly within a few years; and that almost every person can have convenient access to papers by mail; and *printers* know, that the New York papers, designed for circulation in the country, are made up twice a week from

[103] *Poughkeepsie Journal Extra*, Sept. 23, 1795.
[104] Goshen *Orange County Patriot*, Feb. 7, 1820. The third paper in Cayuga County proved to be the saturation point. See the announcement of dissolution in the Auburn *Advocate of the People*, Mar. 4, 1818.
[105] Sag Harbor *Suffolk Gazette*, Feb. 23, 1811.

the daily papers, and published at less expense, than we can publish our country papers—hence they can afford them at a lower price, in proportion to the news they contain, than we can our papers in the country; and thus, in consequence of the facility of the mails, and the cheapness of the city papers, the circulation of our country papers is rapidly diminishing, and ere long many of them must be consigned to oblivion. If the city editors would confine the circulation of their papers to the city, we could then afford to pay the difference ; but whilst their agents are constantly scouring the country picking up every subscriber who can pay *four dollars* a year, and leaving only those who can pay *two,* how can we do it? And if this system is to continue, and increase, as it has done of late years, we shall by and by have very few country papers published, and the poorer class of our population will be doomed to remain in ignorance, like the same class in the monarchies of the old world....[106]

This invasion of the field of the country printer by the city papers led Alden Spooner to begin a daily paper in Brooklyn. The *Brooklyn Evening Star* was an experiment, however, and after three months' trial it was given up as a failure. It could not compete with the New York dailies, so easily circulated in Brooklyn, which were superior to it in the handling of the news. Its printer concluded that his town was but a part of the great city, which it later became.[107] The appearance of semi-weeklies, too, was in part attributable to this condition. In announcing its semi-weekly edition, the *Utica Patriot* asserted that such a paper could disseminate material copied from the dailies as quickly as the semi-weeklies from Albany and New York.[108] Here, too, the outside competition was important.

Yet the Goshen printer was a true prophet, at least with regard to the destiny of the type of paper which he circulated. "The old order changeth." The country printer had reached his eminence and could see the long descent. The future greatness of the city dailies, with their editorial personalities, was beginning to loom. Shortly after 1830 the larger towns, Buffalo, Rochester, and Utica, were incorporated as cities, and their larger newspapers became semi-weeklies or dailies. Mergers took place, and the number of weekly papers was

---

[106] Goshen *Orange County Patriot,* June 11, 1827.
[107] *Brooklyn Evening Star,* June 30, 1827.
[108] *Utica Patriot,* Dec. 26, 1815.

temporarily lessened. In these larger establishments, too, the editor was not the printer, but more often the hired editor as mentioned above. For many years thereafter editors who were also printers published weekly papers in various parts of the state; but the printer-editor was never to occupy the prominent position that he once held. His paper had new competitors—the larger papers of the new cities and the country editions of the New York dailies—and his rôle as a politician and a molder of public opinion was of less consequence. The publisher, too, was less frequently a printer than one who hired others to print for him. The "public" was ceasing to look to the "printer" to be "enlightened."

VIII
CONCLUSION

I T is a truism of the social sciences that no phenomenon of the past can be so isolated as to allow its study independently of its environment. Likewise, contrary to the desire of the natural scientist, it is rarely the purpose of the student of society so to study his subject. He cares less for that which is isolated than for relationships and reactions which he is able to discern and describe. The environment, too, is his study.

So, if the profile and contours of the subject of this sketch, the country printer, are at times blurred and indistinct, there is this apology. The printer has been envisioned as a force in the community life of his town, county, and state. His peculiarities and problems have been related to the environment in which he worked. An attempt has been made to understand his obscurity in the annals of his time and to see in his life story something of the manners and customs of the plain folk whom he served.

Our study began with a consideration of the printer's calling but with no intention of writing the history of the trade, even for this brief period. Our purpose was to show him at work with his tools, striving to meet the problems peculiar to printing in his day. We found that printers, as a group, were bound by the ties of tradition, for the craft was rich in lore and customs. Colonial printers in America carried on these customs, and the printers whom we have studied were under their spell. Apprenticeship, the journeyman class, and some of the customs of the chapel survived.

The tools of the trade, too, were historic. While presses were improved in this period by new devices and sturdier construction, the Ramage press, so generally employed, was but the counterpart of that "common press" of the colonial and early English periods.[1] New and better types were being made

---

[1] The description of the Ramage of this period, *supra,* chap. i, corresponds to the illustration of the "common press" in Stower's *Printer's Grammar* (1808), which L. C. Wroth says was like that of the colonial printers.

in American type foundries, and these often gave a fresh appearance to the country newspaper. Toward the end of our period, too, the introduction of the composition roller for inking was a marked advance. On the whole, however, there were few changes in the mechanics of printing the country newspaper.

Concerning the lot of the workers, more facts were revealed. The apprentice had the same manifold duties. In 1830, however, the lad employed was likely to be older than the boy of 1785 or 1800. He was also better educated or was given more opportunity for schooling; and he probably enjoyed regular wages, at least in the last years of his apprenticeship. The changed conditions of labor in various years, no doubt, were reflected in his status. The growth of the urban labor movement, manifested especially in the late twenties, however, did little to improve conditions. The deplorable situation of "halfway journeymen," or boys plying their trade with insufficient training, was a degrading influence, but this, too, was more particularly the problem of the cities.

The plight of the journeyman grew worse. His vicious habits, as Thurlow Weed remarked, remained unchanged. His wandering propensity was just as strong, though it is evident that this was not entirely his fault. His prospects, in fact, grew worse with the passing years, for there seemed less possibility in 1830 than in 1800 of his emerging as a proprietor of his own establishment. He became increasingly dependent, a wage earner who sold his labor to others. While the successful printer-editor had passed through all the grades of the printing craft from apprentice to master, he realized that the next generation of journalists would not have the same background.

On the other hand, those printer-proprietors whose initial struggles we have watched with such interest, grew up with the land. Men like Bemis, Bogert, Dauby, Prentiss, Redfield, Williams, and many others, demonstrated through their careers the great social strides which had been made in their day. They became successful business men, *entrepreneurs,* and much that has been said about the power of the press and the influence of the editor, properly pertains to them. They had succeeded, and through their establishment of presses in other towns they extended their influence and helped others to succeed also. In a great variety of ways they built up their trade and in so doing benefited the community. They were citizens, in the larger sense, of their respective villages and counties.

In the last decade of the eighteenth century New York's population was growing rapidly. New villages, counties, and towns began to dot the map. They were planted by hardy pioneers with a vision of the future or were created by venturesome land speculators.[2] Once in existence, they began to boast of community achievements. What was done was exaggerated, and what was not done was promised. Progress was the ideal, and the virtue of the country printer was not only that his appearance was an indication of progress but that he, more than anyone else, could speak to the world.[3]

One of the characteristics of such a developing country was its preoccupation with politics. New political units were being created; town and county lines were being drawn; and large "purchases" were being divided. The speculator rushed in, to be sure, but so did the man of constructive views, the empire builder. There was every opportunity for young men. In those days the first judge of a county might be a young man of twenty-one; and the "dean" of printing in western New York, James D. Bemis, was surprisingly youthful.[4] The classic advice of Horace Greeley was, as yet, unuttered, but thousands were attracted by the prospects of the West.

Into this vale of opportunity plunged the printers. From printing offices in the older sections, especially from New England, they set forth. There was no prescribed route or destination. Some took their presses with them, others secured presses later; there were many (providential forces determining their

[2] Cf. Higgins, Ruth L., *Expansion in New York with Special Reference to the Eighteenth Century* (1931).

[3] An outstanding example of this was the establishment of the *Rochester Daily Advertiser*. Henry C. Sleight had a vision of a developing community. The *Daily* was a means of spreading that gospel. H. C. Sleight to Henry O'Reilly, May 20, 1873.

[4] Autobiographical letter, *loc. cit.*

destiny) who drifted Westward and into printing. Whether there was a demand for printers, or whether their appearance in such numbers was due to special conditions, a hothouse germination, it is impossible to ascertain. Their rapid increase in numbers resembled the "raining" of toads after a storm; and that was enough to cause some people to term them pests. In many instances the printers did behave like pests, and it required no new technique for the populace to characterize the whole by the worst part. But, in spite of his bad name, the printer performed an essential service.

Politics may not have created the country printer, but he found his greatest activity in party service; frequently a group of partisans or a faction in the community provided his financial backing. Such supporters quite naturally demanded a newspaper to their liking or even dictated its policies and wrote its editorials. Hence, the printer came to be called a hireling and a tool, although not a few resented the imputation and proved their independence.

Party leaders were aware of the power of the press in molding the public mind and availed themselves of country papers to reach their more remote constituents. The printer, becoming a politician, was not averse to political rewards. Although not all were satisfied, some became postmasters, sheriffs, magistrates, or legislators, thus profiting from their partisan activity. Other forms of reward were government printing, legal notices, and printing for the party organization, all of which the party leaders dispensed.

There was no diminution of this activity as the years passed, but, on the contrary, it increased. Later multiplication of newspapers was often due to the appearance of new factions (Bucktails, Anti-Masonic, or Anti-Regency groups), and thus competition was made intense by virtue of party backing. The rewarding of printers, too, was more pronounced with the coming of Jacksonian democracy. If this signified a new eminence for the editor, he had earned it through his past labors.

Among the rôles played by the printer-editor was that of champion of his party's principles, measures, and candidates.

His zeal in this often led him to a violent attack upon not only the principles but also the personalities of the enemy. Recriminations and charges, recklessly hurled with little prior investigation of their truth, seemed to characterize these attacks. The result was innumerable suits at law and occasional assaults upon the editor's person. Some of these suits were no doubt justified. Others proceeded from a chip-on-the-shoulder attitude or were deliberately utilized as a means of party warfare. At all events, they created an unwholesome situation and served to blacken the reputation of the journalist.

Political convictions, however, were deep seated, and "principle" was held dear. For that reason it was essential that free expression should be permitted and that there should be no recurrence of the sedition legislation of 1798. An attempt to check journalistic abuses by drastic governmental action would have been worse than the evil. Some good results, too, came from this unseemly litigation, for this period witnessed the enactment of better laws regarding libels—an end for which the champions of free speech had long been striving.

As a journalist, it appears that the country printer was the "city editor" of his day. This paradox raises him from the low position to which so often he has been relegated. His purpose was not to publish neighborhood gossip and community happenings. He devoted his attention to the affairs of state and nation and sifted the reports from far and wide to give their broadening "intelligence" to his readers. During most of this period the latter were not reached by the newspapers of the cities. The country editor, then, was a factor in the dissemination of information on all topics (not local) ; and especially in the spread of political doctrines. He was an important link in the great journalistic hook-up. This function of the country printer was passing in 1830, and now has ceased to be.

There are other differences, too, quite as striking, between the country editor and the journalist of today. The characteristic enterprise and resourcefulness of the twentieth century newspaper man seemed nonexistent before 1830. Nor was the country printer alone deficient in this respect. The city dailies were yet to learn from James Gordon Bennett to exploit personalities; from Benjamin H. Day to print a cheap paper for the masses. Editors were yet to see Horace Greeley emerge as an arbiter of opinion who made his judgments and courageously forced them upon a hostile public. A half-century later publishers were to struggle for the maximum of circulation by means of "yellow" sensationalism, scare headlines, and rapid-fire stores.

The gap between the country printer and the man who conducted a city daily was not so great as it is today. A reputation could be earned in Cooperstown or Hudson, and the opinions of a "typesetter" were read with respect by the politically powerful. Expedition in the collection of news was deemed desirable, but the chief enterprise of publishers was not to that end. For a few decades the reportorial "scoop," was confined to the early reproduction of the President's message. The staff of an establishment were, for the most part, engaged in the mechanical operations. When the paid editor was first employed, even for larger semi-weeklies or dailies he often had a part-time job. He practiced law and played politics on the side.

As a factor in the journalistic development of the country the printer is not to be lightly considered. As long as the maintenance of a large subscription list by New York City and Albany newspapers was handicapped by difficulties in distribution, the country sheets, feeding to the public their second-hand clippings from exchanges, were cultivating a reading public, later to be exploited by their successors from both large and small centers. This was no mean achievement. Those who participated in the spread of the newspaper press were the pioneers of journalism more truly than the energetic editors in the growing, large cities.

But, if the political side of the printer has been emphasized, other phases of his activity are not to be neglected. The spawning of new presses throughout the state has been mentioned as an element of expansion. It also holds a place in the great "transit of civilization." The press is a civilizing force; the printer an agent of culture. In the frontier towns and the back country such agents become an important leaven in the social organization. But the reaction upon the agent is often negative, for he is asked to give and he is left poorer. As a result of his service he may become a martyr to the unappreciative public. In this class belong the country doctor, the circuit-riding preacher, and—the country printer. Look down upon his limitations, contrast him with the successful who rose to important positions in the cities, if you will—but mark his service.

The character of the fare in the country newspaper varied with the taste of the editor. With regard to the editorial, as has been pointed out, many printers were incapable of such composition, or were too busy to make the attempt. A few developed their latent editorial talent to good effect, usually in political controversy.

In the miscellaneous "magazine" section there appeared poetry and fiction (some native and much that was pirated from books and periodicals), religious and ethical treatises, practical suggestions or observations upon mechanics and agriculture, and humorous anecdotes.

In another sense, however, the printing office was often the cultural center of the community. The bookstore, run in connection with it, furnished all that was available for cultural improvement. The "reading room" provided by some offices opened to the community the literary resources of the editor and his newspaper exchanges. In the larger establishments the publishing of books became an important cultural service, and their range and variety indicate the tastes of the day. Whereas, schoolbooks, almanacs, and sermons predominated in the output of the smaller and earlier establishments, more ambitious projects in literature, philosophy, and law were not wanting.

Nevertheless, these efforts were subordinated. Instead of being primarily the propagandist of science and religion, the printer was the mouthpiece of politics, and the so-called cultural service which he rendered was secondary. Yet the "literature" in the country newspaper did sustain some modicum of taste and enjoyment in the provincial mind. If it did little to raise the cultural level, it was at least an agent of literacy.

The demands which his meager selection of miscellany made upon the "editor" were enough to raise him above the average citizen. As his English critic would have it, he did get the reputation of being a "smart man." Along with the lawyers, physicians, and clergy, he was one of the "educated," albeit his "college" was the "case."

His place in the community, however, must have been determined to a large extent by economic forces. Like his neighbors, he was in business, and as a business man he must be judged. The newspaper was the advertising medium for merchants and tradesmen. Upon its circulation the efficacy of their notices would depend, and this was important then as now. The average printer circulated five or six hundred copies weekly, a few in the village, but the greater share by post riders. Exchanges and political circulation might account for some, but these were of little consequence commercially. An increasing number, toward the end of our period, received their papers by mail. The reluctance of many subscribers to pay promptly was an alarming condition faced by the printer. His resources were buttressed, however, by the returns from legal notices, if he were fortunate enough to receive them. Not only was he interested in the community which supplied his circulation, but he would be favored by whatever progress or business development promoted his advertising patronage.

With the changes in communication and rapidity in circulating the news from the cities, the prospects of the printer of a country paper faded. His hope lay not in the continuance of those conditions which had attended his rise but in adapting himself to the changes which followed. The printer-editor of this period did not disappear suddenly, of course, nor were the newspapers transformed after 1830. Decades were to pass before the weekly designed for purely local news became common, and before the one man printing office became obsolete. Many of the newspapers which we have discussed were to endure for generations in changed form.[5] Whether the change was an improvement the reader must judge.

The social position of the printer was not a happy one. Struggling in many instances with insufficient support, handicapped by makeshift and primitive implements, he was to be pitied rather than admired. His better impulses were misdirected through the urgency of political connections, and his zeal was often spent in degrading attacks, giving him a reputation for scurrility. In the early days, no doubt, the Federalist printer gained a certain respectability from the prestige of his patron; somewhat later, even this disappeared. The trained printer could not escape some of the opprobrium of the unfortunate class of journeymen, from which he had sprung. His indomitable self-respect, so often dignified in the printed word, enables us to award him the credit denied him by his contemporaries.

[5] French's *Gazetteer* records 67 papers of this period still existing (though most of them under changed names) in 1860, an average of more than one for each county. Among them are a few which have endured and kept their original names to this day: the Fredonia *Censor,* the Catskill *Recorder,* the Canandaigua *Messenger,* and the Cooperstown *Freeman's Journal.* There may be others.

APPENDICES

No class of men in any age of the world, have given evidence of so great versatility of talent—universal knowledge and variety of reading, as the body typographical. The biography of many printers would be both amusing and instructive.—WILLIAM A. WELLES at Printers' Festival, 1846.

APPENDIX I

THE following list of printers, editors, and publishers is appended for two reasons. First, in order to supplement and substantiate the statements and generalizations made in the foregoing treatise; and, second, to serve as a reference list for the benefit of future researchers among newspapers and other contemporary records. In such a list the inclusion of documentation and source references for all information only serves to encumber, if not to confuse, the compilation. Much must be taken on the authority of the compiler, who in all cases has sought the best sources available—the newspapers themselves in most instances. The "Bibliography of American Newspapers, 1690-1820," by Clarence S. Brigham has been used constantly throughout this work, and for the period which it covers is the acknowledged authority. No references are made to it explicitly here, nor to the newspapers. When the compiler has not been satisfied that his information was conclusive he has indicated the secondary works on which he has relied.

The scheme of arranging data needs some explanation. Whenever available, information on each name is given in the following order: (1) dates of birth and death; (2) place of birth; (3) name of wife and date of marriage; (4) apprenticeship, with dates and name of master; (5) service as a journeyman; (6) newspaper connections as printer, editor, or proprietor, with inclusive dates; (7) names of partners and dates of their association in parentheses; (8) political offices held, with dates; and (9) place of death.

Dates for newspaper connections are inclusive, except where only one date is known. Dates of apprenticeship, too, are frequently not inclusive, but represent all that is known, the beginning or end of the period of service. Places mentioned are in New York State, unless otherwise indicated.

It is apparent that information on many of the persons listed is fragmentary, sometimes confined to a single newspaper imprint, or supplied by the somewhat dubious authority of a secondary work. Such partial and unsatisfactory data are submitted, however, in lieu of any other; forenames or initials are omitted only when they are not available. It is to be hoped that future researchers may supplement, and perhaps complete, what is here presented. Where the subject has merited a sketch in the *Dictionary of American Biography,* that fact has been indicated, and details of his career after 1830 are not given.

ABBREVIATIONS

appr.	apprentice
Co	Data taken on the authority of a county history
DAB	Sketch of the subject in the *Dictionary of American Biography*
ed.	editor
Fo	Follett, *History of the Press of Western New York*
Fr	French, *Gazeteer of the State of New York*
He	Hewett, *Traveller and Monthly Gazetteer,* 1828
jrmn.	journeyman
pr.	printer

ABBEY, DOREPHUS, d. 1838; pr. job work, Albany; pr. Albany *Friend,* 1815-1816 (with S. A. Abbey), *Oswego Gazette,* 1817 (with S. A. Abbey), Watertown *Jefferson and Lewis Gazette,* 1817-1819 (with J. H. Lord and S. A. Abbey), Binghamton *Republican Herald,* 1820; took part in Canadian uprising of 1837-1839; hanged at Kingston, Canada.

ABBEY, SETH A., 1798-1880; pr. job work, Albany; pr. Albany *Friend,* 1815-1816 (with D. Abbey), *Oswego Gazette,* 1817 (with D. Abbey), Watertown, *Jefferson and Lewis Gazette,* 1817-1819 (with J. H. Lord and D. Abbey), Watertown *Independent Republican,* 1819-1826, Watertown *Independent Republican and Anti-Masonic Recorder,* 1828-1830.

ABBEY, WILLIAM W., d. 1862; *Oswego Republican,* 1825-1827.[Fr Co]

ADAMS, CHARLES CHAUNCEY, d. 1814; m. Cordelia Delavan, 1811/ 12; pr. Poughkeepsie *Political Barometer,* 1810-1811 (with Joseph Nelson), Poughkeepsie *Republican Herald,* 1811-1814 (with D. Mac-Duffee, 1811-1812); d. Poughkeepsie.

ADAMS, DANIEL PECK, 1801-1872; b. Scipio; m. Maria Seaver, 1829; post rider, Buffalo, 1817; pr. Batavia *People's Press,* 1827-1829 (with J. Thorp and D. C. McCleary), Batavia *Masonic Intelligencer,* 1827-1829 (with J. Thorp), Batavia *Spirit of the Times and People's Press,* 1830-1831, *Medina Herald,* 1832-1834/35,[Fr] *Black Rock Advocate;* d. Batavia.

ADAMS, JOHN, *Syracuse American,* 1825-1826.[Fr]

ADANCOURT, FRANCIS, m. Lucinda Buckley, 1810; came from France with Lafayette, 1784; pr. Lansingburgh *Farmer's Register,* 1803-1807, Troy *Farmer's Register,* 1807-1826, Troy *Farmer's Register and Mechanics' and Manufacturers' Journal,* 1826-1832,[Fr] Troy *Evangelical Restorationist,* 1825; adjut. in militia, 1819.

ADDINGTON, STEPHEN, Mount Pleasant *Westchester Herald and Farmers' Register,* 1818-1819.

ALLEN, ANSON H., b. 1806, Palatine; m. Mary Morehouse, 1828; appr. Middlebury, Vt.; pr. *Keeseville Herald,* 1825-1832 (with E. G. Palmer, 1831-1832), *Keeseville Herald,* 1833-1839, Westport *Essex County Times,* 1841-1844, Keeseville *Old Settler,* 1847-1848, Keeseville *Old Settler,* 1850-1853; took census of Essex County, 1840.

ALLEN, FREDERICK P., Plattsburgh *Northern Intelligencer,* 1822-1825, *Keeseville Herald,* 1825, Malone *Northern Spectator,* 1832-1835, Malone *Palladium,* 1835.

ALLEN, ISAAC SPENCER, 1804-1881, b. Schagticoke; pr. Auburn *Cayuga Patriot,* 1827-1845 (with U. F. Doubleday, 1827-1831; with Willett Lounsbury, 1833-1843), Auburn *Gospel Advocate,* 1828-1831 (with U. F. Doubleday).

ALLEN, PETER K., pr. Kingston *People's Advocate,* 1824-1827 (with S. S. Freer); issued prospectus only, Kingston *Ulster True American,* 1827; pr. Poughkeepsie *Dutchess True American,* 1828-1829, Poughkeepsie *Dutchess Inquirer,* 1829-1830,[Fr] Minisink *Sentinel,* 1833.[Fr]

AMES, CHARLES F., ed. Hudson *Columbia Republican,* 1824-1827/28, Poughkeepsie *Dutchess Intelligencer,* 1828 (with F. T. Parsons), Rochester *Spirit of the Age,* 1830, semi-monthly (with T. B. Barnum.

ANDREWS, WILLIAM, ed. Cooperstown *Impartial Observer,* 1808-1809 (with J. H. Prentiss and H. Prentiss).

ANDRUS, WILLIAM, 1800-1869, b. Harwinton, Conn.; appr. to farmer, 1810-1815; appr. to goldbeater, Hartford, Conn., 1815; in bookstore of his brother, 1816-1817; appr. to printer, New York, 1817-1823; book agent, 1823-1824; pr. *Ithaca Journal,* 1824-1827 (with E. Mack), *Ithaca Journal, Literary Gazette and General Advertiser,* 1827-1828 (with E. Mack), *Ithaca Journal and Advertiser,* 1828-1833 (with E. Mack); later engaged in business with E. Mack, Chas. Woodruff, —— Gauntlett, and —— McChain; supervisor, two terms; trustee of Ithaca village, 1840; d. Ithaca.

AUSTIN, JOHN M., *Troy Republican,* 1828-1830 (with E. Wellington), Troy *Gospel Anchor,* 1833 (with —— Williamson).

AVERILL, JOSEPH KETCHUM, b. 1802, Peru; appr. to A. C. Flagg, Plattsburgh, 1823; pr. *Essex Republican,* 1823-1826, Rouse's Point *Observer and Northern Advertiser,* 1826-1827; prospectus only for *Waterford Republican,* 1826; pr. *Plattsburgh Times,* 1827, Fort Covington *Franklin Republican,* 1827, *Plattsburgh Republican,* 1827-1828 (with H. C. Miller), *Martinsburgh Sentinel and Lewis County Advertiser,* 1829-1830, *Whitehall Republican,* 1832, Plattsburgh *Democratic Press,* 1834.

BABCOCK, JOHN, Lansingburgh *Northern Centinel and Lansingborough [-burgh] Advertiser,* 1787-1788 (with —— Claxton), Albany *Federal Herald,* 1788 (with —— Claxton), Lansingburgh *Federal Herald,* 1788-1790 (with —— Hickock).

BACON, WILLIAM J., ed. *Utica Sentinel and Gazette,* 1825-1828 (with S. D. Dakin).

BAKER, ORAN E., pr. Cazenovia *Pilot,* 1808-1823 (with —— Newton, 1808-1809); adjut. cavalry, 1811; coroner, 1813.

BAKER, PIERPONT, ed. *Lockport Gazette,* 1829, *Lockport Balance,* 1829-1831 (with P. Besancon, Jr.).

BAKER, SOLOMON, *Schoharie Observer,* 1819-1823 (with Fish, 1820-1822).

BALCH, JEREMIAH O., 1785-1875; pr. *Le Roy Gazette,* 1826-1827, *Newark Republican,* 1829-1831, *Vienna Republican,* 1831; d. Chicago, Ill.

BALDWIN, CHARLES N., Tompkinsville *Richmond Republican,* 1827-1831.

BALL, HENRY L., *Detroit Gazette* (Mich.), 1826-1829, *Buffalo Republican,* 1830.

BARBER, JOHN, JR., Lyons *Western Argus,* 1830-1831 (with D. Chapman).

BARBER, JOSEPH W., Newburgh *Mirror,* 1798-1799, Newburgh *Orange County Gazette,* 1799-1800 (with J. Schultz).

BARNARD, WARREN, Whitestown *Farmers' Library,* 1800, Whitestown *Hive,* 1800? [only authority for this paper is a letter of C. R. Webster of Albany to Noah Webster, Aug. 27, 1801].

BARNUM, CHARLES P., 1788-1830, b. Danbury, Conn.; ed. Poughkeepsie *Dutchess Observer,* 1815-1824 (with Richard Nelson, 1815-1820; with Nicholas Jackacks, 1820-1822), Poughkeepsie *Republican Telegraph,* 1825, Poughkeepsie *Republican Telegraph and Observer,* 1826-1830 (with Nathan Myers, 1826-1829; with Egbert B. Killey, 1829-1830), *Albany Argus,* 1825 (with Ed. Croswell and O. R. Van Benthuysen); d. near Albany.

BARNUM, PHILO B., pr. *Syracuse Advertiser,* 1826 (with T. B. Barnum and John F. Wyman).

BARNUM, THOMAS B., m. Clarissa Atwater, 1826; appr. to J. D. Bemis, Canandaigua; pr. Canandaigua *Ontario Republican,* 1821-1823, Canandaigua *Plain Truth,* 1822-1824, Canandaigua *Ontario Freeman,* 1823-1825 (with J. A. Stevens), *Syracuse Advertiser,* 1826-1827 (with P. B. Barnum and John F. Wyman, 1826; with John F. Wyman, 1826-1827), Rochester *Spirit of the Age,* 1830 (with C. F. Ames), *Erie Observer* (Pa.), 1830-1831 (with Beriah Brown).

BARROWS, E. S., pastor of a church, Pompey; ed. Utica *Christian Journal,* 1827-1830.[Fr]

BARTER, JAMES C., m. Elisa Harwood, 1827; Ogdensburg *St. Lawrence Gazette,* 1826-1830 (with Dan Spafford).

BARTLETT, H. S., Herkimer *Republican Farmers' Free Press,* 1830 (with B. B. Hotchkin).

BATES, ISAAC, Ballston Spa *Independent American,* 1810 (with James Comstock).

BATES, MORGAN, 1808-1874; m. Janet Cook, 1828; appr.; jrmn. for James Wright, Sandy Hill, 1823; pr. *Warren Gazette* (Pa.), 1826-1828, Jamestown *Chautauque Republican,* 1828-1833 (as ed. 1830-

1833), *Warren Gazette* (Pa.), 1830-1831; jrmn. foreman on New York *New Yorker;* Detroit *Spy in Michigan,* 1837-1839 (with Harsha, 1839), *Detroit Daily Advertiser* (Mich.), 1839-1843 (with George Dawson, 1839-1842); in "gold rush" to California; *Alta Californian,* 1849, Detroit (Mich.) *Peninsular Fountain,* 1851, Traverse City (Mich.) *Grand Traverse Herald,* 1868; mem. assembly of Mich.; Lieut. Gov. of Mich., 1869-1871; d. Traverse City, Mich.

BEACH, CHAUNCEY, *Rome Republican,* 1825-1830.[Fr]

BEACH, CYRUS, Wardsbridge [Montgomery] *Orange County Republican,* 1806-1808 (with L. Pratt).

BEACH, NATHANIEL, 1791-1819; m. Charlotte Marsh, 1814; pr. Canandaigua *Ontario Repository,* 1814-1816 (with J. D. Bemis); d. Bloomfield.

BEARDSLEE [BEARDSLEY], JAMES, m. Charlotte M. Hopkins, 1828; pr. *Manlius Times,* 18— (with L. Kellogg), Auburn *Cayuga Patriot,* 1816, New Orleans (La.) *Louisiana Advertiser,* 1820; clerk of village, Auburn, 1818.

BEEBEE, ALEXANDER M., ed. Utica *New York Baptist Register,* 1825-1854 (with C. Bennett and J. Colwell, 1826; with D. Bennett, 1828-1830; with D. Bennett and E. A. Bright, 1830-1840; with various publishers, 1840-1854).

BEMIS, JAMES DRAPER, 1783-1857, b. Spencer, Mass.; m. Ruth Williams, 1807; appr., Boston, Mass. (ten months), and Albany, 1794-1801; jrmn. for Backus and Whiting, Albany, 1801-1803; pr. Canandaigua *Western Repository,* 1804-1808 (with John K. Gould), Canandaigua *Ontario Repository,* 1809-1830 (with Nathaniel Beach, 1814-1816; with C. Morse and S. C. Ward; with S. C. Ward, 1830).

BENDER, HASTINGS R., Homer *Farmers' Journal,* 1812-1813.

BENJAMIN, JOSEPH, *Ithaca Gazette and Religious Intelligencer,* 1816-1817 (with E. Shepard and ——— Reed).

BENNETT, ABRAHAM H., m. Desdemona Kidder, 1818; appr. to J. A. Stevens, Canandaigua; pr. *Penn Yan Herald,* 1818-1822, *Penn Yan Democrat,* 1822-1841 (with Alfred Reed, 1836-1841); county clerk, Yates Co., 1823-1831; deputy marshall to take census; postmaster, 1834-1841.

BENNETT, CEPHAS, 1804-1885, b. Homer; m. Stella Kneeland, 1826; appr., Utica, 1817-1824; pr. Utica *New York Baptist Register,* 1825-1828 (with A. M. Beebee and J. Colwell, 1826), *Utica Sentinel and Gazette,* 1826-1828 (with J. Colwell; W. J. Bacon and S. D. Dakin, eds.); to Burma with Adoniram Judson, printer of tracts for missionary enterprise, 1829-1885; d. Rangoon, Burma.

BENNETT, DOLPHUS, b. Homer; appr., Utica; pr. Utica *New York Baptist Register,* 1828-1845 (with A. M. Beebee, 1828-1830; with E. A. Bright and A. M. Beebee, 1830-1840; with other partners, 1840-1845).

BERNARD, DAVID L., ed. Kingston *Ulster Palladium,* 1830-1831 (with C. Frary, pr.).

BESANCON, PETER, JR., appr. to J. H. Prentiss, Cooperstown; pr. *Lockport Journal,* 1829-1831 (with Lot Clark and P. Baker, 1829; with P. Baker, 1829-1831).

BICKNELL, BENNETT, 1781-1841, b. Mansfield, Conn.; ed. Morrisville, *Madison Observer,* 1824-1829,[Fr] Morrisville *Observer and Recorder,* 1829-1832; major, 1812; mem. assembly, 1812; mem. state senate, 1818; county clerk, Madison Co., 1822-1827; mem. Congress, 1837-1839; d. Morrisville.

BILL, JAMES, Catskill *Greene and Delaware Washingtonian,* 1813-1816 (with R. Corss, pr.).

BIRCH, GEORGE L., 1787-1864, b. Limerick, Ireland; appr. to shipping merchant, Brooklyn; clerk and bookkeeper for the New York *National Advocate,* 1821; ed. Brooklyn *Long Island Patriot,* 1821-1829; printer to the common council and custom house, 1821-1828; postmaster, 1821-1825; collector of customs, 1829; librarian, Brooklyn navy yard, 1843-1864.

BISSELL, JOSIAH, JR., *Rochester Observer,* 1827 (with L. Tucker, pr., and G. G. Sill, ed.).

BLANCHARD, ABIJAH, ed. Saratoga Springs *Religious Advocate,* 1822.

BLISS, LUTHER, 1781-1854; m. Mary Ann Walsh, 1811; *Lansingburgh Gazette,* 1806-1826 (with G. Tracy).

BLISS, PELATIAH, 1785-1818, b. Bennington, Vt.; m. Sally Fitch, 1810; *Troy Post,* 1812-1818 (with W. S. Parker).

BLODGETT, BENJAMIN, packhorseman and cook to surveyors on Holland Patent; no regular appr.[Fo]; pr. Batavia *Genesee Intelligencer,* 1807-1808 (with E. Williams), Batavia *Cornucopia,* 1809-1811 (with S. Peek), Batavia *Republican Advocate,* 1811-1815 (with D. C. Miller, 1815); Batavia *People's Press,* 1825-1827.

BLOOMER, HENRY, ed. *Canajoharie Republican,* 1827-1828.[Fr]

BLOOMER, R. M., Ovid *Seneca Emporium, and General Advertiser,* 1827 (with O. B. Clark), Trumansburgh *Lake Light,* 1827 (with W. W. Phelps), Canandaigua *Ontario Phoenix,* 1828 (with W. W. Phelps).

BOGERT, JAMES, 1786-1862, b. New York; appr. to T. and J. Swords, New York, 1802-1805; jrmn. for Daniel Longworth, New York, 1805-1806; pr. Geneva *Expositor,* 1806-1809, *Geneva Gazette,* 1809-

1833 (with W. Bogert, 1816; with E. Shepard, pr., 1828); capt. 1812; major, 1817; lieut. col., 1819; col., 1824; collector of canal tolls, 1833-1838; d. Geneva.

BOIES, OBADIAH, *Cortland Observer,* 1816 (with J. W. Osborn).

BOWMAN, GODFREY, 1781-1822, *Poughkeepsie Journal and Constitutional Republican,* 1805-1809 (with N. Power and J. Aikin, 1805; with P. Potter, 1806; with P. Potter and C. Parsons, 1806-1809); d. Poughkeepsie.

BRADISH, CHARLES, *Palmyra Register,* 1819-1820 (with T. C. Strong).

BRAINARD, HENRY POWERS W., 1800-1828; m. Jane Mead Sutton, 1825; Norwich *People's Advocate,* 1825.

BRIGHAM, BENJAMIN F., *Salina Sentinel,* 1827.

BRIGHT, E. A., Utica *New York Baptist Register,* 1830-1840 (with D. Bennett and A. M. Beebee, ed.), Utica *American Citizen,* 1830 (with D. Bennett, G. S. Wilson, ed.), Utica *Youth's Miscellany,* 1834 (with D. Bennett), Utica *Talisman,* 1835 (with D. Bennett).

BROADWELL, CHARLES P., Plattsburgh *Frontier Spectator,* 1826, *Plattsburgh Republican,* 1826-1827, *Whitehall Republican,* 1828.

BROADWELL, WILLIAM, Caldwell *Warren Recorder,* 1824-1826, Glens Falls *Warren Recorder,* 1826.

BROKAW, ABRAHAM, Schenectady *Mohawk Mercury,* 1794-1795 (with C. P. Wyckoff).

BROOKS, JAMES GORDON, 1801-1841, b. Red Hook; m. Mary Elizabeth Aikin, 1828; ed. New York *Minerva,* 1823-1824 (with Geo. Houston), New York *Literary Gazette,* 1825-1827 (with Geo. Bond, 1825-1826), New York *Morning Courier,* 1827-1829, New York *Courier and Enquirer,* 1829-1830, New York *Daily Sentinel,* Rochester *Craftsman,* 1830 (with E. J. Roberts), Winchester (Va.) *Republican,* 1830; d. Albany; DAB.

BROOKS, JOSHUA, Mount Pleasant *Westchester Herald,* 1819 (with S. Marshall, pr.).

BROWN, SAMUEL R., 1775-1817, pr. Saratoga (Court House Hill) *Aurora Borealis and Saratoga Advertiser,* 1803, Saratoga Springs *Saratoga Patriot,* 1809-1812, *Albany Republican,* 1812-1815, Auburn, *Cayuga Patriot,* 1814-1815; author, "A View of the Campaigns of the Northwestern Army," 1814; "History of the War of 1812"; "The Western Gazetteer; or Emigrant's Directory," 1817; d. Cherry Valley.

BROWNEJOHN, THOMAS, Poughkeepsie *Republican Herald,* 1815-1819 (with D. B. Stockholm).

BROWNSON, ORESTES AUGUSTUS, 1803-1876, b. Stockbridge, Vt.; ed. Auburn *Gospel Advocate,* 1829 (with U. F. Doubleday), Le Roy *Genesee Republican and Herald of Reform,* 1829 (with Freeman &

Son), Fo Ithaca *Philanthropist, 1831-1832;* d. Detroit, Mich.; DAB.

BUCKINGHAM, AUGUSTUS, jrmn. for H. C. Southwick, 1817; pr. *Oswego Gazette,* 1817-1819, Auburn *Cayuga Republican,* 1819 (with T. M. Skinner).

BUEL, JESSE, 1778-1839, b. Coventry, Conn.; m. Susan Peirce, 1801; appr. to ——— Lyons, Rutland, Vt., 1792-1796; jrmn. New York, 1796; jrmn. for J. McDonald, Albany; pr. Troy *Northern Budget,* 1798-1801 (with R. Moffitt), Poughkeepsie *Guardian,* 1801-1802 (with N. Joyner), Poughkeepsie *Political Barometer,* 1802-1805 (with Isaac Mitchell), Kingston *Plebeian,* 1803-1813 (with I. Mitchell, 1803-1805), *Albany Argus,* 1813-1821; judge, Ulster Co.; state printer, 1815-1821; mem. assembly, 1823; candidate for gov. of New York, 1836; regent of Univ. of State of N.Y., 1826-1840; d. Danbury, Conn.; DAB.

BUELL, WILLIAM S., ed. Schenectady *Mohawk Advertiser,* 1810-1811 (with T. Johnson, pr.).

BUNCE, ISAIAH, ed. Ballston Spa *Saratoga Journal,* 1814-1818, *Litchfield Journal* (Conn.), 1818, *Litchfield Republican* (Conn.), 1818-1821, *Litchfield Eagle* (Conn.), 1826, Syracuse *Salina Herald,* 1828-1829; postmaster, Litchfield, Conn., four years.

BUNCE, JONATHAN, Peterboro *Freeholder,* 1807-1813 (with ——— Dockstader, 1807-1808), Peterboro *Madison County Herald,* 1813-1819.

BUNTON, SIMEON, ed. Buffalo *Gospel Advocate,* 1823-1826.Fr

BURDELL, ——— "Dr.," ed. Oswego *Freeman's Herald,* 1829-1830.Fr

BURNAP, FRANCIS, Middlebury (Vt.) *Christian Messenger,* 1817-1819, Malone *Franklin Telegraph,* 1820-1828.He

BURRELL, ABRAHAM, ed. Binghamton *Republican Herald,* 1818-1822.

BURROUGHS, EZEKIEL, m. Maria Applebye, 1822; pr. Warren [Rockland Co.] *Palladium,* 1812,Fr Carmel *Putnam Spectator,* 1823, Peekskill *Columbian Chronicle, and Westchester, Putnam, and Rockland Counties Advertiser,* 1825, Haverstraw *Rockland Register,* 1828.Fr He

BUTLER, GEORGE, ed. Troy *Budget and City Register,* 1826 (with Z. Clark, pr.).

BUTLER, L. B. Ithaca *Museum and Independent Corrector,* 1824 (with G. H. Evans), Havana *Tioga Patriot,* 1828-1829 (with S. Butler).

BUTLER, STEPHEN, Havana *Tioga Patriot,* 1828-1829 (with L. B. Butler), Poughkeepsie *Anti-Mason,* 1830-1831 (with J. M. Vethake).

CADWALLADER, MITCHENOR M., 1798-1864; ed. *New York Journal,* 1826, Lockport, *Niagara Courier,* 1828-1832, *Buffalo Whig and Journal,* 1836-1838 (with D. M Day, and H. R. Stagg); d. Buffalo.

CADY, HEMAN, 1789-1849, b. Cambridge, Vt.; m. Maria Platt, 1812;

Plattsburgh *Republican,* 1811 (with A. C. Flagg) ; mem. assembly, 1830; d. Milwaukee, Wis.

CALDWELL, SAMUEL, ed. *Canajoharie Sentinel,* 1827.[Fr]

CALHOUN, JOHN, d. 1859; m. Pamelia C. Hathaway, 1832; appr. to W. Woodward, Watertown, (ages 16 to 21) ; worked in typefoundry of Starr & Little, Albany; jrmn. on city directory, Troy; pr. Fort Plain *Watch Tower,* (with ——— Pratt), *Watertown Eagle,* 1832, *Chicago Democrat* (Ill.), 1833-1836; d. Chicago.

CAMERON, J. A., Mount Pleasant *Westchester Herald and Farmer's Register,* 1818 (with S. Addington and S. Marshall, pr.).

CAMP, ENOCH ELY, ed. Watertown *Anti-Masonic Sun,* 1830.

CAMP, GEORGE, 1790-1850, b. Glastonbury, Conn.; m. Elizabeth Hitchcock; appr. to Ira Merrell, Utica, 1810; pr. *Utica Patriot,* 1813-1816 (with Ira Merrell), *Sackett's Harbor Gazette,* 1817-1820; d. Sackett's Harbor.

CAMPBELL, B. S., *Cortland Republican,* 1817-1819 (with D. Campbell).

CAMPBELL, DAVID, pr. *Cortland Republican,* 1815-1821 (with J. W. Osborn, 1815-1816; interlude when not connected, Aug. to Dec. 1816; with J. W. Osborn, 1816-1817; with B. S. Campbell, 1817-1819), *Sandusky Clarion* (Ohio), 1828 (with J. K. Campbell).

CAMPBELL, W. S., Syracuse *Onondaga Republican,* 1830.[Fr]

CANFIELD, RUSSEL, Mount Pleasant *Impartial Gazette,* 1800-1801.

CANOLL, ABDIAL, Binghamton *Broome County Republican,* 1824-1839 (with A. Morgan, 1824-1828; with Thomas Collier, 1828-1830; with Edwin T. Evans, 1830-1835; with Benj. T. Cooke, 1835-1839).[Co]

CANTINE, J. J. C., *Cortland Journal,* 1827-1828.

CARLISLE, ——— *Oxford Gazette,* 1825 (with A. M. Howard).

CARPENTER, JOHN, pr. *Herkimer Herald,* 1828-1830,[Fr] *Oswego Palladium,* 1830-1845 (with J. H. Lord, 1845).

CARPENTER, WILLIAM ALLISON, 1780-1858; appr. 1796; pr. Goshen *Orange Eagle,* 1804-1805; jrmn. for S. H. and H. A. Salisbury, Buffalo, 1811; jrmn. for Benj. Blodgett, Batavia, 1811-1813; jrmn. for Salisburys, Buffalo, 1814; jrmn. for D. M. Day, Buffalo, 1815; pr. Fredonia *Chautauque Gazette,* 1817 (with J. Hull), *Buffalo Gazette,* 1818 (with H. A. Salisbury), *Buffalo Patriot,* 1826-1834 (with H. A. Salisbury) ; d. Buffalo.

CARRIQUE, RICHARD, ed. Hudson *Messenger of Peace,* 1824-1825.

CARY, LUCIUS, d. 1804; pr. *Newburgh Packet,* 1795, Geneva *Ontario Gazette,* 1796-1799, Canandaigua *Ontario Gazette,* 1799-1800, Canandaigua *Ontario Gazette and Genesee Advertiser,* 1800-1803; d. Canandaigua.

CHAMBERLAIN, ROYALL T., pr. Union Springs *Cayuga Tocsin,* 1812-1813, Auburn *Cayuga Tocsin,* 1813-1814.

CHAPMAN, D., Lyons *Western Argus,* 1830-1835 (with John Barber, 1830-1831; with G. H. Chapin, 1832-1835).

CHAPMAN, WILLIAM E., m. Harriet Sellick, 1829; pr. Oxford *Chenango Republican,* 1828-1830 (with D. Mack), *Oxford Republican,* 1831-1838 (with T. T. Flagler).

CHATTERTON, STEPHEN S., 1806-1876, b. Troy; Ithaca *Republican Chronicle,* 1828-1830 (with D. D. Spencer), *Ithaca Republican,* 1830-1831, *Owego Free Press,* 1828 [campaign paper, printed Sept. to Nov. in Ithaca], Ithaca *Tompkins American,* 1834, *Owego Republican,* 1832 [campaign paper, printed Sept. to Nov. in Ithaca] (with C. O. Flynn); job printing in New York, 1835-1876; d. New York.

CHERRY, PETER, Rochester *Western Wanderer,* 1828-1830,[Fr] Angelica *Allegany Republican and Internal Improvement Advocate,* 1832-1836, *Angelica Republican and Allegany Whig,* 1836.[Co]

CHESTER, JOHN, "Rev."; Hudson *Columbia Magazine* (with A. Stoddard).

CHEVEE, JAMES A., Goshen *Independent Republican,* 1818-1832.

CHILD, ASA, 1780-1828, b. Woodstock, Conn.; m. Lois Foote, 1806; appr. to Solomon Southwick, Albany; pr. Johnstown *Montgomery Republican,* 1810-1823; d. New York.

CHILD, INCREASE, 1740-1810, b. Woodstock, Conn.; m. Olive Pease, 1762; fought in French and Indian War, 1755; fought in Revolution; Ballston Spa *Saratoga Register: or Farmer's Journal,* 1798-1800 (with William Child); capt.; d. Greenfield.

CHILD, WILLIAM, 1777-1840, b. Woodstock, Conn.; m. Polly Weed; appr. to Solomon Southwick, and Southwick and Barber, Albany; pr. Ballston Spa *Saratago Register: and Farmer's Journal,* 1798-1801 (with Increase Child, 1798-1800), Ballston Spa *Republican Telescope,* 1801-1802, Ballston Spa *Political Magazine,* 1801-1802, Ballston Spa *Saratoga Advertiser,* 1805 (with D. C. Miller and T. White), Johnstown *Montgomery Intelligencer,* 1805-1806, Johnstown *Montgomery Republican,* 1806-1809, Ballston Spa *Independent Republican,* 1808-1811, Waterloo *Seneca Farmer,* 1823-1825, Waterloo *Seneca Farmer and Waterloo Advertiser,* 1826-1831/32 (with H. G. Merrell, 1827-1828), Seneca Falls *Seneca Farmer and Seneca Falls Advertiser,* 1832-1835 (with W. N. Brown, part of time), Penn Yan *Democratic Whig,* 1838; elected judge of Ingham Co., Mich.; d. in Mich.

CHILD, WILLIAM H., m. Susan Hill, 1829; pr. Waterloo *Seneca Farmer and Waterloo Advertiser,* 1826-1827 [a brief interlude in proprietorship of this paper by William Child, *q.v.*], *Skaneateles Gazette,* 1829-1831 (with B. B. Drake, ed.), *Lyons American,* 1835.

CHIPMAN, SAMUEL, ed. *Rochester Observer,* 1829-1830 (with E. Loomis).

CLARK, DANIEL, *Manlius Times,* 1817 (with L. Kellogg), *Onondaga Herald,* 1818.

CLARK, ISRAEL W., 1790-1828; pr. Cherry Valley *Otsego Republican Press,* 1813-1814 (with E. B. Crandal), Cooperstown *Otsego Herald,* 1813-1814 (ed. for H. and E. Phinney), Cooperstown *Watch Tower,* 1814-1817, *Albany Register,* 1817-1819, *Albany Daily Advertiser,* 1819-1824 (assoc. ed. and legislative reporter); ed. *Rochester Daily Telegraph;* presidential elector, 1816; d. Rochester.

CLARK, LOT, 1788-1862, b. Hillsdale; studied law; Norwich *Volunteer,* 1814 (with J. M. Miller, pr.), *Lockport Journal,* 1829 (with P. Besancon and P. Baker); postmaster, Norwich; village clerk, Norwich; dist. atty., Chenango Co., 1822-1823, and 1828; mem. Congress, 1823-1825; mem. assembly, 1846; d. Buffalo.

CLARK, ORASMUS B., m. Prudence Darrow, 1830; Ovid *Seneca Emporium, and General Advertiser,* 1827 (with R. M. Bloomer), Trumansburgh *Lake Light,* 1828 (with R. M. Bloomer; then with R. St. John); proposals only, for Ovid *Anti-Mason,* 1828; proposals only, for Seneca Falls *Truth,* 1829; *Seneca Falls Journal,* 1829-1831; state senator in Michigan.

CLARK, SAMUEL W., 1799-1832; m. Rebecca Davis, 1806; *Wilmington Gazette* (N. C.), 1804, Hudson *Bee,* 1810-1821; d. Hudson.

CLARK, ZENA, *Potsdam Gazette,* (with F. C. Powell).

CLARK, ZEPHANIAH, m. Catherine Coenhoven, 1819; appr. to F. Adancourt, Troy, 1811; pr. Troy *Northern Budget,* 1817-1826, *Troy Budget and City Register,* 1826-1827 (with Geo. Butler, ed., 1826; with J. C. Kemble, ed., 1827).

CLAXTON, ——— Lansingburgh *Northern Centinel and Lansingborough [-burgh] Advertiser,* 1787-1788 (with J. Babcock), Albany *Federal Herald,* 1788 (with J. Babcock).

CLAYTON, JOHN G., Malone *Northern Spectator,* 1830-1832.

CLEMENTS, SAMUEL F., jrmn., Brooklyn; pr. Brooklyn *Long Island Patriot,* 1829; postmaster, Brooklyn, 1829.

CLOSE, REUBEN S., Binghamton *Broome County Patriot,* [before 1815].Co

CLOWES, THOMAS, ed. *Troy Republican,* 1828-1830 (with Austin and Wellington).

COCHRAN, JAMES, ed. *Oswego Democratic Gazette,* 1830;Fr "major."

COFFEEN, HENRY, Watertown *American Eagle,* 1810-1812 (with A. Taylor, pr.), Watertown *Republican Watchman,* 1812-1813.

COLE, MATTHEW M., d. about 1842; m. Abigail Catlin, 1820; pr. Schoharie *Observer,* 1818-1819, *Sackett's Harbor Gazette,* 1820-1821, Sackett's Harbor *Jefferson Republican,* 1822, Albany *Standard,* 1827, Hudson *Columbia Republican,* 1828;[He] d. Washington, D. C.

COLES, DENNIS, pr. Newburgh *Rights of Man,* 1801-1803, Newburgh *Recorder of the Times,* 1803-1806.

COLLIER, THOMAS, pr. Bennington (Vt.) *Ploughman,* 1801-1802, *Troy Gazette,* 1802-1804, Binghamton *Broome County Republican,* 1828-1830 (with A. C. Canoll).[Co]

COLWELL, JOSEPH, m. Sylvia Pierce, 1824; jrmn., Utica, 1823; partner of I. Merrell, Utica; pr. *Utica Sentinel and Gazette,* 1825-1826 (with Geo. Wilson, pr.), Utica *New York Baptist Register,* 1826 (with C. Bennett), *Utica Intelligencer,* 1827-1832 (with W. Tracy, 1827; with E. S. Ely, 1828; with J. H. Buckingham, 1830, as editors).

COMSTOCK, JAMES, 1781-1851, b. Adams, Mass.; m. Mary Sears, 1813; pr. Ballston Spa *Independent American,* 1810-1818 (with I. Bates, 1810; with Wm. Child, 1810-1811), Ballston Spa *People's Watch Tower,* 1818-1820, *Ballston Spa Gazette and Saratoga Farmer,* 1821-1822, *Ballston Spa Gazette,* 1822-1847.[Fr]

COOKE, BENJAMIN T., Norwich *Anti-Masonic Telegraph,* 1829-1835 (with E. P. Pellett), Binghamton *Broome County Republican,* 1835-1840 (with A. C. Canoll, 1835-1839; with J. J. Davis, 1839-1840).

COOLEY, EDWIN A., jrmn. for O. Turner, Lockport, 1827; jrmn. for N. Lathrop and C. P. Turner, 1827-1828; pr. Lockport *Priestcraft Exposed,* 1828-1829 (with L. A. Spaulding, ed.), *Attica Balance,*[Fr] *Attica Democrat,* 1846.[Fr]

COPP, WILLIAM, d. 1798; pr. *Litchfield Monitor* (Conn.), 1784-1785, Kingston *Farmer's Register,* 1792-1793 (with N. Power), Kingston *Rising Sun,* 1793-1798 (with S. Freer); d. New York.

CORSS, RICHARD, 1796-1823; pr. Catskill *Greene and Delaware Washingtonian,* 1813-1816 (with J. Bill), Hudson *Northern Whig,* 1817-1820 (with W. L. Stone, 1817-1819).

CORY, BENJAMIN, pr. Herkimer *Telescope,* 1802-1805, Herkimer *Pelican,* 1807-1810, *Herkimer Intelligencer,* 1810-1811, Herkimer *Honest American,* 1812; jailer in Herkimer, 1805; d. Strafford, Montgomery Co.

CORY, BENJAMIN, m. Leafa Balcom, 1827; Oxford *Chenango Republican,* 1826-1828, *Watertown Register and General Advertiser,* 1830-1831, Watertown *Spirit of '76,* 1834.

COWDERY [COUDERY], [BENJAMIN] FRANKLIN, 1790-1867, b. New Marlborough, Mass.; m. Amanda Munger, 1819; appr., Stockbridge, Mass.; pr. *Moscow Advertiser and Livingston Farmer,* 1817 (with

H. Ripley), Olean *Hamilton Recorder,* 1819-1820 (with B. F. Smead), Angelica *Allegany Republican,* 1820-1822, Angelica *News Record and Allegany Patron of Industry,* 1822, *Newport Patriot,* 1824-1825, Geneva *Ontario Chronicle,* 1828-1829, *Chronicle of Geneva,* 1829, *Geneva Chronicle,* 1829, Albion *Orleans Mercury,* 1832, *Cuylerville Telegraph,* 1847-1848, Rochester *Genesee Olio,* 1847, *Oberlin Evangelist* (Ohio) ; jrmn. on *American* and *Democrat,* Rochester; d. Rochester.

CRANDAL, EDWARD B., m. Mary Todd, 1819; pr. Cherry Valley *Otsego Republican Press,* 1812-1813 (with I. W. Clark), Cooperstown *Watch Tower,* 1817-1831.

CROSBY, WILLIAM, 1790-1817; pr. Geneva *Palladium,* 1816, *Auburn Gazette,* 1816-1817 (with T. M. Skinner) ; d. Auburn.

CROSWELL, EDWIN, 1797-1871, b. Catskill; appr. to father, M. Croswell, 1812; pr. *Catskill Recorder,* 1817-1823 (with M. Croswell, 1817-1820), *Albany Argus,* 1823-1854; state printer, 1824-1840, and 1844-1847; d. Princeton, N. J.; DAB.

CROSWELL, HARRY, 1788-1858, b. Hartford, Conn.; m. Susan Sherman, 1800; appr. to brother, M. Croswell; pr. Catskill *Western Constellation,* 1800-1801 (with M. Croswell), Hudson *Balance and Columbian Repository,* 1801-1808 (with E. Sampson and G. Chittenden, 1801-1804), Hudson *Balance,* 1808 (with J. Frary, and F. Stebbins), Hudson *Wasp,* 1802-1803, Albany *Republican Crisis,* 1808 (with J. Frary), Albany *Balance and New York State Journal,* 1809-1810 (with J. Frary), Albany *Balance and State Journal,* 1811 ; d. New Haven, Conn.; DAB.

CROSWELL, MACKAY, d. 1847; m. (1) Betsey ———, (2) Thankful Saugez; appr. to George Goodwin, Hartford, (age 10) ; jrmn. Philadelphia, Pa., 1791-1792; pr. *Catskill Packet,* 1792-1794 (with T. O'H. Croswell), *Catskill Packet and Western Mail,* 1794-1796 (with T. O'H. Croswell), *Catskill Packet,* 1797-1799, Catskill *Western Constellation,* 1800-1804 (with H. Croswell, 1800-1801), *Catskill Recorder,* 1804-1820 (with E. Croswell, 1817-1820) ; town clerk, 1795; d. Catskill.

CROSWELL, THOMAS O'HARA, d. 1844; *Catskill Packet,* 1792-1794 (with M. Croswell), *Catskill Packet and Western Mail,* 1794-1796 (with M. Croswell) ; postmaster [appointed by Washington], 179?-1844; d. Catskill.

CROWELL, TIMOTHY B., Goshen *Orange County Patriot: or, the Spirit of Seventy-Six,* 1809-1811, Newburgh *Orange County Patriot,* 1811-1812 (with Eldad Lewis, 1811), Goshen *Orange County Patriot,* 1812-1828; town clerk, Goshen, 1820-1821.

CRUGER, DANIEL, JR., 1780-1843, b. Sunbury, Pa.; m. Lydia Shepard;

appr. to Websters, Albany, 1794-1800; pr. Union *American Constellation*, 1800-1801, Owego *American Constellation*, 1802; practiced law, Bath, admitted to bar, 1805; mem. assembly, 1814-1816, and 1826; speaker of assembly, 1816; dist. atty. for 7th N. Y. dist., 1815-1818; dist. atty. for Steuben Co., 1821; mem. Congress, 1817-1819; d. Wheeling, Va.

CRUMBIE, ROBERT, Peekskill *Westchester Gazette; and Peekskill Advertiser* [variant title: *Westchester and Putnam Gazette,* 1814], 1808-1818.

CULLEY, WILLIAM, d. 1849; pr. Kingston *Ulster Sentinel,* 1829-1831 (with Chas. G. De Witt, ed.), Saugerties *Ulster Star,* 1833;[Fr] d. Richmond, Va.

CUNNINGHAM, JOHN, pr. Glens Falls *Warren Republican,* 1813-1820 (with A. Emons, 1817-1819).

CURTIS, DANIEL, Lansingburgh *Farmer's Oracle, and Lansingburgh Weekly Gazette,* 1796-1797 (with L. Pratt); mem. assembly, 1791.

CURTIS, ROBERT I., pr. Erie, Pa. *Northern Centinel,* 1814-1815, Erie, Pa. *Genius of the Lakes,* 1816-1819, Mayville *Chautauque Eagle,* 1819-1820, *Erie Reflector* (Pa.), 1820 [Erie, Pa., edition of the *Eagle*], *Wheeling Gazette* (Va.), 1828.[He]

CURTIS, SAMUEL, JR.; m. Sarah Maria Master, 1829; appr. to C. Morgan, Oxford, 1813; pr. Norwich *Republican Agriculturist,* 1820, Kingston *Craftsman,* 1824-1825 (with E. J. Roberts), Kingston *Ulster Republican,* 1827-1828, Hudson *Columbia Republican,* 1829.

CURTISS, DANIEL, JR., Troy *Farmer's Oracle,* 1797 (with L. Pratt).

CUSHING, MILTON F., d. 1811; *Somers Museum,* 1809-1810 [later added to title: *and Westchester County Advertiser*]; Somers *American Union,* 1811 [title given in obit., no other reference]; postmaster, Somers; d. South Salem.

CUSHMAN, CHARLES U., 1802-1859, b. Washington Co.; m. Mary Birdsall, 1832; appr., Rutland, Vt.; proof reader, American Tract Society, New York; pr. Newburgh *Orange Telegraph,* 1829-1839; mem. assembly, 1853; officer in New York custom house; d. Rhinebeck.

CUTHBERT, LEMUEL, 1802-1829; pr. *Schoharie Republican,* 1823-1829, Schoharie *Evangelical Luminary,* 1824, Schoharie *Lutheran Magazine,* 1827; d. Schoharie.

DAKIN, SAMUEL DANA, 1802-1835, b. Jeffrey, N. H.; m. Mary Mumford, 1827; graduated from Hamilton College, 1821; studied law, Utica; ed. *Utica Sentinel and Gazette,* 1825-1829 (with W. J. Bacon, 1825-1828); inventor of a floating dry dock.

DALY, JAMES D., pr. Lewiston *Niagara Sentinel,* 1822-1826.

DARBE, LEVI, m. Jemima Heermanse, 1822; jrmn., Kingston, 1822-

1823; pr. Rhinebeck *Dutchess Republican,* 1823, *Williamsburgh Gazette,* 1838-1850, *Williamsburgh Daily Gazette,* 1850-1854 (with son.)[Co]

DAUBY, AUGUSTINE G., 1795-1876, b. Mansfield, Mass.; m. Mary C. Parmelee, 1818; appr. to Ira Merrell, Utica, 1810-1816; pr. *Rochester Gazette,* 1816-1821 (with J. P. Sheldon, 1816; later with Oran Follett) [brief interlude in publication after office was destroyed by fire, Dec. 5, 1819], *Utica Observer,* 1821-1823 (with E. Dorchester, ed.), Utica *Oneida Observer,* 1823-1834 (with E. A. Maynard, 1826-1834); Utica *Baptist Register,* 1824-1825, *Utica Magazine,* 1827-1828 (with E. A. Maynard, and D. Skinner, ed.), Utica *Evangelical Magazine,* 1829-1830 (with E. A. Maynard); postmaster, Utica, 1829-1849.

DAVISON, GIDEON MINER, 1791-1869, b. Middletown, Vt.; m. Sarah Mason; appr. to William Fay, Rutland, Vt.; pr. *Rutland Herald* (Vt.), 1813-1819 (with William Fay), Saratoga Springs *Saratoga Sentinel,* 1819-1842 [interlude, 1819-1820, "For the Proprietor" by John A. Murray]; clerk of court, 4th judicial dist., 1823; clerk of court of equity, 1825; clerk of court of chancery, 1830; supposed author, with Samuel Williams, of "Sketches of the War between the U. S. and the British Isles."

DAY, BENJAMIN F., 1806-1831; pr. Canandaigua *Ontario Messenger,* 1827-1831 (with E. Morse).

DAY, DAVID M., 1791-1839; appr. to J. A. Stevens, Canandaigua, 1814; partner with J. A. Stevens, 1814-1815; pr. Buffalo *Niagara Journal,* 1815-1820 (with I. Stillman, 1815-1816), *Buffalo Journal,* 1826, *Buffalo Journal and Mercantile Advertiser,* 1826-1834 (with O. Follett, 1826; with O. Follett and R. W. Haskins, 1827-1830), *Buffalo Whig and Journal,* 1836-1837 (R. W. Haskins, ed.; with M. Cadwallader and H. A. Stagg); d. Buffalo.

DAY, HIRAM T., 1796-1826; pr. proposals only for Canandaigua *Political Repertory,* 1822, *Lyons Advertiser,* 1822-1826; d. Lyons.

DEAN, ——— Rochester *Album,* 1827 (with E. F. Marshall).

DELANO, JOHN, pr. *Levanna Gazette and Onondaga Advertiser,* 1798.

DENNISON, BENJAMIN C., 1810-1853; m. Frances Johnson, 1850; Dansville *Village Chronicle,* 1830-1831 (with D. Mitchel), Geneseo *Livingston Journal,* 1831.

DENNISTON, DAVID, d. 1803; b. New Windsor; ed. Newburgh *Mirror,* 1797-1798 (with P. Van Horne, pr.), New York *American Citizen,* 1800-1803 (with James Cheetham, 1801-1803), New York *Republican Watchtower,* 1800-1803 (with James Cheetham, 1801-1803) [semi-weekly edition of the *Citizen*], Newburgh *Rights of Man,* 1803.

DENTON, GABRIEL, Goshen *Orange County Republican,* 1805-1805/6 (with J. G. Hurtin), Goshen *Orange County Gazette,* 1806-1807 (with J. G. Hurtin, 1806; with Elliott Hopkins, 1807); d. Orange Co.

DE VOE, FREDERICK, pr. proposals only for *New York Farmer,* Brooklyn, 1827; Monticello *Republican Watchman,* 1828 Fr-1829, Monticello *Union Democrat,* 1854.

DEWEY, LAURIN, pr. Manlius *Onondaga Republican,* 1824, Rome *Republican,* 1825, Union Village (Washington Co.) *Anti-Masonic Champion,* 1829-1830, Hamilton *Civilian,* 1830-1831.Fr

DE WITT, CHARLES G., 1789-1839; practiced law, New Paltz; ed. Kingston *Ulster Sentinel,* 1826-1831 (with W. Sands, pr., 1826-1829; with W. Culley, pr., 1829-1831); mem. Congress, 1829-1831; chargé d'affaires to Central America, 1833.

DOCKSTADER, JACOB, *Johnstown Gazette,* 1795-1798, Peterboro *Freeholder,* 1807-1808 (with I. Bunce).

DODD, EDWARD, Salem *Washington County Post and North Star,* 1827-1833 (with Henry W. Dodd), Salem *Washington County Post and Advocate of Popular Education,* 1833-1835 (with Henry W. Dodd, 1833-1834); county clerk, 1834.

DODD, HENRY, 1772-1834; pr. Salem *Northern Centinel,* 1798-1804, Salem *Northern Post,* 1804-1823 (with D. Rumsey, 1804-1814; with D. Rumsey and J. Stevenson, 1814; with J. Stevenson, 1814-1823), Salem *Washington County Post,* 1823-1826 (with J. Stevenson), Salem *Washington County Post and North Star,* 1827; d. Salem.

DODD, HENRY W., 1809-1834; Salem *Washington County Post and North Star,* 1827-1834 (with Edward Dodd); d. Salem.

DORCHESTER, ELIASAPH, 1780-1864; m. Abigail Allen, 1823; taught grammar school, Utica, 1808; pr. Utica *Columbian Gazette,* 1814-1816 (with T. Walker), *Utica Observer,* 1816-1823 (with A. G. Dauby); secretary of board of canvassers, 1822; county clerk, 1821-1823.

DOUBLEDAY, ULYSSES F., 1792-1866, b. Otsego Co.; appr., Cooperstown; jrmn., Utica and Albany; pr. Ballston Spa *Saratoga Courier,* 1816-1818, Auburn *Cayuga Patriot,* 1819-1831 (with I. Allen, 1827-1831), Auburn *Gospel Advocate,* 1828-1831 (with I. S. Allen), Auburn *Cayuga Patriot,* 1845-1846; commissioner of deeds, 1826; mem. Congress, 1831-1833, and 1835-1837; inspector of Auburn prison, 1834.

DOUGLAS, NATHAN, 1759-1806; pr. Danbury (Conn.) *Farmer's Journal,* 1790-1793, Danbury (Conn.) *Republican Journal,* 1793, Poughkeepsie *Republican Journal,* 1795-1796, Danbury (Conn.) *Farmer's Chronicle,* 1796, Danbury (Conn.) *Republican Journal,* 1796-1800; d. Hartford (Washington Co.).

DRAKE, B. B., ed. Waterloo *Enunciator,* 1822, *Waterloo Republican,* 1822-1823, *Skaneateles Gazette,* 1829-1830 (with Wm. H. Child).

DUBOIS, IRA, *Catskill Messenger,* 1830.[Fr]

DUFFY, JOHN, *Ovid Gazette and Seneca County Register,* 1830, *Ithaca Republican,* 1830-1831 (assoc. ed.), *Elmira Republican,* 1831.

DURELL, WILLIAM, pr. *Mount Pleasant Register,* 1798; prosecuted under the Sedition Act; imprisoned, pardoned by President Adams.

DURHAM, JAMES, ed. *Elmira Whig,* 1828-1829.

DURNFORD, JOHN, pr. Syracuse *Onondaga Gazette,* 1823-1824, *Syracuse Gazette,* 1824-1829.

DUTCHER, JOHN W., m. Harriet F. Shepard, 1819; pr. Hudson *Columbia Sentinel,* 1821-1823.

DUTTON, —— Cooperstown *Tocsin,* 1829-1830 (with —— Hewes, 1829-1830; with H. Hopkins, 1830).

EASTON, HENRY LAURENS, 1794-1867, b. Wilmington, Vt.; m. Elizabeth Devendorf, 1827; Lowville *Black River Gazette,* 1825-1827 (with W. L. Easton); justice of peace; mem. assembly, 1837; d. Cedarville.

EASTON, OLIVER P., Whitestown *Western Sentinel,* 1794-1796.

EASTON, WILLIAM LYMAN, 1806-1865, b. Hancock, Mass.; m. Emeline Henry, 1828; Lowville *Black River Gazette,* 1825-1833 (with H. L. Easton, 1825-1827; with J. M. Farr, 1832-1833); surrogate of Lewis Co., 1840-1849; d. Lowville.

EATON, EBENEZER, 1777-1859, b. Mansfield, Conn.; pr. Rome *Columbian Patriotic Gazette,* 1799-1800 (with T. Walker), Geneva *Impartial American, or, Seneca Museum,* 1800-1801 (with T. Walker), Scipio *Western Luminary,* 1801, Danville (Vt.) *North Star,* 1807-1828 [He] (with W. Eaton).

EATON, THEOPHILUS, d. 1820; pr. Norwich *President,* 1808; d. Bethlehem, Pa.

EDDY, S. M., Angelica *Allegany Recorder,* 1826.

EDIE, JAMES, pr. York (Pa.) *Pennsylvania Herald,* 1789-1793, *Bath Gazette,* 1796-1798 (with Wm. Kersey).

EDMUNDS, JOHN W., ed. *Hudson Gazette,* 1824-1826 (with P. Sturtevant); mem. assembly, 1831; mem. state senate, 1832-1834; inspector of Sing Sing prison, 1843; justice of circuit court, 1845; justice of state supreme court, 1847.

EDWARDS, LEWIS B., pr. *Lodi Pioneer,* 1827-1828; jrmn., Erie, Pa., 1830.

ELLIOTT, JOHN M., 1783-1864; appr. to D. Frothingham, Sag Harbor, 1791?-1798; pr. Sag Harbor *Frothingham's Long Island Herald,* 1798 [in absence of D. Frothingham—name not on imprint]; appr.

to Geo. F. Hopkins, New York, 1803; jrmn. for James Oram, Trenton, N. J., 1806; on Miranda expedition to South America—escaped, 1806-1809; jrmn. New York; d. Jersey City, N. J.

ELLIOTT, NATHAN, ed. Catskill *American Eagle,* 1807-1811.

ELLIOTT, NATHAN G., ed. *Catskill Recorder and Greene County Republican,* 1829-1835 (with Chas. Faxon, 1829-1831); lost in Gulf of Mexico on trip to Galveston.

ELY, E. S., ed. *Utica Intelligencer,* 1828-1829 (with J. Colwell, pr.).

ELY, ELIHU, 1780-1851, b. Lyme, Conn.; m. Eliza Maria Ely, 1816; Binghamton *Broome County Patriot,* before 1815.Co

EMONS, ADONIJAH, 1787-1845; lawyer; hotelkeeper; wrote occasional editorials for Glens Falls *Warren Republican;* ed. *Sandy Hill Times,* 1819-1824, Sandy Hill *Sun,* 1826-1828, Sandy Hill *Free Press,* 1832, *Keeseville Argus,* 1832-1837; practiced law, Detroit, Mich.; d. Detroit, Mich.

EVANS, EDWIN T., Binghamton *Broome County Republican,* 1830-1835 (with A. C. Canoll), Binghamton *Iris,* 1841-1853 [semi-monthly],Fr Binghamton *Daily Iris,* 1849 (with Wm. Stuart).Fr

EVANS, G. H., Ithaca *Museum and Independent Corrector,* 1824 (with L. B. Butler).

EVERETT, L. S., "Rev."; ed. Buffalo *Gospel Advocate,* 1826-1828, Auburn *Gospel Advocate,* 1828-1831 (with U. F. Doubleday and I. S. Allen, prs.), Buffalo *Western Evangelist,* 1846-1847.

FAGAN, JOHN, pr. *Onondaga Register,* 1826-1827.

FAIRCHILD, JOHN F., pr. Sherburne *Olive Branch,* 1806-1808 (with E. Phinney, 1806-1807), Norwich *Olive Branch,* 1808 (with ———), Cazenovia *Republican Monitor,* 1825-1841 (with L. L. Rice, 1826-1832; with son, 1832-1840).

FAIRCHILD, PLATT B., Ogdensburgh *St. Lawrence Gazette,* 1815-1824 (with D. R. Strachan).

FARR, JOSEPH M., Greene *Chenango Democrat,* 1830,Fr Lowville *Black River Gazette,* 1830-1833 (with W. L. Easton, 1832-1833).

FARRAND, J. pr. Goshen *Orange Farmer,* 1820-1821 (with S. Williams), Kingston *Craftsman,* 1825.

FAXON, CHARLES, *Catskill Recorder,* 1823-1828 (with R. Field, 1823-1827), *Catskill Recorder and Greene County Republican,* 1829-1831 (with N. G. Elliott, and ——— Gates, ed.).

FAY, THOMAS CHITTENDEN, pr. Goshen *Orange County Gazette,* 1810-1811 (with Elliott Hopkins), Onondaga Hollow *Lynx,* 1811-1812, proposals for book publishing, New York, 1813, *Georgetown Gazette* (N. C.), 1827 [imprisoned six months for libel, 1827]; concerned in getting a press in Georgetown, 1834, for a newspaper in St. Clair, Mich.

FELTHOUSEN, JACOB D., Johnstown *Montgomery Monitor*, 1810-1811 (with Russell Prentice).

FERGUSON, BARTIMEUS, m. Sally Ann Culver, 1818; pr. Middlebury (Vt.) *Columbian Patriot*, 1813-1815, Burlington (Vt.) *Northern Intelligencer*, 1814, *Niagara Spectator* (Upper Canada), 1818-1820 [imprisoned six months for libel on the government], Lewiston *Niagara Democrat*, 1821-1822, *Lockport Observatory*, 1822, *Black Rock Gazette*, 1824-1825, *Niagara Herald* (Upper Canada), 1828.

FIELD, RICHARD, 1798-1827; pr. *Catskill Recorder*, 1822-1827 (pr. for E. Croswell, 1822-1823; with Chas. Faxon, 1823-1827); d. Catskill.

FISH, ——— *Schoharie Observer*, 1820-1821 (with S. Baker).

FISH, N. W. W., *Waterford Reporter*, 1827-1828.[He]

FISH, PAUL J., Saugerties *Ulster Palladium and Manufacturers Journal*, 1828-1829 (with C. Frary), Kingston *Ulster Palladium and Anti-Masonic Journal*, 1829-1830.

FISH, WILLIAM L., *Waterford Reporter*, 1822-1827.

FISK, JOHN, Gaines *Orleans Whig*, 1827.

FLAGG, AZARIAH CUTTING, 1790-1873, b. Orwell, Vt.; m. Phoebe Maria Coe, 1814; appr., Burlington, Vt., 1801-1806; jrmn., 1806; pr. Plattsburgh *Republican*, 1811-1813 (with H. Cady, 1811), *Plattsburgh Republican*, 1813-1825 (with H. C. Miller, pr., 1820); lieut. and quartermaster, N. Y. militia, 1812; mem. assembly, 1822; secretary of state, N. Y., 1826-1833; state comptroller, 1842-1846; comptroller of New York City, 1852-1859; d. New York City; DAB.

FLANDERS, F. D., Fort Covington *Franklin Gazette*, 1827-1847, Malone *Franklin Gazette*, 1847-1859.[Fr]

FLEET, SAMUEL, Huntington *Long Island Journal of Philosophy and Cabinet of Variety*, 1825-1826, Huntington *Portico*, 1826-1827, Brooklyn, proposals only, for *New York Farmer*, 1827, *New York Farmer and American Gardener's Magazine*, 1833-1835, New York *United States Farmer and Journal of American Institute*, 1843,[Fr] New York *American Artisan*, 1847.[Fr]

FLETCHER, ADOLPHUS, 1796-1866, b. Croydon, N. H.; m. (1) Sarah Stow, (2) Caroline E. Brooks; appr. in office of *Massachusetts Spy*, Worcester, Mass.; farming, keeping store and tavern, Ashville, 1818-1825; pr. *Jamestown Journal*, 1826-1846 (with A. Hazeltine, ed., 1826-1829; with E. F. Warren, ed., 1829), Jamestown *Northern Citizen*, 1849-1853, Jamestown *Chautauqua Democrat*, 1855 (with James Parker).

FOLLETT, FREDERICK, 1804-1891, b. Hopewell; m. Sarah Sutherland, 1826; appr. to brother, Oran Follett, 1819-1825; pr. Batavia *Spirit of the Times,* 1825-1830, Batavia *Spirit of the Times and People's Press,* 1830-1836 (with D. P. Adams, 1830-1831); in war for the liberation of Texas under Sam Houston, 1836; in expedition to the copper fields of Lake Superior region; pr. Batavia *Spirit of the Times,* 1837-1840, *Batavia Times and Farmers and Mechanics' Journal,* 1840-1843; postmaster of Batavia, 1843-1849; canal commissioner, 1849-1856; in New York custom house, 1891; author, "The History of the Press of Western New York," 1847; d. New York.

FOLLETT, ORAN, 1798-1894, b. Gorham; m. Nancy Filer, 1821; appr. to J. A. Stevens, Canandaigua; managed J. D. Bemis' interest in bookstore of A. G. Dauby, Rochester; pr. Batavia *Spirit of the Times,* 1819-1825, *Buffalo Journal,* 1826-1830 (with D. M. Day, 1826-1827; with D. M. Day and R. W. Haskins, 1827-1830), Sandusky (O.) *Ohio State Journal;* mem. assembly, 1824; Printer of the Laws of the United States, 1821-1825.

FOWLE, EDWARD J., m. Julia Smith, 1827; appr., Ovid, 1816; jrmn. for Alden Spooner, New York; jrmn. for Harpers', New York; jrmn. for William Ray, Geneva, 1822/23; pr. Penn Yan *Yates Republican,* 1824-1835; merchant.

FRANCIS, JOHN, ed. Poughkeepsie *Republican Telegraph,* 1824-1825.

FRANCIS, SIMEON, 1796-1872, b. Wethersfield, Conn.; m. Eliza Rumsey, 1820; appr., New Haven, Conn.; pr. New London (Conn.) *Republican Advocate,* 1818-1820 (with J. B. Clapp), *Buffalo Emporium,* 1824-1826 (with J. A. Lazell), *Buffalo Emporium and Commercial Advertiser,* 1826-1828 [semi-weekly] (with J. A. Lazell), Springfield (Ill.) *Sangamon County Journal,* 1831-1845 (with J. Francis, A. Francis, and J. Newton), Springfield (Ill.) *Illinois State Journal,* 1845-1856 (co-editor), Portland (Ore.) *Oregonian,* 1862; Indian agent in Oregon, 1841; Paymaster in U. S. Army, 1862; maj.; col.; retired, 1870; d. Portland, Ore.

FRARY, CALVIN, pr. Saugerties *Ulster Palladium and Manufacturers Journal,* 1828-1829 (with P. J. Fish), Kingston *Ulster Palladium and Anti-Masonic Journal,* 1829-1830 (with P. J. Fish), Kingston *Ulster Palladium,* 1830-1831 (with D. L. Barnard), Saugerties *Ulster Star,* 1833.

FRARY, JONATHAN, d. 1829; Hudson *Balance,* 1808 (with H. Croswell), Albany *Republican Crisis,* 1808 (with H. Croswell), Albany *Balance and New York State Journal,* 1809-1810 (with H. Croswell); druggist, killed by the explosion of his soda fountain, Hudson.

FREEMAN, ——— Le Roy *Genesee Republican and Herald of Reform,* 1829 (with son; O. A. Brownson, ed.).

FREER, ANTHONY, 1784-1821; Kingston *Ulster Gazette,* 1816-1821 (with S. S. Freer); d. Kingston.

FREER, SAMUEL, 1741-1804; pr. Kingston *Rising Sun,* 1793-1798 (with William Copp), Kingston *Ulster County Gazette,* 1798-1803 (with S. S. Freer) ; d. Kingston.

FREER, SAMUEL S., 1771-1840; pr. Kingston *Ulster County Gazette,* 1798-1816 (with Samuel Freer, his father, 1798-1803), Kingston *Ulster Gazette,* 1816-1822 (with A. Freer, 1816-1821), Kingston *Ulster Herald,* 1822-1823, Kingston *People's Advocate,* 1824-1827 (with P. K. Allen), Kingston *Ulster Republican,* 1827 (with S. Curtis, Jr.) ; commissioner to acknowledge deeds, 1819; d. Kingston.

FRENCH, BRONSON, ed. Poughkeepsie *Farmers' and Mechanics Repository,* 1809 [fortnightly].

FRISBEE, HENRY CLINTON, 1801-1873, b. Essex Co.; appr. to James Hull, Fredonia, 1817-1819; pr. Fredonia *New York Censor,* 1821-1825, *Fredonia Censor,* 1825-1838; mem. assembly, 1845; d. Fredonia.

FROTHINGHAM, DAVID, 1765-1822?, b. Charlestown, Mass.; m. Nancy Pell; appr. Boston, Mass.; pr. Sag Harbor *Frothingham's Long Island Herald,* 1791-1798; jrmn. on *Greenleaf's New York Journal and Patriotic Register,* 1799; convicted of libel on Alexander Hamilton, sentenced to Bridewell for four months; fate uncertain—lost at sea? or in Congo, Africa?

GAMAGE, G. A., ed. Auburn *Cayuga Republican,* 1824-1825 (with T. Skinner), *Albany Patriot and Commercial Advertiser,* 1825-1826 (with G. Galpin), New York *Howard Gazette and New York Phoenix,* 1826.

GANT, S. M. S., Fort Plain *Watch Tower,* 1827,[Fr] Canajoharie *Montgomery Argus,* 1832-1836.[Fr]

GARDNER, GEORGE, Upton *Columbian Courier,* 1794 (with James Hill), *Lansingburgh Recorder,* 1794-1795 (with James Hill), Troy *Recorder,* 1795 (with James Hill; later with N. Billings).

GATES, ——— ed. *Catskill Recorder and Greene County Republican,* 1829 (with N. G. Elliott and Charles Faxon).

GATES, HIRAM, *Waterloo Gazette,* 1826.

GAZLAY, WARD M., 1782-1856, b. Pennsylvania; m. Elizabeth Carter, 1822; pr. Newburgh *Political Index,* 1806-1829; magistrate, Newburgh; d. Newburgh.

GERRISH, GEORGE, pr. Chestertown (Md.) *Apollo,* 1793 (with R. Saunders, Jr.), Salem *Times, or National Courier,* 1794-1795 (with St. John Honeywood), Reading (Pa.) *Impartial Reading Herald,* 1796-1797 (with J. Schneider), Reading (Pa.) *Unpartheyische Reading Adler,* 1797.

GIBSON, JAMES B., d. 1827; ed. Salem *Washington Register,* 1819-1822.

GILBERT, JOHN H., Palmyra *Wayne Sentinel,* 1824-1827 (with P. Tucker).

GOODALE, R., "Dr.," ed. Watertown *Constellation,* 1830-1831 (with D. D. Stephenson, pr.).

GOODENOW, STERLING, *Troy Gazette,* 1805-1808 (with J. C. Wright and H. Stockwell).

GOODRICH, J., ed. *Warsaw Sentinel,* 1830.

GOULD, JOHN KEEP, 1781-1808; jrmn., office of *Albany Centinel;* pr. Canandaigua *Western Repository and Genesee Advertiser,* 1803, Canandaigua *Western Repository,* 1803-1808 (with Russell E. Post, 1803-1804; with J. D. Bemis, 1804-1808); d. Canandaigua.

GRACE, OLIVER, pr. Lewiston *Niagara Sentinel,* 1826-1827, Lockport *Sentinel and Observatory,* 1827 (with O. Turner).

GRANDIN, EGBERT B., ed. Palmyra *Wayne Sentinel,* 1827-1832 (with Theron R. Strong, 1832); published "Book of Mormon," 1829-1830.

GREENMAN, JOSEPH G., Catskill *American Eagle,* 1811.

GREGORY, —— *Troy Sentinel,* 1827-1830 (with N. Tuttle), *Troy Daily Sentinel,* 1830-1831 (with N. Tuttle, O. Holley, ed.).

GRIFFING, EDWARD M., pr. Little Falls *People's Friend,* 1821-1830, Little Falls *People's Friend and Little Falls Gazette,* 1830-1834, Little Falls *Enterprise,* 1839-1841.

GROESBECK, JOHN C. G., Schoharie *American Herald,* 1809-1810.

GROSS, THOMAS, "Rev.," ed. Buffalo *Gospel Advocate,* 1822-1823.[Fr]

HADLEY, JONATHAN A., appr. Rochester, 1825; pr. *Palmyra Freeman,* 1829, *Lyons Countryman,* 1831 (with Myron Holley, ed.), Penn Yan *Yates Republican,* 1835, Warsaw *American Citizen,* 1836-1837; jrmn., foreman on *Rochester Daily Democrat,* 1847;[Fo] Watertown (Wis.) *Chronicle;* justice of peace, in Wis., 1855; asst. U. S. assessor, Watertown, Wis., 1867; employee of secretary of state, Wis.

HALE, SENECA, *Manlius Times,* 1817-1818 [for a while in this period].

HALL, —— Cazenovia *Madison Observer,* 1821-1822 (with L. L. Rice), Morrisville *Madison Observer,* 1822-1823 (with L. L. Rice).

HALL, ALBERT G., pr. *Rochester Observer,* 1830 (with S. Chipman and Co., proprietors).

HALLAND, HENRY, m. Phebe Race, 1811; pr. Hudson *Bee,* 1810 (with Charles Holt).

HARKNESS, ABNER, Newtown [Elmira] *Telegraph,* 1818-1819 (with E. Harkness).

HARKNESS, EDSON, pr. Newtown [Elmira] *Telegraph,* 1818-1819 (with A. Harkness).

HARRINGTON, ELISHA, pr. *Utica Sentinel,* 1821 (with William Williams).

HARRIS, ABIATHAR M., *Brockport Recorder,* 1828-1830, *Brockport Free Press,* 1831-1832 (with T. H. Hyatt).

HARVEY, ASAHEL, 1798-1834, b. Surry, N. H.; Geneseo *Livingston Journal,* 1821-1828 (with C. Morse, 1821-1825), Canandaigua *Ontario Repository,* 1830 (with S. C. Ward and C. Morse); d. Canandaigua.

HARVEY, HENRY L., Watertown *Genius of Philanthropy,* 1828, Watertown *Register,* 1828, Watertown *Voice of Jefferson,* 1828 (with —————— Hunt), *Watertown Register,* 1829, *Watertown Register and General Advertiser,* 1830-1831 (with Benj. Cory).

HASKELL, TRUMAN W., Watertown *Freeman's Advocate,* 1824, Sackett's Harbor *Freeman's Advocate,* 1826?-1828.[Fr Co]

HASKINS, ROSSWELL WILLSON, 1796-1870, b. Salem, Mass.; m. (1) Eliza Caryl, 1823, (2) Emma Stowe, 1840; appr. to bookbinder, Brattleboro, Vt.; jrmn. bookbinder, Hudson; jrmn. bookbinder for J. D. Bemis, Canandaigua, 1817; jrmn. bookbinder for A. G. Dauby, Rochester; ed. *Buffalo Journal,* 1827-1831 (with D. M. Day and O. Follett); Buffalo bookstore, 1831-1832; ed. *Buffalo Whig,* 1834, Buffalo *National Pilot,* 1845-1846, Buffalo *Morning Express;* author, "History and Progress of Phrenology," 1839; "Astronomy for Schools," 1841; d. Buffalo.

HASTINGS, CHARLES, Utica *Western Recorder,* 1824-1832 (with Thos. Hastings and A. Merrell, 1824-1826; with Thos. Hastings and G. Tracy, 1826).

HASTINGS, THOMAS, ed. Utica *Western Recorder,* 1824-1832 (with Chas. Hastings and A. Merrell, 1824-1826; with Chas. Hastings and G. Tracy, 1826-1832).

HASTINGS, TRUMAN, *Troy Review, or Religious and Musical Repository,* 1826-1827 (with N. Tuttle and S. Richards).

HATHAWAY, J. G., pr. Auburn *Cayuga Patriot,* 1814, Ovid *Seneca Patriot,* 1815-1817 (with George Lewis and S. R. Brown), Fayette *Seneca Patriot,* 1817; jrmn. for H. Leavenworth, on *Waterloo Gazette* [Dec. 1817, claimed rights to this press and seized it; was arrested and imprisoned].

HAVENS, PETER B., *Hamilton Recorder,* 1817-1819 (with J. G. Stower).

HAYES, MICHAEL, pr. *Ovid Gazette,* 1816-1827, Ovid *Seneca Republican,* 1827-1830, *Ovid Gazette and Seneca County Register,* 1830.

HAYWARD, BILLINGS, Buffalo *Western Advertiser,* 1827-1828 (with Chas. Sentell).

HAZELTINE, ABNER, 1793-1879, b. Windham, Vt.; graduated, Williams College, 1815; practiced law, Warren, Pa.; ed. *Jamestown Journal,* 1826-1829 (with A. Fletcher, pr.); mem. assembly, 1829-

1830; mem. Congress, 1833-1837; prosecuting attorney, Chautauqua Co., 1847-1850; judge of Chautauqua Co., 1859-1863; d. Jamestown.

HENDRIE, ROBERT C. S., ed. Goshen *Orange County Patriot,* 1828-1834 (with ―――― Wright, 1831-1834), Goshen *True Whig,* 1842-1845.

HERON, JOHN, Newburgh *Orange County Gazette,* 1810 (with E. Hopkins).

HERON, SAMUEL, Rochester *Anti-Masonic Enquirer,* 1828-1829 (with Thurlow Weed).

HERSKELL, HIRAM, m. Caroline Amelia Bunce, 1823; pr. Huntington *American Eagle,* 1823-1826 (with S. Fleet).

HEWES, ―――― Cooperstown *Tocsin,* 1829-1830 (with ―――― Dutton).

HICKOK, ―――― Lansingburgh *Federal Herald,* 1788-1790 (with J. Babcock).

HICKOX, ―――― Fredonia *Chautauque Gazette,* 1821-1822 (with J. Hull).

HILL, EBENEZER, m. Mary Bryans, 1824; Troy *Northern Budget,* 1814/15-1817, Fayetteville (Tenn.) *Village Messenger,* 1823.

HILL, JAMES, pr. Upton *Columbian Courier,* 1794 (with Geo. Gardner), *Lansingburgh Recorder,* 1794-1795 (with Geo. Gardner), Troy *Recorder,* 1795 (with Geo. Gardner), *Burlington Mercury* (Vt.), 1796.

HILL, RICHARD, pr. Warren, (Pa.) *Western Courier,* Ellicottville *Western Courier,* 1826-1827, Ellicottville *Cattaraugus Gazette,* 1827-1828, *Greensville Gazette* (Pa.), 1830.

HINCHMAN, ROBERT, Newburgh *Rights of Man,* 1803-1804 (with D. Denniston, ed.).

HOARD, SAMUEL, Fort Covington *Franklin Republican,* 1827-1833 (with J. Long, 1828), Ogdensburg *St. Lawrence Republican,* 1833.

HOFFMAN, LEWIS G., 1800-1879; m. Caroline Jewett, 1823; appr. to Jesse Buel, Albany, 1816-1820; sent by S. Southwick with M. M. Cole to Sackett's Harbor—broke with Cole on account of a political dispute; pr. Lowville *Lewis County Gazette,* 1821-1822, *Black Rock Beacon,* 1823-1824, *Albany Christian Register,* 1827-1828,[He] Albany *American Masonic Register,* 1839-1843; justice of peace, Waterford.

HOLDEN, DAVID, *Johnstown Gazette,* 1798 (with James Smith).

HOLLAND, WILLIAM, Johnstown *Montgomery Republican,* 1823-1825.[Fr]

HOLLEY, ORVILLE LUTHER, 1791-1861, b. Salisbury, Conn.; graduate, Harvard, 1813; studied law, New York; ed. *Troy Sentinel,* 1823-1828/29 (with W. S. Parker, 1823-1824; with N. Tuttle and S. Richards, 1824-1828/29 [interlude 1826-1827 in which Holley was

not connected with paper]), *New York Weekly Whig,* 1831 (with
H. D. Ward), Canandaigua *Ontario Repository and Freeman,* 1836-
1837, *Albany Daily Advertiser,* 1842-1844; surveyor-general of state,
1838; in office of secretary of state, Albany; author, "Description of
the City of New York," 1847, and "Life of Franklin," 1856; d.
Albany.

HOLT, CHARLES, m. Mary Dobbs, 1800; pr. New London (Conn.)
Bee, 1797-1802 [arrested under the Sedition Act, 1799, fined $200,
and imprisoned three months], Hudson *Bee,* 1802-1810; New York
Columbian, 1809-1816 (with B. Irvine, 1815-1816); ward justice in
New York; employed in New York customs house.

HOLT, DAVID, pr. Herkimer *Farmer's Monitor,* 1805-1807 (with J. B.
Robbins), Herkimer *Bunker Hill,* 1809-1810 (with J. G. Phinney),
Herkimer *Republican Farmer's Free Press,* 1830; jailer; collector of
U. S. internal revenue, 1813; postmaster of Herkimer, 1820; county
judge, 1821-1823.

HOOGHKERK, HENRY, 1806-1829; pr. *Canajoharie Telegraph,* 1825-
1829; d. Canajoharie.

HOOPER, ——— *Troy Budget and City Register,* 1830-1837 Co (with
J. C. Kemble, 1830-1835/36).

HOPKINS, ELLIOTT, 1774-1815, b. Charlotte; Goshen *Orange County
Gazette,* 1807-1814 (with G. Denton, 1807; with J. Heron, 1810;
with T. C. Fay, 1810-1811); d. Cincinnati, O.

HOPKINS, HENRY, Cooperstown *Tocsin,* 1830 (with ——— Dutton),
Cooperstown *Otsego Republican,* one year (with A. W. Clark).Fr

HOSKINS, TIMOTHY, Salem *Washington Register,* 1816-1818 (with J.
B. Gibson), Caldwell *Lake George Watchman,* 1818-1820.

HOTCHKIN, BERIAH B., m. Elizabeth A. Fitch, 1827; ed. *Le Roy
Gazette,* 1827-1828 (with Elisha Starr), proposals only for a
monthly, *Western Preacher,* 1828, *Palmyra Freeman,* 1828, Utica
Elucidator, 1829-1833 (with William Williams, 1830-1833), Her-
kimer *Republican Farmer's Free Press,* 1830-1832 (with H. S.
Bartlett, pr.).

HOUGHTON, ABIJAH OTIS, 1792-1855, b. Sterling, Mass.; m. Eliza
Farrand, 1815; Goshen *Orange County Gazette,* 1814-1818 (with
T. L. Houghton), Durbee (Vt.) *Northern Osiris, Rahway Herald*
(N. J.), *New York Observer;* capt., 1812; col.; customs-house offi-
cial; d. Rahway, N. J.

HOUGHTON, THEOPHILUS LILLY, 1785-1872; m. Mrs. Ann Apple-
gate, 1821; pr. Haverhill (N. H.) *Coos Courier,* 1808-1810, Haverhill (N. H.) *Advertiser,* 1810, Goshen *Orange County Gazette,*
1814-1818 (with A. O. Houghton), Newburgh *Orange County
Gazette,* 1818-1819; d. Brooklyn.

HOVEY, LEVI, b. 1792; m. Betsey Bishop, 1816; Geneseo *Livingston Journal,* 1829-1831; d. New Orleans, La.

HOWARD, ANSON M., pr. Binghamton *Phoenix,* 1818-1820, *Oxford Gazette,* 1823-1825 (with George Hunt, 1823; with —— Carlisle, 1825).Co

HOWARD, LUTHER, bookbinder, Ithaca, 1820; Palmyra *Western Spectator and Public Advertiser,* 1830-1831, Palmyra *Western Spectator and Anti-Masonic Star,* 1831 (with E. Shepard).

HOWE, JOHN, pr. Ballston *Rural Visitor,* 1812 (with S. R. Brown).

HOWELL, BENONI H., pr. Newburgh *Rights of Man,* 1799-1800 (with E. Winfield).

HUBBARD, JOHN F., 1795-1876, b. Columbia Co.; m. Almira Mead, 1820; appr. to H. & E. Phinney, Cooperstown; jrmn., Harrisburg, Pa.; pr. *Norwich Journal,* 1816-1847 [sold establishment to Thurlow Weed, 1818, but resumed publication under old name, 1819] (with Ralph Johnson, 1828-1834); mem. assembly, 1824; mem. state senate, 1829-1836; justice of peace; commissioner to acknowledge deeds; d. Norwich.

HUGHS, WILLIAM, Potsdam *Patriot,* 1830-1831.

HULL, C. JR., Catskill *Greene County Republican,* 1828.

HULL, D. G., pr. Homer *Western Courier,* 1820-1821 (with E. J. Roberts), Delhi *Delaware Republican,* 1823.Fr

HULL, JAMES, 1789-1867; m. Betsey Crosby, 1818; pr. Fredonia *Chautauque Gazette,* 1817-1822 Fr (with William Carpenter and James Percival, 1817), Fredonia *Chautauque Advertiser,* 1824-1826, *Fredonia Gazette,* 1826-1827 (with William S. Snow), *Dunkirk Gazette,* 1827-1828, Westfield *Chautauqua Phenix,* 1828-1831 (with H. Newcomb).

HULL, SAMUEL P., pr. *Geneva Palladium,* 1817-1822/23, Geneva *Miscellaneous Register,* 1822 (with William Ray, ed.), Angelica *Allegany Republican,* 1823-1826, Morristown, (N.J.) *Jerseyman,* 1826, and 1844-1852.

HUNT, —— Rochester *Album,* 1825-1826 (with E. F. Marshall and O. Spalding).Fr

HUNT, ALVIN, Watertown *Voice of Jefferson,* 1828 (with H. L. Harvey), *Watertown Eagle,* 1833. Watertown *Aurora,* 1840.

HUNT, GEORGE, *Oxford Gazette,* 1823-1825 (with Eben. Noyes, 1824-1825).

HUNT, HENRY W., 1774-1852, b. Boston, Mass.; m. (1) Sally Congdon, 1800, (2) Frances Elizabeth Howard, 1816; appr. to Isaiah Thomas, as a bookbinder, Worcester, Mass., 1790-1794; in Haiti, 1804-1809, where he was made colonel by Christophe; ed. Sag Harbor *Corrector,* 1822-1852; d. Sag Harbor.

HURTIN, JOHN G., *Goshen Repository,* 1796-1799 (with William Hurtin, 1798; again 1799 [published for an interval in 1797 by William Hurtin, Jr.]), Goshen *Orange Patrol,* 1800-1801, Goshen *Orange County Gazette,* 1805 (with G. Denton).

HURTIN, WILLIAM, Newton (N. J.) *Farmer's Journal and Newton Advertiser,* 1796-1797, *Goshen Repository,* 1797-1798.

HURTIN, WILLIAM, JR., 1775-1797; appr. to Thomas Greenleaf, New York; pr. New York *Mott and Hurtin's New York Weekly Chronicle,* 1795 (with ———— Mott), *Goshen Repository,* 1797; d. Goshen.

HUTCHINSON, WILLIAM, Hempstead *Long Island Telegraph and General Advertiser,* 1830 (with C. F. LeFevre).Fr

HUTTON, DAVID M., *Tonawanda Recorder,* 1824 [only information of the existence of this paper is a letter, signed by Hutton as editor, in *Black Rock Gazette,* Dec. 21, 1824].

HYER, WILLIAM G., Norwich *People's Advocate,* 1825-1826, Oxford *Chenango Republican,* 1826, Catskill *Greene County Republican,* 1826-1827.

INGERSOLL, JONATHAN, JR., b. 1792, Stockbridge, Mass.; m. Eliza Chapman, 1816; pr. Utica *Club,* 1815, Ithaca *Seneca Republican,* 1815-1816; jrmn. for H. C. Southwick, Auburn, 1817.

JACKACKS, NICHOLAS, m. Mary Dakin, 1827; Poughkeepsie *Dutchess Observer,* 1820-1822 (with C. P. Barnum).

JACKSON, O. P., *Geneva Chronicle,* 1827-1828 (with George Willson).

JANSEN, BENJAMIN G., Kingston *Craftsman,* 1820-1821.

JEHAN, D., Waterford *Saratoga Recorder and Anti-Masonic Democrat,* 1830-1831 (with I. Sackett).

JOHNSON, DAVID, Delhi *Delaware Gazette,* 1822-1828.

JOHNSON, JOHN BURGESS, pr. Norwich *Chenango Patriot,* 1809-1810, Norwich *Volunteer,* 1816, Morrisville *Madison County Gazette,* 1817 (with son), Morrisville *Gazette and Madison County Advertiser,* 1819 (with son), Morrisville *Madison County Advertiser,* 1822.Fr

JOHNSON, JOHN C., Waterford *Anti-Masonic Recorder,* 1820-1830, Troy *Daily News,* 1830.

JOHNSON, RALPH, m. Mary Randall, 1829; pr. Catskill *Greene County Republican,* 1827-1828, *Norwich Journal,* 1828-1834 (with John F. Hubbard).

JOHNSON, T., pr. Schenectady *Mohawk Advertiser,* 1810-1811 (with W. S. Buell).

JOYNER, NATHANIEL, d. 1812; pr. Poughkeepsie *Guardian,* 1801-1802 (with J. Buell) ; d. New York.

JUDD, SILAS, *Canastota Register,* 1830-1831 (with H. B. Mattison).

KAPPEL, MICHAEL J., Catskill *Greene and Delaware Washingtonian,* 1814.

KELLOGG, LEONARD, 1781-1817; m. Sally French, 1808; pr. Manlius *Herald of the Times,* 1808-1809, *Manlius Times,* 1809-1817 (with D. C. Clark, 1817; with J. Beardslee) ; capt. rifle corps, 1812; d. Manlius.

KELLOGG, RICHARD K., Jamestown, *Chautauqua Republican,* 1830-1830/31 (with M. Bates).

KEMBLE, JOHN C., ed. *Troy Budget and City Register,* 1826-1835/36 (with Z. Clark, pr., 1826-1827; with ———— Hooper, 1835/36) ; mem. assembly, 1832; mem. state senate, 1834-1836.

KEMPSHALL, J., Albion *American Standard,* 1830-1832.

KERSEY, WILLIAM, ed. *Bath Gazette,* 1796-1798 (with James Edie) ; judge, Steuben Co., 1803.

KILLEY, EGBERT B., d. 1852; m. Julia Ann Turner, 1829; ed. Poughkeepsie *Republican Telegraph and Observer,* 1829-1849 (with C. P. Barnum, 1829-1830; with Aaron Low, 1830-1835; with B. J. Lossing, 1835-1849), Poughkeepsie *Telegraph,* 1841 (with B. J. Lossing) ; *Poughkeepsie Casket,* 1836 (with B. J. Lossing) ; postmaster, 1846-1851.

KING, NATHANIEL, Hamilton *Madison Farmer,* 1828-1829.

KING, PRESTON, 1806-1865, b. Ogdensburg; graduate, Union College, 1827; ed. *Canton Advertiser and St. Lawrence Republican,* 1827-1830 (with W. W. Wyman, *q.v.*), Ogdensburg *St. Lawrence Republican,* 1830-1833; postmaster, 1831-1834; mem. assembly, 1835-1848; mem. Congress, 1843-1853; mem. U. S. Senate, 1857-1863; d. New York; DAB.

KING, SYLVESTER, Johnstown *Montgomery Monitor,* 1818.

KINNEY, MILTON A., 1803-1861; pr. Homer *Cortland Observer,* 1825-1833, *Skaneateles Columbian,* 1833-1853 (with L. A. Pratt, and E. S. Keeney, 1837-1838; with George M. Kinney, 1851-1853) ; mem. assembly, 1854, d. Skaneateles.

KIPP, JOHN C., *Ogdensburgh Palladium,* 1810-1812 (with T. C. Strong, 1810-1811; with L. Kipp, 1811-1812).

KIPP, L., *Ogdensburgh Palladium,* 1811-1812 (with J. C. Kipp).

KIRK, THOMAS, pr. Brooklyn *Courier and Long Island Advertiser,* 1799, Brooklyn *Courier and New York and Long Island Advertiser,* 1799, Brooklyn *Long Island Courier,* 1800-1802; Brooklyn *Long Island Star,* 1809-1811; postmaster, Brooklyn, 1825-1826.

LADD, THOMAS M., Utica *Mechanics Free Press,* 1829 (with W. Schram).

LANPHIER, WILLIAM B., White Plains *Westchester Spy,* 1830.

LANSING, DIRCK C., "Rev.," ed. Auburn *Evangelical Recorder,* 1818 (with T. Skinner).

LAPPON, JOHN JAY, pr. Cooperstown *Freeman's Journal, and Otsego County Advertiser,* 1817-1819, Delhi *Delaware Gazette,* 1819-1822.

LATHROP, NEAL D., b. 1807, Ballston; appr. to Oliver Grace, Lewiston-Lockport, 1827; pr. Lockport *Sentinel and Observatory,* 1827-1828 (with C. P. Turner); jrmn. on *Niagara Courier,* 1828-1829.

LAZELL, JOHN A., proposals for Worcester (Mass.) *Masonic Cabinet and Miscellaneous Magazine,* 1817, Buffalo *Emporium,* 1824-1826 (with S. Francis), *Buffalo Emporium and Commercial Advertiser,* 1826-1829 [semi-weekly] (with S. Francis, 1826-1828), Columbus (O.) *Ohio State Bulletin,* 1829-1831 (with John A. Bryan, 1829-1830).

LEAVENWORTH, HIRAM, 1797-1857, b. New Canaan; m. Lavinia Holden, 1819; pr. *Waterloo Gazette,* 1817-1821 (with J. McLean, Jr., 1818), St. Catherines (Canada) *Journal;* d. St. Catherines, Canada.

LE FEVRE, C. F., Hempstead *Long Island Telegraph and General Advertiser,* 1830 Fr (with William Hutchinson).

LEONARD, STEPHEN BANKS, 1793-1876, b. New York; m. Henrietta Sperry, 1818; appr. to S. Mack, Owego, 1806; jrmn. for S. Southwick, Albany, 1813; pr. Owego *American Farmer,* 1813-1814 (with S. Mack), *Owego Gazette,* 1814-1849 (with E. Mack, 1815-1816; with J. B. Shurtleff, 1827-1829; with John C. Cantine, 1833-1835); postmaster, Owego, 1816-1820, and 1844-1849; village trustee, 1822-1823; supervisor, 1854-1856; deputy U. S. marshall, 1857-1861; mem. Congress, 1835-1837, and 1839-1841; d. Owego.

LEWIS, ELDAD, *Troy Gazette and Rensselaer Philanthropist,* 1809-1810, *Troy Gazette,* 1810 (with R. Schermerhorn), *Newburgh Republican,* 1811, Newburgh *Orange County Patriot,* 1811 (with T. B. Crowell); book publishing, Newburgh.

LEWIS, GEORGE, d. 1839; jrmn. Manlius; pr. Ovid *Seneca Patriot,* 1815-1816 (with J. G. Hathaway and S. R. Brown), *Waterloo Gazette,* 1817, *Lyons Republican,* 1821-1822; d. Pennsylvania.

LINDSEY, EDWIN GALLOWAY, m. Amarillis Skinner, 1828; pr. *Glens Falls Observer,* 1827-1828, Hudson *Columbia and Greene Co. Envoy,* 1831-1833.Fr

LINTNER, GEORGE A., minister; ed. Schoharie *Evangelical Luminary,* 1824-1825 (with L. Cuthbert, pr.), Schoharie *Lutheran Magazine,* 1827 (with L. Cuthbert).

LISHER, GEORGE B., "Rev.," ed. Glens Falls *Gospel Inquirer,* 1825, Utica *Universalist,* 1825-1826.

LITTLE, WILLIAM, Brooklyn *Long Island Weekly Intelligencer,* 1806-

1807 (with Wm. C. Robinson), *Brooklyn Minerva and Long Island Advertiser,* 1807.

LOOKER, JOHN MILTON, d. 1812; m. Sally Brown, 1803; pr. *Waterford Gazette,* 1802 (with H. H. Wadsworth), Salem *Washington Register,* 1803-1805; d. Cincinnati, O.

LOOMIS, ELISHA, ed. *Rochester Observer,* 1829-1830 (joint editor and proprietor).

LOPEZ, M., West Farms *West Chester Patriot,* 1813.

LORD, JOHN HAINES, 1793-1858; jrmn. for D. and S. A. Abbey, Albany; pr. Watertown *Jefferson and Lewis Gazette,* 1817-1819, *Oswego Palladium,* 1819-1830; postmaster, Oswego, 1840-1841.

LOTHROP, JOHN H., 1771-1829, b. New Haven, Conn.; m. Jerusha Kirkland, 1797; studied law, Hartford, Conn.; ed. Utica *Whitestown Gazette and Cato's Patrol,* 1803, *Utica Patriot,* 1803-1811 (with I. Merrell and A. Seward, 1803-1806; with I. Merrell, 1806-1811); copyist, county clerk's office.

LOTT, ABRAHAM, *New Windsor Gazette,* 1797-1799 (with J. Schultz).

LOW, AARON, m. Mary C. Dean, 1830; pr. Poughkeepsie *Republican Telegraph and Observer,* 1830-1835 (with E. B. Killey).

LOWELL, SAMUEL, d. 1850; Plattsburgh *American Monitor,* 1809-1810 (with George W. Nichols, 1809), Plattsburgh *Clinton Advertiser,* 1810-1811, Plattsburgh *Political Observatory,* 1811, Plattsburgh *Northern Herald,* 1812-1813.

LYON, OLIVER, 1783-1821; m. Nancy [Mrs. Robert] Moffitt, 1809; pr. Troy *Northern Budget,* 1804-1814/15 (with Robert Moffitt, 1804-1807); d. Caldwell.

LYON, ZEBULON, pr. Troy *Northern Budget,* 1801-1804 (with Robert Moffitt).

McCLEARY, DAVID C., ed. Batavia *People's Press,* 1829-1830 (with D. P. Adams, 1829; with A. P. Parker, 1829-1830); d. Vermont.

McCONNELL, CEPHAS S., pr. Ballston Spa *Saratoga Patriot,* 1813-1814 (with R. Prentice), Onondaga Hill *Onondaga Journal,* 1821-1827, Geneva *Republican Phalanx and Geneva Journal of the Times,* 1828-1829, Albion *Orleans Republican,* 1829-1841, *Rochester Daily Advertiser,* 1841, Albion *Orleans Republican,* 1846-1848.

McDONALD, DANIEL, Johnstown *Montgomery Monitor,* 1824-1828 (with Duncan McDonald).[Fr]

McDONALD, DUNCAN, Johnstown *Montgomery Monitor,* 1824-1828 (with Daniel McDonald),[Fr] Johnstown *Free Press,* 1829-1830 (with W. McDonald), *Schoharie Free Press,* 1830-1832,[Fr] *Esperance Sentinel and Schoharie and Montgomery Reporter,* 1832-1835/36.[Fr]

McDONALD, W., Johnstown *Free Press,* 1829-1830 (with Duncan McDonald).

MacDUFFEE, DANIEL, appr. to J. Buel, Kingston; pr. Poughkeepsie *Republican Herald,* 1811-1812 (with C. C. Adams), Kingston *Plebeian,* 1813-1814, Goshen *Independent Republican,* 1816-1817.

MACK, DANIEL, 1801-1830; m. Electa Jane Morehouse, 1825; appr. to Mack and Shepard, Ithaca, 1818; jrmn. to Mack and Shepard, Ithaca, 1819 [in Feb. 1819 signed the indenture of J. N. Bogert of Geneva]; pr. Oxford *Chenango Republican, or Oxford Gazette and People's Advocate,* 1828-1830 (with William E. Chapman); d. Oxford.

MACK, EBENEZER, 1791-1849; m. Ellenor Dey, 1820; appr.; jrmn. foreman for Charles Holt, New York, 1812-1815; pr. *Owego Gazette,* 1815-1816 (with S. B. Leonard), Ithaca *American Journal,* 1817-1823 (with E. Shepard, 1817-1819; with A. P. Searing, 1819; with A. P. Searing, 1820-1821; with C. Morgan, 1823), *Ithaca Journal, Literary Gazette and General Advertiser,* 1827-1828 (with William Andrus), *Ithaca Journal and Advertiser,* 1828-1833 (with William Andrus); continued in business, Mack and Andrus, 1833-1835; Mack, Andrus and Woodruff, 1835-1842; printer to the senate of the state; trustee of village, Ithaca; postmaster, Ithaca; mem. assembly, 1830; mem. state senate, 1833-1837; d. Ithaca.

MACK, STEPHEN, 1765-1814, b. Mass.; m. (1) ———, (2) Mary Sargent, 1797; storekeeper, Cooperstown; Owego *American Farmer,* 1803-1814 (with S. B. Leonard, 1813-1814); assessor; justice of peace; commissioner of highways; excise commissioner; constable; supervisor, 1807-1808, and 1811-1812; First Judge, court of common pleas, 1812-1814; d. Owego.

McLEAN, JOHN, JR., ed. *Waterloo Gazette,* 1818 (with H. Leavenworth, pr.); First Judge, Seneca County, 1818-1823.

McLEAN, WILLIAM, 1774-1848, b. Hartford, Conn.; m. (1) Susan Williams, (2) Louisa Andrews, 1830; pr. *Whitestown Gazette,* 1796-1798 (with S. Wells, 1796), Utica *Whitestown Gazette, and Cato's Patrol,* 1798-1803; Lebanon (O.) *Western Star,* 1814-1816, Cherry Valley *Gazette,* 1848; d. Cherry Valley.

McVEAN, J., *Canajoharie Republican,* 1828 (with D. F. Sacia),[Fr] Canajoharie *Montgomery Argus,* 1831-1832.[Fr]

MANDEVILLE, DAVID, Goshen *Repository,* 1789-1792 (with D. Westcott).

MARKS, SAMUEL, New York *Olio,* 1813-1814, Peekskill *Westchester and Putnam Sentinel,* 1830-1832.

MARSH, LUTHER, 1784-1816, b. Oakham, Mass.; m. Laury Frisbee; pr. Plattsburgh *American Monitor,* 1809 (with George W. Nichols),

Elizabethtown *Reveille,* 1812-1816 (with William Ray, ed., 1812);
d. Elizabethtown.

MARSHALL, ELIHU F., Rochester *Album,* 1825-1827 (with Spalding
and Hunt, 1825-1826; with —— Dean, 1827), Rochester *New
Genesee Farmer,* 1839/40 (with M. F. Bateman); city treasurer of
Rochester.

MARSHALL, STEPHEN, m. Margaret Sherwood, 1820; pr. Mount
Pleasant *Westchester Herald and Farmer's Register,* 1818-1825;
clerk of school district, 1820; postmaster, Mount Pleasant, 1825.

MARTIN, ROBERT, jrmn., Albany; pr. *Albany Daily Advertiser,* 1824-
1833 (with James Hunter and G. W. Ryckman), *Rochester Daily
Telegraph,* 1826-1829 (with Thurlow Weed, 1826), *Rochester
Daily Advertiser and Telegraph,* 1829 (with Luther Tucker),
Batavia *Free Press,* 1827 (with D. P. Adams), Batavia *Masonic In-
telligencer,* 1827 (ed.).

MASON, EBENEZER P., Waterloo *Western Times,* 1830.[Fr]

MATTISON, H. B., *Canastota Register,* 1830-1831 (with S. Judd).

MAYNARD, ELISHA A., Utica *Oneida Observer,* 1826-1834 (with A. G.
Dauby).

MAYNARD, WILLIAM H., d. 1832; b. Mass.; graduate, Williams College, 1810; studied law, New Hartford, 1810; ed. *Utica Patriot,*
1811-1815 (editorial connection, 1811-1814); mem. state senate,
1829-1832.

MERRELL, ANDREW, 1791-1826; Utica *Western Recorder,* 1824-1826
(with Charles Hastings); d. Utica.

MERRELL, HIRAM G., m. Julia Ann Lawton, 1830; Seneca Falls *Seneca
Farmer,* 1827-1828 (with William Child).

MERRELL, IRA, m. Nancy Camp; appr. to William McLean, Utica,
1803; pr. *Utica Patriot,* 1803-1806 (with A. Seward); jrmn.
foreman for Seward and Williams, 1806-1808; pr. *Utica Patriot,*
1808-1814 (with George Camp, 1813-1814), *Utica Patriot
and Patrol,* 1816-1817, *Utica Intelligencer,* 1826-1827, *Geneva
Courier.*

MERRILL, JOHN C., *Geneva Courier,* 1830-1833.[Fr]

MILLER, CHARLES W., appr. to his father, D. C. Miller, Batavia;
jrmn., Batavia, 1826-1828; pr. Batavia *Republican Advocate,* 1828-
1831 (with Charles Sentell, 1828) [ceased active management in
1830].

MILLER, DAVID C., pr. Ballston Spa *Saratoga Advertiser,* 1804-1809
(with J. Swaine, T. White, and W. Child, 1804-1805; with I. Riggs,
1808; with S. R. Brown, 1809), Ballston Spa *Aurora Borealis, and
Saratoga Advertiser,* 1809-1810, Ballston Spa *Advertiser,* 1810,
Johnstown *Montgomery Monitor,* 1809-1810, Batavia *Republican*

Advocate, 1815-1828 (with B. Blodgett, 1815), prospectus only for Buffalo *Western Advertiser,* 1827; supervisor, 1825; county clerk, 1828-1831; moved to Cleveland, O.

MILLER, HENRY C., pr. *Plattsburgh Republican,* 1820-1828 Co (with A. C. Flagg, 1820; with J. K. Averill, 1827-1828).

MILLER, JAMES M., 1792-1838; pr. for Father Gabriel Richards, Detroit, Mich., 1809-1810; pr. Detroit *Michigan Essay or Impartial Observer,* 1809; jrmn. for S. R. Brown, Ballston Spa, 1811-1812; pr. Norwich *Telegraph,* 1812-1814, Norwich *Volunteer,* 1814 (with Lot Clark, proprietor); jrmn. for H. C. Southwick, Auburn, 1817; pr. Auburn *Castigator,* 1819, Ithaca *Castigator,* 1823-1824 [not continuous]; d. Ithaca.

MILLS, P. S., Union Village *Anti-Masonic Champion,* 1829-1830 (with L. Dewey).

MITCHELL, DAVID, Dansville *Village Chronicle,* 1830-1831 (with B. C. Dennison), *Dansville Chronicle,* and *Steuben and Allegany Intelligencer,* 1831.

MITCHELL, ISAAC, 1760-1812; schoolmaster of the Dutchess academy; ed. Poughkeepsie *American Farmer,* 1798 (with John Woods), Poughkeepsie *Political Barometer,* 1802-1806 (with J. Buel, 1802-1805), Kingston *Plebeian,* 1803-1805 (with J. Buel), Albany *Republican Crisis,* 1806-1807, Poughkeepsie *Northern Politician,* 1812; author, "Alonzo and Melissa"; d. Poughkeepsie.

MIX, PETER, 1792-1866, b. Half Moon, Saratoga Co.; appr., Utica, 1808; pr. Johnstown *Montgomery Republican,* 1825-1836 [office burned, 1834], *Schoharie Patriot,* 1838-1860 Fr (later with S. H. Mix.); d. Schoharie.

MOFFITT, ROBERT, 1775-1807; m. Nancy Young, 1805; appr. to S. Tiffany, Lansingburgh, 1792; appr. to W. Wands, Lansingburgh, 1792; pr. *Albany Chronicle,* 1797 (with J. McDonald), Albany *Northern Budget,* 1797 (with J. McDonald), Troy *Northern Budget,* 1798-1807 (with J. Buel, 1798-1801; with Z. Lyon, 1801-1804; with O. Lyon, 1804-1807); d. Troy.

MOON, EBER P., m. Elizabeth G. Sholes, 1829; appr. in office of *Ontario Repository,* Canandaigua, 1828; pr. *Waterloo Observer,* 1828-1829 (with M. Severance), *Clyde Standard,* 1830.Co

MOORE, S. H., Manlius *Spirit of the Press,* 1816-1817.

MORGAN, AUGUSTUS, d. 1869; m. Ambrosia Robinson, 1817; appr. to I. Merrell, Utica, 1810; pr. Binghamton *Phoenix,* 1817, Binghamton *Broome County Republican,* 1823-1828 (with A. C. Canoll).

MORGAN, CHAUNCEY, m. Betsey N. Bessac, 1813; appr. to Ira Merrell, Utica, 1810; pr. Binghamton *Broome County Patriot,* 1812, *Oxford Gazette,* 1813-1823, Ithaca *American Journal,* 1823 (with E.

Mack), *Ithaca Journal,* 1823 (with E. Mack), *Elmira Republican,* 1830-1831 (with W. Murphy, pr.) ; deputy sheriff, 1821-1822.

MORSE, CHAUNCEY, 1794-1882? b. Stratford, Conn.; appr. and jrmn. for J. D. Bemis, Canandaigua, 1811-1814; pr. Onondaga Hollow *Onondaga Register,* 1817-1818 (with L. H. Redfield), Canandaigua *Ontario Repository,* 1818-1821 (with J. D. Bemis, 1818-1819; with J. D. Bemis and S. Ward, 1819-1821), Geneseo *Livingston Journal,* 1821-1825 (with A. Harvey), Canandaigua *Ontario Repository,* 1828-1830 (with S. C. Ward, 1828-1829; with S. C. Ward and A. Harvey, 1830) ; bookseller in Detroit, Mich., 1843-1854; d. Detroit?

MORSE, EVANDER, JR., m. Maria West, 1818; pr. Onondaga Court House *Gazette and Onondaga Advertiser,* 1816-1818 (with William Ray, ed., 1816) ; d. Cincinnati, O.

MORSE, PITT, "Rev."; ed. Watertown *Herald of Salvation,* 1822-1824 [semi-monthly].

MORTON, ABNER, *Watertown Censor,* 1830, Watertown *Jefferson Reporter,* 1832-1834; Co removed to Monroe, Mich.

MOXON, JOHN, "Rev."; ed. Schenectady *Protestant Sentinel,* 1830-1835/37.Co

MURPHY, WILLIAM, 1795-1875, b. Ireland; settled in Williamsport, Pa.; pr. Newton [Elmira] *Telegraph,* 1815-1818 (with ——— Brindle and A. and E. Harkness), Newton *Vedette,* 1818-1819, *Elmira Gazette,* 1829, *Elmira Republican,* 1829-1830 (with C. Morgan, ed.) ; lived in Peoria, Ill., 1838-1875; d. Buckhead, Ga.

MURRAY, JOHN A., pr. Saratoga Springs *Saratoga Sentinel,* 1820-1821 (with G. M. Davison).

MYERS, NATHAN, JR., appr. or jrmn. in office of *Dutchess Observer,* Poughkeepsie, 1822-1824; pr. Poughkeepsie *Dutchess Observer,* 1824-1825 (with Orrin Osborn), Poughkeepsie *Republican Telegraph and Observer,* 1826-1828 (with C. P. Barnum).

NELSON, JOSEPH, 1787-1812; jrmn. foreman of *Political Barometer,* Poughkeepsie; pr. Poughkeepsie *Political Barometer,* 1806-1811 (with Thomas Nelson, 1806-1808; with C. C. Adams, 1810-1811) ; capt. of artillery; d. New York.

NELSON, RICHARD, m. Cordelia [Mrs. C. C.] Adams, 1818; Poughkeepsie *Dutchess Observer,* 1815-1819 (with C. P. Barnum).

NELSON, THOMAS, Poughkeepsie *Political Barometer,* 1806-1808 (with Joseph Nelson).

NEWCOMB, GEORGE WASHINGTON, 1799-1854, b. Thetford, Vt.; m. (1) Lodoiska Philena Keeney, 1829, (2) Catherine Price; teacher; Westfield *Chautauqua Phenix,* 1828-1831 (with J. Hull and H. Newcomb), Westfield *American Eagle,* 1831-1833; minister, Bellevue, Mich.; d. Mt. Clemens, Mich.

NEWCOMB, HARVEY, 1803-1863, b. Thetford, Vt.; m. Alithea A. Wells, 1830; teacher, Alfred, 1818; appr. to Franklin Cowdery, 1822 [ran away on this date]; pr. Westfield *Western Star,* 1826-1828, Westfield *Chautauqua Phenix,* 1828-1829 (with J. Hull and G. W. Newcomb), *Buffalo Patriot,* 1829-1830 (ed.), Pittsburgh *Christian Herald,* 1830-1831 (pr.), Boston *Traveller,* 1849 (ass't ed.), *New York Observer,* 1850-1851 (ed.); deputy county clerk, 1829; justice of peace, 1827; author of 178 volumes, mostly juvenile; author, "Newcomb's Cyclopedia of Missions," 1855; d. Brooklyn.

NEWTON, GEORGE, Cazenovia *Pilot,* 1808-1809 (with O. E. Baker).

NICHOLS, CHARLES, Martinsburgh *Lewis County Sentinel,* 1824-1825, Troy *Evangelical Restorationist,* 1825 [semi-monthly].

NICHOLS, GEORGE W., Walpole, N. H., *Farmer's Weekly Museum,* 1804-1807, Walpole, N. H. *Political Observatory,* 1807-1809, Plattsburgh *American Monitor,* 1809 (with S. Lowell; later with L. Marsh).

NORTHWAY, RUFUS, d. 1871; appr. to Ira Merrell, Utica, 1825; pr. *Utica Sentinel and Gazette,* 1826-1834 (with C. Bennett, 1826-1828; with D. S. Porter, 1828-1831), Utica *Elucidator,* 1830 (with D. S. Porter), Utica *Oneida Whig,* 1834-1848, *Utica Daily Herald,* 1842; d. in Illinois.

NOYES, EBENEZER, *Oxford Gazette,* 1824-1825 (with George Hunt).

OLIPHANT, HENRY, pr. *Auburn Free Press,* 1829-1833, *Auburn Journal and Advertiser,* 1833-1846 (with T. M. Skinner, to 1839), *Auburn Daily Advertiser,* 1846.

OLIPHANT, RICHARD, 1801-1846, b. London, England ; m. Ann H. Jones, 1826; appr., Auburn, 1814; jrmn. for Skinner and Crosby, Auburn, 1816; jrmn. for J. Durnford, Syracuse, 1823; pr. Auburn *Free Press,* 1824-1829, *Oswego Free Press,* 1830-1834, Oswego *Equal Rights,* 1837, *Oswego County Whig,* 1837-1844 (with J. Jones, 1837); Oswego, job printing; author, "The Western Wanderer," 1818; d. Oswego.

O'REILLY, HENRY, 1806-1886, b. Carricknacross, Ireland; m. Marcia F. Brooks, 1829; appr. to Baptiste Irvine, New York, 1816-1817; appr. to Clayton & Kingsford, 1817; jrmn. on New York *Patriot,* 1823; pr. *Kinderhook Herald,* 1826 (with P. Van Schaack, Jr.), *Rochester Daily Advertiser,* 1826-1830 (with L. Tucker; H. C. Sleight, to 1828), *Rochester Republican, Rochester Post and Western New Yorker,* 1841 (ed.), *Albany Atlas,* 1843-1844; postmaster of Rochester, 1838-1842; deputy collector for Genesee district, 1832; d. Rochester, DAB.

ORR, WILLIAM, Poughkeepsie *Republican Herald,* 1823.

OSBORN, JOHN W., Homer *Farmers' Journal,* 1812-1813, *Cortland*

Repository, 1813 (with J. Searl), *Cortland Republican,* 1815-1817 (with D. Campbell, 1815-1816; with O. Boies, 1816; with D. Campbell, 1816-1817), Vincennes (Ind.) *Western Sun,* 1819-1820 (with E. Stout), Terre Haute (Ind.) *Western Recorder,* 1821, Vincennes (Ind.) *Farmers and Mechanics Journal,* 1823 (with A. Kinney), Greencastle (Ind.) *Hoosier Play Boy,* 1830.

OSBORN, ORRIN, 1799-1829; pr. Poughkeepsie *Dutchess Observer,* 1824-1825 (with N. Myers), *Danbury Recorder* (Conn.), 1828; d. Danbury, Conn.

OSBORN, SELLECK, 1783-1826, b. Trumbull, Conn.; m. (1) ——— 1801, (2) Mary Hammond, 1810; appr. Danbury, Conn., 1795; jrmn. for D. Denniston, New York, 1801-1802; pr. Sag Harbor *Suffolk County Herald,* 1802-1803, Danbury (Conn.) *Republican Farmer,* 1804-1805, Litchfield (Conn.) *Witness,* 1806-1807 [imprisoned for libel, 1806], *Boston Democrat,* 1807-1808 (ed.), Wilmington (Del.) *American Watchman,* 1817-1822, *New York Patriot,* 1823-1824 (assoc. ed. with C. K. Gardner); lieut. of dragoons, 1808-1811; capt. 1814; author, "Poems," 1823; d. Philadelphia, Pa.; DAB.

OSGOOD, SAMUEL, *Oswego Gazette and Advertiser,* 1827.

OSGOOD, SEWELL M.; m. Elhira [sic] Brown, 1828; *Cortland Chronicle,* 1828-1829 (with R. A. Reed).

PACE, HENRY, pr. Richmond (Va.) *Recorder,* 1801-1803, *Aurora Gazette,* 1805-1809 (with J. Pace), Auburn *Western Federalist,* 1809-1816 (with J. Pace).

PACE, JAMES, *Aurora Gazette,* 1805-1809 (with H. Pace), Auburn *Western Federalist,* 1809-1816 (with H. Pace).

PALMER, A., Rensselaerville *Rural Folio,* 1828-1830 (with C. G. Palmer), *Schenectady Democrat,* 1828 (with C. G. Palmer),[Fr] *Schenectady County Whig,* 1830-1834 [Fr] (with C. G. Palmer).

PALMER, C. G., Rensselaerville *Rural Folio,* 1828-1830 (with A. Palmer), *Schenectady Democrat,* 1828 (with A. Palmer), *Schenectady County Whig,* 1830-1834 [Fr] (with A. Palmer).

PARKER, A. P., Batavia *People's Press,* 1829-1830 (with D. C. McCleary).

PARKER, WILLIAM S., *Troy Post,* 1812-1823 (with P. Bliss, 1812-1818), *Troy Sentinel,* 1823-1824 [semi-weekly] (with O. Holley, ed.).

PARMENTER, SAMUEL, *Newburgh Gazette,* 1825-1832 (with J. D. Spalding).

PARSONS, CHESTER, *Poughkeepsie Journal and Constitutional Republican,* 1806-1809 (with P. Potter and G. Bowman).

PARSONS, FREDERICK T., pr. Poughkeepsie *Dutchess Intelligencer,*

1828-1829 (with C. F. Ames, 1828; with I. Platt, 1828-1829), *Goshen Democrat,* 1834.[Fr]

PARSONS, THERON, Watertown *Freeman's Advocate,* 1824, Watertown *Thursday's Post,* 1826-1828, Adams *Censor,* 1828-1829, Watertown *Censor,* 1829-1830.

PATERSON, J. P., Salem *Washington Register,* 1826-1830,[Fr] *Union Village Courant,* 1830.

PATTERSON, JOHN, *Mount Pleasant Courier,* 1799.

PEARSON, ——— *Martinsburgh Sentinel,* 1828-1830.[Fr]

PECK, EVERARD, 1791-1854, b. Berlin, Conn.; m. (1) Chloe Porter, 1820, (2) Martha Farley, 1836, (3) Mrs. Alice Bacon Walker, 1852; appr., Hartford, Conn.; jrmn., Albany; bookstore and job printing office, Rochester, 1816-1818; pr. *Rochester Telegraph,* 1818-1825 (with T. Weed, ed. part time); owner of paper mill, burned, 1831.

PEEK, SAMUEL, 1784-1811; pr. Batavia *Cornucopia,* 1809-1811 (with B. Blodgett); d. Batavia.

PELLETT, ELIAS P., 1804-1840, b. in Conn.; m. Editha Ann Pellett, 1820; appr. irregular;[Fo] pr. Norwich *Anti-Masonic Telegraph,* 1829-1840 (with B. T. Cooke, 1829-1835); d. Norwich.

PERCIVAL, JAMES, pr. Sherburne *Morning Star,* 1810, Sherburne *Republican Messenger,* 1810 (with J. Pettit), Homer *Cortland Courier,* 1810-1812 (with S. Percival, 1810), *Cortland Republican,* 1815, Fredonia *Chautauque Gazette,* 1818, Geneseo *Livingston Register,* 1824-1832 [interlude, not published, 1829-1831]; moved to Ohio; mem. assembly, 1831.

PERCIVAL, SAMUEL, Homer *Cortland Courier,* 1810 (with J. Percival).

PERSON, LEWIS, pr. Elizabethtown *Essex Patriot,* 1817-1818 (with O. Person), Essex *Essex County Republican,* 1826-1832 (with ——— Walton, 1826-1828).

PERSON, OLIVER, Elizabethtown *Essex Patriot,* 1817-1818 (with L. Person).

PHELPS, W. W., ed. Trumansburgh *Lake Light,* 1827 (with R. M. Bloomer), Canandaigua *Ontario Phoenix,* 1828-1831 (with R. M. Bloomer, 1828-1830); joined Mormons; prospectus for Independence (Mo.) *Evening and Morning Star;* moved to Council Bluffs, Ia.

PHILLIPS, A. N., Canandaigua *Ontario Republican and Canal Advocate,* 1821.

PHILLIPS, SAMUEL, 1792-1859, b. Mt. Sinai; m. Mrs. Jane Crowell, 1822; taught school, 1822; ed. Sag Harbor *Republican Watchman,* 1826-1844, Greenport (L. I.) *Republican Watchman,* 1844-1857; postmaster, Sag Harbor, 1829; sheriff, 1852-1855; justice of peace.

PHINNEY, ELIHU, 1755-1813; enlisted in Revolutionary army, 1775; partner in management of a store and inn, New Canaan, 1786-1791; pr. Canaan *Columbian Mercury,* 1794-1795, Cooperstown *Otsego Herald,* 1795-1813; judge, court of common pleas, 1799-1801; d. Cooperstown.

PHINNEY, ELIHU, 1785-1863; son of the above; m. Nancy Whiting Tiffany, 1815; bookseller, with brother Henry, Cooperstown; pr. Cooperstown *Otsego Herald,* 1813-1821 (with Henry Phinney); publishing business, 1821-1863; clerk, board of supervisors, 1818.

PHINNEY, GEORGE GORDON, 1788-1828, b. Canaan; pr. *Herkimer Herald,* 1808-1809, Herkimer *Bunker Hill,* 1809-1810, Herkimer *Honest American,* 1811-1812.

PHINNEY, HENRY, 1782-1850; son of Elihu Phinney; bookseller with brother, Elihu, Cooperstown; pr. Cooperstown *Otsego Herald,* 1813-1821 (with Elihu Phinney); publishing business, 1821-1850.

PITTS, ELIAS, 1810-1854, b. Columbia Co.; m. (1) Elizabeth Jamison, (2) Margaret Whited; appr. on *Kinderhook Sentinel;* pr. Kinderhook *Columbia Sentinel,* 1832-1834, *Rochester Daily Advertiser,* (ed.), *Newburgh Telegraph,* 1840-1850, *Poughkeepsie American,* 1850-1853; clerk in Department of State, Washington, D. C.

PLATT, ——— Fort Plain *Watch Tower* (with J. Calhoun).Fr

PLATT, ISAAC, 1803-1872; appr. to Paraclete Potter, Poughkeepsie, 1821-1824; pr. Poughkeepsie *Republican Telegraph,* 1824-1826 (with William Sands), Poughkeepsie *Dutchess Intelligencer,* 1828-1833 (with F. T. Parsons, 1828-1829), Poughkeepsie *Intelligencer and Republican,* 1833-1834 (with T. S. Ranney), *Poughkeepsie Eagle,* 1834-1872 (with T. S. Ranney, 1834-1843; with W. Schram, 1865; with John I. Platt, 1865-1872); postmaster, Poughkeepsie, 1851-1853.

PORTER, D. S., pr. *Utica Sentinel and Gazette,* 1828-1830 (with R. Northway).

POST, RUSSELL E., Canandaigua *Western Repository,* 1803-1804 (with J. K. Gould).

POTTER, PARACLETE, b. 1784, Beekmans; pr. *Poughkeepsie Journal and Constitutional Republican,* 1806-1815 (with G. Bowman, 1806; with G. Bowman and C. Parsons, 1806-1809), *Poughkeepsie Journal,* 1815-1834; bookseller, Poughkeepsie, 1814-1841; removed to Milwaukee, Wis., 1841.

POWELL, FREDERIC C., Plattsburgh *Northern Herald,* 1813-1814, *Potsdam Gazette,* 1816-1823 (with Zena Clark),Fr *Potsdam American,* 1824-1829 (with ——— Redington).Fr

POWER, NICHOLAS, 1760-1811; appr., New York; jrmn. for John Holt, Mrs. Holt, and S. Loudon, New York; pr. Poughkeepsie *Coun-*

try Journal and Poughkeepsie Advertiser, 1785-1788, Poughkeepsie *Country Journal, and Dutchess and Ulster County Farmer's Register,* 1788-1789, *Poughkeepsie Journal,* 1789-1802 (with Richard Vanderburgh, 1796; with H. C. Southwick, 1798-1800), Kingston *Farmer's Register,* 1792-1793 (with William Copp), proposals for Kingston *Rural Casket,* a literary weekly, 1798, *Poughkeepsie Journal and Constitutional Republican,* 1802-1806 (with John Aikin, 1802-1805; with G. Bowman and John Aikin, 1805-1806); postmaster, Poughkeepsie, 1792-1802; d. Poughkeepsie.

PRATT, LUTHER, m. Mary Wilson, 1806; pr. Lansingburgh *Farmer's Oracle, and Lansingburgh Weekly Gazette,* 1796-1797 (with Daniel Curtis), Troy *Farmer's Oracle,* 1797-1798 (with Daniel Curtiss, Jr., 1797), Wardsbridge *Orange County Republican,* 1806-1808 (with Cyrus Beach), Montgomery *Independent Republican,* 1813-1816, New York *Masonic Chronicle,* 1819 (with George F. Busby), Skaneateles *Juvenile Repository,* 1838-1840.[Fr]

PRENTICE, RUSSELL, Ballston Spa *Saratoga Advertiser,* 1810 (with S. R. Brown), Johnstown *Montgomery Monitor,* 1810-1814 (with J. Felthousen, 1810-1811), Ballston Spa *Saratoga Patriot,* 1813-1814 (with C. S. McConnell).

PRENTISS, HENRY, 1786/87-1875; appr. to John Prentiss, Keene, N. H.; pr. Cooperstown *Impartial Observer,* 1808-1809 (with J. H. Prentiss), Herkimer *American,* 1810-1812 (with J. H. Prentiss); d. Rome.

PRENTISS, JOHN HOLMES, 1784-1861, b. Worcester, Mass.; m. (1) Catherine Cox Morris, 1815, (2) Urilla Shankland, 1828; pr. New York *People's Friend,* 1807; jrmn. foreman of New York *Evening Post,* 1808; pr. Cooperstown *Impartial Observer,* 1808-1809 (with H. Prentiss and W. Andrews), *Cooperstown Federalist,* 1809-1817 (with H. Prentiss, 1809-1813), Herkimer *American,* 1810-1813 (with H. Prentiss, 1810-1812), Cooperstown *Freeman's Journal,* 1819-1849; postmaster, Cooperstown, 1833-1837; mem. Congress, 1837-1841; mem. and vice-pres., state constitutional convention, 1861; d. Cooperstown.

PRINCE, FREDERICK, jrmn. for Thomas Skinner, Auburn, 1816-1819; pr. Auburn *Cayuga Republican,* 1819-1821 (with T. Skinner), New York *Ladies Literary Cabinet,* 1823 (with S. Woodworth), *New York Mirror,* 1823 (with S. Woodworth); jrmn. on *Syracuse Gazette,* 1823-1827; pr. *Weedsport Advertiser,* 1827-1829, Weedsport *Northern Phoenix,* 1830, *Jordan Courier,* 1830-1831, *Salina Courier,* 1831, *Auburn Democrat,* 1833, *Auburn Miscellany,* 1835, *Auburn Daily News,* 1838; jrmn. foreman, Port Byron *Western*

Banner, 1844; pr. *Port Byron Herald*, 1844; job printing, Port Byron, to 1849; author, "Tales of Fort Hill."

RANDALL, NATHAN, pr. Greene *Chenango Patriot*, 1830, *Pulaski Banner*, 1830-1832,[Fr] *Ithaca Journal and Advertiser*, 1833-1837,[Fr] *Ithaca Journal and General Advertiser*, 1837-1838 (with ———— Mattison).

RAWSON, NORMAN, 1793-1872; m. Betsey Pratt; *Syracuse Advertiser*, 1826-1829 (with J. F. Wyman, 1826; with J. F. Wyman and T. B. Barnum, 1827; with J. F. Wyman, 1827-1829).[Fr]

RAY, WILLIAM, 1771-1826, b. Litchfield, Conn.; school teacher, Dover, Dutchess Co., 1790-1792; mercantile business, failure, 1792; offered position as editor, Philadelphia, 1803; naval service, frigate "Philadelphia," 1803-1806, and captivity in Tripoli; mercantile business, Essex, 1809-1812; ed. Elizabethtown *Reveille*, 1812 (with L. Marsh, pr.); druggist, Skaneateles, 1814-1816; ed. Onondaga Court House *Onondaga Gazette*, 1816 (with Evander Morse), Geneva *Miscellaneous Register*, 1822 (with S. P. Hull); major, militia brigade quartermaster, 1812-1813; justice of peace, Essex, 1809; justice of peace, magistrate, Onondaga, 1816-1821; commissioner of court of record, Onondaga; justice of peace, Geneva, 1823; author, "Horrors of Slavery; or, The American Tars in Tripoli," 1808; "Poems," 1821, and 1826; d. Auburn.

REDFIELD, LEWIS HAMILTON, 1792-1882, b. Farmington, Conn.; appr. to James D. Bemis, Canandaigua, 1808-1814; pr. Onondaga Hollow *Onondaga Register*, 1814-1829 (with J. D. Bemis, 1814-1817; with Chauncey Morse, 1817-1818; [interlude, 1826-1827, when it was published by John Fagan]), Syracuse *Onondaga Register and Syracuse Gazette*, 1829-1831; bookstore, Syracuse, 1832-1842; postmaster, 1820-1829; pres. village, Syracuse, 1834; presidential elector, 1872; d. Syracuse.

REDINGTON, ———— *Potsdam American*, 1824-1829 (with F. C. Powell).[Fr]

REED, ———— *Ithaca Gazette and Religious Intelligencer*, 1816-1817 (with E. Shepard and J. Benjamin).

REED, RUFUS A., *Cortland Chronicle*, 1829-1832 (with S. M. Osgood, 1828-1829), *Cortland Republican*, 1832-1837, Cortland *Republican and Eagle*, 1837, Homer *Cortland County Whig*, 1846;[Fo] county clerk, 1849.

REYNOLDS, JOHN P., 1782-1858, b. Dutchess Co.; m. (1) Rebecca Newell, 1807, (2) Laura P. Willson; pr. Salem *Washington Register*, 1805-1816; removed to Cincinnati, O.; printer of state laws, for the "Western District," 1806-1809; d. Hamilton, O.

REYNOLDS, LINUS J., 1790-1838, b. Dutchess Co.; m. Alice Baker,

1815; appr. to brother, John P. Reynolds, Salem; pr. Plattsburgh *Republican,* 1811, Glens Falls *Adviser,* 1815, *Hamilton Gazette,* 1816, Salem *Washington Register,* 1825-1827 (with Ansel Warren, 1825-1826), Poultney (Vt.) *Northern Spectator,* 1828-1831/32 (ed.); pastor of church, Port Byron; d. Port Byron.

REYNOLDS, PHILIP, JR., pr. *Johnstown Herald,* 1825-1829, *Johnstown Republican,* 1830.

REYNOLDS, SAMUEL, Goshen *Independent Republican,* 1817.

RICE, LEWIS L., Cazenovia *Madison Observer,* 1821-1822 (with —— Hall), Morrisville *Madison Observer,* 1822-1823 (with —— Hall), Morrisville, *Republican Monitor,* 1823-1826 (with J. F. Fairchild, 1826), New York *Beacon,* Ravenna (O.), *Ohio Star,* 1830.

RICH, JAIRUS, Watertown *Northern Luminary,* 1813-1814, Watertown *American Advocate,* 1814-1817.

RICHARDS, SETH, *Troy Sentinel,* 1824-1827 (with N. Tuttle), *Troy Press,* 1832-1834 (with William Yates), Troy *State Journal,* 1836-1837 (with —— Martin).

RIGGS, ISAAC, appr. "near five years," 1808; pr. Ballston Spa *Saratoga Advertiser,* 1808 (with D. C. Miller), Schenectady *Western Budget,* 1808-1810, Schenectady *Cabinet,* 1810-1823 (with H. Stevens, 1814-1816), *Schenectady Cabinet,* 1824-1830 (with S. S. Riggs, 1830); justice of peace, 1811; coroner, 1811, sheriff, 1818-1821; mem. assembly, 1824.

RIGGS, STEPHEN SEAMAN, m. Julia V. Hammer, 1831; pr. *Schenectady Cabinet,* 1830-1837 (with I. Riggs, ed., 1830), Schenectady *Freedom's Sentinel,* 1837-1840,[Co] *Schenectady Cabinet and Freedom's Sentinel,* Schenectady *Cabinet,* 1856.[Co]

RIPLEY, HEZEKIAH, pr. *Bridgeport Advertiser* (Conn.), 1806-1810, Moscow *Genesee Farmer,* 1817, *Moscow Advertiser and Genesee Farmer,* 1817 (with F. Cowdery), *Moscow Advertiser,* 1817-1824; removed to Belvidere, Ill.

RITCHIE, GEORGE, JR., pr. Schenectady *Mohawk Sentinel,* 1824-1825.

RITTER, FRED W., jrmn. foreman on *Ithaca Journal,* 1829; pr. *Havana Observer,* 1829, Fishkill *Free Press,* 1841.[Fr]

ROBBINS, JAMES B., jrmn. on Albany *Register;* pr. Herkimer *Farmer's Monitor,* 1805 (with D. Holt), Johnstown *Montgomery Intelligencer,* 1806-1807, Martinsburgh *Black River Gazette,* 1807-1808, *Watertown Herald,* 1808-1809.

ROBERTS, ELIJAH JACKSON, 1802-1851, b. Newton, Conn.; m. Lydia Smith, 1822; appr. to Jesse Buel, Albany, 1815; studied law with Erastus Root; pr. Homer *Western Courier,* 1820-1821 (with —— Hull), Delhi *Delaware Republican,* 1822-1824 (with —— Hull),

Kingston *Craftsman,* 1824, *New York National Advocate,* 1824-1826 (with M. M. Noah, ed.), Rochester *Craftsman,* 1829-1831 (with J. G. Brooks, 1830), *Rochester Morning Courier,* 1830, Rochester *Examiner and Spirit of the Age,* 1830, Albany *Daily Craftsman,* 1831-1832 (with H. James), Buffalo *Daily Advertiser,* 1834-1835, Buffalo *Transcript,* 1835 (ed.); practiced law, Detroit, Mich., 1835-1843; ed. Detroit (Mich.) *Craftsman in Michigan,* 1838, Detroit (Mich.) *Morning Post and Craftsman,* 1838-1840 (with ———— Kingsbury); aide-de-camp to Gen. Root, 1812; clerk of House of Representatives, Mich., 1836; justice of peace, 1835; brig. gen. in Canadian "Patriot War," 1837-1838; adjut. gen. of militia, Mich., 1842-1844; ass't mineral inspector for U. S., 1845; prosecuting atty. for Haughton Co., Mich.; mem. state constitutional convention, Mich., 1850; mem. legislature, Mich., 1851; codified state law, Mich. (with E. B. Huntington); d. Detroit.

ROBERTS, SYLVESTER, Hudson *Republican Fountain,* 1806-1807.

ROBINSON, TRACY, 1778-1855, b. Tolland, Conn.; m. Sarah Cleveland, 1799; opened drug store, Binghamton, 1810; ed. Binghamton *Phoenix,* 1814-1818; practiced medicine, M.D.; operated hotel, Binghamton, 1819-1829; dry goods business, Binghamton; justice of peace, 1811; common pleas judge; First Judge, 1823-1843; d. Binghamton.

ROBINSON, WILLIAM C., Brooklyn *Long Island Weekly Intelligencer,* 1806-1807 (with William Little).

ROMEYN, ABRAHAM, Sherburne *Western Oracle,* 1804-1806, Manlius *Derne Gazette,* 1806-1807.

RUDD, JOHN C., "Rev.," ed. Auburn *Gospel Messenger,* 1827-1828, Utica *Gospel Messenger and Church Record,* 1835.

RUDD, REUBEN B., ed. Poughkeepsie *Republican Herald,* 1814-1815 (with D. B. Stockholm).

RUMSEY, DAVID, pr. Salem *Northern Post,* 1804-1814 (with H. Dodd), Bath *Farmer's Gazette,* 1816-1819, Auburn *Cayuga Patriot,* 1819, Bath *Steuben Messenger,* 1828.

SACIA, D. F., *Canajoharie Republican,* 1828 (with J. McVean).[Fr]

SACKETT, ISRAEL, 1809-1880; m. Margaret J. Allen, 1832; Waterford *Saratoga Recorder and Anti-Masonic Democrat,* 1830-1831 (with D. Jehan), Ballston Spa *Schenectady and Saratoga Standard,* 1832-1833.[Co]

ST. JOHN, REUBEN, m. Sophia Pitts, 1827; pr. *Salina Sentinel,* 1826-1827, Trumansburgh *Lake Light,* 1828-1829 (with O. B. Clark, 1828), Trumansburgh *Anti-Masonic Sentinel,* 1829.[Co]

SALISBURY, HEZEKIAH A., 1789-1856; m. (1) Betsey Osbourne, 1815, (2) Phoebe Osbourne, 1829; appr. to James D. Bemis, Canandaigua, 1811; pr. *Buffalo Gazette,* 1811-1815 (with S. H. Salisbury),

Buffalo Gazette and Niagara Intelligencer, 1815 (with S. H. Salisbury), *Buffalo Gazette,* 1816-1818 (with S. H. Salisbury; with W. A. Carpenter, 1818), Buffalo *Niagara Patriot,* 1818-1821, *Buffalo Patriot,* 1821-1836 (with W. A. Carpenter, 1826-1829; with W. A. Carpenter and H. Newcomb, ed., 1829-1830; with W. A. Carpenter, 1830-1834) ; d. Buffalo.

SALISBURY, SMITH H., 1786-1832; m. Nancy Hyde, 1810; appr. to James D. Bemis, Canandaigua, 1810; pr. *Buffalo Gazette,* 1811-1815 (with J. D. Bemis, 1811; with H. A. Salisbury, 1811-1815), *Buffalo Gazette and Niagara Intelligencer,* 1815 (with H. A. Salisbury, pr.), *Buffalo Gazette,* 1816-1818 (with H. A. Salisbury), *Black Rock Gazette,* 1825-1828, *Buffalo and Black Rock Gazette,* Rochester *Craftsman,* 1830 (pr. for E. J. Roberts) ; d. Rochester.

SANDS, WILLIAM, jrmn. foreman for Poughkeepsie *Republican Herald,* 1822; pr. Poughkeepsie *Republican Herald,* 1822-1824 (with C. P. Barnum, ed.), Poughkeepsie *Republican Telegraph,* 1824-1825 (with I. Platt, and short while with J. Francis), Kingston *Ulster Sentinel,* 1826-1829 (with C. G. De Witt, ed. and proprietor).

SCHERMERHORN, RYER, pr. Schenectady *Mohawk Advertiser,* 1807-1810, *Troy Gazette,* 1810-1812 (with Eldad Lewis, 1810), *Schenectady Gazette,* 1812.

SCHRAM, WILLIAM, b. 1807; m. Sarah H. Hallock; appr. to A. G. Dauby, Utica, 1824-1826; jrmn. for A. G. Dauby, Utica, 1826; pr. Utica *Mechanics Press,* 1829 (with F. W. Ladd), *Poughkeepsie Journal,* 1834-1844 (with ——— Jackson), *Poughkeepsie Eagle,* 1844-1865 (with I. Platt) ; job printing, Newburgh, 1868.

SCHULTZ, JACOB, 1776-1859, b. New Windsor; m. Anna Denniston, 1799; *New Windsor Gazette,* 1797-1799 (with A. Lott), Newburgh *Orange County Gazette,* 1799-1800 (with J. W. Barber) ; dry goods store, 1814; mill in New Windsor; in business, Newburgh, 1818.

SCRANTOM, EDWIN, 1803-1880, b. Durham, Conn.; m. Mary Ann Sibley, 1825; appr. to A. G. Dauby, Rochester, 1816; pr. Rochester *Monroe Republican,* 1825-1827 (with F. Whittlesey and ——— Mumford), Rochester *Gem,* 1829-1838 [semi-monthy] ; auctioneer and commission merchant, Rochester; pr. Rochester *Gem,* 1877; printer of the laws of the U. S., 1826-1827; author, historical portion of "Monroe County," 1877.

SEABURY, SAMUEL A., d. 1824; appr. to Alden Spooner, Sag Harbor; pr. Sag Harbor *Suffolk County Recorder,* 1816-1817, Sag Harbor *American Eagle,* 1817-1821, Huntington *American Eagle,* 1821-1823; d. Stonington, Conn.

SEARING, AUGUSTIN P., pr. Ithaca *American Journal,* 1819 (with E.

Mack); job printing, Ithaca, 1822; pr. Ithaca *Museum and Independent Corrector,* 1824 (with G. H. Evans and L. B. Butler), Ithaca *Western Messenger,* 1826-1828;[Fr] village clerk, Ithaca, 1822.

SEARL, JESSE, b. Southampton, Mass.; studied medicine; ed. Homer *Cortland Repository,* 1813-1825 (with J. W. Osborn, pr.).

SENTELL, CHARLES, pr. Batavia *Republican Advocate,* 1828 (with Charles W. Miller), Buffalo *Western Advertiser,* 1827-1828 (with B. Hayward), Pittsburgh, Pa., [an Anti-Masonic paper], 1829, *Waterloo Observer,* 1829-1866 (with some interruption, and with successive partners: Smith & Co., Pew & Marsh, M. C. Hough, Sentell & Pew, Sentell & Vreeland).[Co]

SEVERANCE, M., Waterloo *Republican Observer,* 1828, *Waterloo Observer,* 1828-1829 (with E. P. Moon).

SEWARD, ASAHEL, 1781-1835, b. Waterbury, Conn.; m. Martha Williams, 1812; appr. to William McLean, New Hartford, 1796-1803; jrmn. for Isaiah Thomas, Worcester, Mass.; jrmn. on New York *Morning Chronicle;* jrmn., Boston, Mass.; pr. Utica *Patriot,* 1803-1804 (with I. Merrell), *Utica Patriot,* 1804-1806 (with I. Merrell), *Utica Patrol,* 1815-1816 (with William Williams), *Utica Patriot and Patrol,* 1816-1821 (with W. Williams, I. Merrell, and W. H. Maynard, 1816-1817; with I. Merrell and W. H. Maynard, 1817-1821), *Utica Sentinel,* 1821-1825 (with W. Williams; E. Harrington, pr. 1821).

SEYMOUR, EDWARD P., pr. *Herkimer American,* 1815-1831.

SHELDON, JOHN P., 1792-1871; appr. to John C. Wright, Troy, 1805-1810; jrmn. for J. H. Prentiss, Cooperstown, 1810-1812; pr. *Ogdensburgh Palladium,* 1812-1814; jrmn. for Seward and Williams, Utica, 1814; pr. *Rochester Gazette,* 1816 (with A. G. Dauby), *Detroit Gazette* (Mich.), 1817-1830 (with E. Reed, 1817-1825; with H. L. Ball, 1828-1830; S. McKnight, 1830), Detroit (Mich.) *Free Press,* 1831-1833 (with S. McKnight), Mineral Point (Mich.) *Miners Free Press,* 1840 [contributor], Madison (Wis.) *Wisconsin Democrat,* 1843-1844 (with George Hyer); clerk in government dept., Washington, D. C., supt. of lead mines, Willow Springs, Wis.; printer to city of Detroit, 1825, and 1830; several times printer of Mich. Territory; d. Winfield, Ill.

SHEPARD, ERASTUS, b. 1796, Hartford, Conn.; m. ———, 1817; appr. to Ira Merrell, Utica, 1810-1816; pr. *Ithaca Gazette,* 1816-1817 (with J. Benjamin and ——— Reed), Ithaca *American Journal,* 1817-1819 (with E. Mack), [Elmira] *Newtown Telegraph,* 1819, Bath *Western Republican,* 1819-1822 (with W. B. Rochester, ed., 1820); jrmn. foreman for James Bogert, Geneva, 1822-1830; pr. Palmyra *Western Spectator and Public Advertiser,* 1830-1831 (with

Luther Howard), Palmyra *Western Spectator and Anti-Masonic Star,* 1831, Rochester *Western New Yorker,* 1843,[Fr] Rochester *Penny Preacher.*[Fr]

SHOPE, WILLIAM C., m. Harriet Morse, 1827; *Oswego Gazette and Advertiser,* 1827-1828, *Oswego Advertiser,* 1828-1829.

SHURTLEFF, JONAS BALL, 1805-1844, b. Fitzwilliam, N. H.; m. Elizabeth C. Taylor, 1831; *Owego Gazette,* 1827-1838 (with S. B. Leonard, 1827-1829; with —— Ball, 1835-1836; with J. Frank, 1837-1838); d. Dunkirk.

SIBLEY, DERICK, d. 1875; m. Abbey ——; ed. Montpelier (Vt.) *Freeman's Press,* 1809-1812 (with S. Wright, 1811-1812); Rochester *Monroe Republican,* 1821-1825 (with L. W. Sibley); mem. assembly, 1835, 1838, and 1840; d. Cincinnati, O.

SIBLEY, LEVI W., d. 1844; m. Nancy Remington, 1824; pr. Rochester *Monroe Republican,* 1821-1825 (with D. Sibley); printer of laws of U. S., 1825; d. Rochester.

SILL, G. G., "Rev."; ed. *Rochester Observer,* 1827 (with L. Tucker, and J. Bissell).[Fr]

SKINNER, DOLPHUS, "Rev."; ed. Troy *Evangelical Restorationist,* 1825-1826 [semi-monthly], *Utica Magazine,* 1827-1828, Utica *Evangelical Magazine,* 1828-1830, Utica *Evangelical Magazine and Gospel Advocate,* 1830.

SKINNER, THOMAS M., m. Elizabeth Durnford; pr. *Auburn Gazette,* 1816-1817 (with William Crosby), Auburn *Cayuga Republican,* 1817-1833 (with A. Buckingham, 1819; with F. Prince, 1819-1821; with G. A. Gamage, ed., 1824-1825), *Auburn Journal and Advertiser,* 1833-1839/41.[Fo]

SLEIGHT, HENRY C., 1792-1877, b. New York; m. (1) Cornelia Hildreth, (2) Jane Keese, 1831/2; appr. to Alden Spooner, Sag Harbor, 1807-1811, Brooklyn, 1811-1812; with militia, 1812; pr. Lexington (Ky.) *Western Monitor,* 1814-1815 (with J. Fishback), Russellville (Ky.) *Messenger,* 1815-1817; mercantile business, 1817-1818; pr. Jamaica *Long Island Farmer,* 1821-1826, Jamaica-Brooklyn *Star,* 1825 (with A. Spooner), *Rochester Daily Advertiser,* 1826-1828 (with L. Tucker), *Rochester Mercury,* 1827 (with L. Tucker), Rochester *Monroe Republican and Rochester Mercury,* 1827-1828 (with L. Tucker); publishing business, New York, c. 1830; removed to Genesee, Ill.; return to Sag Harbor, 1868.

SMEAD, BENJAMIN, 1775-1858; pr. Brattleboro (Vt.) *Federal Galaxy,* 1797-1803, Bennington (Vt.) *Epitome of the World,* 1807, Bennington (Vt.) *World,* 1807-1809, Bennington (Vt.) *Green Mountain Farmer,* 1809-1816; jrmn. for J. Buel, Albany, 1816; pr. Bath

Steuben Patriot, 1816-1817, Bath *Steuben and Allegany Patriot,* 1817-1823 (with son); capt., 1812; d. Bath.

SMEAD, BENJAMIN FRANKLIN, m. Eliza Demick, 1824; pr. Hamilton [Olean] *Allegany Mercury,* 1818,[Fr] *Hamilton Recorder,* 1819 (with F. Cowdery), Bath *Farmer's Advocate,* 1823-1830 (with H. D. Smead, part of time), *Angelica Republican and Farmer's and Mechanics Press,* 1832.

SMEAD, HENRY D., pr. Bath *Farmer's Advocate,* 1823-1830 (with B. F. Smead; sole pr. 1830).

SMITH, ABIEL, Glens Falls *Warren Messenger,* 1828-1832.

SMITH, DAN, 1804-1827; pr. *Cortland Journal,* 1824[Co]-1827; d. Cortland.

SMITH, JAMES, *Johnstown Gazette,* 1798 (with David Holden).

SMITH, JOB A., m. Susan Fulton, 1830; Newtown [Elmira] *Investigator,* 1820-1824 (with ———— Brindle, part time), Elmira *Tioga Register,* 1824-1828, *Elmira Gazette,* 1829-1835 (with B. Paine, 1831-1833).

SMITH, PETER C., ed. White Plains *Westchester Spy,* 1830.

SMITH, VIVUS W., 1804-1881, b. Lanesborough, Mass.; m. (1) Caroline Earll, 1831, (2) Theodora Morey; appr. in newspaper office, Westfield, Mass.; pr. Onondaga Hill *Onondaga Journal,* 1827-1829, Syracuse *Onondaga Standard,* 1829 (with J. F. Wyman), Syracuse *Western State Journal,* 1839 (with J. F. Smith), *Syracuse Daily Journal,* 1841, Columbus (O.) *Ohio State Journal,* 1841-1844, *Syracuse Weekly Journal,* 1849-1852; county clerk, 1846-1849; supt. Onondaga salt works, 1855-1865; canal appraiser, 1873-1880; d. Syracuse.

SNOW, WILLIAM S., pr. Forestville *People's Gazette,* 1824-1826, *Fredonia Gazette,* 1826-1827 (with James Hull), *Buffalo Republican,* 1828 (with S. H. Salisbury); postmaster, Forestville, 1825.

SOUTHWICK, HENRY COLLINS, 1776-1821; pr. Newport (R. I.) *Rhode Island Museum,* 1794, *Albany Chronicle,* 1797-1798, *Poughkeepsie Journal,* 1798-1800 (with N. Power); jrmn. foreman on New York *American Citizen,* three years; partner in firm, Hardcastle and Southwick, New York, 1806; pr. *Albany Register,* 1812-1816, Albany *Christian Visitant,* 1815-1816, Auburn *Advocate of the People,* 1816-1818; state printer, 1814; d. New York.

SPAFFORD, DAN, Ogdensburg *St. Lawrence Gazette,* 1826-1830 (with J. C. Barter).

SPAFFORD, HORATIO GATES, 1778-1832; ed. Albany *American Magazine,* 1815-1816, Ballston Spa *Saratoga Farmer,* 1820-1821; author, "Gazetteer of the State of New York," 1813, revised, 1824; "Observations on the Construction of Wheel Carriages," 1815.

SPALDING, JOHN D., 1800-1853, b. Salem, Mass.; m. Elizabeth L. Johnston; appr. to W. M. Gazlay, Newburgh, 1815; pr. *Newburgh Gazette,* 1822-1836 (with S. Parmenter, 1825-1832), *Newburgh Journal,* 1833/34-1843, *Highland Courier,* 1843-1853 [continued by Mrs. Spalding until 1855].

SPALDING, ORMOND, 1802-1826, b. Scipio; m. Olivia Stearns, 1825; appr. to E. Scrantom; pr. Rochester *Album,* 1825-1826 (with E. F. Marshall, and ——— Hunt).

SPAULDING, LYMAN A., ed. Lockport *Priestcraft Exposed,* 1828-1830 (with E. A. Cooley, pr.).[Fr]

SPEAR, OLIVER, Geneva *Palladium,* 1823 (with J. T. Wilson).

SPENCER, ANSON, 1808-1876, b. near Canandaigua; appr. to brother, D. D. Spencer, Ithaca, 1820; jrmn. for L. and B. Butler, Havana, 1828; pr. *Ithaca Chronicle,* 1830-1863 (with D. D. Spencer, 1830-1853), *Ithaca Democrat,* 1876; d. Ithaca.

SPENCER, DAVID D., 1799-1855; m. Melissa Lord, 1823; appr. to L. H. Redfield, Onondaga, 1820; pr. Ithaca *Republican Chronicle,* 1820-1830 (with H. S. Stockton, 1820-1823; with S. S. Chatterton, 1826?-1830), *Ithaca Chronicle,* 1830-1853 (with Anson Spencer); inspector of state prisons, 1847-1850; d. Ithaca.

SPOONER, ALDEN, 1783-1849, b. Westminster, Vt.; m. (1) Rebecca Jermain, (2) Mary Ann Wetmore, 1831; appr. to Samuel Green, New London, Conn.; pr. Sag Harbor *Suffolk Gazette,* 1804-1811, Brooklyn *Long Island Star,* 1811-1819 (with H. C. Sleight, 1812-1813; with E. Worthington, 1817-1819), *New York Columbian,* 1817-1821, *New York Journal and Patron of Industry,* 1821 (with George W. Prentiss), Brooklyn *Long Island Star,* 1821-1823, Brooklyn *Star,* 1823-1825 (with H. C. Sleight, 1825), Brooklyn *Long Island Star,* 1826-1840 (with E. B. and G. W. Spooner, 1836-1839; with E. B. Spooner, 1839-1840), *Brooklyn Evening Star,* 1827; 2d lieut. artillery, 1810; capt., 1819; col., 1826; surrogate, 1841.

SPRAGUE, DANIEL N., m. Rhoda Thompson, 1829; job printing, Rochester, 1827; pr. Rochester *Anti-Masonic Enquirer,* 1829-1830 (with Thurlow Weed), *Wooster Democrat* (Ohio), 1832/34-1846.

STARR, ELISHA, m. Sarah Elizabeth Hosmer, 1829; appr., Canandaigua; pr. *Le Roy Gazette,* 1827-1830 (with B. B. Hotchkin, 1827-1828; with H. D. Ward, 1828-1830).

STARR, GEORGE N., [Gowanda] *Lodi Pioneer,* 1828-1833.[Fr]

STEBBINS, FRANCIS, pr. Springfield (Mass.) *Federal Spy,* 1794-1799, Savannah (Ga.) *Columbian Museum,* 1802-1804, Hudson *Balance,* 1808, Hudson *Northern Whig,* 1809-1814, *Savannah Museum* (Ga.), 1815 (ed. and joint proprietor).

STEPHENSON, D. D., m. (1) Lydia ———, (2) Maria Gibbs, 1828;
pr. *Rochester Balance,* 1827-1828 (ed.), *Palmyra Freeman,* 1828-
1830 (with J. A. Hadley), Watertown *Constellation,* 1831 (with
B. Goodale).

STEVENS, H., Schenectady *Cabinet,* 1812-1816 (with I. Riggs).

STEVENS, JOHN ABBOTT, m. (1) Phoebe Bates, 1810, (2) Amelia
Ackley, 1826; pr. Canandaigua *Ontario Freeman,* 1804-1806, Canandaigua *Genesee Messenger,* 1806-1810, Canandaigua *Ontario Messenger,* 1810-1823 (with D. M. Day, 1814-1815), Canandaigua
Ontario Freeman, 1823-1827 (with T. B. Barnum); mem. assembly,
1819; printer of the laws of U. S., 1819-1820; d. Monroe Co.

STEVENSON, JAMES, JR., Salem *Northern Post,* 1814-1823 (with H.
Dodd, and D. Rumsey, 1814; H. Dodd, 1814-1823), Salem *Washington County Post,* 1823-1826 (with H. Dodd).

STEVENSON, JOHN L., Schenectady *Gazette,* 1799-1801, Schenectady
Western Spectator; or, Schenectady Weekly Advertiser, 1802-1807.

STEWARD, HENRY, pr. Owego *American Farmer,* 1803-1804 (with S.
Mack).

STILES, BERIAH, Salem *Washington Register,* 1822-1825.Co

STILLMAN, ISAIAH, Buffalo *Niagara Journal,* 1815-1816 (with D. M.
Day).

STOCKHOLM, DERICK B., m. Maria Keese, 1815; ed. Poughkeepsie
Republican Herald, 1814-1823 (with R. B. Rudd, 1814-1815; with
T. Brownejohn, 1815-1819); practice law, Ithaca, 1825.

STOCKTON, HENRY K., Ithaca *Republican Chronicle,* 1820-1823 (with
D. D. Spencer).

STOCKWELL, HENRY, *Troy Gazette,* 1804-1808 (with J. C. Wright
and Solomon Wilbur, 1804-1805; with J. C. Wright and S. Goodenow, 1805-1808).

STODDARD, ASHBEL, 1762-1840; appr. in office of Hartford (Conn.)
Courant; pr. *Hudson Weekly Gazette,* 1785-1791/92 (with C. R.
Webster, 1785-1786), *Hudson Gazette,* 1792-1803, Hudson *Colum-
bia Magazine* (with Rev. John Chester, ed.), Hudson *Messenger of
Peace,* 1824-1825 (with Richard Carrique, ed.).

STONE, EBENEZER G., 1802-1828; pr. Poultney (Vt.) *Northern Spectator,* 1826, *Lansingburgh Gazette,* 1826-1827; d. East Ridge (Wayne
Co.).

STONE, WILLIAM LEETE, 1792-1844, b. New Paltz; m. Susanna Way-
land, 1817; appr. to John H. Prentiss, Cooperstown, 1809-1812;
pr. *Herkimer American,* 1813-1815, Hudson *Northern Whig,* 1815-
1819 (with Richard L. Corss, 1817-1819), Hudson *Lounger* [maga-
zine, before Apr. 1817], *Albany Gazette and Daily Advertiser,* 1817-
1818 (with T. V. W. Gould, pr., and Websters and Skinners), *Al-*

bany Gazette for the Country, 1817-1818 [semi-weekly] (same partners), proposals for Troy *State Gazette,* 1818, Hartford (Conn.) *Connecticut Mirror,* 1818-1821 (with Simeon Lincoln), New York *Commercial Advertiser,* 1821-1844; county supt. of schools, 1843-1844; d. Saratoga Springs; DAB.

STORER, E. GILMAN, Arlington (Vt.) *American Register,* 1816-1817, Arlington (Vt.) *Union Magazine,* 1817-1818, Sandy Hill *Times,* 1818-1819 (with Adonijah Emons, ed.) ; removed to Poultney, Vt.

STORER, WILLIAM, JR., m. Mary Street, 1823; Sandy Hill *Times,* 1819-1820, Caldwell *Guardian,* 1821-1823.

STOWER, JOHN G., *Hamilton Recorder,* 1817-1819 (with P. B. Havens; with —— Williams, 1819), mem. state senate, 1833-1835; surrogate, 1827-1829; mem. Congress, 1827-1829.

STRACHAN, DAVID R., Ogdensburg *St. Lawrence Gazette,* 1815-1826 (with P. B. Fairchild, 1815-1824).

STRONG, TIMOTHY C., pr. *Ogdensburgh Palladium and St. Lawrence Advertiser,* 1810-1811 (with John C. Kip), Middlebury (Vt.) *Vermont Mirror,* 1812-1816, Middlebury (Vt.) *Christian Herald,* 1816, Middlebury (Vt.) *Christian Messenger,* 1816-1817, *Palmyra Register,* 1817-1821 (with C. Bradish, 1819-1820), Palmyra *Western Farmer,* 1821-1822, *Palmyra Herald and Canal Advertiser,* 1822-1823; proposals for Detroit (Mich.) *Michigan Emporium,* 1824; pr. *Newport Patriot,* 1825, Newport *Orleans Advocate,* 1828, Newport *Orleans Advocate and Anti-Masonic Telegraph,* 1828, Newport *Orleans Anti-Masonic Telegraph,* 1828, Newport *Orleans Telegraph,* 1828-1829, Newport *American Standard,* 1830, Geneva *Independent American,* 1830, Albion *Orleans American,* 1832-1844.

STURTEVANT, PETER, *Hudson Gazette,* 1824-1826 (with J. W. Edmunds, ed.).

SUTHERLAND, J. T., *Syracuse Weekly Bulletin,* 1828.

SWAIN, WILLIAM N., Bath *Steuben Whig,* 1828.[Fr]

SWAINE, J., Ballston Spa *Saratoga Advertiser,* 1804-1805 (with D. C. Miller).

TAPPEN, JOHN, 1766-1831; ed. Kingston *Ulster Plebeian,* 1814-1826, Kingston *Plebeian and Ulster County Advertiser,* 1826-1831; d. Kingston.

TAPPEN, JOHN JANSEN, Bloomingburgh *Sullivan Whig,* 1820-1828, Monticello *Sullivan Whig,* 1828; postmaster, 1824.

TAYLOR, ABRAHAM, pr. Johnstown *Montgomery Republican,* 1809, Watertown *Hemisphere,* 1809-1810, Watertown *American Eagle,* 1810 (with H. Coffeen).

TENNERY, JOSEPH, *Cambridge Gazette,* 1803-1804, Athens *Monitor,* 1805-1806.

TENNY, JOSEPH, pr. Sangerfield *Christian's Weekly Monitor, or Sabbath Morning Report,* 1814-1817, Sangerfield *Civil and Religious Intelligencer,* 1816-1817, Sangerfield *Civil and Religious Intelligencer, or, The Gleaner and Monitor,* 1817-1823, *Sangerfield Intelligencer, and Madison and Oneida Counties Gleaner,* 1830-1833/35,[Co] Franklin Village [Fabius] *American Patriot,* 1835-1836.

THORP, JOHN, Batavia *People's Press,* 1827-1828 (with D. P. Adams), Batavia *Masonic Intelligencer,* 1827-1828 (with D. P. Adams); d. New Orleans, La.

THROOP, S. G., ed. *Oxford Gazette,* 1817 (with C. Morgan).

TIFFANY, SILVESTER, 1760-1811; m. Frances Ralstone; pr. Lansingburgh *American Spy,* 1791-1792 (with William Wands, 1792), Lansingburgh *Tiffany's Recorder,* 1793-1794; removed to Niagara, U. C., where he was "King's Printer" [Fo]; pr. Canandaigua *Ontario Freeman,* 1803-1805; county clerk, Ontario Co., 1804-1808.

TILLMAN, THOMAS M., Schoharie *True American,* 1809-1810.

TODD, BETHEL, *Cherry Valley Gazette,* 1818-1821 (with L. Todd).

TODD, LEMUEL, *Cherry Valley Gazette,* 1818-1821 (with B. Todd).

TODD, LEWIS C., "Rev.," 1794-1863; m. Ellen Stedman; ed. Jamestown *Genius of Liberty,* 1829-1831, Jamestown *Chautauqua Republican.*

TRACY, GARDINER, *Lansingburgh Gazette,* 1798-1826 (with Luther Bliss, 1806-1826), Utica *Western Recorder,* 1832-1834 (with Thomas Hastings, 1832-1833); mem. assembly, 1822.

TRACY, SEYMOUR, pr. Gaines *Newspaper,* 1825.

TRACY, WILLIAM, ed. *Utica Intelligencer,* 1826-1828 (with I. Merrell and J. Colwell, prs.).

TUCKER, J. N., pr. Lyons *Western Argus,* 1830-1831 (with J. Barber and D. Chapman).

TUCKER, LUTHER, 1802-1873, b. Brandon, Vt.; m. (1) Naomi Sparhawk, 1827, (2) ———; appr. to T. C. Strong, Middlebury (Vt.), 1816-1817, Palmyra, 1817-1819; jrmn. in Philadelphia, Pa., Baltimore, Md., Washington, D. C., and on New York *Patriot,* 1823-1824; jrmn. for H. C. Sleight, Jamaica, L. I., 1824-1826; pr. *Rochester Daily Advertiser,* 1826-1828 (with H. C. Sleight), *Rochester Daily Advertiser and Telegraph,* 1829-1839 (with Robt. Martin, 1829, at various times with, H. O'Reilly, H. L. Stevens, T. W. Flagg, and H. Humphreys), *Rochester Mercury,* 1827, *Rochester Republican,* 1827-1839 (with partners), Rochester *Genesee Farmer,* 1831-1839 (with H. L. Stevens, 1831; with N. Goodsell, ed., 1831-1839); director of state museum, 1845; d. Albany.

TUCKER, POMEROY, 1802-1870, b. Woodstock, Conn.; m. Lucy Rogers, 1824; appr. to J. A. Stevens, Canandaigua; pr. Palmyra *Wayne Sentinel,* 1823-1855 (with John H. Gilbert, 1824-1827; with G. W.

Cuyler, 1834-1835; with O. H. Palmer and F. A. Goldsmith, 1840; with William L. Tucker, 1843-1845; [interludes, when not connected with publication: 1827-1834, and 1835-1840]); mem. assembly, 1837; d. Palmyra.

TURNER, CHIPMAN P., pr. Lockport *Sentinel and Observatory,* 1827-1828 (with N. D. Lathrop); deputy collector of port of Black Rock, 1847.[Fo]

TURNER, ORSAMUS, 1801-1855; appr. (in part) to James D. Bemis; pr. *Lockport Observatory,* 1822-1827, Lockport *Sentinel and Observatory,* 1827, *Lockport Balance,* 1831 (ed.); collector of canal tolls, Lockport; U. S. Marshall to take census, 1830; author, "Pioneer History of the Holland Purchase of Western New York," 1849; "History of the Pioneer Settlement of the Phelps and Gorham Purchase," 1851.

TUTHILL, DANIEL S., Milton (Ulster Co.) *National Pioneer,* 1830.[Fr]

TUTTLE, NORMAN, 1787-1858; m. Sally Phillips, 1810; *Troy Sentinel,* 1824-1831 (with S. Richards, O. Holley, ed., 1824-1827; with ——— Gregory, 1827-1831; [daily, 1827-1831]), *Troy Review, or, Religious and Musical Repository,* 1827 [bi-monthly] (with S. Richards and T. Hastings).

VAN CLEVE, EDW. J., m. Orpha Ives, 1830; *Lansingburgh Gazette,* 1827-1832 (with E. G. Stone, 1827), Troy *American,* 1833-1834.

VANDERBURGH, RICHARD, d. 1806; pr. *Whitestown Gazette,* 1793, Poughkeepsie *Republican Journal,* 1796 (& Co.), *Poughkeepsie Journal,* 1796 (with N. Power); d. Montgomery.

VAN HORNE, PHILIP, Newburgh *Mirror,* 1797-1798.

VAN SCHAACK, PETER, JR., *Kinderhook Sentinel,* 1825-1832 [Fr] (*Kinderhook Herald,* 1826, with H. O'Reilly, according to a letter of O'Reilly), Kinderhook *Columbia's Sentinel,* 1832-1834.

VAN SICE, J. P., *Hamilton Recorder,*[Fr] Rome *Oneida Republican,* 1828-1830,[Fr] Rome *Republican,* 1830-1831.[Fr]

VAN VEGHTEN, CORNELIUS, Schenectady *Western Budget,* 1807 (with D. Van Veghten).

VAN VEGHTEN, DERICK, d. 1844; appr., Schenectady; pr. Schenectady *Western Budget,* 1807-1808 (with C. Van Veghten, 1807), Schoharie *American Herald,* 1810-1811, *Schoharie Herald,* 1812,[Co] *Schoharie Budget,* 1817-1819, *Schoharie Republican,* 1819-1820.

VETHAKE, JOHN M., Poughkeepsie *Anti-Mason,* 1830-1831 (with Stephen Butler).[Fr]

WADSWORTH, HORACE H., *Waterford Gazette,* 1801-1812 (with J. M. Looker, 1802).

WALKER, L., Warsaw *Genesee Register,* 1828 (with W. Walker).

WALKER, THOMAS, 1777-1863, b. Rehoboth, Mass.; m. Mary Eaton;

appr. to Isaiah Thomas, Worcester, Mass.; pr. Rome *Columbian Patriotic Gazette,* 1799-1803 (with Eben Eaton), Utica *Columbian Gazette,* 1803-1825 (with E. Dorchester, 1814-1816); agent of the Postmaster General in establishing post roads; collector of U. S. revenue, 1812-1815; printer of state laws for the "Western District," 1806-1807.

WALKER, W., Warsaw *Genesee Register,* 1828 (with L. Walker).

WALLACE, JONATHAN, d. 1827/28; Potsdam *St. Lawrence Republican,* 1827 (with William Wyman), Potsdam *Day Star,* 1827 [semimonthly] (ed.), Canton *St. Lawrence Republican,* 1827-1828.

WALTON, ——— Essex *Essex County Republican,* 1826-1828 (with Lewis Person).

WANDS, WILLIAM W., d. 1810; pr. Salem *Washington Patrol,* 1795 (with St. John Honeywood, ed.), Lansingburgh *American Spy,* 1792-1797 (with S. Tiffany, 1792); collector for the Philadelphia (Pa.) *American Daily Advertiser;* postmaster, Lansingburgh, 1796; d. Philadelphia, Pa.

WARD, HENRY DANA, 1797-1884, b. Shrewsbury, Mass.; m. (1) Abigail P. Jones, (2) Charlotte Galbraith; ed. New York *Anti-Masonic Review,* 1828-1830, *Le Roy Gazette,* 1828-1830 (with E. Starr), *New York Whig,* 1831 (with O. L. Holley); d. Philadelphia, Pa.

WARD, SAMUEL, C., m. Emily Stanley, 1821; pr. Canandaigua *Ontario Repository,* 1819-1830 (with J. D. Bemis and C. Morse, 1819-1821; with C. Morse, 1828-1829; with J. D. Bemis, 1830; with C. Morse and Asahel Harvey, 1830).

WARNER, ALLEN, Geneseo *Livingston Register,* 1829-1831 (with A. M. Weed).

WARREN, ANSEL, pr. Salem *Washington Register,* 1825-1826 (with L. J. Reynolds), Poultney (Vt.) *Northern Spectator,* 1828, Watervliet *New York Palladium,* 1829, Ballston Spa *New York Palladium,* 1830-1831 (with C. A. Warren) [office burned, May 5, 1831], Lyons *Western Argus,* 1831-1832 (with J. Barber, and D. Chapman), Perry *American Citizen,* 1837-1840 (with ——— Mitchell), Perry *Watchtower,* 1839-1840, Perry *Free Citizen,* 1846-1847.

WARREN, C. A., Ballston Spa *New York Palladium,* 1830-1831 (with Ansel Warren).

WEBB, THOMAS, Homer *Farmer's Journal,* 1812-1822 (with H. B. Bender, proprietor).

WEBSTER, CHARLES, *Waterford Gazette,* 1812-1815.

WEBSTER, CHARLES RICHARD, 1762-1834, b. Hartford, Conn.; m. (1) Rachel Steele, 1787, (2) Cynthia Steele, 1796; appr. to Hudson and Goodwin, Hartford, Conn., 1769; pr. Albany *New York Gazetteer, or Northern Intelligencer,* 1782-1783 (with S. Balentine), *New*

York Gazette, 1783, *Hudson Weekly Gazette,* 1784-1789 (with Ashbel Stoddard), *Albany Gazette,* 1784-1806 (with George Webster, 1789-1806 [semi-weekly]), *Albany Journal, or, The Montgomery, Washington and Columbia Intelligencer,* 1788-1789 (with George Webster), *Albany Gazette,* 1806-1817 (with George Webster and Elisha Skinner, 1806-1811; with George Webster, Elisha, Hezekiah, and Daniel Skinner: "Websters and Skinners," 1811-1817), *Albany Gazette and Daily Advertiser,* 1817-1823 (with T. V. W. Gould, pr., published by W. L. Stone, for Websters and Skinners, 1817-1818; with T. V. W. Gould, pr. for Websters and Skinners, 1818-1819; with Websters and Skinners, 1819-1823; bookselling, printing and binding business, with E. W. Skinner and Co., 1821-1834); capt. Albany artillery co.; act'g deputy county clerk; d. Saratoga Springs.

WEBSTER, TRUMAN, d. 1852; b. West Hartford, Conn.; m. Frances Perkins, 1813; *Waterford Gazette,* 1815-1818, Waterford *Agriculturalist,* 1820-1821; d. Brooklyn.

WEED, ANSON M., d. 1831; Geneseo *Livingston Register,* 1829-1831 (with A. Warner).

WEED, THURLOW, 1797-1882, b. Acra (Greene Co.); m. Catherine Ostrander, 1818; appr. to T. C. Fay, Onondaga Hollow, 1811-1812; appr. to R. T. Chamberlain, Union Springs, 1812; appr. to William Williams, Utica, 1812-1813; appr. to Seward and Williams, Utica, 1813; appr. to Thomas Walker, Utica, 1813; jrmn. for Websters and Skinners, Albany, 1813; jrmn. for W. L. Stone, Herkimer, 1814; jrmn. for H. and E. Phinney, Cooperstown, 1814; jrmn. for S. R. Brown, Auburn, 1814-1815; jrmn. for H. C. Southwick, Albany, 1815-1816; jrmn. for Jesse Buel, on state printing, Albany, 1816; jrmn. on book printing, successively for: Van Winkle and Wiley, B. Fanshawe, George Lang, S. Woods and Son, B. Gardenier, Jonathan Seymour, and William A. Mercein, New York, 1816-1817; jrmn. for I. W. Clark, Albany, 1817-1818; pr. Norwich *Republican Agriculturist,* 1818-1820; jrmn. on *Albany Argus,* 1821; jrmn. for Packard and Van Benthuysen, Albany, 1821; pr. Manlius *Onondaga Republican,* 1821-1822, Rochester *Telegraph,* 1822-1826 (with E. Peck, proprietor, 1822-1825; with R. Martin, 1826), *Rochester Daily Telegraph,* 1826 (with R. Martin), Rochester *Anti-Masonic Enquirer,* 1828-1830 (with S. Heron, 1828-1829; with D. N. Sprague, 1829-1830), *Albany Evening Journal,* 1830-1863 (with, successively: Benj. D. Packard, Chauncey Webster, Benj. Hoffman; later George Dawson); commissioner to acknowledge deeds, 1819; mem. assembly, 1825 and 1830; state printer, 1840-1843, d. New York; DAB.

WELD, JOHN R., pr. *Troy Gazette,* 1807-1808 (with Wright, Good-enow and Stockwell).

WELLINGTON, E., *Troy Republican,* 1828-1830 (with J. M. Austin), Troy *Northern Watchman,* 1831-1832,[Fr] Troy *Watchman,* 1832-1833,[Fr] *Troy Daily Mail,* 1837-1841.[Fr]

WELLS, DARIUS, 1800-1875, b. Johnstown; appr. to William Child; pr. Amsterdam *Mohawk Herald,* 1821-1823; manufacturer of wood type (with E. R. Webb), New York, 1828-1856; postmaster, Paterson, N. J. (13 years).

WELLS, SAMUEL, *Whitestown Gazette,* 1796 (with William McLean).

WESTCOTT, DAVID M., b. Cornwall; appr., Philadelphia; pr. *Goshen Repository,* 1789-1795/96 (with David Mandeville, 1789-1792); merchant and farmer; county clerk, 1815-1821; supervisor, 1820; mem. assembly, 1828; state senator, 1831-1834.

WHEELER, JAMES, Martinsburgh *Lewis County Republican,* 1830-1837.[Fr]

WHITNEY, EPHRAIM J., m. Susan J. Perrine, 1827; *Lyons Advertiser,* 1826-1827, Lyons *Wayne County Gazette,*[Fr] *Lyons Argus* (with W. W. Whitney),[Fr] Lyons *Wayne County Patriot,* 1829-1830 (with W. W. Whitney).

WHITNEY, W. W., *Lyons Argus,* (with E. J. Whitney),[Fr] Lyons *Wayne County Patriot,* 1829-1830 (with E. J. Whitney).

WHITTLESEY, FREDERICK, 1799-1851, b. New Preston, Conn.; graduate, Yale, 1818; admitted to bar, Utica, 1821; practiced law, Cooperstown, 1822, Rochester, 1822; ed. Rochester *Monroe Republican,* 1827 (with E. Scrantom); treasurer, Monroe County, 1829-1830; clerk of circuit court, 1825; mem. Congress, 1831-1835; vice-chancellor, state court of chancery, 1839; puisne judge, state supreme court, 1847-1848; d. Rochester.

WILBUR, HIRAM, m. Hannah Haviland, 1819; pr. Hudson *Columbia Republican,* 1823-1824, *Hudson Gazette,* 1826-1834.

WILBUR, SOLOMON, JR., m. Rhoda Martindale, 1805; *Troy Gazette,* 1804-1805 (with J. C. Wright; later with H. Stockwell), Hudson *Columbia Republican,* 1820-1822.

WILCOCKE, SAMUEL HALL, Montreal (Canada) *Scribbler,* 1820, Burlington (Vt.) *Scribbler,* 1823, Rouse's Point, *Scribbler,* 1823-1826,[Co] *Rouse's Point Harbinger and Champlain Political and Literary Compendium,* 1823-1825,[Co] Plattsburgh *Scribbler,* 1826, Plattsburgh *Colonial Magazine*[Co]; reporter for parliament, Quebec, Canada.

WILLARD, J. D., ed. *Troy Sentinel,* 1826-1827 (with S. Richards and N. Tuttle).

WILLIAMS, ELIAS, Batavia *Genesee Intelligencer,* 1808 (with B. Blodgett), Malone *Franklin Telegraph,* 1829.

WILLIAMS, SAMUEL, 1789-1878, b. Vermont; appr. to S. Southwick, Albany; jrmn. for Jesse Buel, Albany, 1816; pr. Goshen *Orange Farmer,* 1820-1825 (with J. Farrand, 1820-1821); d. Rondout.

WILLIAMS, WILLIAM, 1787-1850, b. Framingham, Mass.; appr. to William McLean, Utica, 1800-1803; appr. to Lothrop and Seward, and Merrell and Seward, Utica, 1803-1807; pr. Utica *Club,* 1814 (with A. Seward, and J. Ingersoll), Utica *Patrol,* 1815-1816 (with A. Seward), *Utica Patriot and Patrol,* 1816-1817 (with A. Seward and W. H. Maynard), *Utica Sentinel,* 1821-1825 (with A. Seward), *Utica Christian Repository,* 1822-1828[He] (with Merrel and Hastings), Utica Elucidator, 1830-1834 (with B. H. Hotchkin, 1830-1833; with S. P. Lyman, ed. 1833-1834), Utica *American Citizen,* 1830 (with George S. Wilson, ed.); capt., volunteers, 1812; d. Utica.

WILLSON, GEORGE, ed. *Geneva Chronicle,* 1827-1828 (with O. P. Jackson), Canandaigua *Ontario Repository,* 1828-1829 (with C. Morse).

WILSON, GEORGE S., 1803-1841, b. Manlius; appr. to Seward and Williams, Utica, 1819; pr. Utica *Sunday School Visitant; Utica Sentinel and Gazette,* 1825-1826 (with J. Colwell), Utica *American Citizen,* 1830 (with William Williams, pr.); preacher at Windsor, Vt., Sackett's Harbor, and Gouverneur; d. Gouverneur.

WILSON, JAMES R., "Rev.," ed. Newburgh *Evangelical Witness,* 1824 [monthly].[Fr]

WILSON, JOHN T., Geneva *Palladium,* 1823-1825 (with Oliver Spear, 1823), *Geneva Palladium,* 1826-1828.

WILSON, SAMUEL C., Angelica *Alleghany Republican,* 1828.[He]

WILSON, THOMAS, pr. Newburgh *Rights of Man,* 1804-1806, Poughkeepsie *Farmer,* 1806-1807.

WINFIELD, ELIAS, ed. Newburgh *Rights of Man,* 1799-1801 (with Benoni Howell, pr. 1799-1800).

WOOD, WILLIAM P. M., ed. *Morristown Palladium* (N. J.), 1827, *Buffalo Republican,* 1828 (with H. A. Salisbury); reputed to be writing for New York *Evening Post.*

WOODS, JOHN, pr. Poughkeepsie *American Farmer, and Dutchess County Advertiser,* 1798-1800 (with I. Mitchell, ed.).

WOODWARD, W., *Watertown Freeman,* 1824-1833.

WORTHINGTON, ERASTUS, JR., 1789-1827; appr., Brooklyn; jrmn., Brooklyn, 1811; pr. Brooklyn *Long Island Star,* 1817-1827 (with A. Spooner, 1817-1818; with A. Spooner, proprietor, 1821-1827); d. York, Pa.

WRIGHT, J. N., *Sandy Hill Herald,* 1828-1829 (with James Wright).

WRIGHT, JAMES, d. 1858; m. (1) ———, (2) Charity T. Baker; appr. in office of Middlebury (Vt.) *Standard;* pr. Sandy Hill *Times,* 1822-1824 (with Adonijah Emons), Sandy Hill *Political Herald,*

1824-1825, *Sandy Hill Herald,* 1825-1841 (with J. N. Wright, 1828-1829) ; mem. assembly, 1834; postmaster, 1829-1841; d. Sandy Hill.

WRIGHT, JOHN CRAFTS, 1784-1861, b. Rocky Hill, Conn.; m. Mary Buell Collier, 1805; appr. to John Collier, Litchfield, Conn.; pr. *Troy Gazette,* 1804-1809 (with S. Wilbur, 1804; with S. Wilbur and H. Stockwell, 1804-1805; with H. Stockwell and S. Goodenow, 1805-1807; with J. Weld, pr., S. Goodenow, and H. Stockwell, 1807-1808; with S. Goodenow and H. Stockwell, 1808; for the proprietors, 1808-1809), ed. *Cincinnati Gazette* (Ohio), 1840-1853; dist. atty., 1817; mem. Congress, from Ohio, 1821-1829; justice of supreme court, Ohio, 1831-1835; delegate to the "Peace Conference," Washington, 1861; d. Washington, D. C.

WRIGHTHOUSE, WILLIAM B., ed. Newburgh *Beacon,* 1828.

WYCKOFF, CORNELIUS P., 1767-1851; m. Elizabeth Richmond; Schenectady *Mohawk Mercury,* 1794-1798 (with A. Brokaw, 1794-1795).

WYMAN, JOHN F., *Syracuse Advertiser,* 1826-1829 (with P. B. Barnum, T. B. Barnum, and Norman Rawson,[Fr] successively, 1826; with T. B. Barnum and N. Rawson, 1827),[Fr] Syracuse *Onondaga Standard,* 1829 (with V. W. Smith).

WYMAN, WILLIAM W., Potsdam *St. Lawrence Republican,* 1827 (with J. Wallace), *Canton Advertiser and St. Lawrence Republican,* 1828-1829 (with P. King, ed.[Fr]), Canton *Republican and Advertiser,* 1829-1830 (with P. King, ed.[Fr]).

YOUNG, ANDREW W., *Warsaw Sentinel,* 1830-1831 (with J. Goodrich, ed.), Batavia *Republican Advocate,* 1831; Warsaw *American Citizen,* 1836 (with J. A. Hadley, pr.) ; mem. assembly, 1845-1846; mem. constitutional convention, 1846.

YOUNG, JEREMIAH, Lansingburgh *Rensselaer County Gazette,* 1826 (with J. C. Young).

YOUNG, JESSE C., Lansingburgh *Rensselaer County Gazette,* 1826-1827 (with Jeremiah Young, 1826), *Lansingburgh Democrat,* 1828.[He]

YOUNG, STEPHEN, d. 1816; pr. Geneva *Palladium,* 1816 (with W. Crosby, at first) ; d. Geneva.

APPENDIX II: TABLE I

STATISTICAL ANALYSIS OF THE COUNTRY WEEKLY

Percentage of columnar space, measured to the nearest half inch, calculated to the nearest hundredth of one per cent, of given categories of content; years and newspapers selected at random.

1809

Kind of Matter[a]	Canandaigua Western Repository	Cazenovia Pilot	Geneva Expositor Gazette[b]	Hudson Northern Whig	Utica Patriot
Domestic	10.91	10.74	12.90	4.69	5.39
Foreign	10.94	16.62	16.73	11.81	10.70
Documentary	9.32	6.47	9.27	9.84	6.93
Political	15.71	20.26	5.16	16.37	12.92
Literary	4.77	16.81	2.30	6.19	0.38
Editorial	1.28	0.78	0.27	9.24	1.26
Advertising	47.07	28.36	53.37	41.84	62.43
Acknowledged as copied[c]	16.75	23.92	10.64	22.07	13.63

[a] For explanation of the categories in this column see page 313.
[b] Geneva *Expositor* changed to the *Geneva Gazette* in the course of this year.
[c] This category overlaps those above.

1812

Kind of Matter	Canandaigua Ontario Repository	Cazenovia Pilot	Geneva Gazette	Hudson Northern Whig	Newburgh Political Index
Domestic	19.14	10.91	21.22	10.37	14.77
Foreign	5.70	2.99	6.72	6.34	4.44
Documentary	7.11	8.15	8.17	19.06	9.99
Political	13.03	10.52	8.20	10.27	3.70
Literary	4.89	11.72	3.84	2.60	0.89
Editorial	1.46	0.12	0.47	8.62	0.56
Advertising	48.68	55.59	51.38	42.73	65.66
Acknowledged as copied	10.09	16.46	15.48	17.24	5.12

1818

Kind of Matter	*Auburn Gazette*	Cazenovia Pilot	*Geneva Gazette*	*Onondaga Register*	Canandaigua Ontario Repository
Domestic	15.95	9.31	17.31	15.45	16.71
Foreign	5.02	4.36	5.56	6.11	5.84
Documentary	3.39	3.67	3.74	9.31	4.25
Political	1.58	2.85	0.95	3.60	4.01
Literary	16.93	8.55	13.22	14.12	9.77
Editorial	0.43	0.37	0.16	1.24	1.06
Advertising	56.71	70.87	59.06	50.17	58.34
Acknowledged as copied	19.14	11.42	20.98	19.72	15.41

1823

Kind of Matter	Auburn Cayuga Republican	Canandaigua Ontario Repository	*Onondaga Register*	Utica Columbian Gazette
Domestic	11.48	15.42	18.00	15.98
Foreign	17.28	10.69	9.03	8.82
Documentary	1.54	2.83	2.72	3.20
Political	4.63	2.93	5.60	2.31
Literary	9.57	15.37	13.02	9.22
Editorial	0.47	1.74	1.08	0.05
Advertising	55.04	51.02	50.55	60.41
Acknowledged as copied	24.49	16.63	22.56	15.93

1828

Kind of Matter	Auburn Cayuga Republican	Cooperstown Freeman's Journal	*Geneva Gazette*	*Onondaga Register*
Domestic	14.32	23.32	11.87	16.43
Foreign	4.74	8.77	5.29	3.79
Documentary	2.99	4.22	2.60	1.93
Political	21.81	16.11	10.59	21.70
Literary	6.92	16.36	13.81	13.61
Editorial	4.27	0.78	3.94	2.20
Advertising	44.95	30.45	51.91	40.33
Acknowledged as copied	22.28	24.94	18.66	19.69

EXPLANATION OF CATEGORIES

Domestic: News of the United States (as distinguished from "Foreign"); marriages, deaths, political events narrated; proceedings of Congress summarized; prices current, bank-note table, marine list.

Foreign: Foreign news, including news from Canada and other points outside the United States; report of British Parliamentary proceedings; extracts from foreign newspapers; treaties and foreign documents.

Documentary: Public documents of the United States or several states; President's message and accompanying documents; reports of officials of the Government; governor's messages; laws of the state; titles of acts passed, listed.

Political: Political opinion, partisan dispute; quoted opinion on public affairs; letters to the editor on politics; resolutions of political meetings.

Literary: Magazine material; poetry, essays, moral and religious material; miscellany, jokes and anecdotes; remarks on works of literature, contemporary and projected; agricultural information; murderer's confessions.

Editorial: Original comment (not communicated from outside sources), expression of opinion (exclusive of the editor's summary of events).

Advertising: Commercial advertising, legal notices, paid personals, as well as advertising of the printer and his bookstore.

Acknowledged as copied: Matter extracted from other papers or periodicals, for which credit is given. This overlaps other categories, i.e., especially "Political," "Domestic," "Foreign," "Literary," and occasionally "Documentary." It obviously does not include any of the material under "Editorial" or "Advertising."

APPENDIX III: TABLE II

LIBEL*a* SUITS VS. COUNTRY PRINTERS, 1798-1830

Date	Printer-Editor	Plaintiff	Result
		CRIMINAL LIBEL SUITS	
1798	William Durell	People	Four months; fine: $50
1804	H. Croswell	People	Dropped after appeal; test case
1804	S. S. Freer	People	Fine: $10
1830	Elijah J. Roberts	People	Fine: $50
1830	Harvey Newcomb	People	... ...
		CIVIL LIBEL SUITS	
1803	J. Buel & I. Mitchell	Barent Gardinier	... ...
1803	F. Adancourt	J. B. Dole	... ...
1803	H. Croswell	Ambrose Spencer	Damages: $120
1803	H. Croswell	Ebenezer Foot	Damages: 6 cents (plaintiff to pay costs)
1803	G. Tracy	Morgan Lewis	Not guilty
1804	Mackay Croswell	De Witt Clinton	... ...
1804	Ezra Sampson	Ambrose Spencer	Withdrawn, retraction printed; defendant paid costs
1804	G. Tracy	Ebenezer Foot	Damages: $200
1805	Power, Bowman & Co.	Isaac Mitchell	... ...
1805	Power, Bowman & Co.	Thomas Tillotson	... ...
1806	Jesse Buel	James Cheetham	... ...
1806	Isaac Mitchell	James Cheetham	... ...
1807	John C. Wright	Col. Albert Pawling	$50 bail; settled after flight
1807	F. Adancourt	John C. Wright	Damages of $800 and costs; settled later
1807	Thomas Nelson	De Witt Clinton	... ...
1808	T. Eaton	Stephen O. Runyan	Settled; retraction printed
1808	John C. Wright	Charles Selden	Settled, costs paid; retraction printed
1809	Henry Dodd	David Thomas	Damages: $50
1809	J. H. Prentiss	Jabez D. Hammond	Settled; retraction printed
1809	J. H. Prentiss	Elihu Phinney	... ...

a The term "libel" is taken broadly for the purposes of this tabulation, including criminal, civil, and seditious libels. Thus the case of Durell (prosecuted under the Sedition Act), and of S. S. Freer (guilty of contempt), are included along with the more common prosecution for defamation of character. In arguing the case of Freer, Hamilton made his plea on the basis of the law of libel; while Section 3 of the Sedition Act of 1798 referred to the punishable offense as a "libel." This list does not include libel suits against printers in Albany or New York, nor those against country printers, such as Buel, Mitchell, or Croswell, who were in Albany or New York as editors when the suit was begun.

Date	Printer-Editor	Plaintiff	Result
1810	James D. Bemis	Micah Brooks	Damages: $250
1810	Nathan Elliott	Moses I. Cantine	Damages: $150
1811	Alden Spooner	J. B. Clarke	... ...
1812	James Bogert	John C. Spencer	Settled
1812	Ira Merrell	Pascal C. I. de Angelis	Damages: $500
1813	John A. Stevens	Solomon Southwick	Damages: $640
1813	Oliver Lyon	James Dole	Damages: $150
1814	Francis Stebbins	Martin Van Buren	... ...
1817	Stockholm & Brownejohn	James Tallmadge Jr.	... ...
1818	A. O. Houghton	Amzi L. Ball	Damages: $25
1818	T. L. Houghton	Amzi L. Ball	... ...
1818	S. H. & H. A. Salisbury	Daniel Penfield	Damages: $8,000
1819	Barnum & Nelson	William Bell	... ...
1819	James Comstock	James Thompson	Settled; retraction printed
1820	Zephaniah Clark	William McManus	Damages: $200
1820	Oran Follett	Samuel M. Hopkins	... ...
1820	Erastus Shepard	Ambrose Spencer	... ...
1821	A. H. Bennett	Robert Troup	Pleaded clemency; damages of $10
1821	Oran E. Baker	Bennett Bicknell	
1823	Alden Spooner	Christopher Scanlan	Damages: $300
1825	William Child	Jesse Clark	No bill; dismissed
1825	David M. Day	Peter B. Porter	Settled; retraction printed
1825	Azariah C. Flagg	Jonas Platt	... ...
1825	Richard Oliphant	Gershom Powers	Dropped
1827	Thomas Skinner	Gershom Powers	Damages: $300
1827	T. W. Haskell	M. Sterling	Damages: $50
1827	George L. Birch	W. Hegeman	Damages of $25 and apology
1827	H. O'Reilly & L. Tucker	Thurlow Weed	Settled; payment of costs
1828	Thurlow Weed	O'Reilly & Tucker	Delayed until 1841; dismissed
1828	Henry O'Reilly	I. J. Richardson	Jury did not agree
1828	Robert Martin	Washington, N. J., Banking Company	... ...
1828	William H. Maynard	Samuel Beardsley	Damages: $446
1829	E. B. Grandin	I. J. Richardson	Acquittal
1829	Thurlow Weed	Jacob Gould	Damages: $400
1829	Daniel P. Adams	H. A. Reed	... ...
1830	P. Baker & E. A. Cooley	J. Center	Damages: $20
1830	James Comstock	Col. Young	... ...
1830	Morgan Bates	Hiram R. Bowers	... ...
1830	John F. Fairchild	Bennett Bicknell	Damages: $60
1830	J. C. Barter & D. Spafford	Geo. W. Strong	Damages: $112

BIBLIOGRAPHY

WHILE newspaper files and collections have formed the principal sources for this study, they are not listed below. Not only would such a list be extremely long, but it would be in several ways a duplication of material to be found elsewhere. Footnotes give detailed citations to the newspapers utilized; and the connections of printers with these papers are included in the Appendix. Students desiring to refer to newspapers will use the admirable "Bibliography of American Newspapers, 1690-1820," by Clarence S. Brigham, which is now being revised, and will eventually have the benefit of the "Union List of Newspapers," being prepared under the auspices of the Bibliographical Society of America, for the period after 1820. These lists possess the additional advantage of giving the location of files.

BIBLIOGRAPHIES AND CHECK LISTS

Barber, John Warner, *Historical Collections of the State of New York.* New York, 1851.

Brigham, Clarence S., "Bibliography of American Newspapers, 1690-1820," American Antiquarian Society *Proceedings,* Worcester, Mass., 1913-1924. Vols. XXVII-XXVIII contain the lists for New York.

Cannon, Carl L., *Journalism: a Bibliography.* New York, 1924.

Evans, Charles, *American Bibliography,* 10 vols., Chicago, 1930.

Fox, Louis H., "New York City Newspapers, 1820-1850, a Bibliography." Bibliographical Society of America *Papers,* Vol. XXI, Chicago, 1928.

Gavit, Joseph, *A List of American Newspaper Reprints.* [Reprinted from the *Bulletin* of the New York Public Library.] New York, 1931.

Griffin, Appleton Prentiss Clark, *Bibliography of American Historical Societies.* American Historical Association *Annual Report,* 1905, Vol. II, Washington, 1907.

Haskell, Daniel C., *Check List of Newspapers and Official Gazettes in the New York Public Library.* New York, 1915.

Heartman, Charles Frederick, *Check List of Printers in the United States.* From Stephen Daye to the Close of the War of Independence, with a List of Places in Which Printing Was Done. New York, 1915.

Ingram, John Van Ness, *A Check List of American Eighteenth Century Newspapers in the Library of Congress.* Washington, 1912.

Nelson, William, *Some Account of American Newspapers, Particularly of the 18th Century, and Libraries in Which They Are Found.* New Jersey Archives, 1st series, Vols. XI-XII, XIX. Paterson, N. J., 1894-1897.

Pittsburgh and Allegheny County, Pennsylvania, Inventory of Files of American Newspapers in. Western Pennsylvania Historical Survey, Pittsburgh, 1933.

Scott, Franklin William, *Newspapers and Periodicals of Illinois, 1814-1879.* Springfield, Ill., 1910.

Severance, Frank Hayward, "Contributions towards a Bibliography of Buffalo and the Niagara Region." Buffalo Historical Society *Publications,* Vol. XIX, Buffalo, 1915.

Slauson, A. B., *Check List of American Newspapers in the Library of Congress.* Washington, 1901.

Watkins, G. T., *Bibliography of Printing in America.* Boston, 1906.

MANUSCRIPT SOURCES

American Antiquarian Society

Matthew Carey Accounts. These are 36 vols. of the account books of M. Carey, and Carey, Lea & Carey, of Philadelphia. The wholesale transactions of this firm covered a large area, and a number of printers' names are found in the comprehensive index.

Munsell, Joel, "Typographical Collections—Consisting of Fugitive Pieces relating to Printing and Its Cognate Arts / instaurata / studio et labore." These eight bound volumes of Joel Munsell of Albany are chiefly in his own hand. Albany, 1857-1867.

―――― *Typographical Miscellany,* Albany, 1850. This is the author's own copy, with extra leaves bound in and many additions in his hand and with numerous clippings. It is very valuable.

Canandaigua

The scrapbooks of the late Charles F. Milliken, former editor of the *Ontario County Times,* containing clippings on the early history of Ontario county, were used at his home.

East Hampton Free Library, Morton Pennypacker Long Island Collection

Letters of David Frothingham, Selleck Osborn, Alden Spooner, and others concerning the press at Sag Harbor.

New York Historical Society

A manuscript of Harry Croswell explains his activities in Hudson, and especially his publication of *The Wasp.* It is an important source in connection with his famous trial for seditious libel.

The Scrapbook of Henry O'Reilly, with a copy of the "first book printed in Western New York," was presented by him to the Society.

New York Public Library

Azariah C. Flagg Papers. These contain much political correspondence, including that with a number of editors in the state.

Harry Croswell ads. the People. This is a manuscript volume in the hand of Justice James Kent, giving the details of the Croswell trial, the notes of Hamilton's speech, and of subsequent legislation regarding libels.

Jedidiah Morse Papers, 1789-1826.

Noah Webster Papers. These include his correspondence with printers in connection with his proposed newspaper survey.

Additional manuscripts concerning printers were found in the general collections, filed under the names of Charles Holt, Thurlow Weed, Edwin Croswell, Jesse Buel, and others.

New York State Library

Papers from the attorney general's office dealing with the accounts of printers for the publication of legal notices include a number of letters by printers.

Onondaga Historical Association

The Scrapbook of Mrs. Anna M. T. Redfield contains letters addressed to Lewis H. Redfield as postmaster and as editor of the *Onondaga Register*.

Rochester Historical Society

O'Reilly Collection. This large collection of the papers of Henry O'Reilly contains letters by him and from Henry C. Sleight, Luther Tucker, James D. Bemis, Lewis H. Redfield, and Frederick Follett.

Scrapbook of Edwin Scrantom. This contains clippings of newspaper articles by Scrantom, with his recollections of his early experiences in Rochester. Many of these were published in a series entitled, "Old Citizen."

PRINTED SOURCES

The Technique of Printing

Bullen, Henry Lewis, "The Evolution of American Printing Presses, 1776-1926." *The American Printer,* July 5, 1926.

De Vinne, Theodore L., ed., *Moxon's Mechanick Exercises; or, the Doctrine of Handy-Works Applied to the Art of Printing;* A Literal Reprint in Two Volumes of the First Edition Published in the Year 1683. New York, 1896.

Hoe, Robert, *A Short History of the Printing Press.* New York, 1902.

Mackellar, Thomas, *The American Printer; a Manual of Typography.* Philadelphia, 1872.

Pasko, W. W., *American Dictionary of Printing and Bookmaking.* New York, 1894.

Stower, Charles, *The Printer's Grammar.* London, 1808.

Updike, Daniel B., *The History, Forms and Uses of Printing Types.* Cambridge, 1922.

Van Winkle, C. S., *The Printer's Guide; or, an Introduction to the Art of Printing.* New York, 1818.

Wray, George E., "Business Methods of Printers." *The American Printer,* July 5, 1926.

Wroth, Lawrence C., *The Colonial Printers.* New York, 1931.

Conditions of Labor

Barnett, G. E., "The Printers." American Economic Association *Publications,* Vol. X, 3d series, October, 1909.

Burk, Addison B., *Apprenticeship as It Was and Is, with Some Suggestions about Industrial Schools for the Training of Workmen.* Philadelphia, 1882.

Commons, John R., ed., *A Documentary History of American Industrial Society,* 10 vols. Cleveland, 1909-1911.

―――― and associates, *History of Labour in the United States.* 2 vols. New York, 1918.

Douglas, Paul Howard, *American Apprenticeship and Industrial Education.* New York, 1921.

Morgan, Charlotte E., *The Origin and History of the New York Employing Printers' Association.* New York, 1930.

Scrimshaw, Stewart, *Apprenticeship, Principles, Relationship, Procedures.* New York, 1932.

Seybolt, Robert Francis, *Apprenticeship and Apprenticeship Education in Colonial New England and New York.* New York, 1917.

Southwick, Solomon, *Address...at the opening of the Apprentices' Library in the City of Albany, January* 1, 1821. Albany, 1821.

Stevens, George A., *New York Typographical Union No. 6,* Albany, 1912. Another edition, Albany, 1913. The scope of this study is far broader than its title indicates. It contains much source material on the conditions of early printing.

Stewart, Ethelbert, *A Documentary History of Early Organizations of Printers.* U. S. Bureau of Labor Bulletin No. 61, Washington, 1905.

Whitney, James S., *Apprenticeship and a Boy's Prospect of a Livelihood.* Philadelphia, 1872.

Whittemore, Charles H., *Albany Typographical Union No. 4.* Albany, 1905.

Biographical and Personal Data

Barnes, Thurlow Weed, *Memoir of Thurlow Weed.* Boston, 1884. Published with the cover title, *Life of Thurlow Weed,* Vol. II, of which his *Autobiography* was Vol. I.

Bradsher, Earl L., *Matthew Carey, Editor, Author and Publisher.* New York, 1912.

Brockway, Beman, *Fifty Years in Journalism.* Watertown, N. Y., 1891.

Brown, Samuel R., *The Western Gazetteer or Emigrant's Directory.* Auburn, 1817.

Buckingham, Joseph Tinker, *Personal Memoirs and Recollections of Editorial Life.* Boston, 1852.

Child, Elias, *Genealogy of the Child, Childs and Childe Families.* Utica, 1881.

Dean, Amos, *Eulogy on the Life and Character of the Late Judge Jesse Buel.* Albany, 1840.

Draper, Thomas Waln-Morgan, *The Bemis History and Genealogy.* San Francisco, 1900.

Faÿ, Bernard, *The Two Franklins: Fathers of American Democracy.* Boston, 1933.

Ford, Paul Leicester, ed., *The Journals of Hugh Gaine, Printer.* 2 vols. New York, 1902.

Greeley, Horace, *Recollections of a Busy Life.* New York, 1868.

Hamilton, John C., ed., *The Works of Alexander Hamilton.* 8 vols., New York, 1851.

Hamlin, L. Belle, ed., "Selections from the Follett Papers." *Quarterly Publication* of the Historical and Philosophical Society of Ohio, Vols. V-XIII, Cincinnati, 1910-1918. Contains the papers of Oran Follett, formerly of Buffalo and Batavia.

Johnson, Allen and Malone, Dumas, eds., *Dictionary of American Biography.* 16 vols. in progress. New York, 1928-1935.

Mehling, Mary Bryant Alverson, *Cowdrey-Cowdery-Cowdray Genealogy.* New York, 1911.

Newcomb, John Bearse, *Genealogical Memoir of the Newcomb Family.* Elgin, Ill., 1874.

Osborn, Selleck, *Poems.* Boston, 1823.

Paltsits, Victor Hugo, *John Holt, Printer and Postmaster.* [Reprinted from the *Bulletin* of the New York Public Library.] New York, 1920.

Parton, James, *The Life of Horace Greeley.* Boston, 1877.

Pennypacker, Morton, *Long Island's First Printer's Devil.* Privately printed, Kew Gardens, Long Island, 1927. John M. Elliott, apprentice to David Frothingham.

Ranney, Ruth Whitaker, *A Sketch of the Lives and Missionary Work of Rev. Cephas Bennett and His Wife, Stella Kneeland Bennett.* Boston, 1892.

Ray, William, *Poems . . . to Which Is Added a Brief Sketch of the Author's Life, and of His Captivity and Sufferings among the Turks and Barbarians of Tripoli on the Coast of Africa—Written by Himself.* Auburn, 1821. Another edition was issued in 1826.

—— *The American Tars in Tripolitan Slavery.* Troy, 1808. Reprinted in the *Magazine of History,* New York, 1911.

Redfield, John Howard, *Genealogical History of the Redfield Family in the United States.* Albany, 1860.

Reynolds, Marion H., *The History and Descendants of John and Sarah Reynolds.* Brooklyn, 1924.

Sellstedt, Laurentius G., "Rosswell Willson Haskins," Buffalo Historical Society *Publications,* Vol. IV, Buffalo, 1896.

Sleight, Mary B., "Henry C. Sleight," Rochester Historical Society *Publication Fund,* Vol. VI, Rochester, 1927.

Stanton, Henry B., *Random Recollections.* New York, 1886.

Stone, William L., *The Life and Times of Sa-go-ye-wat-ka, or Red Jacket.* With a memoir of the author, by his son. Albany, 1866.

—— "From New York to Niagara; Journal of a Tour, in Part by the Erie Canal, in the year 1829," in *The Holland Land Company.* Buffalo, 1910.

Strong, Thomas C., *Memorial Discourse of William Andrus.* Ithaca, 1870.

Treman, Ebenezer Mack, and Poole, Murray E., *The History of the Treman, Tremaine, Truman Family in America: with the Related Families of Mack, Dey, Board and Ayers.* Ithaca, 1901.

Tucker, Ephraim, *Genealogy of the Tucker Family.* Worcester, Mass., 1895.

Tuckerman, Bayard, ed., *The Diary of Philip Hone, 1828-1851.* 2 vols. New York, 1889.

Warner, H. W., *Report of the Trial of Charles N. Baldwin for a Libel. . . .* New York, 1818.

Weed, Thurlow, *Autobiography of Thurlow Weed.* Edited by his daughter, Harriet A. Weed, Boston, 1883. Vol. I of the *Life of*

Thurlow Weed. This is a principal source for the early journalistic history of New York.

——— *Selections from the Newspaper Articles of Thurlow Weed.* Albany, 1877.

Williams, John Camp, *An Oneida County Printer,* William Williams, printer, publisher, editor, with a bibliography of the press at Utica, Oneida County, N. Y., 1803-1838. New York, 1906. A fine study of an influential printer.

Wilson, James Grant, and Fiske, John, eds., *Appleton's Cyclopaedia of American Biography.* 6 vols. New York, 1887-1889.

Wold, Ansel, compiler, *Biographical Directory of the American Congress,* 1774-1927. Washington, 1928.

Wright, Curtis, *Genealogical and Biographical Notices of the Descendants of Sir John Wright*... Carthage, Mo., 1915.

Journalism: Its Growth and Influence

"American Newspapers—Their Appearance, Character, &c." *The Penny Magazine* (London), X, 243-244, June 26, 1841.

Atwood, Millard Van Marter, *The Country Newspaper.* Chicago, 1923.

Bing, Phil C., *The Country Weekly.* A manual for the rural journalist and for students of the country field. New York, 1917.

Bleyer, Willard Grosvenor, *Main Currents in the History of American Journalism.* Boston, 1927. This is the latest and best of the histories of journalism, with an excellent chapter on the political journalism of this period, 1800-1833.

Buckingham, Joseph Tinker, *Specimens of Newspaper Literature,* 1779-1861, with personal memoirs, anecdotes, and reminiscences. Boston, 1850.

Cook, Elizabeth Christine, *Literary Influences in Colonial Newspapers, 1704-1750.* New York, 1912.

——— "Colonial Newspapers and Magazines," *The Cambridge History of American Literature,* Vol. I, chap. vii. New York, 1917.

Duniway, Clyde Augustus, *The Development of Freedom of the Press in Massachusetts.* New York, 1906. An excellent treatment, with general significance.

Evans, Liston P., "How a Country Newspaper Was Published Sixty Years Ago," Maine Press Association *Annual Report of Proceedings,* No. 37, Portland, Me., 1900. Details about the *Piscataquis Observer* compare with those of New York papers.

Follett, Frederick, *History of the Press of Western New York.* Prepared at the request of a Committee... Together with the Proceedings of the Printers' Festival, Held on the 141st Anniversary of the Birthday of Franklin, in the City of Rochester, on Monday, Jan. 18,

1847. Rochester, 1847. This is the most important work for the history of the country press in this period. The original edition is rare, and the author has used the reprint, listed below, for most purposes. The reprint, unfortunately, did not include all of the correspondence and proceedings. When this material has been quoted in the text the date (1847) is given with the citation.

—— *History of the Press in Western New York.* From the Beginning to the Middle of the Nineteenth Century. With a Preface By Wilberforce Eames. Ninety-one Copies Reprinted for Charles F. Heartman, New York, 1920.

Hale, William G., *The Law of the Press,* St. Paul, Minn., 1923.

Hamilton, Milton W., "The Spread of the Newspaper Press in New York Before 1830," *New York History,* April, 1933. Also reprinted as a pamphlet.

Hewett, D[aniel], *Traveller and Monthly Gazetteer.* Philadelphia, 1828. Contains a list of the newspapers of the United States, the names of their publishers, locations, and prices. The copy of Isaiah Thomas in the American Antiquarian Society is the only one known. I have used this copy and also the list in photostat.

Hildeburn, Charles R., *Sketches of Printers and Printing in Colonial New York.* New York, 1895.

Hooker, Richard, *The Story of an Independent Newspaper.* One Hundred Years of the *Springfield Republican,* 1824-1924. New York, 1924.

Howells, William Dean, *The Country Printer.* An essay. Norwood, Mass., 1896.

Hudson, Frederic, *Journalism in the United States.* From 1690 to 1872. New York, 1873. Contains much detail on this period, but is discursive and anecdotal in its treatment.

Jordan, Philip D., "The Portrait of a Pioneer Printer," Illinois State Historical Society *Journal,* Vol. XXIII, April, 1930. The story of a migration westward.

Lee, James Melvin, *History of American Journalism.* Boston, 1917. Revised edition, Boston, 1923.

McCormick, Medill, "The American Newspaper," *The Making of America.* Vol. I, Chicago, 1905.

McMurtie, Douglas C., *Early Printing in Michigan.* With a bibliography of the Michigan Press, 1796-1850. Chicago, 1931.

—— *Early Printing in Milwaukee.* Milwaukee, 1930.

—— *Early Printing in Wisconsin.* With a bibliography of the issues of the press, 1833-1850. Seattle, Wash., 1931.

——*The First Printers of Chicago.* With a bibliography of the issues of the Chicago Press, 1836-1850. Chicago, 1927.

McMurtie, Douglas C., "Pioneer Printing in Kansas," *Kansas Historical Quarterly,* Vol. I, Nov., 1931.

——— "The Westward Migration of the Printing Press, 1786-1836," *Gutenberg Jahrbuch,* Mainz, Germany, 1930.

Mitchell, Edward Page, "Colonial Journalism in New York," New York State Historical Association *Proceedings,* Vol. XVI. Albany, 1917.

Moore, John Weeks, *Moore's Historical, Biographical, and Miscellaneous Gatherings;* in the form of disconnected notes relative to the printing, printers, publishing, and editing of books, newspapers, magazines, and other literary productions, 1420-1886. Concord, New Hampshire, 1886.

Munsell, Joel, *Typographical Miscellany,* Albany, 1850. This is a valuable collection of data, arranged chronologically, by an outstanding antiquarian and printer.

Murphy, Lawrence W., "The Illinois Editorial Hall of Fame," in *Editor and Publisher,* Sept., 1930. Contains a sketch of Simeon Francis.

Nelson, William, "The American Newspapers of the Eighteenth Century as Sources of History," American Historical Association *Annual Report,* 1908, Vol. I, Washington, 1910.

——— *Notes toward a History of the American Newspaper.* New York, 1918.

Nevins, Allan, *American Press Opinion, Washington to Coolidge;* a Documentary Record of Editorial Leadership and Criticism, 1785-1927. New York, 1928. Contains admirable introductory essays to each of the four sections. The first deals with this period, 1783-1835.

——— *The Evening Post; a Century of Journalism.* New York, 1922. One of the best of the histories of single newspapers, very valuable for this period.

New York Press Association, *Reports* of the Annual Conventions. 20th (1876); 21st (1877); 22d (1878); 25th (1881). Dansville, N. Y. These elusive, and almost-forgotten, reports often contain reminiscences and letters concerning early New York printers.

Nolan, J. Bennett, *The First Decade of Printing in Reading, Pennsylvania.* Reading, Pa., 1930. Records facts about George Gerrish, formerly of New York.

North, S. N. D., *History and Present Condition of the Newspaper and Periodical Press of the United States.* Washington, 1884. A publication of the tenth census.

O'Brien, Frank M., *The Story of The Sun, 1833-1918.* New York, 1918.

O'Reilly, Henry, "The March of Empire—Progress of Typography Westward," *The Historical Magazine,* Vol. I, second series, No. 4, April, 1867.

Oswald, John Clyde, *A History of Printing; Its Development Through Five Hundred Years.* New York, 1928.

Payne, George Henry, *History of Journalism in the United States.* New York, 1920.

Peddie, Robert A., ed., *Printing. A Short History of the Art,* London, 1927. The article on North America is by L. C. Wroth.

Perrin, W. H., *Pioneer Press of Kentucky,* Filson Club *Publications,* No. 3, Louisville, 1888.

Presbrey, Frank, *The History and Development of Advertising.* New York, 1929.

Rutherfurd, Livingston, *John Peter Zenger, His Press, His Trial and a Bibliography of Zenger Imprints.* New York, 1904.

Salmon, Lucy Maynard, *The Newspaper and Authority.* New York, 1923.

—— *The Newspaper and the Historian.* New York, 1923.

Scott, Frank W., "Newspapers, 1775-1860," in *Cambridge History of American Literature,* Book II, chap. xxi. New York, 1917-1921.

Siebert, Frederick Seaton, *The Rights and Privileges of the Press.* New York, 1934.

Spaulding, E. Wilder, "The 'Connecticut Courant,' a Representative Newspaper in the Eighteenth Century." *New England Quarterly,* July, 1930.

Tassin, Algernon de Vivier, *The Magazine in America.* New York, 1916.

Thomas, Isaiah, *History of Printing in America.* 2 vols. Worcester, 1810. 2d ed., Albany, 1874. This was the first history of American journalism and is a primary source for the study of this period.

—— *Diary of Isaiah Thomas, 1805-1828.* Edited with an introduction by Benjamin Thomas Hill. Worcester, Mass., 1909.

Thwaites, Reuben Gold, "The Ohio Valley Press before the War of 1812-1815," American Antiquarian Society *Proceedings,* Vol. XIX, Worcester, 1908-1909.

Vail, Robert W. G., *The Ulster County Gazette and Its Illegitimate Offspring.* New York, 1931.

Weeks, Stephen Beauregard, *The Press of North Carolina in the Eighteenth Century.* With biographical sketches of printers, an account of the manufacture of paper, and a bibliography of issues. Brooklyn, 1891.

Willey, Malcolm MacDonald, *The Country Newspaper; a Study of Socialization and Newspaper Content.* Chapel Hill, N. C., 1926.

Winterich, John T., *Early American Books & Printing*. Boston-New York, 1935.

Woodward, Julian Lawrence, *Foreign News in American Morning Newspapers;* a Study in Public Opinion. New York, 1930. An example of the quantitative study of newspaper content.

Worth, Gorham A., and others, *Sketches of the Character of the New York Press*. New York, 1844.

State, County, and Local Histories

Adams, James Truslow, *History of the Town of Southampton*. Bridge-hampton, L. I., 1918.

Aldrich, Lewis Cass, *History of Ontario County, New York*. Syracuse, 1893.

———— *History of Yates County, N. Y.* Syracuse, 1892.

Alexander, De Alva Stanwood, *A Political History of the State of New York*. 3 vols. New York, 1906.

Allegany County, History of. New York, 1879.

Anderson, Arthur Wellington, *The Conquest of Chautauqua*. Jamestown, 1932.

Anderson, George Baker, *Landmarks of Rensselaer County*. Syracuse, 1897.

———— *Our County and Its People: Saratoga County*. Boston, 1899.

Bagg, Moses Mears, *Memorial History of Utica*. Syracuse, 1892.

———— *Pioneers of Utica*. Utica, 1877.

Baird, Charles W., *History of Rye, New York*. New York, 1871.

Barrett, Walter, pseudonym, *The Old Merchants of New York City*. 2d series. New York, 1863. One of a series prepared by J. A. Scoville.

Bayles, Richard M., *History of Richmond County, New York*, 1887.

Beardsley, Levi, *Reminiscences;* personal and other incidents; early history of Otsego County... New York, 1852.

Beauchamp, William Martin, *Past and Present of Syracuse and Onondaga County, New York*. New York, 1808.

Benton, Nathaniel S., *A History of Herkimer County*. Albany, 1856.

Bradford, Sarah H., "History of Geneva," in *Brigham's Geneva, Seneca Falls and Waterloo Directory*. Geneva, 1862.

Brayman, J. C., "When Our Press Was Young," in Buffalo Historical Society *Publications,* Vol. XIX. Buffalo, 1915.

Brown, George Levi, *Pleasant Valley;* a History of Elizabethtown, Essex County, New York. Elizabethtown, 1905. Valuable letters of William Ray given in full.

Bruce, Dwight Hall, *Memorial History of Syracuse, N. Y.* Syracuse, 1891.

Bruce, Dwight Hall, *Onondaga's Centennial.* 2 vols. Boston, 1896.

Bunnell, A. O., *Dansville.* Dansville, 1902.

Burr, George, *Historical Address Relating to the County of Broome.* Binghamton, 1876.

Cattaraugus County, History of. Philadelphia, 1879.

Child, Hamilton, *Gazetteer and Business Directory of Columbia County, N. Y. for 1871-72.* Syracuse, 1871.

Churchill, John C., and others, *Landmarks of Oswego.* Syracuse, 1895.

Clark, Hiram C., *History of Chenango County.* Norwich, 1850.

Clark, J. H. V., *Onondaga.* 2 vols. Syracuse, 1849.

Clayton, W. Woodford, *History of Onondaga County, New York.* Syracuse, 1878.

—— *History of Steuben County,* New York, Philadelphia, 1879. Contains complete correspondence of Benjamin Smead and Daniel Cruger.

Clearwater, A. T., *History of Ulster County.* Kingston, 1907.

Cleveland, Stafford C., *History of Yates County.* Penn Yan, 1873.

Cole, David, *History of Rockland County.* New York, 1884.

Columbia County at the End of the Century. 2 vols. Hudson, 1900.

Cowles, George W., and others, *Landmarks of Wayne County.* Syracuse, 1895.

Devoz, John, *History of the City of Buffalo and Niagara Falls.* Buffalo, 1896.

Downs, J. P., *History of Chautauqua County.* Boston, 1921.

Durant, Plina A., *History of Oneida County.* Philadelphia, 1878.

Ellis, Franklin, *History of Columbia County.* Philadelphia, 1878.

Emerson, Edgar C., *Jefferson County.* Boston, 1898.

Fitch, Charles E., *The Press of Onondaga;* a Lecture Delivered before the Onondaga Historical Association. Syracuse, 1868.

Flick, Alexander C., ed., *History of the State of New York,* 10 vols., New York, 1933-1936.

Foreman, Edward R., ed., Rochester Historical Society *Publications.* Vols. VIII-IX, Rochester, 1930-1931.

Fox, Dixon Ryan, *The Decline of the Aristocracy in the Politics of New York.* New York, 1919. Contains the best account of political parties in the state for this period.

French, J. H., *Gazetteer of the State of New York.* Syracuse, 1860. The footnotes supply a detailed record of the press of each county, which is extremely valuable.

Frothingham, Washington, *History of Fulton County.* Syracuse, 1892.

Furman, Gabriel, *Antiquities of Long Island;* to Which Is Added a Bibliography of Long Island by Henry Onderdonk, Jr. New York, 1875.

Galpin, Henry J., *Annals of Oxford, New York*. Oxford, 1906.

Gay, W. B., *Historical Gazetteer of Tioga County, New York*. Syracuse, 1888.

Gazetteer of the State of New York, with general statistics, including the census of 1840. Albany, 1842.

Goodwin, H. C., *Pioneer History of Cortland County*. New York, 1859.

Gordon, Thomas F., *Gazetteer of the State of New York*. Philadelphia, 1836.

Green, Frank Bertangue, *The History of Rockland County*. New York, 1886.

Grose, Edward F., *Centennial History of the Village of Ballston Spa*. Ballston Spa, 1907.

Haddock, John A., *Growth of a Century: as Illustrated in the History of Jefferson County, New York*. Albany, 1895.

Hakes, Harlo, and others, *Landmarks of Steuben County*. Syracuse, 1896.

Hall, N. K., and Blossom, Thomas, "The Postal Service of the United States in Connection with the Local History of Buffalo," Buffalo Historical Society *Publications,* Vol. IV, Buffalo, 1896.

Hammond, Jabez Delano, *History of Political Parties in the State of New York*. 2 vols. Cooperstown, 1846. A primary source for the politics of this period.

Hammond, Mrs. L. M., *History of Madison County,* Syracuse, 1872.

Hatch, V. A., *History of Jamestown*. Jamestown, 1900. An article by A. B. Fletcher deals with the press of Jamestown.

Hazeltine, Gilbert W., *The Early History of the Town of Ellicott,* Chautauqua County, N. Y., compiled largely from the personal recollections of the author. Jamestown, 1887. By the nephew of Abner Hazeltine, editor of the *Jamestown Journal*.

Headley, Russell, *History of Orange County,* New York. Middletown, 1908.

Hill, William H., *A Brief History of the Printing Press in Washington, Saratoga, and Warren Counties*. Together with a check list of their publications prior to 1825 and a selection of books relating particularly to the vicinity. Privately printed, Fort Edward, 1930.

Hotchkin, James Hervey, *History of the Purchase and Settlement of Western New York,* and of the Presbyterian Church. New York, 1848.

Hough, Franklin B., *History of Jefferson County, New York*. Albany, 1854.

—— *History of Lewis County, New York*. Albany, 1860.

——— *History of St. Lawrence and Franklin Counties, New York.* Albany, 1853.

Howell, George R., *Early History of Southampton, L. I.,* Albany, 1887.

——— and Tenney, Jonathan, *History of the County of Albany, New York.* New York, 1886.

Hufeland, Otto, *A Check List of the Books, Maps, Pictures, and Other Printed Matter Relating to the Counties of Westchester and Bronx.* White Plains, 1929.

Hull, Nora, ed. *Official Records of the Centennial Celebration, Bath, N. Y.* Bath, 1893.

Hurd, Duane Hamilton, *History of Clinton and Franklin Counties.* Philadelphia, 1880.

Jenkins, John Stilwell, *History of Political Parties in the State of New York.* Auburn, 1849.

Johnson, Crisfield, *Centennial History of Erie County.* Buffalo, 1876.
——— *History of Washington County.* Philadelphia, 1878.

Jones, Pomroy, *Annals and Recollections of Oneida County.* Rome, 1851.

Ketchum, William, *History of the City of Buffalo,* 2 vols. Buffalo, 1865.

Kurtz, D. Morris, *Ithaca and Its Resources.* Ithaca, 1883.

Lawyer, William S., *Binghamton, Its Settlement, Growth and Development... 1800-1900.* n. p., 1900.

Livermore, S. T., *A Condensed History of Cooperstown.* Albany, 1862.

McBain, Howard Lee, *De Witt Clinton and the Origin of the Spoils System in New York.* New York, 1907.

McKinstry, Louis, "The Press of Chautauqua," in *Centennial History of Chautauqua County.* Jamestown, 1904. Author was editor of the Fredonia *Censor.*

McKinstry, W., "The Pioneer Press of Chautauqua County," an Address Read by W. McKinstry Before the Fredonia Historical Society, Friday Evening, March 14, 1879. Jamestown *Chautauqua Democrat,* April 2, 1879.

McMaster, Guy H., *History of the Settlement of Steuben County.* Bath, 1853.

Manly, John, *Cattaraugus County.* Little Valley, N. Y., 1857.

Miller, Stephen B., *Historical Sketches of Hudson.* Hudson, 1862.

Milliken, Charles F., *A History of Ontario County, New York, and Its People.* 2 vols. New York, 1911.

Minard, J. S., *Allegany County and Its People.* Alfred, N. Y., 1896.

Monroe County, New York, History of. Philadelphia, 1877.

Monroe, Joel Henry, *Historical Records of a Hundred and Twenty Years, Auburn, N. Y.,* Geneva, 1913.

────── *Schenectady, Ancient and Modern.* Geneva, 1914.

Morris, Ira K., *Morris's Memorial History of Staten Island.* 2 vols. West New Brighton, 1900.

Near, Irvin W., *History of Steuben County, New York.* Chicago, 1911.

New York (State). *Laws of the State of New York,* (1806), Albany, 1806.

────── *Laws of the State of New York,* (1845), Albany, 1845.

────── *Revised Statutes of the State of New York,* Albany, 1829.

Nutt, John J., *Newburgh, Her Institutions, Industries, and Leading Citizens.* Newburgh, 1891.

Oakes, R. A., *Genealogical and Family History of the County of Jefferson, New York.* Chicago, 1905.

O'Callaghan, Edmund Bailey, *The Documentary History of the State of New York,* 4 vols. Albany, 1849-1851. Volume II contains documents relating to the first printing in Ontario county.

O'Reilly, Henry, "The First Daily Newspaper in the West, and the First Telegraph Line between the Atlantic and the Mississippi Valley," (Dawson's) *Historical Magazine,* Vol. I, 2d series, January, 1867.

────── *Sketches of Rochester.* Rochester, 1838.

Oswego County, New York, History of. Philadelphia, 1877.

Parker, Amasa Junius, *Landmarks of Albany County.* Syracuse, 1897.

Parker, Jenny Marsh, *Rochester, a Story Historical.* Rochester, 1884.

Peck, William Farley, *History of Rochester and Monroe County.* New York and Chicago, 1908.

────── *Landmarks of Monroe County, New York.* Boston, 1895.

Peirce, Henry B., and Hurd, D. H., *History of Tioga, Chemung, Tompkins and Schuyler Counties, New York,* Philadelphia, 1879. Contains an article on the press of Chemung by C. G. Fairman.

Pinckney, James D., *Reminiscences of Catskill.* Local sketches by the late James D. Pinckney, together with interesting articles by Thurlow Weed, Edwin Croswell, S. Sherwood Day, and Joseph Hallock, Esqs. Catskill, 1868.

Platt, Edmund, *The Eagle's History of Poughkeepsie.* Poughkeepsie, 1901.

Pool, William, *Landmarks of Niagara County.* Syracuse, 1897.

Prime, Nathaniel S., *A History of Long Island.* New York, 1845.

Roberts, Millard Fillmore, *Historical Gazetteer of Steuben County.* Syracuse, 1891.

Roscoe, William E., *History of Schoharie County*. Syracuse, 1882.

Ross, Peter, *A History of Long Island*. 3 vols. New York and Chicago, 1903.

Royce, Caroline Halstead, *Bessboro: a History of Westport, Essex County, N. Y.* Privately printed, 1902.

Ruttenber, Edward M., *History of the County of Orange,* with a History of the Town and City of Newburgh. Newburgh, 1875. Ruttenber was a newspaper man and gave considerable attention to the press in his histories.

——— *History of Orange County*. Philadelphia, 1881.

——— *History of the Town of Newburgh*. Newburgh, 1859.

Salisbury, Guy H., "Early History of the Press of Erie County," Buffalo Historical Society *Publications,* Vol. II, Buffalo, 1880. Some of this material was gathered for Follett's history. The author was the son of Smith H. Salisbury, pioneer printer of Buffalo.

Scharff, J. Thomas, *History of Westchester County, New York*. 2 vols. Philadelphia, 1886.

Schoonmaker, Marius, *History of Kingston*. New York, 1888.

St. Lawrence County, History of. Philadelphia, 1878.

Selkreg, John H., *Landmarks of Tompkins County*. Syracuse, 1894.

Seneca County, History of. Philadelphia, 1876.

Severance, Frank H., "The Periodical Press." Buffalo Historical Society *Publications,* Vol. XIX, Buffalo, 1915.

Seward, William Foote, ed., *History of Binghamton and Broome County*. New York and Chicago, 1924.

Seymour, Norman, *The Genesee County Pioneer Association*. Annual address, June 11, 1878. Batavia, 1879.

Shaw, S. M., *A Centennial Offering. Being a Brief History of Cooperstown*. Cooperstown, 1886. Shaw was the editor of the *Freeman's Journal,* the successor of J. H. Prentiss.

Signor, Isaac Smith, and others, *Landmarks of Orleans County*. Syracuse, 1894.

Sleight, Harry D., *Sleights of Sag Harbor*. Privately printed, Sag Harbor, 1929.

Smith, Carroll E., *Pioneer Times in the Onondaga Country*. Compiled by and dedicated to his father by Charles Carroll Smith. Syracuse, 1904.

Smith, George W., "Newspapers of Herkimer County," Herkimer County Historical Society *Papers,* Vol. I, Herkimer, 1898.

Smith, H. Perry, *History of the City of Buffalo and Erie County,* Syracuse, 1884.

——— *History of Cortland County,* Syracuse, 1885.

——— *History of Essex County,* Syracuse, 1885.

Smith, James Hadden, *History of Chenango and Madison Counties.* Syracuse, 1880.

—— *History of Dutchess County, New York.* Syracuse, 1882.

—— and Cale, H. H., *History of Livingston County, New York.* Syracuse, 1881.

Smith, John E., *Our County and Its People...Madison County, New York.* Boston, 1899.

Spafford, Horatio Gates, *Gazetteer of the State of New York.* Albany, 1813; revised, 1824.

Spaulding, E. Wilder, *New York in the Critical Period, 1783-1789.* New York, 1932. An excellent treatment of the political campaigns, including the part played by the press.

Stiles, Henry R., *A History of Brooklyn.* 3 vols. Brooklyn, 1869-1870.

—— *History of Kings County.* Including the city of Brooklyn. Brooklyn and New York, 1884.

Stone, William L., *Washington County, New York.* New York, 1901. The newspaper press was treated by T. A. Wright.

Storke, Elliott G., "History of the Press of Cayuga County, N. Y., 1798-1877." Cayuga County Historical Society *Collections,* No. 7, Auburn, 1889.

—— and Smith, James H., *History of Cayuga County.* Syracuse, 1879.

Strong, Augustus Hopkins, *Reminiscences of Early Rochester.* A paper read before the Rochester Historical Society, Dec. 27, 1915. Rochester, 1916.

Suffolk County, Portrait and Biographical Record of. Chicago, 1896.

Sylvester, Nathaniel Bartlett, *History of Rensselaer County.* Philadelphia, 1880.

—— *History of Saratoga County.* Philadelphia, 1878.

—— *History of Ulster County.* Philadelphia, 1880.

Thompson, Benjamin F., *History of Long Island.* 2d ed., 2 vols. New York, 1843.

Tooker, W. W., "Early Sag Harbor Printers." Paper read before the Sag Harbor Historical Society, 1902. *Sag Harbor Express,* Jan. 23, 1902.

Turner, Orsamus, *History of the Pioneer Settlement of the Phelps and Gorham Purchase.* With the pioneer history of Monroe County. Rochester, 1851. Turner was a printer of this period in Niagara County, and his work, therefore, is a primary source.

—— *Pioneer History of the Holland Purchase of Western New York.* Buffalo, 1849.

Tyler, R. H., *Oswego County Fifty Years Ago.* Address delivered before the Old Settlers Association of Mexico, August 21, 1879. Fulton, N. Y., 1880.

Wager, Daniel E., *Our County and Its People...Oneida County*. Boston, 1896.

Warren, Emory F., *Sketches of the History of Chautauque County*. Jamestown, 1846.

Washington County, History and Biography of. And the Town of Queensbury, New York. Richmond, Ind., 1894.

Watson, Winslow C., *Military and Civil History of the County of Essex, New York*. Albany, 1869.

Weise, Arthur James, *History of the City of Troy*. Troy, 1876.

—— *History of Lansingburgh, New York*. Troy, 1877.

—— *Troy's One Hundred Years, 1789-1889*. Troy, 1891.

Werner, Edgar A., *Civil List and Constitutional History of the Colony and State of New York*. Albany, 1884. Issued annually for a time after 1883. It is very useful for identification of printers and in determining what public services they rendered.

White, Truman C., *Our County and Its People—Erie*. Boston, 1898.

Wilkinson, J. B., *Annals of Binghamton*. Binghamton, 1840.

Williams, Edward Theodore, *Niagara County, New York*. A Concise Record of Her Progress and People, 1821-1921. 2 vols. Chicago, 1921.

Williams, M. Parker, *Columbia County at the End of the Century*. Hudson, 1900.

Woodworth, John, *Reminiscences of Troy*. 2d ed. with notes. Albany, 1860.

Worth, Gorham A., *Random Recollections of Albany from 1800-1808*. Albany, 1849. 2d ed., Albany, 1850, contains "Recollections of Hudson." 3d ed., Albany, 1866, contains notes by Joel Munsell.

Yates, Austin A., *Schenectady County*. New York, 1902.

Young, Andrew White, *History of Chautauqua County, New York*. Buffalo, 1875.

General and Miscellaneous

Adams, Henry, *History of the United States of America during the Administrations of Jefferson and Madison*. 9 vols. New York, 1889-1891.

Anderson, Frank M., "The Enforcement of the Alien and Sedition Laws." American Historical Association *Annual Report,* 1912. pp. 115-126.

Bacon, Matthew, *A New Abridgement of the Law*. 3d edition, London, 1768.

Chafee, Zechariah, Jr., *Freedom of Speech*. New York, 1920.

Channing, Edward, *History of the United States*. 6 vols. New York, 1905-1925.

Clark, L. H., *Report of the Trial of an Action on the Case Brought by Silvanus Miller, Esq., Late Surrogate of the City and County of New York against Mordecai M. Noah, Esq., Editor of the National Advocate, for an Alleged Libel*. New York, 1823.

Clay, Henry, Secretary of State, *Report on Newspapers*. House Executive Document, No. 41, 19th Congress, 1st Session. A List of Newspapers in which the laws of the United States have been published during the years 1824 and 1825, and the papers in which the publication thereof has been directed to be made during the year 1826. Jan. 16, 1826. Washington, 1826.

Cooper, Thomas, *A Treatise on the Law of Libel and the Liberty of the Press*. New York, 1830.

Depew, Chauncey M., *One Hundred Years of American Commerce*. 2 vols. New York, 1895.

Hamilton, Thomas, *Men and Manners in America*. 2d American ed. 2 vols. Philadelphia, 1832.

Kerr, Robert Washington, *History of the Government Printing Office; with a Brief History of the Public Printing for a Century, 1789-1881*. Lancaster, Pa., 1881.

McCarthy, Charles, "The Antimasonic Party: A Study of Political Antimasonry in the United States, 1827-1840." American Historical Association *Annual Report*, 1902, Vol. I, pp. 365-574.

McMaster, John Bach, *A History of the People of the United States*. 9 vols. New York, 1883-1927. The early volumes, which cover this period, were based largely on newspapers.

Melish, John, *Travels in the United States, in the Years 1806, 1807, and 1809-1811*. 2 vols. Philadelphia, 1812.

Munsell, Joel, *A Chronology of Paper and Paper-Making*. Albany, 1857.

Nevins, Allan, *The American States during and after the Revolution, 1775-1789*. New York, 1924.

Rammelkamp, C. H., "The Campaign of 1824 in New York," American Historical Association *Annual Report*, 1904, pp. 175-201.

Rusk, Ralph Leslie, *The Literature of the Middle Western Frontier*. 2 vols. New York, 1925. One section is devoted to newspapers and magazines.

Tocqueville, Alexis de, *Democracy in America*. 3d American ed. 2 vols. New York, 1839.

United States. *Statutes of the United States*. Printed by Francis Childs, New York, 1795.

United States. *Statutes of the United States.* Printed by Richard Folwell, Philadelphia, 1799.

—— *Statutes of the United States.* Printed by Samuel Green, New London, 1799.

—— *Laws of the United States.* 1814.

—— *United States Statutes.* Laws of the 8th Congress, 1st Session, 1804.

Veeder, Van Vechten, "The History of the Law of Defamation," *Select Essays in Anglo-American Legal History,* III, 446-473, Boston, 1909.

Wansey, Henry, *An Excursion to the United States of North America in the Summer of 1794.* Salisbury, England, 1798.

Weeks, Lyman Horace, *A History of Paper Manufacturing in the United States, 1690-1916.* New York, 1916.

Wertenbaker, Thomas Jefferson, *The First Americans, 1607-1690.* Vol. II of A History of American Life. New York, 1927.

INDEX

PLACES listed are in New York State unless otherwise indicated. Newspapers mentioned in the text, only, are listed under the title. No references are made to the biographical Appendix, although persons and newspapers mentioned in Tables I and II are listed.